Time Out

Shanghai

timeout.com/shanghai

D1341224

Published by Time Out Guides Ltd, a wholly owned subsidiary of Time Out Group Ltd.
Time Out and the Time Out logo are trademarks of Time Out Group Ltd.

© Time Out Group Ltd 2008
Previous editions 2004, 2006.

10 9 8 7 6 5 4 3 2 1

This edition first published in Great Britain in 2008 by Ebury Publishing
A Random House Group Company
20 Vauxhall Bridge Road, London SW1V 2SA

Random House UK Limited Reg. No. 954009

Random House Australia Pty Limited 20 Alfred Street, Milsons Point, Sydney, New South Wales 2061, Australia
Random House New Zealand Limited 18 Poland Road, Glenfield, Auckland 10, New Zealand
Random House South Africa (Pty) Limited Isle of Houghton, Corner Boundary Road & Carse O'Gowrie,
Houghton 2198, South Africa

Distributed in the US by Publishers Group West
Distributed in Canada by Publishers Group Canada

For further distribution details, see www.timeout.com

ISBN: 978-1-84670-067-5

A CIP catalogue record for this book is available from the British Library.

Printed and bound by Firmengruppe APPL, aprinta druck, Wemding, Germany.

The Random House Group Limited supports The Forest Stewardship Council (FSC), the leading international forest
certification organisation. All our titles that are printed on Greenpeace approved FSC certified paper carry the FSC
logo. Our paper procurement policy can be found at www.rbooks.co.uk/environment.

Time Out carbon-offsets all its flights with Trees for Cities (www.treesforcities.org).

Time Out Guides Limited
Universal House
251 Tottenham Court Road
London W1T 7AB
Tel + 44 (0)20 7813 3000
Fax + 44 (0)20 7813 6001
Email guides@timeout.com
www.timeout.com

Contributors

Introduction Amy Fabris-Shi. **History** Andrew Humphreys, Tom Pattinson (*Calendar girls* Sherisse Pham; *Mem-Mao-ries* Gary Bowerman). **Shanghai Today** Tom Pattinson. **Expo 2010** Tom Pattinson. **Where to Stay** Amy Fabris-Shi. **Sightseeing Introduction** Kathryn Tomasetti. **The Bund** Peter Hibbard. **People's Square & Nanjing Dong Lu** Kathryn Tomasetti. **Jingan** Kathryn Tomasetti. **The Old City** Spencer Dodington (*Walk on* Simon Ostheimer/Panthea Lee). **Xintiandi** Tristan Rutherford. **French Concession** Spencer Dodington. **Xujiahui & Hongqiao** Helen Elfer (*Little Britain* Tristan Rutherford). **Pudong** Tristan Rutherford. **Hongkou** Helen Elfer (*Liquid refreshment* Dan Bignold). **Restaurants & Cafés** Christopher St Cavish. **Pubs & Bars** Dan Bignold. **Shops & Services** Sophie Lloyd (*Tea-time* Kathryn Tomasetti). **Festivals & Events** Panthea Lee. **Children** Carl Krause. **Film** Lynn Chen. **Galleries** Lynn Chen. **Gay & Lesbian** Kenneth Tan. **Mind & Body** Megan Shank. **Music** Lisa Movius. **Nightlife** Panthea Lee. **Performing Arts** Lynn Chen. **Sport & Fitness** Lauren Hansen (*All the tees in China* Gary Bowerman). **Getting Started** Megan Shank. **The Canal Towns** Panthea Lee. **Hangzhou & Moganshan** Traci Meadows (*Moganshan* Mark Kitto). **Suzhou** Will McClung (*Pei designs* Panthea Lee). **Putuoshan** Lim Hui Sin. **Directory** Megan Shank (*Shanghai uncensored* Margaret Devereaux).

Maps john@jsgraphics.co.uk, except page 256.

Photography by Jackson Lowen, except: pages 3, 50, 58, 68, 72, 73, 74, 83, 86, 90, 93, 96, 98, 104, 105, 108, 109, 122, 123, 128, 147, 197, 162, 171, 172, 191, 199, 201, 202, 205, 209, 212 Mark Parren Taylor; page 10 Central Press/Getty Images; page 11 akg-images/VISIOARS; page 12 Roger-Viollet/Topfoto; page 17 EH ENG KOON/AFP/Getty Images; page 126 Dai Wanxiang.

The following images were provided by the featured establishments/artists: pages 23, 124, 149, 150, 152, 158, 160, 166, 167, 176, 177, 187, 190, 208, 210.

The Editor would like to thank Matt Chesterton and Dominic Thomas, and all contributors to previous editions of *Time Out Shanghai*, whose work forms the basis for parts of this book.

Contents

Introduction

Few cities have so enraptured the world media in the first decade of the new millennium as Shanghai. Frequently dubbed, with breathless fascination, the world's 'hottest', 'fastest-moving' and 'most happening' city, Shanghai is nothing if not compelling – a megalopolis whose wildly hedonistic past and still wilder future ambitions collide in a feverish present.

Shanghai picked up the habit of making headlines in the decadent 1920s and '30s, and its rediscovered craving for international acclaim pushed it to bid for, and win, the right to host the 2010 World Expo. Subsequently, this city of 18 million – which was already hurtling along the economic express lane – went into overdrive. The city government has invested in a pre-2010 infrastructure upgrade of vast, almost inconceivable, proportions. It will yield a new portfolio of trophy skytowers and trendy urban renewals, as well as two expanded airports, a cruise port, extended road and metro networks, and citywide Wi-Fi.

By the time Shanghai hosts the longest World Expo in history, it will have 13 metro lines (up from just three in 2006) and more underwater expressway tunnels than any other city, while a double-decker tunnel beneath the historic Bund will free up the riverfront for a pedestrian boulevard of grassy parklands and glass pavilions.

Heady stuff to be sure – but try not to lose yourself among the eye-catching icons of 'new China', as Shanghai's soul is still to be found in its older neighbourhoods. While the wrecking ball is pulverising vast swathes of old Shanghai for redevelopment, traditional street life survives in residential laneways, markets and parks. The tree-lined streets of the former French Concession camouflage stylish villas, doddering lane houses and weathered art deco gems, and streetside hawkers serve savoury snacks from blackened griddles and bamboo steamers.

Best of all, the cosmopolitan atmosphere and freewheeling, sometimes rakish spirit that defined the 'Paris of the East' in its 1930s heyday endures today in exciting new ways – especially after dark, when haute cuisine dining rooms, glitzy cocktail lounges and smoky jazz clubs turn on the razzle-dazzle. Daytime is for making money; nighttime is for making whoopee. And, like most simple formulas, it works.

Boundless ambition and an insatiable appetite for internationalisation mean that Shanghai will continue to polish up its act, often at the expense of its grittier, most atmospheric districts. So enjoy the diversity while you can – the fast-track ride to the future seems to recognise no speed limit.

ABOUT TIME OUT CITY GUIDES

This is the third edition of *Time Out Shanghai*, one of an expanding series of more than 50 guides produced by the people behind the successful listings magazines in London, New York, Chicago, Sydney and many more cities around the world. Our guides are all written and updated by resident experts who have striven to provide you with the most up-to-date information you'll need to explore Shanghai, whether you're a local or a first-time visitor.

THE LOWDOWN ON THE LISTINGS

Above all, we've tried to make this book as useful as possible. Addresses, telephone numbers, websites, transport information, opening times, admission prices and credit card details have all been included in the listings, as have details of other selected services and facilities. However, owners and managers can change their arrangements at any time. Before you go out of your way, we strongly advise you to call and check opening times and other particulars. While every effort has been made to ensure the accuracy of the information contained in this guide, the publishers cannot accept responsibility for any errors it may contain.

PRICES AND PAYMENT

Our listings detail which of the four major credit cards – American Express (AmEx), Diners Club (DC), MasterCard (MC) and Visa (V) – are accepted by individual venues. Many businesses will also accept other cards, such as Maestro and Carte Blanche, as well as travellers' cheques issued by a major financial institution.

Prices in this book are given in Chinese *renminbi* (RMB). At the time of going to press exchange rates were around RMB 13.5 to the pound and about RMB 7 to the dollar.

The prices we've supplied should be treated as guidelines, not gospel. Fluctuating exchange

rates and inflation can cause charges, particularly in shops and restaurants, to change rapidly. If prices vary wildly from those we've quoted, ask whether there's a good reason, then please email to let us know. We aim to give the best and most up-to-date advice, and we always want to know if you've been badly treated or overcharged.

THE LIE OF THE LAND

Shanghai is massive, but the areas of interest covered by this book are restricted to a manageable few square kilometres of the city centre, either side of the banks of the Huangpu River. This central district is easy to fathom, and small enough to explore on foot. For further details of the city's geography, see p46.

Street signs are in both English and Chinese. Because many streets are so long they are often prefixed by 'north', 'south', 'east', 'west' or 'central'. So the main highway Yanan Lu progresses from Yanan Xi Lu (West Yanan Road) to Yanan Zhong Lu (Central Yanan Road) to Yanan Dong Lu (East Yanan Road). Maoming Lu is either Maoming Nan Lu (South Maoming Lu) or Maoming Bei Lu (North Maoming Lu).

Travelling around on public transport is made difficult by the language barrier, but the metro is partially signed in English so we've included metro details with each listing. For more information on getting around and the various transport options, see pp216-218.

For all addresses given in the book, we've included a cross-street, details of the nearest public transport option(s) and a reference to the series of fully indexed colour maps at the back of this guide, which start on page 240. The precise locations of hotels (❶), restaurants (❶) and bars (❶) have all been pinpointed on these maps; the section also includes a transport map and a street index.

TELEPHONE NUMBERS

The international dialling code for China is 86 and the code for Shanghai is 021 (drop the zero if calling from overseas). Follow with the eight-figure number as given in this guide. We've identified premium-rate and mobile numbers, which will incur extra calling costs.

For more on phones, including information on free and premium-rate numbers, see p226.

ESSENTIAL INFORMATION

For all the practical information you might need for visiting the city, including customs and immigration information, disabled access, emergency telephone numbers, the lowdown on the local transport network and a list of useful websites, turn to the Directory at the back of this guide. It starts on page 215.

LET US KNOW WHAT YOU THINK

We hope you enjoy *Time Out Shanghai*, and we'd like to know what you think of it. We welcome tips for places that you consider we should include in future editions, and take notice of your criticism of our choices. You can email us at guides@timeout.com.

There is an online version of this guide, along with guides to more than 50 other international cities, at **www.timeout.com**.

Time Out
Travel Guides
Worldwide

All our guides are
written by a team of
local experts with a
unique and stylish
insider perspective.
We offer essential tips,
trusted advice and
honest reviews for
everything you need
to know in the city.

Over 50 destinations
available at all good
bookshops and at
timeout.com/shop

Time Out
Guides

影星周璇

In Context

The **International Settlement**. See p12.

History

The story of how East met West to create China's most cosmopolitan city.

Throughout its history Shanghai has been shaped by lucrative trade, cheap and plentiful labour, and relative calm compared with the rest of China. While wars and unrest plagued the rest of the country, for most of the late 19th and early 20th centuries, Shanghai was largely safeguarded by business-motivated Chinese-Western coalitions. This gave the city's residents an aloof feeling that they were impervious to the ills of the rest of China. Indeed, were they part of China at all?

Prior to 1842, Shanghai was a prosperous but slightly isolated Chinese town. Its position on the Yangtze River delta with a safe harbour on the tributary Huangpu River guaranteed its importance as a trading port.

Rice, cotton and other crops were brought to Shanghai to be carried on barges and sampans up the Yangtze and its tributaries, or to be shipped down the coast and thence inland again along China's extensive canal network.

Shanghai at this time was a pleasant sight: a bustling, modestly sized centre of commerce encircled by a wall three and a half miles (5.6 kilometres) in circumference. Local leaders had built the city walls in the 16th century to protect themselves from Japanese raiders. On the flat marshy delta that stretched around were numerous fishing and farming villages, but otherwise, the landscape was featureless.

Unlike most cities built upon trade, Shanghai, along with China's other ports, remained exclusively Chinese. It had long been the desire of the ruling Qing Dynasty (1644-1912) to keep the borders sealed from the outside world. Opinion at the Beijing court was that foreigners were uncivilised, thus there could be no reason to interact with them.

This did not mean that there was no contact at all. Since the late 18th century, the British East India Company and others had exported Chinese tea, silks and porcelain to Britain. However, they never had anything of equal value to sell to China. To redress this situation the enterprising, if unprincipled British decided to capitalise on the Chinese penchant for opium smoking. They introduced an Indian-grown product that was more refined than the Chinese version. In a short time, the balance of trade was reversed.

Unable to curb the increasingly widespread opium addiction among its populace, the Qing court instead concentrated on shutting down the drug industry. Britain responded by sending gunboats under the pretext of protecting free trade in an action that came to be known as the First Opium War. The expected results were swift: a few skirmishes on the coast were followed by Chinese acquiescence to all British demands at the 1842 Treaty of Nanking. Among those demands was that China cede Hong Kong to Britain and the British right to trade and reside in five mainland Chinese cities: Ningbo, Amoy (Xiamen), Fuzhou, Guangzhou and Shanghai. In 1843, the first British traders duly arrived in Shanghai and were allotted a small area of muddy riverbank, just to the north of the walled city.

HARDSHIP CITY

The British called their land the British Settlement, reflecting the fact that it was neither a leased territory nor a government-controlled colony. They named their stretch of riverfront the Bund, a Hindi word meaning 'embankment' that the traders brought with them from India. These early traders governed themselves under the laws of their own country, a right called extraterritoriality. The US and France jealously claimed the same concessions from the beleaguered Qing court. The Americans settled north of Suzhou Creek while the French were sandwiched in between the British Settlement and the Chinese walled city to the south.

As late as 1848, there were fewer than 100 resident foreigners in Shanghai. Their mudflat settlements resembled the colonial bungalow style favoured in South-east Asia and India, with wide verandas to shade the buildings from the heat of summer. The city at this time was considered a 'hardship post' on account of the bitter winters and stiflingly hot summers, regular flooding, pestilential mosquitoes and foul stenches. 'As regards the people who live in this region,' wrote an early arrival, quoted in Pat Barr's *To China With Love: the Lives & Times of Protestant Missionaries in China*, 'the dampness moistens them, the saltiness stiffens them, the wind shrivels them and the stagnant waters poison them.' There was also an almost complete absence of European females. Foreign men found sexual solace in service professionals from China, the Philippines and elsewhere. Otherwise, leisure conformed to the traditional British Empire pursuits of horses and shooting. Early expatriates constructed Shanghai's first racetrack just inland from the Bund (later to be superseded by a larger track on what is now People's Square).

Small and underpopulated, the foreign settlements found themselves at risk from the rising tide of the Taiping Rebellion. In 1837, a village schoolmaster near Canton took the teaching of a Methodist missionary from America to heart and declared himself 'God's Chinese Son', or Tien Wang, the Celestial King. His religious preaching quickly turned into propaganda of rebellion against the ruling Qings. His movement to create Taiping, the 'reign of eternal peace', spread to become effectively a civil war in which 20 to 30 million people are believed to have died.

In 1860 and 1862, Taiping forces menaced Shanghai, but were repulsed by British and French expeditionary forces led by a 30-year-old general, Charles George Gordon, who would later go on to be immortalised as the imperial Victorian hero Gordon of Khartoum.

CONSOLIDATION OF FOREIGN POWER

The rebellion irrevocably altered Shanghai. Before the insurrection, the foreign-controlled part of Shanghai had been dwarfed by the larger Chinese city. By the end of hostilities the reverse was true. Foreign militias had proven their overwhelming strength and ability to protect property and civilians. Not so in the Chinese city where gangsters known as the 'Small Swords', as well as militant factions allied to either Qing or Taiping, were destroying property and terrorising residents. The foreign settlements took pity on the Chinese and offered shelter – but at a price. Driven by Chinese demand, the cost of an acre of land soared from £50 in 1850 to £20,000 in 1862. Shanghai's first fortunes were amassed by an emerging elite of property barons, of

Shunzi, the first Qing emperor of China.

whom some of the most successful were three family dynasties of Baghdadi Jews: the Sassoons, the Kadoories (*see p31* **Past forward**) and the Hardoons.

At this time Shanghai's foreign settlements housed some 300,000. In 1863, alarmed by the Taiping episode, the Americans had joined with the British to form one International Settlement.

The new unified Settlement governed itself through the auspices of the Shanghai Municipal Council, which was made up of a small number of representatives of British and American landowners. Leaders of the French Concession declined to join the English-speakers, instead formalising their governing body as an extension of the French colonial government

City of sin

In addition to being the wealthiest, most sophisticated and most cosmopolitan city in all Asia, 1920s Shanghai was naturally the most vice-ridden and dangerous too. Opportunity was there for all: not just the upper-crust British financiers, Jewish property tycoons, Japanese industrialists and Chinese revolutionaries, but also Chinese gangsters, Filipino musicians and Russian thugs, as well as cardsharps, pickpockets, murderers for hire and, of course, prostitutes of all nationalities.

At one time the International Settlement alone boasted almost 700 brothels and one in every 13 women in the city was reckoned to be a prostitute. At the same time, more illegal drugs were seized in Shanghai each year than in the whole of the United States. Kidnapping, extortion and violence were a constant threat, as reflected in the city's lexicography by Blood Alley (rue Chu Pao-san) in the French Concession, so named for the frequency of brawls there.

Most of Shanghai's shady characters at the time were small fry compared to

Du Yuesheng, also known as Big-Eared Du. His not-so-secret triad, the Green Gang, controlled every organised labour group, from beggars to stevedores and upwards, including Chinese municipal employees. Du also ran a handful of respectable businesses, notably the Chung Wai Bank, one of the largest Chinese financial concerns of the day, although his real power lay in the money he made from his monopoly on the opium trade. He also had a nice line in kidnapping, organising the snatches then offering his services as a mediator, taking 50 per cent of the ransom. The French Concession authorities were in his pocket, as were several prominent members of the Municipal Council. Even future Nationalist leader Chiang Kaishek was a good friend.

Du's power lasted as long as capitalistic ambition was respectable in Shanghai. When the Communists won the battle for control of the mainland in 1949, the crime lord fled to Hong Kong, where he lingered in ill health for another two years, but his lavish spending and drug habits meant that Du died poor.

in Hanoi. Both the International Settlement and the French Concession took advantage of their superior military strength in the face of Qing weakness to expand their respective territories into the surrounding Chinese countryside. By the early 20th century, the two territories occupied no less than 12 square miles (31 square kilometres).

Throughout the second half of the 19th century, the International Settlement and French Concession prospered. Increasingly settled and self-confident, residents built ever more handsome structures backed by an impressive infrastructure. Shanghai boasted not only China's best roads and hotels, but also its first gaslights (1865), telephones (1881), electric power (1882), running water (1884), cars (1901) and trams (1908).

Shanghai's next great change came in the aftermath of the Sino-Japanese war of 1895. Acceding to victorious Japan's terms, the Qing court granted Japan similar rights to those it had allowed the Western powers earlier in the century. Japan, however, asked for one other concession: the right to open factories in Shanghai. The Western powers valued the city for its market and raw materials; the Japanese saw greater potential in its cheap and pliable labour. Other countries copied, taking the line that a concession to one was a concession to all.

The city's Chinese population was employed to spin silk, mill grain, roll cigarettes... Workers' conditions were grim and wages pitiful – so much so that already, in 1905, there were the first stirrings of organised unrest. This moment can be seen as the beginning of modern Shanghai – even modern China. On the one hand were the rich foreign capitalists, on the other the masses of uneducated but increasingly organised labourers.

In 1912, the feeble Qing Dynasty gave way to a fledgling republic headed by the revolutionary figure of Sun Yatsen. In short order Sun and his followers were ousted from Beijing by a power-hungry rival and, forming a new Nationalist Party, or Kuomintang, they relocated to the southern city of Canton. Attracted by the safety of the Settlements, Sun also kept a house in Shanghai's French Concession (see p77), which he shared with his bride Soong Qingling.

COMMUNIST THREATS AND A BRUTAL RESPONSE

In 1917, events that were happening far beyond China's borders were soon to have a major impact on Shanghai. Communist victory in the Russian Revolution resulted in the flight of the defeated 'White Russians'. Over 40,000 made their way overland across Siberia to Vladivostok, which was only a few days' sail from Shanghai. As many as could afford the passage made the Chinese city their new home.

The Russians influenced Shanghai life in many ways. They introduced a new cosmopolitanism with their music, food and fashion. Parts of the French Concession, in particular around the central expanse of avenue Joffre (now Huaihai Zhonglu), took on a Slavic air with bakeries, dance and music studios, and Muscovite cafés. However, many came bereft of belongings and funds, and were forced to take the most menial or unsavoury work to survive.

'Chinese students led anti-Japanese strikes.'

High-born women eked out an existence selling their jewellery and family heirlooms, or working as nightclub hostesses and prostitutes. Such is the fate of the Countess Sofia Belinskya as played by Natasha Richardson in 2005's Merchant Ivory movie *The White Countess*. Many in the city's long-term foreign resident community resented the Russians for destroying the myth of the omnipotent foreigner: for the first time the Chinese could see Caucasians performing the same sort of demeaning tasks that up until then had been exclusively the lot of Asiatics.

Shanghai was also buffeted by one other significant repercussion of the war in Europe. Under the terms of the concluding Treaty of Versailles, the Chinese territories belonging to defeated Germany were to be handed back not to China but to Imperial Japan.

Chinese student leaders led anti-Japanese and anti-Western strikes accompanied by boycotts of foreign goods. This was part of a general wave of protest that came to be known as the 4 May Movement. Leftist-leaning leaders of the Movement formed links with international Communism and, in 1922, Mao Zedong and others held the first meeting of the Chinese Communist Party in a small lane house in Xintiandi (see p75).

Order in Shanghai was increasingly difficult to maintain for its foreign rulers. They counterattacked with anti-Communist propaganda and the main English-language newspaper the *North China Daily News* carried instructions on 'How to Spot Communists at Moving Picture Shows and Other Public Gatherings'. Strikes were becoming more disruptive. In 1925, a Japanese foreman shot a striking Chinese worker in a Shanghai textile mill, triggering mass protests on the streets. On 30 May, a mob surrounded the headquarters of the Municipal Police hoping to free students held inside; police shot directly into the crowd, instantly creating 11 martyrs.

Anti-foreign sentiment was channelled into mass support for the Kuomintang under its new leader Chiang Kaishek, who had succeeded Sun Yatsen on his death in 1925. On a mission to unite China and rid the country of imperialists the Kuomintang marched north out of Canton. In 1927, the 'Northern Expedition' reached Shanghai where the Communists, in alliance with the Kuomintang, had organised a city-wide strike. But what the Communists didn't know was that Chiang had struck a deal with arch-capitalist-cum-gangster Du Yuesheng and together the two parties had agreed to do the dirty work of the beleaguered Shanghai Municipal Council and rid the city of its disruptive Communist elements.

On 12 April 1927, Green Gang thugs and Nationalist soldiers rounded up thousands of suspected Communists and strike leaders and executed the lot, by decapitation, often in full public view. Chiang's motive for partaking in the massacre was to win the support of the wealthy bankers, traders, property barons and industrialists of Shanghai. Job done, the Kuomintang retreated to headquarters in Nanjing where money from Shanghai poured into Nationalist coffers.

THE SHANG-HIGH LIFE

With the political uncertainties and labour unrest of the 1920s out of the way, the Shanghailanders (the name given to the city's long-term foreign residents) and Shanghainese could concentrate on what they did best: making money. The average man in the street was untroubled by the collusion of Shanghai municipal leadership, Chinese military power and Shanghai organised crime. All they knew was that the city was booming. Over the next decade, despite unprecedented aggression from Japan just outside Shanghai's borders, cultural and business life within the city was at its apex. In pursuit of profit, Shanghai became the most international metropolis ever seen.

An article published in US magazine *Fortune* in 1935 describes Shanghai as 'the fifth city of the earth, the megalopolis of continental Asia, inheritor of ancient Baghdad, of pre-War Constantinople, of nineteenth-century London, of twentieth-century Manhattan.' It ascribes to Shanghai the tallest buildings outside the American continent, 50,000 junks at the city's wharves and the 'greatest concentrated silver hoard on earth'. This vast wealth is 'justly claimed', according to *Fortune*, by 'just a few thousand white men,' which, broken down by nation, included 9,331 British, 3,614 Americans, 1,776 French and 1,592 Germans.

Life for Shanghai's foreign business elite (known as taipans) revolved around the club, the most exclusive of which was the great, gloomy Shanghai Club with its Long Bar – Noël Coward, laying his cheek on the bar, said he could see the curvature of the earth. Then there were the races, dinners, fancy-dress balls and nightclubs, particularly the Chinese dance palaces with their 'taxi dancers' – slim girls clad in *qipaos* slit to the hip whose company on the dancefloor was bought with a ticket. Though not exactly prostitutes, the girls would become concubines to the men with money to pay for them.

During the 1920s and '30s, the city became a legend. It was the city of money, gangsters, drugs, warlords, brothels and spy rings but, above all, also of opportunity. In addition to Coward, other famous figures flocked to see for themselves this so-called 'whore of the Orient', including Christopher Isherwood and WH Auden (whose socialist leanings the city offended), George Bernard Shaw and Charlie Chaplin. It was during this time that the Bund, the ultimate account of Shanghai's foreign-dominated wealth, took its familiar shape; 1923 saw the completion of the grandiose domed Hongkong & Shanghai Bank building, while the imposing brown-stone cliff-face of the Cathay Hotel (now the Peace Hotel) was added in 1929 (*see p40* **Keeping the peace**).

Even as the rest of the world suffered in the lead-up to World War II, Shanghai experienced its greatest exuberance. Its citizens must have thought that the magic that had so far blessed their city would shield it forever. Japan, however, had other ideas.

SCORCHED BY THE RISING SUN

China's political weakness – as proved by its inability to form a strong national government since the fall of the Qing Dynasty – was an irresistible temptation to natural resource-poor Japan. It had already seized Manchuria from China in 1931 by creating its puppet 'Last Emperor' regime. From there it menaced Beijing and Tianjin. In 1932, Japanese troops had invaded the Chinese-run parts of Shanghai following anti-Japanese rioting. International condemnation, however, had forced them to relinquish their gains. Events were to prove more dangerous a second time around.

By 1937, Japanese forces had conquered much of northern China. As they menaced Shanghai, Chiang Kaishek mobilised his forces in the Chinese quarters of Shanghai. The ensuing fighting brought heavy casualties to both sides and almost total destruction to Chinese Shanghai (these events form the backdrop to Kazuo Ishiguro's haunting novel *When We Were*

Calendar girls

When the foreign population of Shanghai skyrocketed in the early 20th century, an influx of foreign goods soon followed. Eager to tap in to Chinese markets, international companies began tailoring advertisements to local tastes. Their first attempts missed the mark: foreign merchants thought richly printed, colourful ads would appeal to Chinese customers. But the portraits of Abraham Lincoln and scenes from Europe they featured were unsurprisingly met with indifference among locals.

Merchants went back to the drawing board, taking inspiration from the genre of block-printed Chinese New Year posters found in most Chinese households, which feature the 24 seasonal division points and often pictured the Kitchen God. At the same time, the *Shanghai News* was already printing Western calendars as reader gifts, showing both the Western year and the Chinese seasonal divisions, bordered by sober pictures of 24 historical figures. The subsequent move to replace old bearded statesmen with nubile girls in racy *qipaos* was, in modern parlance, a no-brainer.

Eventually the *yuefenpai* calendar advert aesthetic – an iconic graphic style marrying art deco with Chinese brush painting – would be used to sell everything from clothing to cigarettes. The lavish images, unmistakably Chinese yet clearly wearing the influence of cosmopolitan Western tastes, captured the look and feel of the city at the time.

Almost a century later, the image of a smiling young woman dressed in the signature Shanghai *qipao* holds great aesthetic and historical appeal, and authentic *yuefenpai* posters fetch high prices among collectors. Many boutiques in Shanghai, however, cater to casual buyers, selling high-quality reproductions. These vintage-looking posters make excellent gifts or souvenirs and can be found at **Dongtai Lu Antiques Market** (*see p146*) and **Madame Mao's Dowry** (*see p144*). Contemporary twists on the iconic images (on notepads, paperweights, homewares and so on) can be found at decor stores like **Simply Life** (*see p144*).

Orphans). Death also came to the International Settlement when Chinese pilots mistakenly dropped bombs on the Bund's Palace Hotel and on entertainment complex Great World, where Chinese refugees fleeing the Japanese had taken shelter – over 1,000 were killed and another 1,000 wounded in the largest ever death toll from a single bomb until Hiroshima.

The Japanese were victorious and this time no amount of international pressure could get them to relinquish their territorial gains. With control over a large part of the International Settlement, Japanese leaders pressured the Municipal Council for a greater role in city politics. The more prescient could see that swallowing only part of Shanghai would not sate Japanese hunger. Many civilians left the city and ominously Britain and America began to scale back their military presence, citing the overwhelming Japanese numerical superiority.

On the morning of 8 December 1941, at almost the same time as Japanese bombers were destroying Pearl Harbor, Japanese forces attacked the two remaining gunships of the Anglo-Saxon powers, which were moored off the Bund (an event powerfully described in the opening chapters of JG Ballard's *Empire of the Sun*). They then invaded the International Settlement and in early 1942 interned Allied nationals in detention centres around the city, where they remained for the next three years, until the Japanese surrendered to the Americans on 15 August 1945.

LIBERATION: THE FUN STOPS HERE

The US navy moved to occupy Japan in late 1945, also taking the reins in Shanghai. During the war, both the International Settlement and the French Concession had ceased to exist, thus the Americans filled a power vacuum in the first-ever united Shanghai. They held control of the city for only a year before handing over to Chiang Kaishek.

From the end of 1945 until 1948, Shanghai attempted to rebuild its former glory. Returning industrialists invested in new factories and built new homes. However, it was to be something of a last hurrah, as by late 1948 Chiang's government was on its last legs, having lost countless military campaigns to the Communists. The Nationalists started to plan for an evacuation to Taiwan, the capitalists headed for Hong Kong. Believers in the 'New China' stayed put. On 25 May 1949, in an event known as the 'Liberation', the Communists marched silently into a Shanghai that had already been abandoned by the Nationalist leadership and its army. The peasant conquerors, who still carried emergency rations of crushed locusts strapped to their backs, must have gazed in wonder at the towering buildings and the department store windows filled with imported luxury items.

'Shanghai's rebirth came with the death of Mao.'

Most Shanghainese accepted the new state of affairs with their usual pragmatic stoicism. The middle classes – still donning their business suits and hats for another day at the office on the day of Liberation – presumed that nothing much would change. At first what change did occur took place slowly. Those foreign and Chinese industrialists who had chosen not to abandon their businesses found themselves gradually pressed with crippling demands, as comparatively prosperous Shanghai was milked to finance schemes in the rest of China. Then, in 1953, the Communists announced that all Shanghai companies were henceforth to be 'owned by the people'. The last group of Westerners left. Surviving dance halls and privately owned villas were converted into 'cultural palaces' and the stylish apparel that the peacocks of the former 'Paris of the East' were known for was traded in for grey unisex tunics and caps.

In 1966, Mao launched his Cultural Revolution, aimed at consolidating his own power by exposing those leaders and Party members who did not follow the Maoist line. Shanghai was the headquarters for a group later termed the 'Gang of Four' – Zhang Chunqiao, Yao Wenyuan, Wang Hongwen and Mao's wife, Jiang Qing. They were fervent supporters of Mao's policies and exerted great control over the activities of the new revolutionary, militant Red Guards, whose job it was to rid the country of

the 'Four Olds': old culture, old customs, old habits and old ways of thinking. There was no exact definition of 'old' and it was left to the Red Guards to decide – in other words it was a licence to create chaos. Shanghai's streets were renamed, buildings were destroyed (notably Jingan Temple, while Xujiahui Cathedral had its spires lopped off) and large numbers of Shanghainese – who the average Chinese viewed as tainted by Western decadent ways – were forced into demeaning public self-criticism sessions before being locked up.

By the early 1970s, when President Nixon visited Shanghai for his historic meeting with Zhou Enlai, the city that had enjoyed the first electricity and cars in China was completely dark at nightfall. Shops stood empty. The city's residents were cowed and had to watch what they said in case someone overheard and reported them. The vibrant, decadent capitalist paradise of the 1930s had been put to death.

THE LIGHTS COME BACK ON

The start of the rebirth came in 1976 with the death of Mao. A more moderate Communist Party leadership arrested the reviled Gang of Four. A shell-shocked Shanghai reopened its schools and factories. In 1978, Deng Xiaoping became China's new leader and launched an era of reform. The benefits were slow to come to Shanghai. The city's industries were used for the greater good of greater China and over 80 per cent of all revenues were directed to Beijing. With no investment the city stagnated. In 1988, the tallest building in town remained the Park Hotel built in 1934. But there was one event with irrefutable impact: this was the Anglo-Chinese Joint Declaration in 1984 agreeing the handover of the British colony of Hong Kong. Now there would be a city in China that was even more foreign and tainted than Shanghai.

In 1990, the government in Beijing decreed that Shanghai was to become the country's new economic powerhouse. The city government was allowed to use fiscal revenues to develop long-neglected infrastructure. While South-east Asia experienced crisis and new-returnee Hong Kong stumbled, the 1990s were a boom time for Shanghai. The skyline changed beyond recognition as the city attempted to make up for the 40 years that it had lost under Communism.

THE MODERN MEGALOPOLIS

On the surface, Shanghai at the beginning of the 21st century appears very much like the modern city it aims to be. Its German-built Maglev train is the fastest in the world, while the thriving designer heritage mall Xintiandi and the Rolls-Royce dealership at the Westin hotel seem to uphold the rosy statistics illustrating the city's rediscovered economic might. But such rapid growth rarely comes without pain, and the average citizen is paying dearly for development. The rich are most certainly getting richer but at the foot of skyscrapers elderly beggars rummage through garbage bins. The city in which everyone once cycled to work in identical blue overalls now rivals Brazil's as the most unequal on earth. Similarly, while the speed of growth is exhilarating, many fear it is coming at the expense of the city's architectural and cultural heritage as the government seems hell bent on pulling down all pre-war structures to replace them with skyscrapers. Prosperity is attracting ever-increasing numbers of migrants from the hinterland who need to be provided with more housing, which, in turn, sends the city sprawling outwards with more roads, more congestion, more pollution.

In such a climate of hyper capitalism and open discussion, it's easy to forget that all of this is being overseen by a Communist state. Clues remain, however, in a fondness for sloganeering and finger-wagging. The red banners have gone but they've been replaced with enamelled plaques warning against the 'Seven no-nos'. These range from SARS-sensible 'No spitting' to the prissy 'No foul language'. According to the government, this is necessary to bring Chinese behaviour in line with that of 'global citizens'. Which is in some

Mem-Mao-ries

Although Shanghai is the official birthplace of communism in China, tracking the legacy of the movement's most iconic and influential figure, Mao Zedong, isn't as easy as you might expect. Of course, you will see the face of the ruthless dictator, who ruled China on and off between 1949 and 1976, every day on Chinese currency notes. But now that consumerism has ousted communism, he is scarcely seen on the streets of Shanghai. Many of the old wall murals have been painted over and, while you can still find a large Mao statue at the gates of Fudan University, don't make the common mistake of assuming the statue on the Bund (at the end of Nanjing Lu) is the Great Helmsman – it is actually Chen Yi, Shanghai's first post-Revolution mayor.

In a strikingly ironic turn, the cradle of Chinese communism is now an adjunct to the high-end Xintiandi dining and shopping enclave. Here, in July 1921, 13 communist intellectuals, including a young Mao, held the first clandestine congress of China's Communist Party. The meeting site has been brutally converted and is now a propaganda-friendly museum (Museum of the First National Congress of the Chinese Communist Party; see p75) featuring a *Last Supper*-like installation of a standing Mao addressing the group seated at dinner.

As Mao tightened his grip on power, his personality cult tightened its grip on the Chinese people. The **Propaganda Poster Art Centre** (see p84) has a colourful collection of Cultural Revolution posters painted to Mao's orders, depicting him in various nation-saving poses: announcing the founding of the

People's Republic, greeting devoted peasant workers with a blazing red sun shining on the fields of rural China, and so on.

Purchasing Maomorabilia has become a guilty pleasure among tourists, and street markets pedal cheap Mao watches, clocks and Little Red Books. **Madame Mao's Dowry** (see p144) offers classier lines, featuring subtle Mao-themed paintings, mirrors and ceramics – and a giant, peeling wooden statue of the Chairman himself.

ways ironic: Shanghai, after all, is the place that initiated the concept of the modern global city.

As the property market gives way to the stock market, the march of capitalism continues. Pudong rises higher into the sky with the new World Financial Centre taking the crown of China's tallest building from the neighbouring Jinmao Tower. A new wave of five-star hotels has sprung up along the Bund, in Pudong and deeper into the city to cater for the 70 million visitors expected to attend the 2010 World Expo. But the Shanghainese will be closely watching the government's reactions to a recent rollercoaster of national emotions, including protests in Tibet, storms, floods and the biggest earthquake in 30 years, killing tens of thousands. Natural disasters have traditionally preceded the downfall of an empire in Chinese history, and the authorities are well aware of that.

Shanghai has also challenged the state's all-providing power by donating huge amounts of private funds to charities supporting fellow nationals who suffered so profoundly in 2008 – previously almost unheard of in China. In addition, the 18-year sentence the city's Party boss received for misuse of social funds was in no small part influenced by the local protests of people who expect increased accountability from their leaders. All the while, the party's 'one step forward, two steps back' attitude to freedom of the press; the slow response to corruption; and the lack of transparency and rule of law leave the city's population in little doubt they are still ruled by Communists.

Key events

1684 Following Emperor Kangxi's green light to maritime trade, Shanghai flourishes as a nexus of trade along the Yangtze River.
1839 British and Chinese forces clash in the First Opium War.
1842 The embattled Qing court signs the Treaty of Nanjing, giving Britain the right to trade and settle in Shanghai.
1843 A British settlement is established on a muddy patch of ground near the Huangpu River and Suzhou Creek. The Brits name it the Bund.
1849 The French negotiate the same rights as the British, and set up the French Concession.
1853 Taiping Rebellion forces capture Nanjing and begin a campaign of violence against Shanghai. Settlement troops defend the city.
1863 The British and American settlements combine forces to form the International Settlement.
1895 The Qing court is defeated in the Sino-Japanese war. The Japanese win the right to trade, settle and open factories in Shanghai.
1905 First organised labour protest.
1911 The weak Qing Dynasty concedes power to early Republican forces.
1917 An international decree makes opium illegal; Shanghai is filled with smugglers.
1919 The Treaty of Versailles awards Germany's Chinese territories to Japan. Chinese students protest, sparking labour unrest.
1922 The first meeting of the Chinese Communist Party takes place in a small lane house in the French Concession.
1927 Gangster Du Yuesheng strikes a deal with Nationalist leaders to kill off the

Communist faction in Shanghai. The coalition is a success and fosters economic prosperity.
1937 Japanese troops take increasing control of China, including Shanghai.
1941 On the same morning they bomb Pearl Harbor, the Japanese seize the International Settlement. The French Concession is already captured by default of the Vichy Government.
1945 American forces occupy Shanghai following Japan's surrender.
1946 Chiang Kaishek's Nationalist government is reinstalled in Nanjing.
1949 The Communist People's Liberation Army marches into Shanghai. Mao forms the People's Republic of China.
1966 The Gang of Four, which includes Mao's wife, instigates the bloody Cultural Revolution.
1976 Mao dies and the Gang of Four is arrested and tried.
1978 Deng Xiaoping pledges to reform and open up the Chinese economy.
1989 The Tiananmen Square anti-government protests leave Shanghai largely unaffected.
1990 Shanghai is earmarked by the government as the economic hope for China. Pudong is declared a Special Economic Zone.
1993 The Oriental Pearl Tower goes up and becomes an icon of the new Shanghai.
2003 The Maglev, the world's fastest train, goes into service running between Pudong International Airport and the city.
2006 Shanghai hosts the sixth summit of the Shanghai Cooperation Organisation (SCO), watched keenly by international diplomats.
2010 Shanghai hosts the World Expo.

Shanghai Today

A city built on burning ambition.

'Pearl of the East', 'Paris of the East', 'Whore of the Orient', 'Paradise for adventurers'… Like most great world cities with colourful pasts, Shanghai has been nicknamed and typecast as much as any actor. But what are we to we call it now? 'Powerhouse of the unstoppable Chinese economy' doesn't deliver quite the same exotic effect, but the fruits of the city's latest economic revolution are every bit as exciting. With a dazzling new face, Shanghai has re-emerged, with a confident swagger, on to the world stage.

Bathing in its boomtown exuberance, 21st-century Shanghai radiates a sense of impatience, energy and adventure. As increasing numbers of businesses from Hong Kong and Singapore relocate to the mainland, and Beijing's Olympic buzz gradually fades to a gentle hum, it is Shanghai that is picking up the lion's share of Asia's business leaders, entrepreneurs, celebrities and economic adventurers.

But then money-making is nothing new to Shanghai – it has always been a city of purpose and ambition, and the Shanghainese are renowned for their business nous and drive.

While personal connections (known as *guanxi*) are a vital part of doing business of any sort in China, the Shanghainese are willing to put their money unhesitatingly where their mouth is and to clock up the hours to achieve their goals. From the sharply dressed young men in Pudong's financial district to the sharp-minded old ladies in Xuhui playing with their stock portfolios, all kinds of Shanghai folks are hustling, haggling and occasionally hitting it big.

Many of the new millionaires quaffing in Lounge 18 (*see p121*) – the latest hotspot on the champagne-drenched Bund – made their fortune on the property market. Being in the right place at the right time (and with the right connections, of course) made many developers wealthy beyond their wildest dreams, as vast areas of the city were parcelled up and sold off at the turn of the millennium. The bubble created by rising real estate prices is, however, beginning to deflate, and investors are moving their capital into the riskier terrain of stocks and equities. Still, the markets suit the style of the Shanghainese perfectly – high stakes, with potentially high gains.

THE ART OF LIFE

Those who make money in Shanghai like to flaunt it. From Alexander McQueen suits to Jimmy Choo shoes to Hermès dresses, super-high-end goods and accessories (that sound you're hearing is Lenin and Mao spinning in their tombs) are hugely coveted symbols of wealth, and the city has one of the fastest-growing luxury goods markets in the world. But as wealth increases and diffuses, these days the Shanghai social climber needs more than a YSL bag to mark his or her status. Golf classes for children, custom-made Bentleys, million-dollar yachts and suburban villas are the bare necessities for the city's nouveaux riches.

Chinese art is acquiring a high cachet too, not only with investors from Switzerland and London but also with newly rich Shanghainese. Stroll along Moganshan Lu, the underground-turned-overground art enclave, and you'll see dozens of galleries doing a brisk trade in local art (big names include Zhou Tiehai, Li Shan, Xu Zhen) with pieces regularly going for hundreds of thousands of dollars.

The art scene, now freed (relatively speaking) from the shackles of censorship and indoctrination, is flourishing for the first time in over 70 years. The same authorities that once banned anything with even a hint of the avant-garde now seem to be enthusiastically

promoting it – albeit on their own terms. The old warehouse docklands of Suzhou Creek, made famous for underground culture when artists moved in to the low-rent spaces in the 1990s, is being revamped with government sponsorship to create a slick creative district in time for 2010 (*see p95* **Liquid refreshment**).

Communist propaganda, while still endemic across print, radio and TV media, is loosening its stranglehold on the modern arts, and a new and vivid kind of social commentary is emerging. Art displayed openly in galleries depicts the city's economic story, Lazarus-like in its dramatic resurrection, as well as the inequalities and paradoxes such rapid economic growth entrains. Many of the works are also full of warmth and wit, traits that are characteristically Chinese but have been long suppressed under the Communists.

THE CULTURE COMPLEX

If Beijing is the scruffy waif of the north then Shanghai is the high-maintenance lady reclining on her chaise longue in the south. The capital has always been a rough literary and creative centre where rock stars, dissidents and avant-gardists convene in furtive huddles to slurp noodles and argue politics. Shanghai, on the other hand, tends to wrinkle her nose at the merest whiff of bohemia. In lieu of grungy bars and centres of academic excellence, she favours champagne, designer dresses and blue-chip corporations.

'Arrogant' and 'cocky' are two adjectives frequently used to describe the Shanghainese, particularly by their northern rivals in Beijing. These jibes are, of course, as much coloured by envy as disdain. The Shanghainese are self-confident; they don't fear the erosion of their past by international cultures, fashions and trends because it was largely these forces that established their city in the first place. The cosmopolitan Shanghainese have always been the main consumers of Western brands and concepts in China, and their compatriots tend to regard this East-meets-West mentality with some scepticism, suspecting that the Shanghainese are less reverent of local tradition than they should be.

Shanghai was built by the British and French, and almost continuously occupied by foreign nations until the 1949 Liberation. It was the Chinese Communists, not foreign invaders, who tried to make Shanghai conform. The process of economic and cultural liberalisation of the past two decades has seen Shanghai re-emerge as a global city, rather than invent itself as one. In this bubble of Westernism in the heart of the Orient, politics play second fiddle to business, and culture is considered a work in

Greening up?

A survey of the stats confirms that China is a world super-polluter: it is home to 16 of the world's 20 most polluted cities, a new coal-fired power station is built every two weeks and ecological disasters take place almost monthly. However, at the 17th Party Congress in 2007, President Hu Jintao pushed the importance of an 'ecological civilisation', and in recent years, Shanghai has shown itself to be at the cutting edge of green ideas and reforms, as dead rivers, sulphur-belching factories and gridlocked streets gradually become an image from the city's past.

By 2009, Shanghai will be using China IV standard fuel for all cars in the city (the same as European emission standards and higher than American standards), and projects such as the 12-year long cleaning-up of Suzhou Creek (*see p95* **Liquid refreshment**) have brought about remarkable improvements. Fish have even returned to the stretch of the creek known as 'stinky river', effectively the city's toilet for the best part of a century.

The 2010 Expo – with the slogan 'Better City, Better Life' – has been crucial in upping the city's eco-conscience. The event is to be powered entirely by renewable energy and produce zero waste, and it will also showcase numerous ground-breaking green ventures, not least an enormous (and rather ambitious) temperature-controlled underground city, which will be entirely sustainable, solar-powered and carbon-free.

Most dramatically of all, just north of Shanghai on China's second largest island, Chongming, a Sino-British venture is making the capital city of **Dongtan**, a self-sustaining urban environment, and the world's first ever 'eco-city'. With initial plans to support a 'demonstrator' population of 50,000 by 2012, the island estimates it will sustain a population of half a million by 2050.

Critics argue that this showpiece gesture is a mere drop in the ocean when you consider the environmental damage dealt by China as a whole, but if some of the projects trialled here can be implemented throughout China, then the effects could be huge.

Aside from national and regional policies, and technological showpieces, there is increasing eco-awareness among private companies. Shanghai has become a major international hub of carbon traders, and the city is home to the country's only carbon-neutral hotel. Built with recycled and locally sourced materials, all carbon produced at the **URBN** hotel (*see p37*) is offset with carbon credits. Taking it ten steps further, the soon-to-open **Songjiang Hotel** is being built dramatically into an old quarry on the outskirts of the city; it will use geothermal energy for electricity and heating, and will have a 'green roof'. It's a small and largely symbolic step – but as the Chinese know better than anyone else, most revolutions begin that way.

progress rather than a slave to tradition. But as more of Old Shanghai is knocked down to be replaced with shiny, plastic towers – the poor left stranded while the middle classes move into their new village green residences – many fear that in the end Shanghai's concession to an international future may prove as politically unpopular as its foreign concessions of the past.

CHANGES AT STREET LEVEL

Pudong is exhibit 'A' in the story of Shanghai's modern reinvention. With its gleaming towers, 21st-century parks and sites designated for the coming World Expo (see p23 **Expo 2010**), it's hard to believe that just two decades ago it was a bleak marshland. Comparisons with the New York of the 1950s or the Hong Kong of the 1980s abound, but a closer look reveals that Shanghai is not so much emulating other cities as creating its own blueprint. Purging itself of the mimetic instinct that once made it proud to be called the 'Paris of the East', it is busy forging its own identity with ground-breaking eco-towns (see p21 **Greening up?**), underground cities and record-breaking structures.

> ### 'Old Shanghai is beginning to fade to sepia, only living on in the odd dusty museum.'

As Shanghai's skyline changes beyond recognition, so inevitably does the way of life of its citizens. Until the 1990s, the majority of Shanghainese lived in a type of terraced dwelling both unique and quintessential to the city, the *shikumen* or lane houses (see p74 **Changing lanes**); precious few now remain. Ten square miles of *shikumen* were razed to make way for the new city in the '90s, with further bulldozing sprees in recent years.

Along with the old bricks and mortar has gone the extraordinarily rich street life that once typified Shanghainese culture. Where locals might once have gathered in the communal alleyway to talk, or to play mah-jong, they now convene in the air-conditioned comfort of a private apartment. You can still find vignettes of old Shanghainese life – laundry hanging from bamboo poles, locals going about their business in pyjamas or taking a nap in a rattan chair – but, with the total number of skyscrapers over 100 metres set to reach 5,000 by 2010 (more than New York), such scenes are becoming rare. As the generation that remembers the days of pre-Communist Liberation dies out, and the buildings they grew up in are gradually demolished, the collective memory of old Shanghai is beginning to fade to sepia, only

living on in the odd dusty museum, or in the foreign-owned retro bars and restaurants on the Bund or in the French Concession.

THE PRICE OF PROGRESS

The city's newfound wealth is obvious at all levels – but prosperity has come at a price. The cost of food has been rising as quickly as a Shanghai skyscraper, with the price of pork rising by 59 per cent between 2007 and 2008 – and rises in rents and petrol prices have also outpaced salaries, many of which have hardly changed in a decade. While the state hopes to hold inflation down to 4.5 per cent in 2008, experts are predicting the figure will be closer to 8.5 per cent. Many independent shops, restaurants and enterprises are being forced out of the market, and streetside restaurants are disappearing in favour of fast-food chains.

As land prices downtown have increased to four times that of the surrounding districts, homes in the centre are fast being replaced by offices, and local markets with mega malls. Poorer residents are being forced to the outskirts, where policing, healthcare and infrastructure are weaker, crime is on the rise and fear is rife that ghettos are just around the corner.

FUTURE SHOCKS?

Old Shanghai, typified by the Bund and the former Concessions, was a testament to Western achievement. The Shanghai being built today is being shaped by Chinese hands, hearts and minds, and this renaissance could even surpass the boom of the colonial era. Will the bubble burst? It's anyone's guess. Despite general optimism in China, there are some signs that the country's tigerish economy is losing some of its bounce, and any slowdown can be expected to be felt deeply in Shanghai.

Meanwhile, corruption continues as the city struggles to cope with its sudden wealth. The Communist Party boss, Chen Liangyu, was jailed for 18 years in April 2008 for misuse of social security funds. Trouble in Tibet, the 2008 earthquake and the Olympic games have refreshed memories around the world of much that is good about China – the earthquake rescue was a model effort when compared with the Burmese junta's appalling failure to feed its own cyclone victims – as well as much that is not (a less than spotless human rights record, a widening wealth gap, choking pollution).

Shanghai's fortunes look set to rise so long as China remains in the world's spotlight. And, given the growth rate of its GDP (11.4 per cent in 2007), its immense impact on the global economy and the country's increasing cultural engagement with the rest of the world, that looks like being a very long time indeed.

Expo 2010

Making over the megalopolis.

Like a pair of spoiled kids, Shanghai and Beijing have always vied for attention, so it came as no surprise to find that, after the capital was awarded the Olympic Games in 2001, Shanghai was gunning for a share of the limelight. In December of the following year, Shanghai beat four other countries to host the World Expo 2010, kick-starting a frenzy of building, bettering and – more controversially – bulldozing. The Expo will launch on 1 May 2010 and run for six months until 31 October, during which time it is expected to draw a record-breaking 70 million visitors.

This being dynamic, driven Shanghai, the preparations for the exhibition are radically, ambitiously and expensively transforming the face of city. The Expo site itself symbolically straddles the Huangpu River, the arterial axis that divides the old city of Puxi from the new city of Pudong. Here, the old industrial areas by the river are being remodelled almost beyond recognition, with cutting-edge performance spaces, hotels, pavilions and even a skyscraper-sized rollercoaster, moving in where houses, warehouses and factories once stood.

THE BIG MAKEOVER

The World Expo 'village' sprawls over 5.3 square kilometres (two square miles) between Nanpu Bridge and Lupu Bridge, on both sides of the river, making it Shanghai's largest ever construction project. It is also the biggest site in the Expo's history, particularly impressive considering the city-centre location. Most cities build their sites in the suburbs but Shanghai is transforming an area of high-density manufacturing units and docks in the heart of the metropolis. Like the rejuvenation of the London Docklands, the Shanghai dockyards will be converted into high-profile exhibition venues; but unlike London, many of the buildings slated for redevelopment were still in use. Controversially, over 18,000 households and 272 active factories were relocated, at great personal and financial cost, to make way for the jamboree.

The scale and pace of construction for 2010 is certainly impressive, but for many it is also alarming. Residents can only look on as swathes of old Shanghai are razed – and gradually erased from the picture. As with the rebuilding of Beijing for the 2008 Olympics, the authorities have, in their eagerness to build a modern 'global city', sidelined heritage issues to a controversial degree. A series of large-scale environmental projects may well benefit the city's residents in the long term, but in the meanwhile the thousands of locals forcibly relocated, the communities displaced and the historic buildings destroyed testify to the government's desire to do what is best for the people – whether the people like it or not. But Shanghai Party chief Yu Zhengsheng insists that the Expo is about 'improving the lives and environment of people in the city', and sustainability is a central theme.

THE GREEN THEME

For many, the environmental theme of the Expo – 'Better City, Better Life' – is ironic, given that the host country's environmental problems frequently make world headlines. China struggles to cope with high carbon emissions, water pollution, soil erosion, air pollution and desertification. The authorities are busy using the Expo as a vehicle to prove to the world that

the country is waking up to the importance of green living and sustainability, and a variety of ultra-high-profile projects are getting their point across effectively. Of them, the biggest eco statement by far is the costly creation of the world's first 'eco-city' in Dongtan, on the nearby island of Chongming (*see p21* **Greening up?**).

The sheer volume of people expected at the Expo is presenting huge challenges for organisers, as they try to avert problems with access, pollution and congestion. Temperatures reach the high 30s during the summer months, and the imagined scene of tens of thousands of people fainting with heatstroke was enough to make organisers prepare solar panels to power cooling facilities and introduce misting systems under canopies to keep visitors cool. While better than many urban areas in China, Shanghai's air quality is still poor. In a bid to clean it up, factories are continually being relocated out of the city centre, and by the end of 2009, all new vehicles in Shanghai must meet EU-standard emissions. Things are improving but the city is a long way from being 'clean'.

Meaning in the mascot

Like all Chinese events, the Expo will have a mascot. Haibao, as it is called, is meant to look like the Chinese character 'ren' – meaning 'people' – and all its features have special significance, including his Elvis quiff, which is actually a wave representing his 'open character and birthplace'. However, when Haibao made his debut at the end of 2007, he was accused of looking like everything from an oral hygiene ad to a blue condom. The creator of the mascot, Shao

Longtu, then had to defend his creation after web users accused Haibao of being a look-alike Gumby from 1980s sit-com *Growing Pains*. Haibao has started appearing on merchandise around the city, but the negative press has meant that his trademark 'big round eyes, to show his anticipation of the city' and 'round body to present a comfortable life' has been faked a lot less than the very popular Beijing Olympic mascots, the Friendlies.

If the pollution, or the heat, proves too much, Expo visitors can escape to a vast underground network being built below the site. Designed to create further space for pedestrians to get around the exhibition in the shade, it will also house retail outlets and cafés. The network will be supported by advanced ventilation technologies, apparently making it more of an underground garden of Eden than your average basement car park. The underground city will eventually take up a whopping 500,000 square metres (5.3 million square feet), making it the largest underground 'city' in the world.

CULTURAL ENSEMBLE

Named the 'Crown of the East' and unsurprisingly red in colour, the Expo's China Pavilion will be the biggest of the permament pavilions, with each of the mainland's provinces given 600 square metres (6,400 square feet) of exhibition space with which to show off their 'modern achievements'. Expect lots of displays about the country's environmental protection programmes and not a lot about, say, the deadly outbreaks of algae from nitrogen and phosphorus contamination across the lakes and rivers of south-west China in recent years. As the Expo is being dubbed the 'Business Olympics', provinces will also be trying to encourage international corporations (those specialising in heavy industry included) to invest in their provinces. As well as featuring separate Hong Kong and Macao pavilions, this will also be the first time Taiwan has attended a World Expo since the island lost its United Nations Security Council seat to China in 1971.

Participating countries are trying to ingratiate themselves with the Chinese authorities by designing modern Chineseified pavilions. The British Pavilion, designed by Heatherwick Studio, is to be on the east bank of the Huangpu River and will see a huge centrally lit cube with thousands of what will appear to be free standing spines, each tipped with coloured lights; it will cost up to £12 million – with funding split between sponsors and taxpayers – and British officials are hoping to attract 50,000 visitors per day to their showcase of the best of British culture, education and business.

There will be an estimated 20,000 cultural performances during the six-month event, including live music, theatre, dance and performance art from countries as far-flung as Tuvalu and El Salvador. China is also keen to promote its traditional art forms, so expect plenty of Chinese opera (*see p189*), as well as performances from some of China's lesser-known ethnic groups, including the colourfully dressed Bai and Miao, and the musical and matriarchal Naxi.

TRAINS, PLANES AND AUTOMOBILES

Cars and taxis are banned from the Expo site. Instead, a 26-square-kilometre (ten-square-mile) transport hub is being built in the Hongqiao area (and Hongqiao airport will get a second runway and a new terminal). As well as providing access to the airport terminals, expressways, trains, long-distance buses, taxis and Metro lines, Hongqiao will be the point of ingress to the Expo site. Public transport, including free Expo Buses, will be available to shuttle people in and out.

In 2006, it was announced that the Maglev train, which currently shuttles the 31 kilometres (19 miles) from Pudong airport to Longyang Lu station in just seven minutes and 20 seconds, would be extended to tie in with the Expo. The world's fastest train was to take commuters from Shanghai to the nearby city of Hangzhou, stopping at the Expo site. However, residents affected by the proposed route protested that the radiation from the electromagnetic field was dangerous, and that the forced relocation of many households in the route of the development was unjustifiable. Others questioned whether any train could be worth $4.5 billion dollars in state funding.

In 2007, the main cheerleader of the project and the then head of Shanghai's Communist Party, Chen Liangyu, was found guilty of misusing funds and in May the project was shelved. For many the Maglev was just another narcissistic monument to the not-so-beloved leader. As of early 2008, the project was said to be back on; however, transport officials state that completion in time for the Expo is now impossible. At time of writing, the Maglev extension was still under review.

LOOKING AHEAD

Tickets for the Expo will go on sale in late September 2008, tentatively priced at RMB 160. Whether this relatively high price-tag will lower numbers remains to be seen. In May 2008, with two years to go, a World Expo Exhibition Centre opened at the Hong Kong New World Tower on Huaihai Lu to generate further interest and support among city residents, some of whom question if – and how – the Expo will ultimately benefit them.

Nine years in the making, and with billions of dollars spent on infrastructure, architecture and environmental development, the Shanghai World Expo 2010 will change the face of the city for another century. What has been torn down will not be rebuilt, although the structures flying up are expected to stand the test of time. But the question remains: will the new face of the city be as attractive and enduring as the old one? Only time will tell.

ANNABEL LEE
SHANGHAI

Located in a quiet lane on the Bund, Annabel Lee Shanghai's flagship store showcases the sophisticated and elegant pieces in the finest Chinese silk, linen, cashmere and the radiance of traditional embroidery. To imbed the beautiful traditional Chinese culture into this vibrant city's modern lifestyle, the up-scale gift store is able to make it a totally unique experience for high society and clued-in cosmopolitan traveler by its comforting linen and silk home wear, breath-taking hand-embroidered shawls and scarfs, and last but not the least intricate silk gifts.

To ditch more stories of this famous shop among local expats we are able to find out the design power behind the Shanghai-based luxury home accessories brand is a group of pure domestic designers fascinated by profound Chinese traditions and culture. If you are willing to spend a little bit more for something with real value other than what you expect from a lousy souvenir market, then any piece of Annabel Lee Shanghai would be a great souvenir!

Product range

Gift - jewelry, Chinese motif cases, etc.
Home wear - pajamas, sleep dresses, kimonos, etc.
interior item - silk table sets, cashmere blankets, etc.
fashion accessories - evening bags, scarves, shawls, etc.

Bund Flagship Store

No.1, Lane 8, Zhongshan Dong Yi Lu, the Bund
(64458218/www.annabel-lee.com)
Open 10am-10pm daily.

Xin Tian Di Store

Unit 3, House 3, North Block, Xintiandi, Lane 181, Taicang Lu
(63200045)
Open 10.30am-10.30pm daily.

Where to Stay

Jia Shanghai. *See p36*.

Where to Stay

Boutiques move in to fill the gaps between modern monsters and budget beds.

Luxury with a 21st-century twist at **Hyatt on the Bund**.

As befits a boom town with a World Expo on the horizon, Shanghai's hotel industry is going through a growth spurt of dramatic dimensions. More than 25 new hotels have opened in Shanghai since our last edition – that's 11,000 new rooms in the space of two years. And with record international and domestic visitor numbers expected to continue, the hotel trade is set firmly on an upward course. 'Up' being the operative word. The city is now home to the two highest hotels in the world – the **Park Hyatt**, which opened in 2008 atop the spanking new 101-storey Shanghai World Finance Centre, and sister property the **Grand Hyatt** right next door in the 88-floor Jinmao Tower – and thousands of other lofty lodgings. Shanghai's crop of new five-stars put on a truly world-class show, featuring haute design, high-tech conveniences and ever-ascending room rates.

Though the Shanghai hotel industry, being predominantly business-led, majors in modern luxury, a handful of boutique properties (the stars among them being **Jia Shanghai** and **Mansion Hotel**) have thankfully also entered the fray in recent years, their quirky

individuality and intimacy providing a much-needed alternative to the branded palaces – even if service standards aren't always quite as polished. Chinese-run chains like **Motel 168** and **Jinjiang Inn** meanwhile dominate the budget segment, offering basic rooms aimed at the local market.

COMING SOON

The next couple of years are set to see yet more activity. Established five-stars like the **Ritz Carlton**, **Shangri-La** and **Four Seasons** will open second properties. **Peninsula**, **W**, **Langham**, **Conrad** and **Jumeirah** will also sweep into the market, while **Fairmont** is poised to usher in a new era of decadence for the iconic Peace Hotel (*see p40* **Keeping the Peace**). There is also set to be a **Banyan Tree** beside the Huangpu River and an **Aman** in the old British Consulate on the Bund.

Business hotels tend to congregate along the shopping high street of Nanjing Xi Lu, or in the Pudong financial district. In between the two, the Bund offers heritage architecture, upscale drinking and dining, and is reasonably convenient for the Old City and People's Square. Another popular area is the French Concession, the charming residential heartland of Shanghai, lined with leafy streets, cafés and lively bars. Be warned: grinding traffic can make a room in the wrong part of town a real frustration.

CHAIN HOTELS
Shanghai's booming economy has inevitably attracted the global chains in numbers. In addition to the hotels reviewed below, other internationals that have set up shop include Crowne Plaza, Hilton, Holiday Inn, Howard Johnson, Novotel, Ramada, Regent, Sheraton, Sofitel, St Regis and Swissotel; check the group websites for details. Don't expect a great deal of character, but you will, of course, get the same standards of service and comfort as you last found at the same chain's outlet in Dallas, Kuala Lumpur, Zurich…

BOOKING AND RATES
Booking a room in advance is highly recommended. Rack rates are rising across the board but, with so many hotels opening in Shanghai, so is competition. Check the hotel websites for the best daily rate or package specials, and you may score a surprisingly good deal at weekends. Note that hotels in the budget category – and even some of the mid-range places – may not have a competent English-speaking reservation line. The best bet is to email where possible, or to fax with a request that the hotel acknowledges receipt. Alternatively, for ease of booking and some genuinely good accommodation rates try www.english.ctrip.com.

The Bund

The Bund's historic Peace Hotel – the city's most famous hotel – is undergoing renovation and will reopen as the **Fairmont Peace Hotel Shanghai** in the first half of 2010, *see p40* **Keeping the Peace**. In 2009, the northern Bund will see the arrival of the **Peninsula Shanghai** (*see p31* **Past forward**).

Expensive

Fairmont Peace Hotel
20 Nanjing Dong Lu, by Zhongshan Dong Yi Lu (6321 6888/www.shanghaipeacehotel.com). Metro Nanjing Dong Lu. **Rates** call for details. **Credit** call for details. **Map** p245 M4 ❶

> ▶ ❶ Green numbers given in this chapter correspond to the location of each hotel as marked on the street maps. *See pp240-249.*

As we went to press, China's most famous hotel was closed for renovation and due to open in 2010. *See p40* **Keeping the Peace**.

Hyatt on the Bund
199 Huangpu Lu, by Wuchang Lu (6393 1234/www.shanghai.bund.hyatt.com). Metro Nanjing Dong Lu then walk. **Rates** from RMB 1,600 single/double. **Rooms** 631. **Credit** AmEx, DC, MC, V. **Map** p245 N3 ❷

The 'on the Bund' title is actually a bit of a stretch, geographically speaking – the Hyatt is in reality situated on the North Bund towards the international cruise terminal. Despite the hike necessary to reach the Bund proper, the Hyatt's up-and-coming location, straddling a sharp bend of the Huangpu River, affords some of the city's best views of both the neo-classical sweep of the Bund and Pudong's futuristic skyline. Built in 2007, the Hyatt has all the modern design flair and mod cons you might expect; the lobby is all glass and steel, and the fresh-faced lounges have a soundtrack compiled by, ahem, American 'music stylists'. All 631 rooms across two towers (the entire east wing is an Executive Tower)

The best Hotels

For banking on views
On a sharp bend of the Huangpu River, **Hyatt on the Bund**'s panoramic views take in the sharp juxtaposition of Shanghai's old and new skylines facing off across the muddy waters. *See above.*

For designer living
The *Wallpaper**-worthy interiors of boutique residence **Jia Shanghai** attract the design crowd. *See p36.*

For heady heights
Occupying the 79th to 93rd floors of the Shanghai World Financial Centre, the new **Park Hyatt Shanghai** is the world's highest hotel. *See p44.*

For location for less
Tucked behind the Portman Ritz Carlton, **Baolong Home Hotel**'s low prices belie its smart location and design. *See p37.*

For 1930s gangster paradise
Former opium den turned luxury digs, **Mansion Hotel** revives '30s Shanghai decadence with glorious aplomb. *See p40.*

For wiping your footprint
China's first carbon neutral hotel **URBN** puts your environmental conscience at ease in funky style surrounds. *See p37.*

Airline flights are one of the biggest producers of the global warming gas CO_2. But with **The CarbonNeutral Company** you can make your travel a little greener.

Go to **www.carbonneutral.com** to calculate your flight emissions then 'neutralise' them through international projects which save exactly the same amount of carbon dioxide.

Contact us at **shop@carbonneutral.com** or call into the office on **0870 199 99 88** for more details.

CarbonNeutral®flights

Past forward

The Kadoories, a family of wealthy Baghdadi Jews, arrived in Shanghai in 1880, making their fortune in real estate, banking, rubber production and hotels. When the Hong Kong Hotel Company – of which brothers Elly and Ellis Kadoorie owned a major stake – merged with Shanghai Hotels in 1923 to form the Hong Kong & Shanghai Hotels, its portfolio included three of Shanghai's ritziest addresses – the Astor House (now, ironically, occupied by the budget Pujiang Hotel; *see p33*), and the Palace and Majestic Hotels – with the Peninsula Hong Kong soon following in 1928. When the company dissolved its interests on the Chinese mainland after World War II, the Kowloon grand dame assumed the mantle of the company's flagship, now considered one of the world's finest hotels.

Eighty-six years and eight Peninsulas later, Hong Kong & Shanghai Hotels is returning to its roots with the opening of the **Peninsula Shanghai** (*see below*) in 2009. The Kadoories are still major shareholders of Asia's oldest hotel company, and the current chairman, Sir Michael Kadoorie, is none other than Sir

Elly's grandson. Forbes rated him the fourth-richest man in greater China in 2007, with a cool nine billion to his name.

The 15-floor, 235-room **Peninsula Shanghai** is to be located at the northern end of the Bund in the Waitanyuan precinct, with views of the Bund, the Huangpu River and the former British Consulate next door. Along with classic Peninsula indulgences, there is more than a nod to the Shanghai golden era in its art deco interiors, Sunday afternoon tea dances and the 'Salon de Ning', a clubby lounge concept inspired by the exotic travels of celebrated Shanghai socialite and jetsetter Madame Ning.

The Kadoorie family rose alongside the Sassoons (*see p40* **Keeping the Peace**) to become a major force in Shanghai's Sephardi Jewish community, and their lifestyle was matched by their philanthropy. The old Shanghai family home – named Marble Hall after its vast swathes of imported Italian marble – still stands today as the **Shanghai Children's Palace** (*see p66*), on the corner of Nanjing Xi Lu and Wulumuqi Zhong Lu.

boast expansive water views, along with 32-inch plasma TVs, DVDs, iPod docks and integrated bathrooms. Glass lifts at the back of the hotel overlook the rapidly disappearing heritage neighbourhoods of the Hongkou district. The entire lower level is dedicated to the luxurious Yuan Spa (*see p177*), with a 25-metre swimming pool, yin and yang plunge pools, a fitness centre, hair salon, organic juice bar and even an indoor river. Part-alfresco Chinese restaurant Xindalu (*see p100*) specialises in perfect Peking duck from its custom-built clay oven. Even if your budget doesn't stretch to a Hyatt sojourn, it is well worth a visit to two-storey bar Vue (*see p121*), which has sensational city views. *Photo p28.*
Bars (2). Concierge. Disabled-adapted rooms (5). Gym. Internet (high-speed). No-smoking floors. Parking (free). Pools (1 indoor). Restaurants (4). Room service (24hrs). Spa. TV.

Peninsula Shanghai
32 Zhongshan Dong Yi Lu, by Hankou Lu (www.peninsula.com/shanghai). Metro Nanjing Dong Lu. **Rates** call for details. **Rooms** 235. **Credit** AmEx, DC, MC, V. **Map** p245 M5 ❸
Shanghai's Peninsula is due to open in 2009, returning the Kadoorie family to the forefront of Shanghai hoteliers. *See above* **Past forward**.
Bars (2). Concierge. Disabled-adapted rooms. Gym. Internet (high-speed). Pool. Restaurants (2). Room service (24hrs). Spa. TV.

Westin
Bund Centre, 88 Henan Zhong Lu, by Guangdong Lu (6335 1888/www.westin.com/shanghai). Metro Nanjing Dong Lu. **Rates** RMB 1,688 single/double. **Rooms** 500. **Credit** AmEx, DC, MC, V. **Map** p244 L5 ❹
Part of the Bund Centre complex, and dominated by a 50-storey tiara-topped tower that sparkles on the Puxi skyline, the Westin Shanghai carries off the more humdrum business of bed and board with remarkable panache. The dramatic main atrium turns on the razzle-dazzle with a show of pertrified palms, reflection pools and a Vegas-style cantilevered glass staircase complete with computer-programmed lighting. Things are toned down somewhat in the guestrooms, done out in rich cherrywoods in the original Crown Tower and light, fresh tones with windowside bathtubs in the newer Grand Tower. Italian restaurant Prego does great pizzas, Eest serves Chinese, Japanese and Thai, while the Stage restaurant hosts the most popular Sunday brunch buffet in town. Also on the premises is a 24-hour business centre, two-storey WestinWORKOUT gym, and the exotic Banyan Tree spa (*see p175*), all within easy walking distance of both the Bund and People's Square.
Bars (1). Concierge. Disabled-adapted rooms (3). Gym. Internet (high-speed). No-smoking floors. Parking (RMB 10/hr). Pools (1 indoor). Restaurants (4). Room service (24hr). Spa. TV.

The once (and future?) hotel to the stars: **Pujiang (Astor House) Hotel**.

Moderate

Broadway Mansions Hotel

20 Bei Suzhou Lu, by Wusong Lu (6324 6260/ www.broadwaymansions.com). **Rates** RMB 1,090-1,690 double. **Rooms** 253. **Credit** AmEx, DC, MC, V. **Map** p245 N3 ❺

Built in 1933, Broadway Mansions strikes an angular art deco pose on the banks of Suzhou Creek, between the raised highway of Wusong Lu and the Waibaidu Bridge. Once a luxury residence for foreign correspondents after the war, later phases of renovation have resulted in a hotchpotch of design styles. Happily, a 2007 makeover of the lobby, restaurants and 11th-floor guestrooms goes some way to recapturing a sense of its former elegance, as well as bringing updated facilities. If you do stay here (and again, it's a fringe location), insist on an 11th-storey Bund view room or you'll likely be disappointed. *Bars (1). Business centre. Concierge. Disabled-adapted rooms (1). Internet (high-speed). No-smoking floors. Parking (free). Restaurants (3). Room service (24hrs). TV.*

Seagull on the Bund

60 Huangpu Lu, by Wuchang Lu (6325 1500/ www.seagull-hotel.com). **Rates** RMB 938 single/double. **Rooms** 128. **Credit** AmEx, DC, MC, V. **Map** p245 N3

Taking its cue from the Hyatt on the Bund across the road (*see p29*), the Seagull has also adopted the somewhat misleading 'on the Bund' moniker. At the confluence of the Huangpu River and Suzhou Creek, just east of the Waibaidu Bridge (closed until early 2009), the rooms boast excellent views of the river (and the namesake seagulls), as well as of the sweeping Bund and Pudong skylines. The stained-glass windows and marble floors in the lobby are left over from its days as a navy club, however these are somewhat lost amid the naff decor of a later makeover. In 2005, the 128 guest rooms were refashioned with endearingly kitsch faux-Victorian furnishings, velvet drapes and plasma TVs. Business suites come with PCs, printers and fax machines. There's a gym and mini-golf in the recreation club. It's a bit of a walk to the action, but the enormous neon Epson sign on the roof is a useful beacon when trying to wend your way home. *Bars (1). Concierge. Disabled-adapted rooms (1). Gym. Internet (high-speed). Parking (free). Pools (1 indoor). Restaurants (2). Room service (24hrs). TV.*

Budget

Captain Hostel

37 Fuzhou Lu, by Sichuan Zhong Lu (6323 5053/ www.captainhostel.com.cn). Metro Nanjing Dong Lu. **Rates** RMB 70 dormitory; RMB 450-550 double. **Rooms** 37. **Credit** (doubles & suites only) DC, MC, V. **Map** p245 M5 ❼

While there are a handful of flophouses around, this is the only place in Shanghai where the words

Lonely Planet will elicit recognition. The nautical-themed hostel is simple but clean, the rooms basic but smart. Dormitories have several sets of blond-wood bunk beds (complete with port holes) and share bathroom facilities, while doubles are equivalent to those found in many economy hotels (with en suites and air-con). The location is grand, an attractive 1920s block just a sailor's hornpipe from the Bund and not much further to the Old City, Nanjing Lu or People's Square. There are internet stations in the lobby, bicycles available for rent and a top-floor bar with a great riverside deck (*see p120*). Captain Hostel has a second branch in Pudong, behind Jinmao Tower (527 Laoshan Donglu, 5836 5966). *Bars (1). Business centre. Internet (shared terminals). Room service (24hrs). TV.*

Jinjiang Inn

33 Fujian Nan Lu, by Jingling Zhong Lu (6326 0505/www.jj-inn.com). Metro Nanjing Dong Lu. **Rates** RMB 269 double. **Rooms** 144. **Credit** MC, V. **Map** p244 L6 **8**

Economy hotel chain Jinjiang Inn has multiple locations around town but we favour this one for its strategic locale near the Bund and Yu Gardens, with easy access to the cross-river tunnel heading to Pudong. Targeting the budget-conscious Chinese business traveller, JJ's 144 no-frills rooms come with cable TV, overseas direct dial phones, and free broadband internet. The hotel has benefited from recent renovations, but low prices are the main draw. It is predicted that by 2010 there will be 600+ Jinjiang Inns across the country. *Bars (2). Business centre. Concierge. Disabled-adapted rooms (2). Internet (high-speed). No-smoking floors. Parking (free). Restaurants (3). Room service (24hrs). TV.*

1931 Villas Hotel

306 Guangdong Lu, by Henan Zhong Lu (5158 8666/www.villas1931.com). Metro Nanjing Dong Lu. **Rates** RMB 590 single/double. **Rooms** 76. **Credit** MC, V. **Map** p244 L5 **9**

A 1930s red-brick façade and row of fluttering national flags announce this well-run Chinese establishment. The five-storey residence was originally built as a foreign banking office and later became a branch of Xinhua bookstores, before being refigured as the Villas Hotel in late 2007. All 76 compact but neat guestrooms come with TVs, coffee makers and broadband internet access. Breakfast and afternoon tea is served in the lounge, situated just off the lobby, which still shows hints of original heritage features in the wall castings and antique chandeliers. Friendly service and a convenient location within walking distance of both the Bund and People's Square make this good value for money. *Business centre. Internet (high-speed). TV.*

Pujiang (Astor House) Hotel

15 Huangpu Lu, by Wusong Lu (6324 6388/ www.pujianghotel.com). Metro Nanjing Dong Lu. **Rates** RMB 896 double. **Rooms** 130. **Credit** MC, V. **Map** p245 N3 **10**

Shanghai's perennial budget favourite was once the haunt of the champagne set (when it was called the Astor House Hotel and held decadent dances in the Peacock Hall). The city's first electric lights and telephone also debuted here. Today, the building retains a magically creaky vibe, as well as much of the original Victorian detailing. Hanging in the lobby are black and white photos of distinguished former guests (both Charlie Chaplin and Albert Einstein reputedly stayed here), and staff are knowledgeable on local history. Recent decades of guests are more likely to have been Dirk from Copenhagen on a six-month trip round the world and Shaz looking for work teaching English to fund the coming winter in Chiang Mai. But that may change with persistent whispers that the hotel is to be overhauled to its former five-star splendour. *Bars (2). Business centre. Concierge. Disabled-adapted rooms (2). Internet (high-speed). No-smoking floors. Parking (free). Restaurants (3). Room service (24hrs). TV.*

People's Square

Expensive

JW Marriott

Tomorrow Square, 399 Nanjing Xi Lu (5359 4969/ www.marriotthotels.com/shajw). Metro People's Square. **Rates** RMB 2,400 single/double. **Rooms** 342. **Credit** AmEx, DC, MC, V. **Map** p244 H5 **11**

The five-year-old JW Marriott occupies the upper part of the 60-storey rocket ship that is Tomorrow Square, on the north-west corner of People's Square, a location convenient for just about everywhere. The airy lobby lounge and check-in are on the 38th floor. The guestrooms are a cut above the five-star norm ('JW' is the Marriott's premier league brand), with plenty of space, comfy Revive Beds and hydraulic massage jets in the showers. Best of all are the simply fantastic views over the city through massive picture windows with bench-like sills (this is not a hotel for vertigo sufferers). In addition to all the usual facilities, the JW also boasts a private library on the uppermost floor reached by a winding staircase, a champagne bar with 360-degree views, 24-hour health club and a branch of the renowned Mandara Spa (*see p176*). *Bars (1). Business centre. Concierge. Disabled-adapted rooms (3). Gym. Internet (high-speed). No-smoking floors. Parking (RMB 10/hr). Pools (1 indoor, 1 outdoor). Restaurants (3). Room service (24hrs). Spa. TV.*

Radisson Hotel Shanghai New World

88 Nanjing Xi Lu, by Xizang Zhong Lu (6359 9999/ www.radisson.com). Metro People's Square. **Rates** RMB 1,800 single/double. **Rooms** 520. **Credit** MC, V. **Map** p244 J4 **12**

Radisson Hotel Shanghai New World occupies the Nanjing Lu skyscraper that looks as if a spaceship

URBN: China's first carbon-neutral lodgings. *See p37.*

landed on top of it (the 'spaceship' even flashes and whirls thanks to a 45th floor revolving restaurant). The interiors are exuberant and – in the spirit of the eastern end of this infamous strip – tacky and inexplicably popular. The 520 rooms are decorated with gilt gold excess, a riot of bold patterns and faux-Versace furnishings. However, the spacious family suites (replete with eight-seater dining table, lounge area and two bedrooms with double beds and massive en suites), are a good option for those travelling as a group. Other undeniable advantages of the Radisson are its affordable rates, complimentary broadband internet access in each rooms, and a super-central location in the heart of the action (at exit 7 of People's Square station). There's also an indoor swimming pool, virtual golf and adjoining Shanghai New World Plaza shopping mall with a SEGA World, cinema, iceskating rink and Madame Tussauds wax museum.

Bars (1). Business centre. Concierge. Disabled-adapted rooms (4). Gym. Internet (high-speed). No-smoking floors. Pool (1 indoor). Restaurants (3). Room service (24hrs). Spa. TV.

Le Royal Meridien

789 Nanjing Dong Lu, by Yunnan Lu (3318 9999/ www.starwoodhotels.com/lemeridien). Metro People's Square. **Rates** from RMB 1,750 single/double. **Rooms** 761. **Credit** AmEx, DC, MC, V. **Map** p244 J5 ⑬

Occupying the tallest building in Puxi, marked by two throbbing antennae, 66-storey Le Royal Meridien – the brand's Asia flagship – opened at People's Square in September 2006. The luxury behemoth boasts 761 ultra-modern rooms with glass

bathrooms, 42-inch plasma TVs, DVD/CD players, Wi-Fi and floor-to-ceiling city views. There is no shortage of restaurants and bars, notably Allure for fine French dining, 450-seat Ai Mei Cantonese and three-storey 789 Bar across the uppermost floors. In keeping with Le Meridien's apparent new focus on the 'creative individual', its artist-designed room keys can also be used to 'unlock' a free cultural experience, by giving you free entrance at the Museum of Contemporary Art (MOCA; *see p57*) across the road in People's Park.

Bars (1). Business centre. Concierge. Disabled-adapted rooms (7). Gym. Internet (high-speed). No-smoking floors. Parking (free). Pools (1 indoor). Restaurants (4). Room service (24hrs). Spa. TV.

Moderate

Park Hotel

170 Nanjing Xi Lu, by Huanghe Lu (6327 5225/ www.parkhotel.com.cn). Metro People's Square. **Rates** RMB 1,466-1,566 double. **Rooms** 252. **Credit** MC, V. **Map** p244 H5 ⑭

Today it is dwarfed by skyscraping neighbours, but when it opened in 1934 the Park Hotel was the tallest building in Asia. In those days it overlooked a racecourse, now it addresses the park and cultural institutions of People's Square; it remains a good location, convenient for sightseeing and the shops of Nanjing Lu. Although the dark stone exterior is still imposing, modernisations in 1998 stripped away much of the original character of the interior. The lobby retains some art deco detailing and fabulous black and white photographs documenting the hotel's glory days – sadly, all a far cry from the atmosphere in the poky rooms, which are furnished in identikit fashion, with basic amenities and old bathrooms. The hotel nonetheless hosts a steady stream of delegations and groups.

Bars (1). Business centre. Concierge. Disabled-adapted rooms (1). Gym. Internet (high-speed/ wireless). No-smoking floors. Parking (RMB 30/ day). Restaurants (3). Room service (24hrs). TV.

Jingan

Expensive

Four Seasons

500 Weihai Lu, by Shimen Yi Lu, Jingan (6256 8888/www.fourseasons.com). Metro Nanjing Xi Lu. **Rates** RMB 3,500 single/double. **Rooms** 435. **Credit** AmEx, DC, MC, V. **Map** p243 F5 ⑮

Fans of the particular brand of elegance and sophistication usually associated with the name Four Seasons may find themselves a bit nonplussed by the chain's Shanghai property, a purpose-built 37-storey twin-spired tower. The cavernous lobby and adjacent atrium café are pleasant enough. The same is true of the rooms, which are large but lack that extra oomph that usually sets the Four Seasons apart. Neither is the location too great: the hotel is a short walk from Nanjing Lu but the immediate surroundings are distinctly lacking in glamour.

Bars (1). Business centre. Concierge. Disabled-adapted rooms (2). Gym. Internet (high-speed). No-smoking floors. Parking (RMB 10/hr). Pool (1 indoor). Restaurants (3). Room service (24hrs). Spa. TV.

Jia Shanghai

931 Nanjing Xi Lu, by Taixing Lu (6217 9000/ www.jiashanghai.com). Metro Nanjing Dong Lu. **Rates** 2,600 single/double. **Rooms** 55. **Credit** AmEx, DC, MC, V. **Map** p243 F5 ⑯

Design aficionados will love Jia Shanghai, first sibling of the Philippe Starck-designed Jia in Hong Kong. Housed in a 1920s neoclassical building on thoroughfare Nanjing Lu, Jia sets the bar for Shanghai boutique hotels with its fashionably low-key approach. The 55 quietly theatrical rooms feature dark timber floors, Bisazza-tiled bathrooms and white marble kitchenettes. Entertainment includes 42-inch flat-screen TVs with DVDs, Nintendo and Wii games, MP3 link-ups to a surround-sound speaker system and, if all that sounds too technical, a selection of old-fashioned board games. Glamorous second-floor restaurant Issimo, in collaboration with celebrity chef Salvatore Cuomo, serves rustic-chic Italian fare and excellent wood-fired pizzas, while the trendy hotel clientele mingles over complimentary breakfast, afternoon cakes and evening wines in the private residential lounge.

Bars (1). Business centre. Concierge. Gym. Internet (high-speed). No-smoking floors. Parking (free). Restaurants (1). Room service. Spa. TV.

Portman Ritz-Carlton

Shanghai Centre, 1376 Nanjing Xi Lu, by Xikang Lu, Jingan (6279 8888/www.ritzcarlton.com). Metro Jingan Temple. **Rates** RMB 2,000 single/ double. **Rooms** 628. **Credit** AmEx, DC, MC, V. **Map** p243 E5 ⑰

As part of the Shanghai Centre, the Portman is at the heart of expat life; ranged around the forecourt

are various consulates and airline offices, a Singaporean-run Parkway Health surgery, excellent City Supermarket, cafés Element Fresh (*see p103*) and Paul bakery (*see p109*), a California Pizza Kitchen and the Long Bar. To celebrate its tenth anniversary in 2008, the hotel unveiled a $50 million renovation. Imperial-red columns and a giant fountain now announce the entrance on Nanjing Lu; Tables all-day restaurant and The Bar have trendy new designs; and the 628 rooms over 50 floors have been updated with rich rosewood, Italian marble and LCD TVs. Other bonuses include a 24-hour Club Lounge and gym, on-call 'technology butlers', and one of the city's top Italian restaurants, Palladio. Service throughout is exemplary, although what really wins favour is that despite being one of the city's oldest international five-stars, the Portman still feels like one of the most vibrant and essential places to stay in town.

Bars (1). Business centre. Concierge. Disabled-adapted rooms (2). Gym. Internet (high-speed). No-smoking floors. Parking (free). Pools (1 indoor, 1 outdoor). Restaurants (4). Room service (24hrs). Spa. TV (widescreen/DVD/TV room).

URBN

183 Jiaozhou Lu, by Xinzha Lu (5153 4600/ www.urbnhotels.com). Metro Jingan Temple. **Rates** 2,000 single/double. **Rooms** 26. **Credit** AmEx, DC, MC, V. **Map** p242 C5 ⑱

The 26-room URBN, which opened in 2007 (around the time that China became the world's worst CO_2 polluter), is the nation's first carbon-neutral hotel. Transforming a '70s-era post office block behind Jingan Temple (*see p66*), the hotel pioneers sustainable building practices and offsets remaining energy (including staff commutes, food and beverage delivery, and energy used by guests) by purchasing carbon credits that go towards funding wind farms, hydro-electricity stations and other clean-energy projects around China. Guests have the option of offsetting their flights too. Despite the green theme, Urbn is no rustic-looking retreat. The contemporary Asian-styled rooms come with futons, sunken lounges, open bathtubs, iPod docks and free Wi-Fi. Guests have access to in-room spa treatments and local culture lessons – not to mention the Shanghai social set that congregates at roomtwentyeight restaurant (*see p106*) in the lobby. *Photo p35.*

Bars (1). No-smoking floors. Internet (Wi-Fi). Restaurant (1). Room Service. TV.

Moderate

Ivy Shanghai

709 Jiaozhou Lu, by Yuyao Lu (3221 2600/ www.ivyshanghai.com). **Rates** from RMB 600 single/double. **Rooms** 46. **Credit** AmEx, DC, MC, V. **Map** p242 C3 ⑲

The green army camouflage exterior of this cinema-turned-design-hotel looks laughably conspicuous amid the surrounding flats and abandoned factory buildings on the outskirts of the Jingan district. But then the Ivy isn't going for subtlety. Paris-based interior designer Dillon Garris vamps up the interplay of ancient and modern Chinese design with bright red lattice screens, neon-lit corridors and local pop art. The 46 contemporary-styled rooms are somewhat calmer, with a hint of fun in the red cashmere throws and moon gates separating the four-poster bed from the expansive living quarters. LCD TVs, DVD/CD players, 24-hour butlers and in-room secretarial services are among the high-end offerings.

Bars (1). Business centre. Concierge. Internet (high-speed). No-smoking floors. Parking (free). Restaurants (2). Room service (24hrs). TV.

Budget

Baolong Home Hotel

125 Nanyang Lu, by Xikang Lu (5174 8188/ www.bljj.net.cn). Metro Jingan Temple. **Rates** RMB 349 double. **Rooms** 66. **Credit** AmEx, DC, MC, V. **Map** p242 D5 ⑳

Tucked away behind the Portman Ritz Carlton (in fact, staring straight at its air-conditioning shafts), the Baolong Home Hotel is part of a small budget chain of stylish, well-managed establishments. The small bamboo courtyard, classic Chinese lobby and pristine facilities belie the economy rates. Low-lit corridors connect the 66 guestrooms, equipped with air-conditioning, international direct dial phones, free internet access and traditional Chinese decorative touches. You emerge from the driveway into a vibrant neighbourhood of bars and boutiques.

Internet (high-speed). No-smoking floors. Room service (24hrs). TV.

Lapis Casa Boutique Hotel. *See p39.*

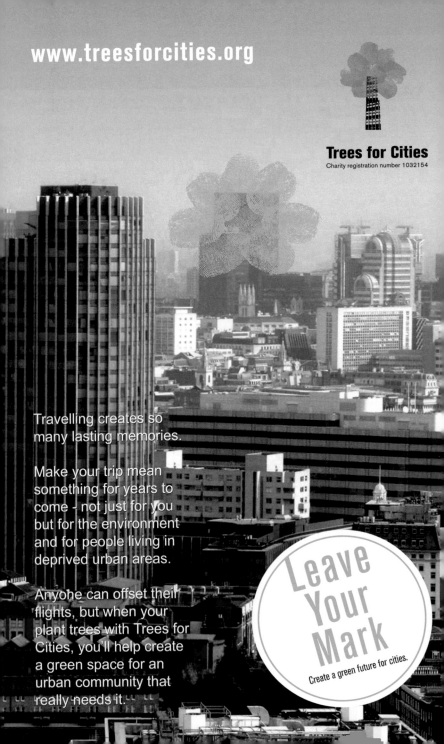

Old City

Moderate

Renaissance Yuyuan Shanghai

*159 Henan Nanlu, by Fuyou Lu (2321 8888/
www.renaissancehotels.com/shasy).* **Rates** from
RMB 1,250 single/double. **Rooms** 341. **Credit**
AmEx, DC, MC, V. **Map** p248 L7 ㉑
The Renaissance Yuyuan Shanghai opened in the
city's famed Yu Gardens in 2007. The four-star
brand's trendy new-look flagship is apparently
designed to appeal to 25- to 40-year-olds.
Accordingly, the 341-room hotel, conceptualised by
Czech glass artist Borek Sipek, is decked out in bold
carpets and quirky blown glass. Cheery light
turquoise and yellow guestrooms feature 32-inch
flat-screen TVs, Wi-Fi internet, glass bathrooms and
tubs in the living area in some cases. Views over the
faux Ming dynasty-styled former Chinese settlement
are especially impressive at night when the winged
rooftops are outlined with fairy lights. A two-storey
Quan Spa is decked out in vibrant hues of aqua,
mauve and lime, with petrified palm trees, Vichy
showers and yet more breathtaking views. There's
also a 24-hour gym and rooftop indoor pool with a
(terrifying) glass infinity wall.
*Bars (1). Business centre. Concierge. Disabled-
adapted rooms (2). Gym. Internet (high-speed).
No-smoking floors. Parking (free). Pool (1 indoor).
Restaurants (2). Room service (24hrs). Spa. TV.*

Xintiandi

Expensive

88 Xintiandi

*380 Huangpi Nan Lu, by Taicang Lu (5383 8833/
www.88xintiandi.com). Metro Huangpi Nan Lu.*
Rates RMB 3,300 single/double. **Rooms** 53.
Credit AmEx, DC, MC, V. **Map** p248 H7 ㉒
Aesthetically speaking, Shanghai could do with
many more ventures like 88 Xintiandi, a boutique
hotel that looks exquisite with its updated Chinese
art deco. Part of the massive Xintiandi shopping and
nightlife complex, 88 is aimed primarily at the
wealthy business traveller, and the high-spec rooms
come with all the requisite creature and technological comforts for the expense-account rich, time-poor
customer, including a kitchenette and complimentary broadband. The best of the 53 rooms overlook the
artificial lake; the others address a busy shopping
plaza. Guests have access to a boutique health club,
spa and swimming pool next door.
*Concierge. Internet (high-speed). No-smoking floors.
Pools (1 indoor). Room service. Spa. TV.*

Lapis Casa Boutique Hotel

*68 Taicang Lu, by Shunchang Lu (5382 1600/
www.lapiscasahotel.com). Metro Huangpi Nan Lu.*
Rates RMB 1,800 double. **Rooms** 18. **Credit**
AmEx, DC, MC, V. **Map** p248 J7 ㉓

The Taiwanese owners of Shanghai restaurant and
rustic ceramic tableware brand Lapis Lazuli have
refreshed a natty old hotel not far from Xintiandi into
18 individually designed rooms. Though small, the
rooms boast a touch of '20s Shanghai decadence in
the club chairs, candelabra and green jade sinks.
Rooms 81 to 84 offer leafy views over Huaihai Park,
and there's a Mediterranean-styled Japanese restaurant and a branch of the Taiwanese Bellagio chain
downstairs – and, of course, all the action of Xintiandi
and Huaihai Lu lie just outside the door. Internet and
the minibar are offered free of charge. *Photo p36.*
*Bar (1). Internet (wireless). Restaurants (1). Room
service. TV.*

Pudi Boutique Hotel Fuxing Parc

*99 Yandang Lu, by Nanchang Lu (5158 5888/
www.boutiquehotel.cc). Metro Huangpi Nan Lu.*
Rates RMB 2,277 suite. **Rooms** 52. **Credit**
AmEx, DC, MC, V. **Map** p247 G8 ㉔
A short walk from Xintiandi, the Accor-managed
Pudi offers 52 generously-sized guestrooms adorned
with original works by contemporary Chinese artists.
The dark, sophisticated rooms with bold copper bath-
rooms target the high-end China clique. Nice touches
include in-room check-in, a pillow menu featuring
exotic green tea and buckwheat varieties, complimen-
tary Wi-Fi and a 'bath master'. Guests can enjoy a
members' lounge with Perrier-Jouet 'Belle Époque'
Champagne Room and a rooftop jacuzzi. Pudi is also
Shanghai's only pet-friendly hotel. Party animals
meanwhile can head downstairs to the Philippe
Starck-designed club, Volar (*see p185*). *Photo p42.*
*Business centre. Disabled-adapted rooms (1). Gym.
Internet (high-speed). No-smoking floors. Parking
(20/day). Restaurants (1). Room service (24hrs). TV.*

French Concession

Expensive

Hengshan Moller Villa

*30 Shaanxi Nan Lu, by Yan'an Zhong Lu (6247
8881/www.mollervilla.com). Metro Shanxi Nan Lu.*
Rates RMB 1,500-1,800 double. **Rooms** 27. **Credit**
AmEx, DC, MC, V. **Map** p243 E6 ㉕
Popular mythology has it that Eric Moller, a wealthy
Jewish businessman, built Moller Residence in 1936
to a design dreamt up by his 12-year-old daughter.
It seems a plausible enough explanation for the
steeples, spires, pointy red gables and patterned
brickwork that give the place the look of a gaudy
Gothic castle. The house was later used as offices by
the Shanghai Communist Youth League, and converted to a hotel in 2001, benefiting from a prime (if
slightly noisy) location near Shanghai's shopping
streets. A major makeover in 2008, though taking a
few structural liberties, tuned up and toned down
the interiors, introducing flat-screen TVs and other
contemporary luxuries while retaining its classic
European style and fairytale aura. All 27 guestrooms are set back off the street in Building Two,

Keeping the Peace

Travellers visiting Sir Victor Sassoon's Cathay Hotel on the Bund during its 1930s heyday were greeted by a thrusting art deco symbol of Shanghai's modernity and international glamour. They would feast on Parisian foie gras and Californian peaches in the marble-clad dining rooms; shop for Rolex watches or Lalique glass in the luxury arcades; and join Shanghai's social set for classical concerts and cocktail parties. They might even bump into famous guests like Charlie Chaplin or Noel Coward, who reputedly penned *Private Lives* in the Cathay Suite.

In stark contrast, before the Peace Hotel closed its doors for much-needed restoration in April 2007, visitors would be lucky to get some stale peanuts and a serenade from the octogenarian jazz band in the dimly lit lounge. The 80-year-old icon was in a state of slow decay, wearing the scars of a tumultuous past that saw it ravaged by wartime bombs, requisitioned by Nationalists and made redundant by the Communists. Most destructive of all were the rounds of 'modernisations' from the 1950s to the '90s, which systematically stripped the interior of much of its charm and treasures.

The revitalisation of the landmark hotel was hotly contested for years among luxury global players until finally, with the 2010 World Expo a looming yardstick, Jin Jiang International Group appointed Fairmont Hotels & Resorts to manage a new five-star icon, to be known as the **Fairmont Peace Hotel Shanghai** (*see p29*). Shanghai-based architectural firm Allied Architects International and hospitality design heavyweights Hirsch Bedner Associates were charged with the restoration, working carefully with Tongji University, the Shanghai Design Institute and a handful of respected consultants, including 80-year-old architectural expert Luo Xiao, local historian Peter Hibbard and art deco specialists.

The reawakening of this grand dame is an exciting project to be sure, but one that has been fraught with challenges. The first being an acute lack of detailed information on the building, prompting a worldwide quest for photographic and documentary evidence to help piece together a better understanding of how the hotel began life and evolved over time. The hotel site also underwent a detailed

while the front building contains restaurants and function rooms leading out to a picturesque garden, which is a popular spot for Chinese newlyweds to pose for their wedding day photos.
Bars (1). Business centre. Concierge. Internet (high-speed). No-smoking floors. Parking (free). Restaurants (2). Room service (24-hour). TV.

Mansion Hotel

82 Xinle Lu, by Xiangyang Bei Lu (5403 9888/ www.chinamansionhotel.com). Metro Shanxi Nan Lu. **Rates** from RMB 1,980 single/double. **Rooms** 32. **Credit** AmEx, DC, MC, V. **Map** p247 E7 ㉖
Many of Shanghai's historic buildings now operate as lacklustre hotels, but Mansion Hotel is an exception. This boutique hotspot had a less than propi-

tious past – it was the headquarters of Shanghai mafia boss Du Yuesheng in the 1930s. At the height of Shanghai's gangster era, it is believed that up to 40 per cent of the world's opium passed through the building. The hotel lobby is a veritable museum of memorabilia from the owner's private collection, while 32 rooms ooze classical opulence, with 15-foot ceilings, art deco chandeliers, plush-pile carpets and enormous baths. Modern luxuries include Bose iPod docks, printer/scanner/fax, 42-inch flat-screen satellite TVs, CD/radio and free Wi-Fi. The sprawling 150sq m (1,600sq ft) Mansion Suites are among the largest – and most expensive – in town, their private stone terraces overlooking the small Chinese garden below and the onion domes of the Russian Orthodox

structural study to define the precise dimensions and original floor plan, during which time entire hidden floors and mezzanines were discovered.

But perhaps the most difficult aspect of all for the architects was the transformation of the Peace into a functional and profitable modern five-star hotel. When Tug Wilson first designed Sassoon House in 1926, it wasn't actually intended to be a hotel at all, but rather an office building and luxury shopping complex topped with 20 residential apartments. Construction had reached the fourth floor when the edict came from Sassoon to convert the upper section into a luxury hotel. As a result, some floors even shared public washrooms – not an acceptable arrangement for a modern-day luxury hotel.

When the building resumed its former duty in 1956, it was carved in sections around the other tenants, and the back-of-house areas were less than efficient. The design team has therefore had to completely rethink the internal operational systems of kitchens, offices and loading docks, not to mention incorporating the modern requirements of a luxury hotel, like car parking and a health club. Key to facilitating all of this has been the addition of a new construct in a small vacant block at the back of the hotel. The Fairmont Peace Hotel Shanghai is slated to reopen after its three-year overhaul in 2010, aiming to capture Sir Victor Sassoon's vision of the grand hotel of the past, as well as his visionary commitment to Shanghai's bright future.

Church across the road. Service standards can be somewhat inconsistent, but for a taste of authentic 1930s decadence, Mansion's the one.
Bars (1). Concierge. Internet (high-speed). No-smoking floors. Parking (free). Restaurants (1). Room service. Spa. TV.

Okura Garden Hotel

58 Maoming Nan Lu, by Changle Lu (6415 1111/ www.gardenhotelshanghai.com). Metro Shanxi Nan Lu. **Rates** RMB 1,700 double. **Rooms** 492. **Credit** AmEx, DC, MC, V. **Map** p247 F7 ㉗
The Okura looks a bit like a miniature White House (complete with landscaped lawn), which has had a 33-storey concrete monstrosity land behind it. The beautiful baroque building, with its two grand lobbies,

sweeping staircases, art deco detailing and original 1926 oval ballroom, is what remains of the old Cercle Sportif French Club. The hotel later became a favoured retreat of Chairman Mao, at which time a bomb shelter was built beneath the front lawn. The new block contains the accommodation – 492 guestrooms that are comfortable if undistinguished. As part of the Okura group, the hotel is geared to travellers from Japan – staff speak Japanese, the rooms have yukata robes and techno toilets, and there's a fine Japanese restaurant, Yamazato, and a top-floor teppanyaki bar. Stop by for a coffee in the lobby lounge, and soak in the live classical music and elegant colonial atmosphere.
Bars (3). Business centre. Concierge. Disabled-adapted rooms (1). Gym. Internet (high-speed). No-smoking floors. Parking (free). Pool (1 indoor). Restaurants (5). Room service (24hrs). Spa. TV.

Moderate

City Hotel

5-7 Shanxi Nan Lu, by Yanan Zhong Lu (6255 1133/www.cityhotelshanghai.com). **Rates** from RMB 955 single/double. **Rooms** 270. **Credit** AmEx, DC, MC, V. **Map** p243 F6 ㉘
Rising 26 storeys over the French Concession, the four-star City Hotel is a crisp, clean and convenient base midway between the restaurants and nightlife of the French Concession, and the bustling commerce of the Jingan district. The two-decade-old hotel has recently had a full makeover and its 270 rooms are basic but pleasant and well maintained. Request a room on the southern side for sun and views over the residential lanes. There's a large health club with a spa and indoor pool, and a lobby bar with tall windows looking out to the passing parade of fashionistas along Shanxi Nan Lu, a street known locally for its well-priced shoe shops.
Bars (1). Business centre. Concierge. Disabled-adapted rooms (1). Gym. Internet (high-speed). No-smoking floors. Parking (RMB 40/day). Pool (1 indoor). Restaurants (4). Room service (24hrs). Spa. TV.

Donghu Hotel

70 Donghu Lu, by Huaihai Zhong Lu (6415 8158/ www.donghuhotel.com). Metro Changshu Lu or Shanxi Nan Lu. **Rates** RMB 878 double. **Rooms** 271. **Credit** AmEx, DC, MC, V. **Map** p246 D7 ㉙
Donghu Hotel is a collection of seven mansion blocks in walled grounds, dating from the 1920s and '30s, formerly home to infamous gangster Du Yuesheng and his sundry mistresses. In their current demobbed incarnation the assorted buildings offer 271 guestrooms, which come equipped with all the usual facilities. The real draw, however, is the garden setting, lush with trees, flowers and a 25-metre swimming pool. There is a good Korean barbecue restaurant on the premises, with loads more fabulous boutiques, bars and eateries a short walk along Huaihai Lu, and dotted throughout the leafy backstreets and alleys of this charming part of town.

Bars (3). Business centre. Concierge. Disabled-adapted rooms (1). Gym. Internet (high-speed). No-smoking floors. Parking (free). Pool (1 indoor). Restaurants (1). Room service (24hrs). TV (pay movies).

Jinjiang Hotel

59 Maoming Nan Lu, by Changle Lu (6258 2582/ www.jinjianghotels.com). Metro Shanxi Nan Lu. **Rates** RMB 1,058 double. **Rooms** 434. **Credit** AmEx, DC, MC, V. **Map** p247 F7 ③⓪

Built in 1929 as plush residences for the French, the distinctive white-and-dark-brick Jinjiang Hotel occupies a walled garden complex made up of five heritage buildings and acres of manicured lawns. While some of the original fittings can still be glimpsed in the lobby of the main Cathay Building, the guestrooms have unfortunately been renovated into blandness, save their airy three-metre high ceilings. A better option is the Cathay Garden across the courtyard, which was rebuilt in 2005 in the art deco style of its neighbours, and has 208 sophisticated chocolate-and-taupe-toned executive rooms with luxurious beds and spacious bathrooms – all for only slightly more than those in the original block. Be sure to ask for a garden view. Excellent mod-Chinese restaurant The Chinoise Story occupies the main building, while the adjoining 'Jinjiang gourmet street' is home to popular MSG-free Shanghainese restaurant Yin (*see p113*).

Business centre. Concierge. Disabled-adapted rooms (1). Internet (high-speed). No-smoking floors. Parking (free). Pool (1 indoor). Restaurants (4). Room service (24hrs). TV.

The Nine

9 Jianguo Xi Lu, by Taiyuan Lu (6471 9950). Metro Hengshan Lu. **Rates** RMB 800-1,500 single/double. **Rooms** 6. **No credit cards.** **Map** p246 D10 ③①

This beautiful art deco B&B is run in laid-back (albeit slightly exclusive) style, shunning press and soliciting most of its reservations through word of mouth alone. Entering through large wooden gates, the lucky few (there are only six rooms) at once get a sense that this is more private residence than hotel. Exquisite antique furniture and Buddhist sculptures engender an air of taste and tranquillity, as do the peaceful garden and secluded balconies. The guestrooms – all with en suite – have their own unique ambience and objets d'art. Upstairs rooms are brightest and, while the penthouse comes complete with a kitchen and large terrace, we love the junior suite with its own private library. Breakfast is served in the 'mahjong room'. The management sees its guests as friends, but fussy diets, noisy children and bad attitudes are not tolerated.

Internet (high-speed). Room service. TV (TV room).

Old House Inn

No.16, Lane 351, Huashan Lu, by Changshu Lu (6248 6118/www.oldhouse.cn). Metro Changshu Lu. **Rates** RMB 800-1,130 double. **Rooms** 12. **Credit** MC, V. **Map** p242 C7 ③②

The Old House Inn is a small, independently run B&B set tucked away down a typical French Concession residential alley. The 70-year-old lane house has a dozen guestrooms – king, queen, doubles, and singles – with wooden floors, elegant Ming

dynasty-style furniture and stylish bathrooms. Breakfast is served in the hip ground-floor restaurant and bar, A Future Perfect, which spills out into a leafy courtyard garden. The simply stylish residence and homely vibe make this a very popular choice and as a result room rates have risen sharply in recent years, but it nevertheless remains a competitive and very charming place to stay.
Internet (high-speed). No-smoking floors. Room service (24hrs). TV.

Ruijin Guesthouse

118 Ruijin Erlu, by Fuxing Zhonglu (6472 5222/ http://china.showhotel.com/shanghai/ruijing). Metro Shanxi Nan Lu then 20mins walk. **Rates** from RMB 1,320 single/double. **Rooms** 62. **Credit** AmEx, DC, MC, V. **Map** p247 F8 ㉝

What's now a guesthouse used to be the Morriss Estate, home to an eccentric newspaper tycoon and his pack of racing hounds. In its current form the place is composed of five statuesque villas surrounded by lawns, wooded gardens and a small lake. Opt for Building 2, the original 1920s family home, with larger rooms and art deco details. What could be an amazing boutique property remains slightly underwhelming due in large part to poor service and mismanagement. Still, the setting can't be beaten, especially given that one of Shanghai's best bars (Face, *see p124*), with accompanying upstairs Thai restaurant (La Na Thai) and Indian restaurant Hazara are within the beautiful grounds.
Bars (4). Business centre. Concierge. Gym. Internet (high-speed). Parking (RMB 100/day). Pool (1 indoor). Restaurants (4). Room service. Spa. TV.

Taiyuan Villa

160 Taiyuan Lu, by Yongjia Lu (6471 6688/ www.ruijinhotelsh.com). Metro Shanxi Nan Lu then 20mins walk. **Rates** RMB 1,200 double. **Rooms** 23. **Credit** MC, V. **Map** p246 D9 ㉞

This state-owned mansion, built in 1928 by a French nobleman, is best known as the former digs of General George Marshall, who was chief mediator between Nationalist Chinese leader Chiang Kaishek and Communist leader Mao Zedong. After the Communist victory, it became Madame Mao's favourite pied à terre in Shanghai. The beautifully maintained villa, set in several acres of greenery deep in the French Concession, was given a classy makeover in 2007. The 13 guestrooms and reception lounges have been restored to their former French elegance, with black and white marble floors, chandeliers, Persian rugs, elaborate fireplaces and French windows leading out to the manicured lawns.
Business centre. Concierge. No-smoking floors. Parking (free). Pool (1 indoor). Restaurants (2). Room service. TV.

Changning & Hongqiao

Moderate

Millennium Hotel Hongqiao Shanghai

2588 Yanan Xi Lu, by Shuicheng Nan Lu (6208 5888/www.millenniumhotels.com/cn/millennium shanghai). **Rates** RMB 1,100 single/double. **Rooms** 369. **Credit** AmEx, DC, MC, V. **Map** p240 A4 ㉟

Pudi Boutique Hotel Fuxing Parc.
See p39.

Located in the west of the city, just six kilometres (3.7 miles) from Hongqiao domestic airport, and close to Shanghai Mart and the Shanghai Exhibition Centre, the five-star Millennium Hotel is the sort of sleek, contemporary option you'd expect given its business oriented location. Opened in 2007, its 369 comfortably exuberant rooms feature floor-to-ceiling windows, flat-screen TVs, peek-a-boo bathrooms and a spacious layout. There is a selection of Chinese and Western restaurants and lounges on site, and free shuttle buses to the downtown action. Predominantly a business hotel, its fringe location means that prices tend to be more competitive, with special packages sometimes available at weekends. *Bars (2). Business centre. Concierge. Gym. Internet (high-speed). Parking. Pool (1 indoor). Restaurants (4). Room service. Spa. TV.*

Budget

Motel 168
1119 Yanan Xi Lu, by Zhaohua Lu (5117 7777/ www.motel168.com). Metro Jiangsu Lu. **Rates** from RMB 300 double. **Rooms** 510. **Map** p242 A7 ㊱
Started in 2004 by the local Merrilyn group, China's first 'motel' chain already has 20 properties in Shanghai and is rapidly expanding across the country. Offering simple, serviceable accommodation and great value for money, these cheap and cheerful places are naturally extremely popular with Chinese budget travellers, so be sure to call the reservation hotline a few days in advance. Rooms come equipped with basic amenities and free broadband, and strive for some style with feature pebbles, sculptures and a bold colour scheme. We like the Yanan Lu motel, right across from the Regent, with a 24-hour cafeteria and branch of the popular Merrilyn restaurant serving Shanghai, Jiangsu and Zhejiang cuisine. For an extra RMB 100 or so, Motel 268 next door offers a more upscale experience, with trendy contemporary apartments, and use of a communal kitchen and laundry.
Other locations 715 Aomen Lu, by Xikang Lu, 5115 6000; 400 Wanping Nan Lu, by Xietu Lu, Xujiahui, 5157 7788; 365 Shangcheng Lu, by Pucheng Lu, Lujiazui, 5115 6111.
Internet (high-speed). Parking (free). Restaurants (2). Room service (24hrs). TV (pay movies).

Pudong

Expensive

Grand Hyatt
88 Shiji Dadao, by Yincheng Lu (5049 1234/ www.shanghai.hyatt.com). Metro Lujiazui. **Rates** RMB 2,200 single/double. **Rooms** 555. **Credit** AmEx, DC, MC, V. **Map** p245 O5 ㊲
For many years, the Grand Hyatt, which occupies the top 34 floors of the cloud-piercing 88-storey Jinmao Tower, held the title of the world's highest hotel – that is until sister property Park Hyatt (*see below*), in the World Financial Centre right next door, knocked it off its high-flying perch. The Grand Hyatt's central atrium, which soars 33 floors from the hotel lobby, is a breathtaking sci-fi spectacular of seemingly infinite circular galleries. Its 555 spacious guestrooms and suites have floor-to-ceiling windows to make the most of the incredible views; those facing the river on the 40th to 50th floors offer the finest panoramas. The hotel also boasts a clutch of excellent restaurants, including modern-Italian Cucina, and a dream of a bar in the appropriately named Cloud 9 (*see p128*).
Bars (5). Business centre. Concierge. Disabled-adapted rooms (2). Gym. Internet (high-speed). No-smoking floors. Parking (free). Pool (1 indoor). Restaurants (5). Room service. Spa. TV.

Park Hyatt Shanghai
Building 1, 100 Shiji, by Dongtai Lu, Pudong (6888 1234/www.shanghai.park.hyatt.com). Metro Lujiazui. **Rates** call for details. **Rooms** 174. **Credit** AmEx, DC, MC, V. **Map** p245 P5 ㊳
Stealing the crown of world's tallest hotel from its sister property Grand Hyatt right next door, the Park Hyatt Shanghai was poised to open as we went to press. Guests will be able to look down on the rest of the city from the 79th to 93rd floors of the key-shaped Shanghai World Financial Centre (*see p91* **Height matters**) in Pudong. The 174-room property promises to be the vertiginous height of hotel luxury, boasting an aerial tai chi courtyard, and various stylish dining, entertainment and meeting venues across the top three floors.
Bars (2). Business Centre. Concierge. Disabled-adapted rooms. Gym. Internet (high-speed). No-smoking floors. Restaurants (4). Room service (24-hour). Spa. TV.

Pudong Shangri-La
33 Fucheng Lu, by Yincheng Dong Lu (6882 8888/ www.shangri-la.com). Metro Lujiazui. **Rates** RMB 2,320 double. **Rooms** 375. **Credit** AmEx, DC, MC, V. **Map** p245 O5 ㊴
The opening of this $138 million second tower in late 2005 made Pudong Shangri-La the biggest five-star hotel in Shanghai – and one of the very best. The newer glass tower looks like a hip younger sibling of the more flamboyant original building. This sleek contemporary design aesthetic continues into the 375 spacious new rooms and suites, which have 32-inch LCD TVs, DVDs, and floor-to-ceiling views across the river to the Bund (rooms ending in 60, 61 and 62 are best). There's also a heavenly day spa CHI (*see p176*), and 12 excellent drinking and dining destinations. The jewel in the crown – Jade on 36 bar-restaurant (*see p118*) – boasts dazzling 36th-floor views of the Bund, French chef Paul Pairet's deliciously quirky cuisine and fabulously eccentric design elements, like giant Chinese snuff bottles and a jade box bar. A great place to stay.
Bars (3). Business centre. Concierge. Gym. Internet (high-speed). No-smoking floors. Parking (free). Pool (1 indoor). Restaurants (5). Room service (24hrs). Spa. TV (widescreen/DVD).

Sightseeing

Introduction

Shang hi.

In a city where fashion and fortune reign, visitors may feel like they are clutching at straws as they try to get a glimpse of traditional culture and custom. If it's imperial palaces, dynastic tombs and ancient city walls you want, the place to head in Shanghai is the airport – you'll find all of those in Beijing and countless other Chinese cities, but not in Shanghai. While there are a few incense-fogged temples and a pretty ornamental garden with a zigzag bridge, this is a city that doesn't so much thumb its nose at tradition as jump in a bulldozer and flatten it. Which isn't to say that there's nothing to see and do here – far from it – it's just that the quintessential Shanghai experience differs from those of other cities.

Our list of highlights starts with eating. We can't conceive of a finer introduction to the city than an evening at **Bao Luo** (*see p109*), **1221** (*see p118*) or **Yin** (*see p113*), gorging on dish after dish of local specialities.

The next essential experience is to shop. It doesn't matter if the activity is normally anathema to you, in Shanghai it's a whole different ball game – actually, it's not a ball game at all, it's a blood sport. Don't believe us? Then try haggling at one of the city's **markets** (*see p132*). By the end of the day, you will walk out sheepishly with a new suitcase, bought to transport the hoards of Chinese kitsch that you couldn't resist. After all, it was just so cheap!

Shopping done, nights should be spent in old colonial elegance, sipping gin slings on the veranda of a villa that once belonged to a 1920s opium lord, or nibbling canapés on a rooftop terrace while checking out the Vegas-style show that is the city's skyline after dark.

SHANGHAI GEOGRAPHY

Shanghai is divided into a multitude of local municipalities but these are not very helpful to the visitor, so we've instead divided the city up

Essential Shanghai

...in one day

Everyone should start by seeing **the Bund**, where the architectural glories of the past face off against the architectural glories of the future over the water in Pudong. Cross under the river in the zany **Bund Tourist Tunnel** for a coffee at one of a string of **riverside cafés**. Cross back over to the Bund, perhaps by one of the frequent ferries, for a lunch with a view. Afterwards, stroll west down pedestrianised **Nanjing Lu** to experience full-on Chinese commercialism. Exit into People's Square for cultural enlightenment at the **Shanghai Museum** and/or contemplate the city's future at the **Urban Planning Centre**.

Flag down a taxi for **Ruijin Er Lu** and a sundowner on the terrace of **Face** bar or opt for an aperitif with city views on **Mansion Hotel**'s gorgeous terrace. You are now in the heart of the French Concession, with at least a dozen excellent restaurants within easy walking distance, including standouts **Bao Luo**, **Shintori**, **South Beauty** and **Yin**.

Whichever of these you choose, there is an equally outstanding bar just minutes away (People 7, Face, Constellation).

...in two days

Day one, as above; start day two early at **Fuxing Park** in the French Concession, where you can watch Shanghainese of all ages practise tai chi. For images of the country's communist past, amble over to the **Propaganda Poster Art Centre**, taking in the **boutiques** along Maoming Lu and Nanchang Lu along the way. Hop on the metro or head back along upmarket Huaihai Lu, aiming to end up in the ye olde Shanghai precincts of **Xintiandi** for lunch. Spend the early afternoon dallying at **Dongtai Antiques Market**, just east, then continue east along Fangbang Zhong Lu to the bustling **Old City** and the gorgeous **Yu Gardens**, where you can enjoy a bumper dumpling feast at **Nan Xiang**.

Take a taxi ride to the Bund for an **evening cocktail** at one of the glamorous rooftop bars (Glamour Bar, New Heights, Bar Rouge). Raise a toast to China's most vibrant city.

into our own, more easily digestible geographical areas. Thumbnail sketches of these areas might read:

● **The Bund & around** The heart of colonial Shanghai with a grand waterfront promenade and a flamboyant restaurant and bar scene.

● **People's Square & Nanjing Dong Lu** Museum central and the busiest shopping street in the city.

● **Jingan** The central business district with top-end malls and two temples.

● **The Old City** The original Chinese area, with gardens, a temple and an old-style bazaar.

● **Xintiandi** A modern redevelopment of an old quarter, now a top spot for shopping, dining and entertainment.

● **French Concession** Low-rise, tree-lined and pretty… little in the way of sights but lots of superb shopping, dining and drinking.

● **Xujiahui, Hongqiao & Gubei** Far-flung south-western suburbs with an authentic temple, gardens and a bloody history.

● **Pudong** Space-age financial district east of the river with rapidly sprouting skyscrapers.

● **Hongkou** A largely residential area with sites of cultural and Jewish significance.

Shanghai operates on an east–west axis. Its two main streets are **Nanjing Lu** and **Huaihai Lu**. The first connects Jingan with People's Square and the Bund, the other the French Concession with Xintiandi and the Old City. Both are pedestrian-friendly and many of the city's sights are located on or just off one or the other. Running parallel between the two is **Yanan Lu**, an elevated highway for fast-moving traffic. At night, this expressway is lit in red and blue neon – trust Shanghai to make a feature of a flyover.

GETTING AROUND

Despite the immense size of the greater city, the districts that will most interest visitors are closely grouped and manageable in size. Getting around on foot is pretty easy. There's also a good, modern metro system, although it can be crowded and where English-language signage there is isn't easy to spot. We recommend that you make use of taxis, which are both plentiful and cheap. For more information on navigating the city, *see pp216-218.* For our **self-guided walks,** *see p70 & p82.*

TOURS AND CRUISES

Jinjiang Tour Buses (6445 9525) runs a red hop-on, hop-off sightseeing bus that hits all the city's top spots, including People's Square, Yu Gardens, the Bund and the Oriental Pearl Tower. Buses depart every 30 to 45 minutes from the Jinjiang Hotel (*see p42*; 9am-5.15pm

Mon-Fri; 8.45am-5.45pm Sat, Sun; tickets RMB 18). Alternatively, a one-day tour of the city, including all sights and lunch, is priced at RMB 400 per person, with pick-up at the Jinjiang Hotel at 8.40am. Active sorts could join **Bohdi Bikes** (www.bohdi.com.cn) on one of its city bike rides (RMB 200, plus RMB 100 bike & helmet rental, 10am-3pm Sat).

It's also worth checking the website of the **Chinese Culture Club** (www.chinese cultureclub.org). This is an organisation dedicated to introducing China and its culture to foreigners through talks, courses and regular tours around specific parts of the city. **Community Center Shanghai** (www.communitycenter.cn) offers similar activities and day events.

A variety of companies offer river cruises along the Huangpu River, including the **Huangpu River Cruise Company** (127 Zhongshan Dong Er Lu, the Bund, 6374 4461) and **Qiangsheng Cruise Company** (19 Waimalu, by Dongmen Lu, the Bund, 6326 4898). Both offer one-hour river cruises up to the Yangpu Bridge (RMB 50) or a much better three-and-a-half-hour, 60-kilometre (37-mile) round trip up to the Yangtze River. Tickets cost between RMB 100 and RMB 150; the more expensive tickets include refreshments.

Oriental Pearl Tower in **Pudong**.

Sightseeing

The Bund & Around

Pomp and circumstance – and stupendous views of Pudong – on the iconic riverside promenade.

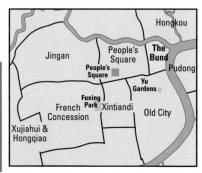

Maps p51 & p245

The Bund (or Waitan to the Chinese), grandly skirting the Huangpu River, is Shanghai's most famous landmark, its skyline the city's umistakable historical signature. By the late 1920s, its kilometre-long waterfront sweep – lined with magnificently grandiose buildings, many of them the former headquarters of Western-owned banks and institutions – cemented Shanghai's standing as Asia's leading financial and commercial centre, and as its only international city.

British-American author Christopher Isherwood, visiting in May 1938, viewed the rampant capitalism with distaste: 'The biggest animals have pushed their way down to the brink of the water'. Just over a decade later, the Communists shared his sentiments wholeheartedly and drove everybody out. The halls and corridors of these great buildings lay largely dormant for 50 years. Upkeep was poor but the Communists, to their credit, destroyed very little. Now the grand old dame is stirring back to life and is once again the most prestigious bit of real estate in all China.

The area was given its name by the British. The word 'Bund', often mistaken for a German expression, in reality derives from Hindustani and means an embankment or an artificial causeway. Apart from their diverse architectural styles, which range from neo-Grecian to Italian Renaissance and art deco, the buildings along the Bund are impressive in terms of scale and height – a number of them

have at some point claimed (and quickly conceded) the title of tallest building in Asia. Amazingly, the bulk of the materials used for their construction and decoration were imported, including tons of rare Italian marble, granite from Japan and just about everything from toilets to pre-moulded ceilings from England. The buildings have seen little outward change over the last half-century, apart from some despoliation during the Cultural Revolution, although many of their grand interiors have been lost. Each has been designated a heritage structure by the Shanghai Municipal Government.

The revival started in 1999 with **M on the Bund** restaurant (*see p101*). Then, in 2002, a law that had nominally zoned the Bund for finance and shipping was dropped, opening the floodgates for countless ambitious developers. Since then, some of the world's most famous retail and hospitality brands have been vying to get a piece of what is looking increasingly like China's Fifth Avenue. The buildings are leased whole, which puts them out of reach of all but the wealthiest of investors, who then need to attract the sort of super-rich tenants that aren't fazed by stratospheric ground rents. **Three on the Bund** has Armani, Evian Spa and a clutch of high-profile international, celeb chef-driven restaurants, while **Bund 18** boasts Cartier, Aquascutum, Boucheron and Ermenegildo Zegna, plus more celebrity chefs. At **6 Bund**, Dolce & Gabbana, with its own Martini Bar, set up shop in 2006. As eye-popping as these developments are, they are almost certainly just the beginning.

For key sights and streets around the Bund written in **Chinese script**, *see pp252-255*.

ALONG THE BUND

To start your tour of the Bund, get a taxi to take you to Three on the Bund (an address most taxi drivers know) and then walk one block south to get to no.1.

You might like to begin your walk with a visit to the extremely modest **Bund Museum** that is housed in the former Meteorological Signal Tower (1907). More worthwhile than the museum is the restaurant and bar located on the upper level, with great views of the Bund from its terrace.

Bund Museum

Meteorological Signal Tower, Zhongshan Dong Yi Lu, by Yan'an Dong Lu (3313 0871). Metro Nanjing Dong Lu. **Open** 9am-noon, 1-5pm daily. **Admission** free. **Map** p245 M5.

Housed in a 49m-high (161ft) tower that once delivered typhoon warnings to local shipping, the Bund Museum has little more than a small collection of old prints and a replica 1855 map of the area.

● **No.1 McBain Building (1915)** A grand seven-storey, neo-classical monolith built by the McBains, a wealthy British trading family. AIA have moved into the back part of the building, while the Bund-facing section was unoccupied at the time of going to press.

● **No.2 Shanghai Club (1911)** A one-time bastion of British old boy snobbery, the Club was the place for toast and marmalade and freshly ironed newspapers at breakfast, pink gins before lunch and martinis at the famed Long Bar at six. It was strictly members only, no women and no Chinese. Noel Barber, in his *The Fall of Shanghai*, tells of how a young banker was caught in the crossfire between Japanese and Chinese soldiers skirmishing on the Bund. He ran for the nearest cover, which happened to be the Shanghai Club, and was promptly ordered off the premises because he wasn't a member. The building later housed the Seaman's Club, with Mao's portrait replacing that of King George V. The building, was closed in 2000 and work on converting it and its surrounding site into a hotel complex commenced in 2008.

● **No.3 Three on the Bund (1915)** Originally built for the Union Insurance Society of Canton. Distinguished as the only fully owned building on the Bund, in the hands of a Singapore-based family and the GITI Group. The services of star American architect Michael Graves were employed to create its magnificent post-modern interior. The ground floor is occupied by a Georgio Armani flagship store, Armani/Casa and Hugo Boss, while the six floors above contain more retail, an Evian Spa (*see p176*), the Shanghai Gallery of Art (*see p165*), and restaurants Laris (*see p101*), Whampoa Club (*see p100*), Jean-Georges (*see p101*) and New Heights (*see p102*). The New Heights bar-restaurant with its rooftop terrace boasts one of the best views in Shanghai.

● **No.5 Huaxia Bank/M on the Bund (1921)** The former HQ of NKK, a Japanese shipping line, is where the trend for the regeneration of the Bund began, when in 1999 the M on the Bund restaurant (*see p101*) became the first high-profile venture to stake a claim to Shanghai's 'best address' (although the entrance is actually round the corner on Guangdong Lu). Others, including teppanyaki restaurant Moonsha and Bund Five Spa, have since moved in. No.5 Bistro opened in the basement in 2008.

● **No.6 6 Bund (1881)** Despite a heritage plaque near its main entrance asserting that the building was opened in 1897 as the Commercial Bank of China, it actually opened many years earlier as the premises for American opium

Night lights along the Bund.

The 'finest building east of Suez.' **No.12 Pudong Development Bank**.

traders, Russell & Co. Upstairs from Dolce & Gabbana an aquarium sets the stage for the Suntory Japanese Dining Sun and Aqua Bar, with Beijing fare courtesy of Tian Di Yi Jia one floor up.

● **No.7 Bangkok Bank (1908)** An attractive four-storey neo-classical manse built for the Great Northern Telegraph Company, which had introduced the telephone to Shanghai as early as 1881 (Britain had to wait until 1884). It's not open to the public.

● **No.9 Shiatzy Chen (1901)** Marking a growing Chinese presence on the Bund, both today and yesterday, it was originally built for the China Merchants Steam Navigation Company and taken over by the Taiwanese fashion guru for her flagship store in 2005. The building occupies the former garden of the oldest surviving building on (now off) the Bund (1855) that was also owned by the company. Almost altered beyond recognition (look out for the stonework and grand arches) it is now home to Annabel Lee, an Italian restaurant, the Studio Rouge Art Gallery, Suzhou Cobblers and Blue Shanghai White.

● **No.12 Pudong Development Bank (1923)** AG Stephen, the Hongkong & Shanghai Bank's chief manager, gave clear orders to architects Palmer & Turner that their

new building should 'dominate the Bund'. When completed in 1923, the resulting bit of stone boastfulness was considered the 'finest building east of Suez'. It was the first major Asian building with central air-conditioning and offered desk space for some 600 employees. It's open to the public, inside and outside banking hours – though note the sign that warns there's no entry for those wearing 'slippery dress'. The building is distinguished by – among other things – two bronze lions flanking the entrance and original interior fittings. There are also some fine mosaic ceilings (uncovered by British restoration architects DIA in 1997), including one adorning a rotunda that depicts Shanghai alongside New York, London and Tokyo – which gives you an idea of the city's one-time historic importance as a world financial hub. The grand banking hall is magnificent. The Bund 12 Cafe on the second floor, with a terrace overlooking the bank's quadrangle, is a great spot for a breather.

● **No.13 Customs House (1927)** Also designed by Palmer & Turner, the Customs House is capped by a huge clock tower that still houses a bell that once chimed in the fashion of Big Ben, hence its nickname 'Big Ching'. During the Cultural Revolution the Westminster chimes were changed to those of the omnipresent

Communist anthem, 'The East is Red.' A new CD version of this plays louder than ever today through a series of 40 speakers placed in four apertures atop the tower. The building remains as the Customs House, so entry is denied to the public, but you can take a peek at the entrance vestibule with its recently restored hall and mosaics depicting Eastern shipping and commerce. The portico wall is splashed with some revolutionary zeal in the form of a sculpture commemorating the Communist seizure of the city in 1949.

● **No.14 Bank of Shanghai (1948)** The last building to be completed on the Bund as the premises for the Bank of Communications, executed in striking art deco style by modernist Hungarian architect CH Gonda.

● **No.15 Shanghai Gold Exchange (1902)** Designed in Italian Renaissance style by German Heinrich Becker for the Russo-Chinese Bank, this was the most modern bank building in China in its time. Closed to the public.

● **No.16 China Merchants Bank (1927)** Another Palmer & Turner building, in neo-Grecian style, which was commissioned as the Bank of Taiwan. Visitors can take a look at the main banking hall, and compare the cheapness of the new black and white marble, with the beautiful original marble that still remains on the balustrade above. *Photo p53.*

● **No.17 American International Assurance (1923)** The AIA has reclaimed a property it originally partly occupied in 1927 – it was one of the first of the Bund's former tenants, who left en masse after 1949, to return. Back then it shared its tall, narrow premises with the offices and printing presses of the *North-China Daily News*, aka 'the Old Lady of the Bund', which ran from 1850 to 1951 and was the mouthpiece of the Shanghai Municipality. Over the ground-floor windows is a series of three fibre-glass relief reproductions of Italian marble panels that were irrevocably encrusted in concrete during the Cultural Revolution. They display the motto of the old newspaper: 'Journalism, Art, Science, Litterature [sic], Commerce, Truth, Printing'.

● **No.18 Bund 18 (1923)** The building was originally the Chartered Bank of India and Australia. It still has magnificent Italian marble columns and facings on the ground floor, which are looking better than ever after $15 million's worth of renovation carried out by Venetian architects prior to launching in 2004 as a glamorous multi-level complex for dining and shopping. There's a gallery, a Who's Who of exclusive retail outlets, and top-end restaurants Sens & Bund (*see p101*) and Tan Wai Lou (*see p100*), all crowned by one of the city's best roof

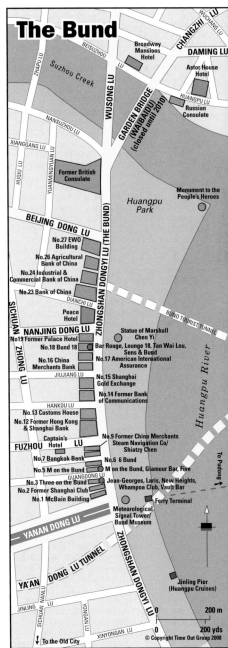

Changing faces

Strolling alongside the roaring multi-lane highway that is the modern-day Bund, it is hard to conceive that it was little more than a muddy towpath 150 years ago. The changes started in the 1880s, when the Shanghai Municipal Council decided to create an esplanade, with fine lawns, by the river – and little else changed until the early 1920s, when motorcars forced the council to widen the Bund and redesign its lawns. Many in the foreign community (the Bund at this point was part of the International Settlement) protested as green space was given over to the new motorised pests, but times were changing: land prices were spiralling upwards, investors were thinking big, and the car was conquering the roads. A host of prestigious companies announced and realised grand plans to rebuild their outdated premises along the Bund in the early 1920s, and, in the early 1930s, a number of the Bund waterside lawns were converted to car parks.

First war and then communism put a halt to further development, to the extent that the face the Bund changed exceptionally little over the following 50 years. By the early 1990s, the motorcar again made its mark as a deafening eleven-lane highway was rolled out along the Bund, and a new ramp for the Yanan Lu elevated highway fashioned a barricade along the waterfront.

In early 2008, it was time for another Bund makeover, this time to to improve the ergonomics of the city's famous strip ahead of Expo 2010, and to allow greater dialogue between the buildings and the waterfront. The project will transform the strip by redirecting traffic underground – the famous ramp has been pulled down and two spans of the centenarian Garden Bridge, at the northern end of the Bund, have been ferried away for restoration. With congestion eased, and major landscaping work and more alfresco options promised, the Bund might yet be the place for that evening promenade popularised in Edwardian times.

And just like in its 1920s and '30s heyday, the changes aren't just at ground level. The first sign of things to come was the mighty mass that is the new 15-storey Peninsula Hotel (see p31), due to open in autumn 2009. After that, more modern towers are destined to appear on, or just behind, the Bund: a high-rise tower will rise behind the Shanghai Club (currently being converted into a boutique hotel), several others are scheduled for the area around the Peninsula Hotel, and more will surely follow. But it's really nothing new at all – investors are still thinking big and tall on China's ritziest strip.

Peter Hibbard is the author of The Bund Shanghai: China Faces West, *Odyssey, 2007.*

---

terraces at Bar Rouge (see p119), which is where Tom Cruise gave his press conference when in town filming *Mission: Impossible III*.

● **No.19 Palace Hotel (1907/1909)** The building on the south side of Nanjing Dong Lu at the Bund began life as the Palace Hotel – though, despite a keystone displaying the date as 1906, one half of it opened in 1907 and the other in 1909. The building was scheduled to be demolished in 1939, but was saved by the advent of World War II. In JG Ballard's *Empire of the Sun*, it's from a river-facing room in the hotel that the 12-year-old Jim witnesses the Japanese gunboat attack on the HMS *Petrel* (December 1941) that signalled the beginning of the end of Concession-era Shanghai. It is now in the hands of the Swatch Group as an 'art palace'.

● **No.20 Cathay Hotel (1929)** Formerly Sassoon House, incorporating the Cathay Hotel. Shanghai's most legendary hotel, both before and after 1949, was closed in April 2007 with some $50 million earmarked for its restoration

and revival as the Fairmont Peace Hotel; see p40 **Keeping the Peace**.

● **No.23 Bank of China (1940s)** Another moderne structure, the Bank of China stands less than a metre lower than Sassoon's legendary hotel next door. Original plans for a twin-towered building climbing over 20 metres (66 feet) higher than the hotel were unrealised and the building, on which work had started in 1936, wasn't occupied by the Bank of China until ten years later. Its original marble interior was discarded in 2006.

● **No.24 Industrial & Commercial Bank of China (1924)** Successfully blending neo-Grecian with Eastern designs, the former Yokohama Specie Bank building was liberally adorned with granite sculptures and bronze work featuring Japanese warriors; only two defaced sculptures have survived above the ground-floor windows.

● **No.26 Agricultural Bank of China (1918)** Originally built as the Yangtsze Insurance Association.

● **No.27 EWO Building (1922)**
Originally built by Jardine Matheson, one of
the most influential British companies in Asia
who were the first to register premises on the
Bund, on the same site in 1843. The company
was presided over by two pillars of British
society, the Keswick brothers. Tony Keswick
acted as chairman of the Shanghai Municipal
Council and was chief of underground
operations in the Far East during World
War II. Destined to become yet another
showcase for those with money and style.
● **No.28 Shanghai Everbright Bank and
the Shanghai Broadcasting, Movie & TV
Group (1923)** Originally erected as premises
for the Glen Line shipping company, it was
later home to the German Consulate and the
American Navy before 1949.
● **No.29 Shanghai Everbright Bank
(1914)** The interior of the former premises of
the Banque de L'Indochine has undergone an
insensitive renovation.
   Next door a new Peninsula Hotel has arisen
around the site of the former NYK Building
(built 1926, quietly demolished 2004), and the
adjacent grassed compound at the northern
end of the Bund, containing two former British
Consulate buildings from the 1870s and 1880s,
is part of a separate boutique hotel scheme.

Huangpu Park

The area between the Bund and the river
was originally created as the Public Gardens
in 1868, although 'public' excluded people of
Chinese origin. (The infamous and frequently
mentioned sign that supposedly read 'No Dogs
or Chinese Allowed' never actually existed,
however.) The Chinese were finally allowed to
enter the park in 1928. It's not so much grass
as concrete that now dominates, and its
Monument to the People's Heroes, designed
by a local university professor, stands tall
as a striking monolith dedicated to those who
gave their lives for their country.
   The northern perimeter of the park is
bounded by Suzhou Creek, which is crossed by
way of the Garden Bridge (Waibaidu Qiao), a
structure built of steel from northern England
that was opened in 1908 to allow an extension
of Shanghai's first tram network. As we went to
press the bridge had been dismantled as part of
a major project to direct traffic under ground
and reconnect the Bund with the river (*see p52*
Changing faces) and will be reassembled in
2009. At the southern end of the park is an
underpass and access to the psychedelic
Bund Tourist Tunnel (*see p90*), which
takes visitors across to Pudong.

The far bank.

Shanghai Natural History Museum.

Inland of the Bund

At the southern end of the Bund, the Yan'an Dong Lu delineates what was once the boundary between the French Concession and the International Settlement. Three blocks inland is the musty **Natural History Museum**. One block north is the Bund Centre, a hulking office complex whose distinctive crown dominates the skyline. Its restaurant and bar, CJW, have some of the best views in town.

A block north again, the intersection of Fuzhou Lu and Jiangxi Zhong Lu is dominated by the Bund Centre of its day, an early 20th-century grouping of imposing corner buildings. The two matching 17-storey art deco monoliths on the east side were built by Sir Victor Sassoon as the Metropole Hotel and Hamilton House in 1932. The former remains a hotel, while the latter houses various offices and residences as was originally intended. The stylish Hamilton House restaurant (*see p100*) opened on the ground floor in 2007. The squat building on the north-west corner (built 1922) is now occupied by government offices, but prior to 1945 it housed the headquarters of the Shanghai Municipal Council. Formed in 1854 to administer the affairs of the British and American settlements, the handful of men who made up the Council – predominantly British to begin with – to all intents and purposes ran the city, operating an international court, police force and, at one point, an international army brigade. The complementary art deco building on the south-west corner was completed for the Commercial Bank of China in 1936.

To the north of the old Shanghai Municipal Council offices, beyond Hankou Lu, the red-brick former Holy Trinity Cathedral, built in the late 1860s, would look very much the part as an English city cathedral (although to the Chinese, it's the Hong Miao, or 'Red Temple'). Its Gothic-inspired architecture was based on the designs of Sir George Gilbert Scott, one of England's most celebrated Victorian architects, responsible for London's Albert Memorial and St Pancras railway station. The cathedral has undergone a faithful restoration to bring it back to its 1928 look, when it was last remodelled as a place of worship, and is set to reopen in 2009.

North of Nanjing Dong Lu are more examples of fine Concession-era architecture. The 12 heritage buildings that form part of the RockBund project, under the direction of British super-architect David Chipperfield, stand out in particular, located on the block between Huqiu Lu and Yuanmingyuan Lu (to the west of the Peninsula Hotel). This high-profile rejuvenation project speaks of the area's world-class aspirations. Take a look at the sleek art deco building on the corner of Suzhou Nan Lu and Huqiu Lu that was opened in 1928 as the Capitol Theatre; it housed the Far Eastern headquarters of all the big American film companies. CH Gonda, the architect of no.14 the Bund, designed it. Huqiu Lu was formerly known as Museum Road because of the foreign-run Shanghai Museum at no.20, housed in the Royal Asiatic Society building where you can still see traces of the 'RAS' sign up on its crown. Some of its exhibits are now on show at the Natural History Museum.

Shanghai Natural History Museum

260 Yanan Dong Lu, by Henan Zhong Lu (6321 3548). Metro Nanjing Dong Lu. **Open** 9am-4.50pm Tue-Sun. **Admission** RMB 5. **No credit cards.** **Map** p244 L5.

This magnificent 1920s building began life as the Cotton Goods Exchange. Converted for its current use in 1950, the structure exhibits the same signs of age as its poorly displayed stuffed exhibits. The main atrium hall, which is where the cotton trading took place, has an impressive display of dinosaur skeletons, but the principal story told here isn't about prehistory so much as a far more recent fall from grandeur – witness the badly neglected state of the old mosaic floors, woodwork and stained-glass windows.

North of Suzhou Creek

The northern side of Suzhou Creek, which used to be known as the Broadway, is dominated by the mighty art deco **Broadway Mansions**. When completed in 1934, the 19-storey block alongside the Park Hotel on today's People's Square stood as the highest buildings in Asia. Its British owners made a fortune by selling to a Japanese government company in 1939. After the war, it was a popular residence for foreign correspondents – they had the best spot in the city from which to observe the triumphant Communist troops parading along the Bund in 1949. Following an ungracious renovation in 2007 it reopened as an anonymous tourist hotel.

A block east is another hostelry, the Astor House Hotel (*see p33*), which catered for budget travellers until its upgrade in 2006. The first hotel on the site opened in 1858 but the present building, in English Renaissance style, opened in 1911. Once one of the best hotels in Asia, it's still worth a visit for a glimpse of the old lobby and newly restored ballroom, which accommodated post-reform China's first securities exchange until its move to Pudong in 1998.

In front of the hotel, where its gardens once unfolded, is one of the few surviving German-

designed buildings in the city. The Russian Consulate was completed in 1916 and is still in use in its intended role. Going east along Huangpu Lu the former Japanese Consulate and many buildings once belonging to the NYK Japanese shipping line still survive opposite the new Hyatt on the Bund hotel.

The surrounding area, designated as the Northern Bund, has experienced a dramatic transformation in recent years as swathes of old housing have been replaced with tower blocks and a new international terminal for cruise ships has opened (just about on the same site as the old one that accommodated round-the-world cruise liners in the 1920s).

A walk along the Hongkou Creek on Jiulong Lu, with its crumbling warehouses and 1920s housing, leads on to one of the city's most exciting new developments. A spectacular art deco Gothic building once housing the Shanghai Municipal Abattoir has been converted into a creative centre: **1933** (10 Shanjing Lu, continuation of Jiulong Lu, at Liyang Lu, no phone, www.1933-shanghai. com), the year in which it was completed.

Along the creek west of Broadway Mansions, the building with a clock tower is the Chinese Post Office, built in 1924 and still functioning as the city's main postal depot. It is also home to the interesting **Shanghai Postal Museum** (250 Suzhou Bei Lu, 6362 9898, closed Mon, Tue, Fri), which has a striking atrium and a rooftop garden. A little further down the creek the elongated ten- (originally seven-) storey art deco apartment block, the largest of its time in Asia, opened as the Embankment Building in 1932. Its owner, Sir Victor Sassoon, allowed part of it to be used as a processing centre for Jews escaping the Nazi regime in 1938.

People's Square & Nanjing Dong Lu

People, people, everywhere – and a park to relieve the pressure.

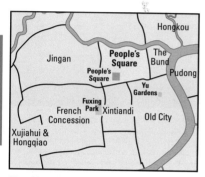

Map p244

Although you'll have a hard time believing it these days, the 22-storey art deco **Park Hotel** (*see p35*), standing proud opposite Remnin Park, was, until 1988, the tallest building in Shanghai. It might now be surrounded by structures of staggering variety and scale, but it is still regarded as Shanghai's point zero, with the cacophonous commerce of Nanjing Dong Lu on one side, the imposing modern cultural institutions of People's Square on the other, and tangles of public transport all around.

Never imperial, regal or grand, **People's Square** (Renmin Guangchang) is a great formless space – part park, part concrete plaza, barely hemmed in by a fringe of buildings and a stretch of elevated highway. In recent years, it has gained a clutch of grand cultural edifices – the largest manifestation of the city leaders' unabashed ambition to bring Shanghai international recognition as a cultural centre – each of them strikingly modern symbols of the city's grand cultural aspirations.

The square's perimeters are loosely defined by two of the city's main east–west arteries, **Nanjing Dong Lu** (Shanghai's answer to Oxford Street) and **Yanan Dong Lu** (the elevated road that traces the old border between the International Settlement and the French Concession). In a bureaucratic fit of copying in triplicate, there are bus stations at the north-eastern, south-eastern and south-western corners of the square – and several metro exits. But keep

your eyes on the prize: people visit this part of town to see four of the city's best museums, including the superb **Shanghai Museum**; *see p60*) and the **Shanghai Grand Theatre** (*see p188*), as well as to enjoy the relative tranquillity of its small green spaces.

For key sights and streets around People's Square and Nanjing Dong Lu in **Chinese script**, *see pp252-255*.

RACEY BEGINNINGS

People's Square started life as the Shanghai racetrack. It was built by the British in 1862 and races were held in the spring and autumn of each year right up until the Japanese occupation in 1941. In the off-season, the ground was used for training, riding and games of polo. The city gentry raced short-nosed Mongolian ponies and laid bets (ladies wagered fans, gloves and bonnets). It was the Far Eastern equivalent of Ascot, a gathering of power and wealth, and a weekly high-society spectacle. It was also one of the finest sources of gossip, intrigue and outrage anywhere east of Suez, including the notable occasion when a Japanese general with a bee in his bonnet about the lack of Nipponese representation on the Municipal Council shot the city's leading British citizen, Sir William Keswick, during post-race celebrations at the clubhouse.

In 1941, when the Japanese seized Shanghai, the racecourse became a holding pen for enemy nationals – Jim, the young protagonist of JG Ballard's novel *Empire of the Sun*, is briefly interned here. Following the 1949 Communist takeover, the racecourse was ploughed out of existence and during the Cultural Revolution it became a venue for pro-government propagandising. The Red Guard used the open area for enforced self-criticism sessions by notorious 'criminals'. It is only in recent decades that the joint square and park have been given a more attractive face. The turning point was perhaps in the mid 1990s, when the municipal government moved to its new home here, abandoning the former Hongkong & Shanghai Bank on the Bund.

Shanghai Museum in a day

When you arrive in People's Square, you can't fail to miss the **Shanghai Museum** (*see p60*), distinctive for its round top in the shape of an ancient Chinese three-legged cooking vessel, or *ding*. The building also embodies the ancient Chinese notion of the square earth under a round sky. Its immense collection carries over 120,000 pieces presented in 11 galleries – which is why you may want to take our whistle-stop tour. Start at the North Entrance. Pick up a free museum map from the atrium helpdesk, and then head straight up the escalators to the top floor.

Your first stop, the **Chinese Minority Gallery** on the top floor, showcases the dress and handicrafts of China's 55 ethnic minorities. Check out the ingenious salmon-skin jacket worn by the Hezhen people from Heilongjiang and the flashy Miao crescent-shaped hat from Guizhou. Terrifying Tibetan skull masks, formerly used in sacrificial rituals, line one wall, along with Tujia *nuo xi* masks dating from the Qing dynasty. Another highlight is a life-sized boat from the Gaoshan people of Taiwan, which bears a striking resemblance to a Native American canoe.

Although you may be tempted to give the **Coin Gallery** a miss, it's worth checking out this small room at the back, which holds a collection of Silk Road coins that spans 2,600 years, including an extremely rare gold Genghis Khan coin from 1221. Stroll through the newly renovated **Jade Gallery**, with its elegant exhibits, ancient symbols of wealth and power; and eye up the refined pieces in the **Ming and Qing Furniture Galleries**, which house two mock Ming rooms.

Below is the **Painting Gallery**. In a masterstroke of conservation and presentation, the museum authorities have installed subtle motion-sensitive lighting that only illuminates each painting when you stand before it. This dramatic effect works best with the must-see collection of vivid hanging scrolls, particularly *Viewing Waves* by famed Qing landscape artist Yuan Jiang.

Pop quickly into the **Calligraphy Gallery** next door for a peek at the 2,000-year-old wooden divination tablets and an authentic oracle bone; however, unless you can read Chinese, the endless rolls of scrolls rapidly become monotonous. Likewise the Chinese Seals Gallery may be another one for enthusiasts only. Instead, ride an escalator down to the second-floor **Ceramics Gallery**. The words at the entrance read 'Pottery belongs to all mankind, but porcelain is China's invention', an impressive claim, and one the fierce-looking Tang Dynasty (AD 618-907) Heavenly Guardians on display would no doubt give their glazed right arm to protect.

Muster your reserves of energy and hustle down to the first floor. First, drop by the stand-out **Bronze Gallery** for its extensive collection of ancient ritual bronzes, the oldest of which date back to the 18th century BC; admire the elaborate ox-shaped wine vessels (6th-13th century BC) and the three-legged *ding* (food vessels). Your final destination, the **Ancient Chinese Sculpture Gallery**, is an ideal spot to meditate on the extraordinary Buddhist carvings, best encapsulated by the *Thousand Buddha Stele* (Northern Zhou, AD 557-581), a slab of stone impressively covered in mini carvings of Buddha.

Round off your trip with a quick drink or bite to eat at the second-floor teahouse or head down to the ground floor, where you'll find the (mediocre) restaurant and a gift shop (there are less impressive kiosks on every floor). When you're ready, leave by the South Exit. People's Square sometimes seems like it has been occupied by half the population of Shanghai; the quickest way to escape the madding crowd is to bear left and in to the nearest metro entrance or taxi.

Sightseeing

Museum of Contemporary Art
Shanghai (MOCA Shanghai).

Museums & parks

The races, horses and stables are gone, but the
clubhouse survives at the corner of Nanjing
Xi Lu and Huangpi Bei Lu. Built in 1934, it's
distinguished by a grand **clocktower**. The
rooftop is now occupied by bar-restaurant
Kathleen's 5 (*see p122*); on the way up note
the insignia of the SRC (Shanghai Race Club)
above the main door; the sepia-toned racing
photos that line the staircase and second-floor
café; and the cast-iron horses' heads worked
into the design of the balustrade.

Back outside, head left around the building
to visit its largest current tenant, the **Shanghai
Art Museum** (*see p60*). Imposing in its time,
the clubhouse is now dwarfed by developments
like **Tomorrow Square**, with its angular glass
tower, crowned with four pincers grasping at
the sky. It's the tallest building this side of the
river and looks like it should be home to a Bond
villain, but instead houses the swanky JW
Marriott (*see p33*). Take the lift up to the 38th
floor reception for a pot of tea in the hotel's
lobby and fantastic views over the square.

Equally emblematic of the new Shanghai
is the striking **Shanghai Grand Theatre**
(*see p188*), which takes the form of a plinth
with a rocker on top. It was designed by French
architect Jean-Marie Charpentier, who explains
his creation thus: 'the layout is a geometrical
square, the perfect shape in Chinese that
symbolises Earth. The curved roof is a
segment of a circle representing the Sky'. It is
undeniably gorgeous at night thanks to some
very effective lighting, and the soaring foyer is
also quite magnificent (and usually open to the
public). The three auditoriums can be visited as
part of a guided tour (9-11am Mon, RMB 40) –
or you could attend a performance.

Beside the theatre is the yawning avenue
Renmin Dadao, of a width tailored to mighty
parades of massed armies and rocket-carrying
trucks (though such parades don't happen any
more). On the north side is **City Hall** (closed to
the public) and the space module that houses
the **Urban Planning Centre** (open to the
public and well worth a visit, *see p61*).

To the south is the centrepiece of People's
Square, the world-class **Shanghai Museum**
(*see p60*), with its highly distinctive profile
inspired by the *ding*, an ancient bronze
cooking vessel. For decades visitors to China
were denied access to its exhibits of ceramics,
calligraphy, bronzes and other antiquities; now
it's not only open, but also free for all. A recent
addition to the list of must-dos in the square
is **MOCA Shanghai** (*see p59*), the first
contemporary art museum in the city and
also the city's first to be privately financed.

The city of the future – and the future of the city – at the **Urban Planning Centre**. *See p61.*

Take a break in the **walled garden** with ponds in the north-west corner of the square, beside Nanjing Xi Lu. Early morning it fills with folk practising tai chi. The open plazas around City Hall and the Shanghai Museum are softened with manicured gardens and flowerbeds, as well as a musical fountain. They are constantly busy with strollers, bench-sitters and kite flyers (flying kites is banned in most parts of the city). Between City Hall and the Grand Theatre is what's known as **English Corner**, where eager citizens gather to practise their spoken language on acquiescent Westerners. Those who want to practise Japanese – the second most common foreign language studied in Shanghai – gather in the walled garden. Those interested in developing a closer relationship with China should head straight to the central square near the **lotus pond**, close to Barbarossa (*see p121*), which has become Shanghai's unofficial matchmaking market. Calculating mothers and fathers spend weekends combing the grounds, looking for the perfect match for their child. Parents often carry photos of their children that bear the child's age, occupation and salary expectations (of the prospective spouse, that is). It's a fascinating glimpse into the Chinese obsession with marriage and the meddlesome nature of Chinese parents.

Not all activity is above ground. Below the square is the Hong Kong Shopping Centre or **D Mall** (*see p133*), which fills a vast former air-raid shelter burrowed out in the 1960s in the wake of the Sino-Soviet split. With low ceilings, low prices and narrow corridors, it makes for a hectic kind of shopping experience, buzzing with giddy teenagers perusing the bargain-basement beauty parlours, cheap accessories stalls and gaming arcades.

Museum of Contemporary Art Shanghai (MOCA Shanghai)

Gate 7, People's Square, 231 Nanjing Xi Lu, by Huangpi Bei Lu (6327 1282/www.mocashanghai. org). Metro People's Square. **Open** 10am-6pm daily (until 10pm Wed). **Admission** RMB 20. **No credit cards. Map** p244 H5.
Billed as a 'platform for the most exciting art from China and the world', MOCA is by far Shanghai's freshest museum. The space alone, an all-glass cocoon (the building was formerly a greenhouse) featuring a leafy themed floor by artist Michael Lin and works by acclaimed Chinese artist Ai Weiwei and photographer Yang Yongliang, is well worth a look. The art, though often trend-conscious, is also accessible and interesting. There is no permanent collection – instead MOCA hosts a series of temporary shows. The 2008 exhibition 'Salvatore Ferragamo: Evolving Legend 1928-2008' saw around 50 pieces of the designer's footwear paired with tiny, flatscreen TVs, each showing a movie in which the shoes were featured. In the past the programme has leant towards animation, design installation and pop-art painting, but since the departure of artistic director Victoria Lu in 2007, the MOCA has been sailing on without a rudder.

Pyjama party

Shanghai may be a modern, cosmopolitan metropolis but, like any other city, it has inherited quirks. The Shanghainese have a particular eccentricity: many of them (around 16 per cent according to a recent survey) like to stroll the streets dressed in their nightwear. Clad in their best – or worst – cotton, flannel or fleece-lined silk, these pyjama fiends dine in brightly patterned jim-jams, run errands in slippers and cycle

around town with dressing gowns flapping in their slipstream. And if this sartorial idiosyncrasy causes them any embarrassment, they certainly hide it well.

Other Shanghainese, easily identified by their insistence on wearing trousers, skirts, shoes and things like that, are less sanguine about having to queue at the ATM behind Wee Willy Winkie; a government campaign (futile, of course) to ban nightwear in public has been ongoing since 2002. The fault line between the pro- and anti-pyjama lobbies is largely generational. As a rule of thumb, younger Shanghainese, intoxicated with the seemingly limitless potential of the new China, abhor anything that smacks of backwardness or parochialism. Their elders, on the other hand, who had to live through decades of war, revolution, food shortages and communal living conditions, will be damned if their children and grandchildren are going to tell them what to wear and when to wear it.

Eager to join the jammie-clad? Pick up flamboyant fashions at **Gujin** (666 Huaihai Lu, by Maoming Nan Lu, 6473 6714, www. sh-gujin.com). The more conservative should hit **Ruijin Lu**, where nos.28 and 92 offer the finest in flannel. Traditional silky Chinese-chic can be had at **Shanghai Tang** in Xintiandi (see p137). Keep an eye www.cityweekend. com.cn and www.smartshanghai.com, where clubs like **Kommune** (no.7, The Yard, Lane 210, Taikang Lu, by Sinan Lu, 6466 2416) advertise pyjama parties, with freebies to guests in their nighttime best.

Hopefully the addition of Art Lab on the top floor, will help to reinvigorate the museum. What had once been an underused space for opening parties and corporate events was reborn in 2008 as a multi-use space featuring a semi-permanent collection of photography, paintings and furniture, plus a performance space, restaurant and bar. Furniture, including jelly bean-like stools and a long snake-seat that trails around the main room, were all specially commissioned. With a strong wine list, tea selection and a sizeable terrace, Art Lab is the ideal post-museum refreshment spot. (Tip: make sure you also look closely at the walls in the bathrooms.)

Shanghai Art Museum

325 Nanjing Xi Lu, People's Square (6327 4030/www.sh-artmuseum.org.cn). Metro People's Square. **Open** 9am-5pm daily. **Admission** RMB 20; RMB 5 under-16s & students. **No credit cards**. **Map** p244 H5.

Located in the city's former racetrack clubhouse, the Shanghai Art Museum exhibits frequently rotating collections of contemporary art, covering everything from pastoral landscapes to photographic cityscapes. It's well worth a look, even if there are very few explanations in English (despite the signs that have advertised it for years, no audio tour exists). The museum has a very good gift shop and bookstore, as well as a small café on its second floor and Kathleen's (see p122) on the top floor. In autumn (even years only), it also hosts the prestigious Shanghai Biennale (see p152).

Shanghai Museum

201 Renmin Dadao, by Xizang Zhong Lu, People's Square (6372 3500/www.shanghaimuseum.net). Metro People's Square. **Open** 9am-5pm daily. **Admission** free. **No credit cards**. **Map** p244 J6. The Shanghai Museum was established in 1952 and originally operated in an old bank building near the

Sightseeing

Bund. This distinctive new building, which opened in 1996 at a cost of around $50 million, was designed by esteemed Shanghai architect Xing Tonghe. Six stone lions and a pair of mythical beasts guard the entrance, and the granite walls are decorated with designs that were inspired by those found on ancient Chinese bronze-ware. The 120,000 or so pieces on show span Chinese history from the Neolithic Age right up to the present day. Superb collections of sculpture, calligraphy, coins, furniture, ceramics, jade-ware, minority ethnic handicrafts and ancient bronzes are shown in state-of-the-art displays.

All of the museum's major displays are annotated in English and a good audio commentary is available for RMB 40 (plus your passport or RMB 400 as deposit), as are free gallery maps and a brief summary of the museum's collections. In addition, the museum hosts top-quality international touring exhibitions, such as the selection of the Amsterdam Rijksmuseum's Rembrandt paintings exhibited in 2008. The museum shop has a fine range of replicas from various collections, and is the city's best source of books on Shanghai and Chinese arts and culture.

For more about how to get the best out of this vast museum, see p57 **Shanghai Museum in a day**.

Urban Planning Centre

100 Renmin Dadao, by Xizang Zhong Lu, People's Square (6318 4477/www.supec.org). Metro People's Square. **Open** 9am-5pm Mon-Thur; 9am-6pm Fri-Sun. **Admission** RMB 30; RMB 15 under-16s & students (temporary exhibitions RMB 40/RMB 20). **No credit cards. Map** p244 J5.

A showcase of the city's ongoing architectural development, this centre evokes past, present and future through fascinating models, dioramas and multimedia displays. A countdown clock, displaying the days left until Shanghai hosts the 2010 World Expo, hammers home the message that this is a city with definite goals and ambitions. These are set out in what's billed as the largest of its kind in the world – a huge model of how the central part of the city should look come 2020. It can be viewed at eye-level on the third floor or from above on the fourth. The fourth floor also highlights a series of key projects for future growth, including redevelopment of areas along the Huangpu River and Suzhou Creek, and plans to make Shanghai a more environmentally friendly city by 2010. Temporary international art exhibitions are shown on the second floor, while the fifth floor is home to a café with great views over the square. An audio tour is available. *Photo p59.*

Around People's Square

High-rise hotels and shopping complexes surround the square – which is just as it has always been. Today, the **JW Marriott** (*see p33*) dominates, but not so long ago it was the **Park Hotel** (*see p35*) that held court. Built by Hungarian-born Ladislaus Hudec in 1934, the rust-coloured tiled exterior remains a monument to art deco design, although the top-floor dance club with retractable roof is sadly now defunct. Although his name is little known outside East Asia, Hudec was hands-down Shanghai's most remarkable pre-war architect. His meticulous attention to detail and human comfort bucked the local trend for building functional boxes and slapping a bit of decoration on the outside. He also eschewed the easy route of undertaking repetitive projects for a few choice clients and instead cultivated an extraordinarily diverse portfolio that included villas and mansion blocks, churches and hospitals.

Running north from the Park is **Huanghe Lu**, which looks exactly like everyone's idea of 'Chinatown': a narrow street crowded with tall neon signs, washtubs of writhing things just off the pavement and tables of people eating cooked, formerly writhing, things, in a myriad of tiny restaurants. Go with an appetite.

What is now the Shanghai Athletics Association building, next to the Park Hotel, was the interrogation centre for enemies of the state during the Cultural Revolution. It was here that the daughter of author Nien Cheng (*Life and Death in Shanghai*) was beaten to death by Red Guards.

At the north-east corner of People's Square twin spires mark another Ladislaus Hudec design, the red-brick **Moore Memorial Church**, built in the late 1920s and named after Texan Arthur J Moore, who donated funds for its construction. Then as now it serves a large community of Chinese Christians.

Nanjing Dong Lu

Nanjing Dong Lu has traditionally been regarded as 'China's number one shopping street'. While the Bund symbolised British imperial might, Da Ma Lu (literally, the 'big road') was always far more egalitarian. Throughout the 20th century, shoppers of every nationality and class thronged its department stores, where, in addition to the finest and most expansive selection of foreign and domestic goods, the retailers competed for attention with rooftop garden terraces and restaurants, in-store cinemas, amusement halls, radio studios where shoppers could watch local singing sensations and even, in one case, an in-store hotel.

Today the road holds little of the cachet it once did and Shanghai's best shopping is most definitely elsewhere. However, as a spectacle of the crowded, gaudy, neon-lit China of coffee-table photo books, it is unbeatable. Evening strollers can expect to be approached with offers of massage and other services from 'Chinese ladies', as well as hash and money (rent) boys. You may also be invited for a drink with 'English students' seeking to practise their language skills. Beware, as this frequent scam may corner you into forking out hundreds of RMB when it's time to pay the bill. If you don't fancy walking, there's a silly little electric 'train' that runs up and down the street, plastered with garish ads for Chinese convenience foods.

Look out for the **Shanghai No.1 Department Store** (800 Nanjing Dong Lu, by Xizang Zhong Lu, 6322 3344, www.shdsno1.com), which for many years was the largest in China and boasted the country's first escalators. A bit further along, across Guizhou Lu, is the unmissable **Shanghai First Foodstore** (720 Nanjing Dong Lu, by Guizhou Lu, 6322 2777, www.firstfood-cn.com). The corner of Guizhou Lu and Nanjing Dong Lu is the site of the 30 May Massacre, where in 1925 British policemen killed 11 Chinese anti-Japan protestors (*see p13*). At no.635, on the corner of Zhejiang Zhong Lu, is the former Wing On, a department store that once boasted two whole floors of entertainments, while no.429 used to be Sincere, so named because it was the first store to feature fixed prices. It was also the first department store on Nanjing Dong Lu, opened in 1917. Ahead of you now is the Bund, but it's also worth exploring the streets to the south.

South of Nanjing Dong Lu

Once known for its brothels and bars, **Fuzhou Lu** is now Shanghai's emporium of books and artist supplies. These range from the tiny suppliers of stationery and paper to the mighty state-owned booksellers. For English-language titles, try **Shanghai City of Books** (*see p135*) or the **Foreign Languages Bookstore** (*see p133*). One block south, Guangdong Lu specialises in small shops selling beauty supplies. Come here for anything from Chinese opera make-up to a camphor-wood comb.

The building tiered like a wedding cake at the corner of Xizang Zhong Lu and Yanan Dong Lu was, prior to 1949, the hub of Shanghai nightlife. Billing itself as **Great World**, it was an adult amusement palace and, in the words of city biographer Stella Dong, 'No one establishment said more about Shanghai during the last decades of semi-colonialism than this hodgepodge of the most déclassé elements of East and West'. Quite innocuous when it was opened in 1916 by a local pharmacist who'd made his fortune with a cure-all tonic, the place become notorious after its takeover by arch-gangster 'Pockmarked' Huang in 1931. Its six storeys offered sing-song girls (whose clothing got more revealing with each successive floor), prostitutes, cabaret and gambling. The rooftop reputedly lacked a safety rail, offering a quick way out of debt for chronic losers. Josef von Sternberg visited in the early 1930s while scouting locations for *Shanghai Express*, a movie that, as Stella Dong writes, 'had film audiences all over the world – except perhaps in Shanghai – wondering what Marlene Dietrich really meant when she said, "It took more than one man to change my name to Shanghai Lily".' During the Communist years, the building survived as a wholesome 'youth palace'; it is currently ringed by scaffolding, closed and awaiting redevelopment.

Nanjing Dong Lu. *See p61.*

Jingan

Corners of colonial and religious heritage survive among the shiny new temples to consumerism.

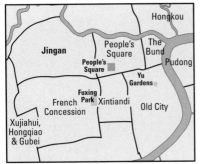

Maps p242 & p243

Once part of the city's International Settlement, Jingan in the 21st century is a humming and hectic urban mix of offices, malls, glass façades and high-end designer boutiques. Starbucks, McDonald's and Häagen-Dazs grace the lower levels of an endless string of shopping complexes, while top-flight brands (including Armani, Prada and Shanghai's first Tiffany & Co.) jostle for space on the floors above. The area is named after its most prominent Buddhist landmark, the Jingan Temple (or Jingan Si), which translates loosely – and these days rather ironically – as 'peace and quiet'. But despite the dominance of business and big buildings, it is still possible – with a little effort – to encounter remnants of a far older Shanghai.

BUBBLING WELL ROAD

Long ago, the Jingan section of Nanjing Xi Lu was quaintly named Bubbling Well Road and was the main artery that facilitated the International Settlement's expansion into the countryside. Unfortunately, the fields surrounding the new suburbia were a major depot for the city's nightsoil, once collected at dawn from doorsteps in every urban centre in China and carted to the outskirts for 'recycling'. Early editions of the *North China Daily News*, the English-language paper established in 1850, frequently published letters and articles complaining of the stink. Those long-gone fields are now covered by perfume and cosmetic shops.

Bubbling Well Road ran from the Shanghai racetrack – today's People's Square – to the western end of the International Settlement,

marked by the Jingan Temple. When it was first laid, the road passed through the centre of the racetrack, which was gated. Non-members of the Jockey Club paid a small toll to use that particular stretch.

By the 1930s, the area around Bubbling Well Road was no longer suburban; it had been swallowed up by the expanding city. The population density sent land prices sky-high, with the result that many owners sold or razed their mansions and erected exclusive clubs, dance halls and residential tower blocks along Bubbling Well Road and other nearby thoroughfares. Some of Shanghai's most celebrated clubs of the era – including DD's and the Majestic – indulged in their particular brand of hedonism just up the road from where the Portman Ritz-Carlton (*see p36*) now stands.

For key sights and streets in Jingan, written in **Chinese script**, *see pp252-255*.

Nanjing Xi Lu

Walking from People's Square, after passing under the north–south Chengdu Bei Lu flyover, head two blocks north on Shimen Er Lu, crossing Beijing Xi Lu, to check out the new,

Jingan Sculpture Park. *See p64.*

Wujiang Lu.

modern-looking **Jingan Sculpture Park** (*photo p63*), inaugurated in March 2008 with 30,000 square metres (323,000 square feet) of much-needed green space. At the time of writing, it was home to a single sculpture, *Angel-Turtle* by French sculptor Georges Saulterre, backed by a wide range of flora, but plans were underway for the addition of other sculptures, and the installation of a new hall for the Shanghai Natural History Museum (*see p54*) on the north side of the park.

Cross Nanjing Xi Lu and head a block west, where a small side street slips down the south side of Nanjing Lu and follows it west, curving back to rejoin it after a couple of blocks. This was Love Lane, which was full of dance halls before the Liberation. Today it is **Wujiang Lu**, one of Shanghai's busiest centres for street food. At midday and during the early evening, the tiny eateries are packed and long queues form outside. This shambolic little street seems to be the one allowance that the authorities have made for the Shanghainese love of *renao* (loosely translated as a noisy or slightly chaotic atmosphere) in their quest to turn downtown Shanghai into a pristine, modern city. Try the fried dumplings (*shengjian*), which are sold at several joints in the middle of the first block, approached from People's Square.

At the time of writing, the final two blocks of Wujiang, beyond the junction with Shimen Yi Lu, were in the process of moving considerably upmarket. Pedestrianised and chic – and showing every promise of living up to its new name, 'Wujiang Road, Leisure Street' – this section of Wujiang looks destined to fall in line

with the Westernised streets that surround it, leaving behind the days of cheap and cheerful Cantonese restaurants and street sellers flogging all manner of dodgy goods.

At the point where Wujiang Lu rejoins Nanjing Xi Lu, it's worth a quick detour south down Maoming Bei Lu for some particularly good examples of *shikumen* housing (*see p74* **Changing lanes**), where women squat on the doorsteps peeling veg while cigarette-chewing, middle-aged gents putter by on noisy motor scooters. Near here, just over Weihai Lu and within the grid of tiny cramped lanes, is the little-visited **Chairman Mao's Residence**.

Chairman Mao's Residence

Lane 120, Maoming Bei Lu, by Weihai Lu (6272 3656). Metro Nanjing Xi Lu. **Open** 9-11am, 1-4pm Tue-Sun. **Admission** RMB 5. **No credit cards**. **Map** p243 F5.

This was the most frequently used of three houses that Mao kept during his early years in Shanghai, and is worth a visit. He shared it with his wife, their two children and his mother-in-law. The well-preserved grey-and-red-brick *shikumen* dwelling features spartan bedrooms, and a large exhibition of photos and letters. Considering the number of places in China where Mao spent five minutes for a nap that are now historical sites, this Shanghai house stands up as a genuine residence. Displays are annotated in English.

Shanghai Centre & around

In an astonishing contrast that says more about the dynamics of modern Shanghai than any amount of economic analysis, just one turn of the corner is a leap of a century, from the

National Geographic world of the *shikumen* housing of Maoming Bei Lu to the 21st-century mall culture of central Nanjing Xi Lu. The scenes of hanging washing and women hunched over pots and pans are replaced by high-heeled, pencil-skirted misses and their dark-suited male counterparts scooting between appointments, streaming rapid-fire speech into palm-sized mobiles. The backdrop is the sheet-glass walls and rounded contours of the Westgate Mall, the CITIC Square, Plaza 66 and Japanese behemoth, Sogo, which overlooks Jingan Temple to the west.

After the CITIC Square mall, take Shanxi Bei Lu north to the old **Ohel Rachel Synagogue** (no.500), built in 1920 by Jacob Sassoon and the spiritual home of the city's Sephardic Jews until their departure in 1949. The building was subsequently used as a stable, warehouse and Communist Party meeting hall. The synagogue isn't open to the public, although you can peek in from the front gates, or the **Shanghai Jewish Centre** (6278 0225, www.chinajewish.org) can arrange access for groups.

Back on Nanjing Xi Lu, one block west of Plaza 66, is the **Shanghai Centre**, the grandaddy of the city's commercial developments, although saying that, it's only 19 years old. More commonly known as the Portman – after its American architect, who was also responsible for the Bund Centre and Tomorrow Square – the complex of apartments and shops was one of the first foreign-backed property ventures in the city after the Communist takeover in 1949. It opened in 1989, shortly after the Tiananmen Square incident.

While most other foreigners were cutting ties with China at the unfair matching of tanks versus students, the money behind the Portman honoured its commitment. Because of this, the place has special rights such as its own telephone exchange (operated by US-based BellSouth), the only one in all China. It also boasted the first HSBC branch and automatic teller in Shanghai.

The central section of the complex is anchored by the five-star **Portman Ritz-Carlton Hotel** (*see p36*). Also located here is the Shanghai Centre Theatre, home to the Shanghai Acrobats, plus a well-stocked, Western-style grocery store on the ground floor, where you can pick up Marmite, Skippy peanut butter and Nutella; a tailor; the HSBC bank and cashpoint; and, inevitably, a Starbucks. On the upper level around the forecourt are six airline offices, a Toni & Guy hair salon and a branch of the French bakery, **Paul** (*see p109*). The building itself houses several consulates (including those of the UK and Canada) and the American Chamber of Commerce.

While the Portman represents Shanghai's enthusiastic embrace of US-style market capitalism, directly across Nanjing Xi Lu is a monument to an earlier ideological union, that between China and the USSR, in the highly Muscovite form of the **Friendship Exhibition Hall** (1000 Yanan Xi Lu, by Tongren Lu, 6247 6980), known as both the Shanghai Exhibition Centre and the 'wedding cake'. During the early 1950s, the Chinese Communist Party had just 'saved' the country from the evil Kuomintang (Nationalist Party), and had also recently helped North Korea beat back the 'imperialist' Americans. To show off the first fruits of the new-won socialist paradise, the city government decided on a grand monument to international Communism, which – oh, sweet revenge – was built on a site formerly occupied by a villa belonging to one of the Concession era's wealthiest foreigners: real estate and opium baron Silas Hardoon.

The Exhibition Hall was spruced up in 2001 and now regularly hosts jamborees of a decidedly unsocialist nature, such as the Shanghai Boat Show, the Wedding Show and various other decadent lifestyle exhibitions, including the Millionaire Fair. Depending on the event being hosted, entry is free or at a price set by the organisers. Either way, as long as something is going on, it's fairly easy to slip in for a look. Most of the rooms have lost their proletariat-lauding mural work, but the Soviet influence remains pervasive in the odd mixture of Bolshevik-cum-beaux arts architecture and crowning red star. All the same, once you have seen one hall, you'll have seen them all.

Temples

A short walk west of the Portman and the Exhibition Hall, past the busy dim sum restaurant **Bi Feng Tang** (*see p104*), is the attractive expanse of greenery that is Jingan Park, formerly Bubbling Well Cemetery. Today, it boasts a scenic lake and a small but beautiful garden (RMB 3), criss-crossed with serpentine pathways and a peaceful pagoda café alongside its tiny pond. On dry days, old men practise big-character calligraphy, with water for ink, on the main path through the park. There's also a re-creation of the well that gave the cemetery and road their names; the original spring was just outside the cemetery gates, at what is now the junction of Nanjing Xi Lu and Wanghang Du Lu, but was paved over in 1919.

The well dated back to at least the third century AD, which was around the time that the first place of worship was erected on the site now occupied by the rebuilt **Jingan Temple** (Temple of Tranquillity; *see below*).

West again along Nanjing Xi Lu, just before the junction with Wulumuqi Zhong Lu, the slightly tattered yet imposing white structure on the south side of the road is the **Shanghai Children's Palace**. Each municipal district has one of these institutions, where gifted children receive special tutoring and perform for visiting dignitaries. Talent-show brats aside, what's interesting about the Palace is its former life as the fabled Marble Hall. Built for wealthy Shanghai Jew Sir Elly Kadoorie, the mansion took six years to complete. Its name derives from the massive amounts of Italian stone imported to ornament the fireplaces. It was the first house in the city to have air-conditioning and boasted a 19-metre-high (65-foot) ballroom with 5.4-metre (18-foot)

chandeliers. Amazingly, the ballroom and chandeliers have survived. You can see them on a tour organised through the tourist office (*see p227*), or you may (or may not) be allowed in for a wander, as long as you agree to stay under the watchful eye of a minder.

A good 30-minute walk north of Nanjing Xi Lu, along Shanxi Bei Lu, is the appealing **Jade Buddha Temple** (*see below*), or Yufo Si. Worth a sneaky peek, just to see Buddhism's latest incarnation in the Middle Kingdom, is the bank-like office just inside the main gate of the temple on the left. Behind glass windows and computer screens, robed Buddhist monks sit like bank tellers, accepting (according to the titles above the windows) 'donations', 'initiations', 'car cleaning' commissions and 'conversions'. Don't try to change your pounds or dollars at the last one, unless of course you want release from the Wheel of Life in return.

North-west of the Jade Temple is the arty district of **Moganshan Lu** (*see p163*).

Jade Buddha Temple

170 Anyuan Lu, by Jiangning Lu (6266 3668/www.yufotemple.org). Metro Shanghai Railway Station.
Open 8am-5pm daily; 5.30am-5pm on 1st & 15th of mth. **Admission** RMB 20 (plus RMB 10 to view Jade Buddha). **No credit cards. Map** p242 D2.
Built in the 1920s, Jade Buddha Temple is distinctly more temple-like than Jingan Temple, with its quiet courtyards surrounded by brightly coloured devotional halls, and a genuine jade, 1.9-metre-high (six-foot) Qing Dynasty Buddha statue, which is hidden upstairs and can be viewed for an additional RMB 10 fee. There being no room for a mall here, the shops are actually inside some of the halls, and vendors flog their trinkets while the faithful pray (for money) right beside them.

Jingan Temple

1686 Nanjing Xi Lu, by Wanhangdu Lu (6256 6366). Metro Jingan Temple. **Open** 7.30am-5pm daily; 5am-5pm on 1st & 15th of mth. **Admission** RMB 10. **No credit cards. Map** p242 C5.
The first temple collapsed in 1216 and was rebuilt in something similar to the form you see today. None of the old structure remains, having been pulled down in the 1990s and relocated to Tongli in the Jiangsu province, where it survives in the private museum of business tycoon Jeffrey Wong. In Jingan it was rebuilt from scratch like many historic structures, which have been replaced with concrete-based, gussied-up lookalikes. Jingan's reincarnation came with an inbuilt shopping mall, and the temple itself looks like it is constantly under partial renovations. While the main hall is a simple, unattractive, concrete box, the smaller halls surrounding the central courtyard are filled with an interesting mix of effigies and saffron-clad monks, often drumming and chanting. By far the most interesting time to visit is during a festival, when the place fills with worshippers.

Jade Buddha Temple.

The Old City

The shock of the old.

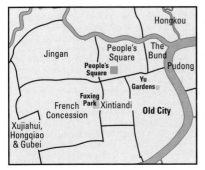

Maps p248 & p249

The first place that most visitors are shown in Shanghai is the 'Old City'. Look at a map of Shanghai and it's easy to identify where the original settlement once lay: it's the yolk in the egg white of the city. The defining, near circular line of the old walls – demolished but now traced by Renmin Lu/Zhonghua Lu – rebuffs the Cartesian grid of the modern city.

What's in a name? 'Old' in this case is merely a descriptor (there has been a Shanghai of sorts at this spot for some 2,000 years), but if it's original buildings and grand historical remnants you seek, you're in the wrong city. Although locals may be proud to tell you Shanghai existed before the Opium Wars of the 19th century, they aren't so quick to mention that their city was a mud-brick town that sold fish products and cotton into the Chinese interior. Larger populations, culture and money in China's central east coast were to be found in Suzhou and Hangzhou. These cities Marco Polo visited, not Shanghai.

Nevertheless, Shanghai's central Old City today presents a sanitised but colourful version of the traditional Qing Dynasty marketplace, complete with a lovely but crowded tea house and garden, a Taoist temple and hawkers galore. Most Shanghainese only come here to purchase traditional red lanterns and other kitsch adornments, or to pay their respects at the temple on lucky days. Chinese from other regions are herded through the market area in tour groups – to them Shanghai is the shining symbol of China's modern growth and affluence. However, don't be discouraged:

the Old City is still a wonderful place to find something of the soul of Shanghai, with Chinese Buddhist, Muslim, Taoist and Confucian temples. Although urban development – skyscrapers, widened roads and even a new metro line – is changing the scale of the district, laneways of traditional houses, small eateries and open markets still fill perhaps half of the one square mile that makes up the Old City.

Yu Gardens & Bazaar

The most visited part of the Old City is the tightly defined block bounded by Jiujiaochang Lu to the west, Fangbang Zhong Lu to the south, Fuyou Lu to the north and Anren Lu to the east. Taking up a large part of this area is Shanghai's number one tourist attraction, the **Yu Gardens** or the Garden of Leisurely Repose – known as Yu Yuan to the locals (and, hence, to your taxi driver). The gardens were originally created in the 16th century for the governor of the Sichuan province, Pan Yunduan. Neglect followed his demise, but the gardens were rescued and restored in the middle of the 18th century. These days, the Yu Gardens are resplendent, with a design that embodies an artistic vision of the world in miniature, ingeniously mixing over 30 pavilions in with hillocks and picturesque bridges, stairs, winding paths and carp-laden lotus ponds. Each section of the gardens is separated by curvaceous white walls, crowned with the head and body of a dragon.

One of the key features to look out for is the **Exquisite Jade Rock**, which stands in front of the Hall of Jade Magnificence. The rock was supposedly destined for the imperial park in Beijing, during the reign of Emperor Hui Zong, but by misfortune its cargo boat sank and it ended up languishing at the bottom of the Huangpu River. It was later rescued by the creators of the Yu Gardens.

Of the pavilions, the **Three Ears of Corn Hall** is the largest; symbols of plenty (rice ears, millet, wheat seedlings, melons and fruit) adorn the doors and windows. The nearby **Hall for Viewing the Grand Rockery** is a beautiful two-storey building overlooking a pond. Upstairs is the 'Chamber for Gathering the Rain', which derives its name from a Tang Dynasty poem by Wang Bo.

Sightseeing

The 'Corridor for Approaching the Best Scenery' (aren't these just the greatest of names?) leads to the heart of the gardens, the **Grand Rockery**, which was built with 2,000 tons of yellow stone quarried from Zhejiang province and the whole thing cemented together with rice glue. At the foot of the rockery is the **Pavilion for Viewing Frolicking Fish** and a neighbouring 200-year-old wisteria, while a gingko tree, reputed to be 400 years old, stands in front of the **Ten Thousand Flower Pavilion**. Also worth a look is the **Hall of Mildness**, which houses a century-old set of furniture skillfully carved from banyan tree roots.

Note that the gardens can get uncomfortably crowded. Our advice is to get there early or visit during the relatively quiet lunchtime period.

Yu Gardens

Opposite Bridge of Nine Turnings, Fuyou Lu, by Anren Jie (6328 2465/www.yugarden.com.cn). **Open** 8.30am-5pm daily. **Admission** RMB 40; RMB 10 children (under 1.4m/4.59ft). **No credit cards**. **Map** p248 M7.

Yu Gardens Bazaar

Just outside the entrance to the Yu Gardens is a large ornamental lake, teeming with carp and crossed by the wonderfully batty **Bridge of Nine Turnings**, which zigzags across the water in lightning-flash fashion. It is built like this to halt evil spirits, which are apparently unable to turn corners. At the centre of the lake sits the **Huxinting Tea House**, immortalised

on dinner plates worldwide as the Willow Pattern Tea House.

There are a number of speciality eateries in the vicinity, notably **Nan Xiang** (*see p106*), a famous little shop that sells delicious steamed dumplings near the entrance to the gardens; it is easy to find simply by following the snaking queues of salivating customers. In a nearby Ming Dynasty-style pavilion, **Lu Bo Lang** (115-131 Yuyuan Lu, by Bridge of Nine Turnings, 6328 0602, www.lubolang.com) serves pricey food and has tea ceremonies.

Around the lake area is the **Yu Gardens Bazaar** (Yuyuan Shangsha), an area of narrow lanes filled with over 100 small stores. The architecture is traditional in style but modern in execution, and the whole thing comes across as a sort of Disneyfied version of 'ye Olde Shanghai'. Of the few places of genuine interest, look out for **Liyunge Shanzhuang** (37 Yuyuan Lao Lu, by Fuyou Lu, 6326 4692), a shop specialising in fans that's been around since 1880, and also the city's oldest medicine store **Tong Hang Chun Traditional Chinese Medicine Store** (20 Yuyuan Xin Lu; *see p144*), where you can stock up on bear bile and preserved antlers.

Temple of the City God

At the heart of the Yu Gardens Bazaar area is what in days gone by was the focal point of the town, the **Temple of the City God** or **Chenghuang Miao**. Originally built in 1403, the temple was traditionally a venue for fairground activities, where entertainers and vendors would gather at festival times. It was believed that the City God had charge of all the other spirits who had once been embodied in the citizens of Shanghai. Following years of neglect and prior use as a factory and shop, the temple was restored a few years back and people still seek advice from the god on private and business matters.

Temple of the City God

249 Fangbang Zhong Lu, by Sanpailou Lu (6386 5700). **Open** 8.30am-4.30pm daily. **Admission** RMB 10. **No credit cards**. **Map** p249 M7.

Fuyou Lu & Shanghai Old Street

North of the Yu Gardens area is **Fuyou Lu**, home to an array of warehouse-like jewellery and festival-supply stores; red lanterns are in abundant supply. More culturally noteworthy is the **Chenxiangge Nunnery** (*see p69*), which was part of the estate of the gardens' original owner. Also on Chenxiangge Lu is the endlessly

Shanghai Old Street.

Nanpu Bridge. See p72.

fascinating curio shop, the **Seal Military** (no.32, 5383 0334), which stocks a variety of Mao memorabilia.

A few minutes' walk west, the **Fuyou Lu Mosque** (378 Fuyou Lu, by Henan Lu, 6328 2135) is one of the oldest surviving buildings in the area, and the oldest mosque in the city. Consisting of three interconnecting halls in traditional Chinese style, it was built in 1870 and reopened in 1979.

South of the Yu Gardens, the street known to locals as Fangbang Zhong Lu is marketed to visitors as **Shanghai Old Street**. It is a picturesque alley of two-storey shop-houses, some of which may be old but most of which were renovated when the street was given a tourist-friendly makeover at the turn of the millennium. Just east of the junction with Jiujiaochang Lu is the **Hua Bao Building**, with an interesting, if expensive, basement antique market.

Travelling west from the junction with Jiujiaochang Lu, Shanghai Old Street is lined with antique, curio and craft stores. Fuyou Lu is home to a lively **antiques market** housed on the north side in the Cang Bao Building (457 Fangbang Zhong Lu, by Henan Nan Lu), just before the *pailou*, or ceremonial arch, that frames the street. The market comes alive at weekends, and especially on Sundays, with an astounding array of antiques and knick-knacks spread over its four levels. It's best to get there early as many stallholders pack up mid afternoon. Bargaining is expected.

Also on this section of Shanghai Old Street are several tea houses, including the touristy **Old Shanghai Tea House** (385 Fangbang Zhong Lu, by Houjia Lu, 5382 1202), which doubles as a small museum. The 1920s and 1930s artefacts and memorabilia on display include clothing, paintings, photos, posters and some old maps.

Chenxiangge Nunnery

29 Chenxiangge Lu, by Jiujiaochang Lu (6320 3431). **Open** 7am-4pm daily. **Admission** RMB 5. **No credit cards. Map** p248 L7.

This nunnery was rebuilt as a temple in the early 19th century and, like all religious edifices in the area, ignobly converted into a factory workshop during the Cultural Revolution. Following five years of careful restoration, it reopened as a place of worship in 1994. Visit for the absolute serenity within – seldom is there anyone there – and the massed figurines of the 348 disciples that adorn the surface of a vault enclosing a gilded statue of Buddha.

West of Henan Lu

To escape the tourist version of Old Shanghai, continue west on Fangbang Zhong Lu across the major north–south thoroughfare **Henan Nan Lu**. This entire area is slated for bulldozing, so get in now to glimpse a slice of undeveloped Shanghai. About 100 metres along are the 100-metre-long ochre-coloured walls of the new part of the **Cixiu Nunnery** (15 Zhenling Jie, by Fangbang Zhong Lu, 6328 8550 admission RMB 10). Continue north around the nunnery on Zhenling Jie to the older and more interesting part of the nunnery. There's a richly decorated small courtyard temple, built in 1870, with a prayer hall on one side and dormitories for the nuns opposite. Visitors are welcome in both parts, though there is no English signage.

Take a left on to Dajing Lu and walk west to the impressive **White Cloud Taoist Temple** (no.239, by Qinglian Jie, 6326 6171 ext 5). This is a fine example of indigenous temple architecture and, though it looks like it's seen a bit of history, it was actually only completed in 2004. Serving as a stage for the daily rituals of Taoist monks, the temple possesses some unique Ming Dynasty bronze statues. The neighbouring 1815 **Dajing Pavilion**

Walk on The Old City

Start/finish: Bridge of Nine Turnings,
Yu Gardens
Length: approx. 3.5km (2.2 miles)

On first impressions, the **Yu Gardens**
(Yu Yuan) and its surroundings seem to
have more in common with Disneyland than
Shanghai: impressive, but also gaudy, full of
shops selling tat and bursting at the seams
with tourists at all times. It is overwhelming
and underwhelming at the same time, and
before long you'll be in need of a refreshment
break – the perfect time to explore the
surrounding streets and alleys.

Start at the heart of Yu Gardens, the
ornamental lake crossed by the **Bridge of
Nine Turnings** (*see p68*). Positioned by the
lake, point yourself due south and head
towards Starbucks (resisting the temptation
to order a double mocha-chocca-lappa-cino)
and veer left. Hang a right at Dairy Queen,
pausing for a peek at the traditional **picture
theatre** (La Yang Pian, RMB 3). Carry on
straight, then take the next left. In front of
you is the **Temple of the City God** (*see p68*).

This is where the walk proper begins, with
a right turn into the shopping arcade before
the temple (you'll see a golden tea kettle
suspended mid-air on your right), past the
cutting-edge shop – it exclusively sells
knives and scissors – also on your right.

Emerging from the cacophony of
shopkeepers' cries, turn right and stroll
west down **Fangbang Zhong Lu** (Shanghai
Old Street; *see p69*), a street full of Mao
memorabilia, Chinese paintings, decorated
chopsticks and all-round tourist kitsch. To fuel
your search, pick up a *rou* or *cai baozi* (meat
or vegetable steamed bun) – RMB 0.50-1.20
– or take your pick of the seasonal fruit being
sold by street-side vendors.

After crossing over Jiujiaochang Lu,
stroll north up Houjia Lu, then head right
on Wangyima Zhong Nong (take a moment
to admire the *shikumen* dwellings near
the entrance, examples of a pre-renovation
Xintiandi; *see p74* **Changing lanes**) to sample
a slice of what the entire locality used to be
like. At the end of the lane, turn left, and then
left again to emerge back out on to Houjia Lu.

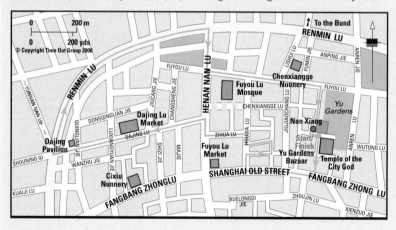

(69 Dajing Lu, by Renmin Lu, 6385 2443)
adjoins the only surviving section of the Ming
Dynasty city wall. It's a two-storey tower that
originally served as a battlement from which
archers could fire on attacking Japanese pirates
in the 16th century. One room was then
converted into the Guangong Temple and
the building also houses a rather primitive

exhibition dedicated to the native city. On the
second floor you'll find a small model of the old
town and a short series of visuals, annotated in
Chinese, that chronicle the area's history.

Across main thoroughfare Renmin Lu,
hawker-lined **Yunnan Lu**, with its chain of
small food stands, stalls and eateries, makes
a beeline north for central People's Square.

From here you will keep heading west. First, cross the street to **Zihua Lu** to soak up the street life. Then head over Henan Nan Lu, bear right, and then take the first left down Dajing Lu.

At times, it seems as if almost every local resident is out on **Dajing Lu** going about their daily business and – judging by the abundance of food stalls – their vocation is mostly eating. This is a great place to try *dabing* (a bread similar to a savoury squashed doughnut, sold at RMB 1), grab a snack of fruit, some roast duck, *shandong jiaozi* (RMB 1 for six fried dumplings) or just pick up a couple of *zongzi* (parcels of glutinous rice and meat, wrapped in banana leaf). The local food market (on your left) makes for compelling browsing, though stalls selling snails, eels and chicken's feet may affect your appetite.

The further you walk down Dajing Lu, you'll find the more half-demolished houses you pass, until you finally emerge at the **White Cloud Taoist Temple**, adjacent to the **Dajing Pavilion** (for both, *see p69*). The latter is the only remnant of the wall that once surrounded the entire Old City. If you're still hungry, take a short detour north up **Yunnan Nan Lu** towards People's Square (Renmin Guangchang) for stalls selling kebabs, *nang* (round bread) and hotpot. Otherwise, follow Renmin Lu as it curves east, past a gargantuan shopping mall dedicated to weddings on your right. Take a right on to Henan Nan Lu – the street is very wide, make sure to take the second possible right turn at the intersection – and then a left on Fuyou Lu, where you can stop by the historic **Fuyou Lu Mosque** (*see p69*).

Continue straight to end back at Yu Gardens, where you can pick up that tablecloth/chopstick set/paper-cutting kit you've decided you can't live without.

Confucius Temple

South on Zhonghua Lu – the lower half of the Old City 'ring road' – a ceremonial arch marks the entrance to Wenmiao Lu. This is the site of the only **Confucius Temple** (*see below*) to have survived in the city. The temple's present appearance dates from 1855, during which days

of blood and thunder it was occupied by the gangster Small Swords Society for an assault on the city. However, much more damage was done to its majesty and riches during the Cultural Revolution, only some of which was rectified during the extensive restoration work of the mid 1990s.

The centrepiece is the recently renovated 20-metre-high (66-foot) **Kuixing Pavilion**, which overlooks the 'Sky and Cloud Reflection Pool' and once commanded views over the whole of the Old City. It's now dwarfed by a rash of neighbouring dwellings, all with more than 20 storeys. The temple features a number of exhibition halls with exhibitions of Chinese crafts, including a teapot museum.

As well as being a centre for worship, the compound was a place of learning, housing the National Library of Shanghai in the 1930s. Students hoping for success in the June national examinations still tie red ribbons around the camphor trees in front of the temple. The main courtyard of the temple also hosts a large and lively parasol-shaded second-hand **book market** each Sunday. While most titles are in Chinese, a good rummage could turn up revolutionary and pre-revolutionary offerings in English. Outside, the street is busy with vendors peddling pirated CDs and DVDs, and street eats. There's another large book market north-east of the complex, just off Xuegong Lu.

A few streets north and east, close to the junction of Fuxing Lu and Henan Lu, is the **Peach Garden Mosque** or Xiaotaoyuan (52 Xiaotaoyuan Lu, by Henan Lu, 6377 5442), tucked down an alley of the same name. Completed in 1927, this historic building with Western, Chinese and Islamic architectural adornments is the major centre for the city's growing Muslim population and serves as the headquarters for the Shanghai Islamic Association. Like everything else around here, it has been recently restored to something like its previous state.

Confucius Temple
215 Wenmiao Lu, by Xueqian Jie (6377 1789). Metro Laoximen. **Open** 8.30am-4.30pm daily. **Admission** RMB 10. **No credit cards.** **Map** p248 L8.

Dongjiadu Lu & Nanpu

South-east of the Old City (as defined by the line of the old walls) is the **Dongjiadu Cathedral**. This Catholic church is Shanghai's oldest standing, and perhaps most beautiful, place of worship. Mass is held every morning; at other times just ring the bell; visitors are welcome. A 1914 school building, once attached to the cathedral, stands across the road.

Sanshan Guild Hall.

A short walk south of Dongjiadu Lu at 399 Lujiabang Lu is the site of Shanghai's **fabric market** (*see p133*). This vast but orderly grouping of 200 small shops is Shanghai's best location for fabrics and tailoring (*see p136* **Made to measure**).

One of the city's most photographed modern landmarks is **Nanpu Bridge** (1410 Nanma Lu, by Zhongshan Nan Lu, open 8.30am-4pm daily, *photo p69*). Completed in 1991, this was the first bridge over the Huangpu River. Cars ascend a spiralling access road to reach its distinctive cable-suspended structure; pedestrians and tourists can take the lift up to the main span for great views upriver and across the city.

As we went to press, the area to the south of the bridge, down to the new Lupu Bridge, had been razed to accommodate one of the main sites for **Expo 2010**. The Spanish are building a steel and wicker cityscape, while the Swiss pavilion will feature a soybean-fibre complex complete with cable cars to whizz you around its dandelion-covered rooftop garden. Many of the pavilions will be temporary structures but one key permanent fixture will be the dramatic redevelopment of the old workshops of the 110-

year-old Nanshi Power Plant. Once a major polluter, the complex will be reborn as one of the Expo's five main pavilions, with the chimney converted into the 201-metre (659-foot) **Expo Harmony Tower** (Wangda Lu), with a futuristic look and a wraparound, helterskelter-style sightseeing 'rollercoaster' on the outside.

Reminiscent of Sydney Harbour Bridge, **Lupu Bridge** (909 Luban Lu, 800 620 0888, www.shanghaiclimb.com, open 8.30am-5pm daily, admission RMB 68), the extension of Luban Lu, opened in 2003, is the world's longest arched bridge. Visitors are encouraged to clamber up its superstructure to enjoy the views from 100 metres (330 feet) above the river. The hike can only be done in good weather and is unavailable to anybody displaying signs of inebriation or ill health. The nearest metro station is Lunan Lu, a 15-minute walk.

One hopes that the authorities have sense enough to avoid the destruction of the **Sanshan Guild Hall**, a precious part of Shanghai history. Up until the 1920s, guilds were very important associations for regulating the economic and social life of migrant workers living in Shanghai. Sanshan, one of the few surviving guild halls, was built in 1909 for its Fujianese community. The magnificent red-brick, stone and wood courtyard building, with opera stage and intricate roof, was restored in 2002 and now serves as the **Shanghai Museum of Folk Collectibles**.

Dongjiadu Cathedral

185 Dongjiadu Lu, by Zhongshan Nan Lu, Huangpu (6378 7214). **Open** noon-3pm daily. **Admission** free. **Map** p249 O9.
Founded in 1849 by a Bishop Besco and an intrepid band of Jesuit missionaries, the Cathedral has a meticulously restored Spanish Baroque-style façade and interior. The bas-relief on the upper sections of the walls adopts traditional Chinese emblems and the bell tower still holds all four original bells. The surrounding area once housed a huge Catholic community, with its own police force and fire brigade – something like China's very own Vatican – which survived until the early 20th century.

Shanghai Museum of Folk Collectibles

1551 Zhongshan Nan Lu, by Nanchezhan Lu, Huangpu (6314 6453). **Open** 9am-4pm daily. **Admission** free. **Map** p248 L11.
The exhibition halls display temporary exhibitions from private collections and offer an intriguing insight into the history of Shanghai through such everyday items as cosmetics, cigarette lighters and cases from the 1920s and '30s, small shoes for bound feet, porcelain and family photos. There are also more general Chinese arts and crafts on display. As we went to press, the museum was closed for renovation but should reopen by the end of 2008.

Xintiandi

Communism's first meeting place becomes a model of consumerism.

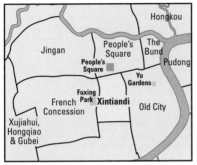

Map p248

In the seven years since Xintiandi (pronounced 'shin-tien-dee') opened to the public, it has become an unlikely centre of entertainment and tourism: entertainment, as it houses better-than-average dining and shopping destinations; and tourism, because it has become something of a cultural icon for China, a model for successful urban development that is being furiously copied throughout the country. This is quite a statement for what is essentially an open-air shopping mall.

Xintiandi's popularity is helped by being just a fifteen-minute walk south of central People's Square. The electronics market inside the nearby Hong Kong Plaza (corner of Huaihai Zhong Lu and Huangpi Nan Lu) draws in additional punters looking for cheap memory sticks and iPods, while **Huaihai Park** a few blocks away offers outdoor cafés and games of Chinese chess in its bamboo-shaded centre.

For an authentic slice of Old Shanghai pre-redevelopment, walk a few blocks east of Xintiandi to the antique and curios market on **Dongtai Lu** (*see p75*) and its side streets. Increasingly encircled by towering skyscrapers, the zone has held out against urban renewal, and remains a mainly unsanitised mix of genuine bargains and plastic tat.

For key sights and streets in Xintiandi written in **Chinese script**, *see pp252-255*.

Park life, Chinese style at **Huaihai Park**.

Changing lanes

Shanghai's population might now be topping 20 million but high population density – and the related housing challenges – is by no means a new theme. In the late 19th century, urban planners were looking for ways to maximise small parcels of land, while incorporating Chinese requirements – such as ancestor-worship halls and south-facing gardens – into dense, middle-class neighbourhoods. The result was the *shikumen* or 'stone-gated' house – grey and brown two-storey tenements arranged in terraces – an architectural form that is unique to Shanghai.

The appearance is more northern England mill town than archetypal China. The houses typically had five rooms upstairs and five down; family members had the best rooms, while servants and paying lodgers took the undesirable north-facing rooms and roomlets off rear staircases. Gardens were often minuscule and paved. Developers built the *shikumen* in south-facing rows, densely squeezed together, with common bathing facilities at the ends of each lane.

The *shikumen* model was standard throughout Shanghai and, by the 1930s, almost every part of town was gridded with them. With the population increase after World War II, most *shikumen* were subdivided, and at one point, half of the population lived in *shikumen* housing. Sadly, economic pressure to develop Shanghai has had a devastating impact on the lanes. Though most Shanghainese were born and raised in these neighbourhoods, precious little is being done to protect this key part of the city's heritage.

Most of the remaining *shikumen* are overcrowded and poorly maintained by non-owning occupants, which only favours the pro-development lobby. And when it comes to development, the chosen method is usually to send in the bulldozers. Finding creative ways to preserve the architecture is rarely an option, although there is the odd exception – notably Xintiandi, where several dilapidated blocks of housing have been overhauled and restyled to create an upmarket mixed-use development. Yet even here no attempt was made to retain the original community: tens of thousands of long-term residents were evicted to pander to the credit card.

To see a good example of *shikumen* in their original state (at least for now), visit 200-303 Maoming Bei Lu, which is between Nanjing Xi Lu and Weihai Lu, close to Nanjing Xi Lu metro station. To learn more about *shikumen*, visit the **Shikumen Open House Museum** (*see p75*).

Xintiandi

If the Bund was the showpiece of early 20th-century Shanghai, then Xintiandi is arguably one of its 21st-century counterparts. But whereas the structures on the Bund were all about bombast, Xintiandi is a celebration of modern Shanghai's ability to fuse old and new, east and west. Its 28 buildings, grouped into North and South blocks, are all examples of renovated or wholly reconstructed *shikumen*, a photogenic fusion of 19th-century English terrace housing and south-of-the-Yangtze traditional Chinese residences. These tenements were originally built in the 1920s and '30s to house the Chinese middle classes.

As part of Xintiandi's redevelopment, teams of international and local architects retained – or built anew – the exteriors, while the interiors were gutted and refitted to modern requirements. Between the buildings run tiny *nongtangs* (alleys) that connect with large open-air plazas suitable for alfresco dining and drinking. The development is subject to the most meticulous touches, such as buttermilk treatment to help grow moss on bricks and the monthly inspection of manhole covers to ensure their proper alignment.

However, for all the care and the veneration of traditional architectural forms, the result in some parts can rather resemble a high-end mall (or, worse, a Disneyfied Shanghai street scene), a Potemkin village of pretty façades aimed at seducing affluent visitors and parting them from their money. Its 100 or so units are filled with ritzy shops such as Cheese & Fizz, which sells the likes of Italian wines and French cheeses, as well as multinational chains of the ilk of Benetton, French Connection, Häagen-Dazs and Vidal Sassoon.

There are several worthwhile places to eat and drink within the complex: we like the French restaurant **KABB** (*see p107*) and, for top-end dining, **T8** (*see p108*), all of which are in the North Block. The South Block has dim sum specialist **Crystal Jade** (*see p107*) and the **UME International Cineplex** (*see p161*). Cultural representation is otherwise limited to the **Shikumen Open House Museum** (*see below*) and, irony of ironies, the **Museum of the First National Congress of the Chinese Communist Party** (*see below*) now anchors the North Block of this most bourgeois of developments.

In recent years, Xintiandi has spread in all directions to include several blocks of high-end apartments and, east across Huangpi Nan Lu, a fabricated but pretty lake. These newly developed sections are designed for the well-heeled long-term leaseholder.

Museum of the First National Congress of the Chinese Communist Party

374 Huangpi Nan Lu, by Xingye Lu (5383 2171). Metro Huangpi Nan Lu. **Open** 9am-4pm daily. **Admission** RMB 3; RMB 2 concessions. **No credit cards. Map** p248 H7.

Here, on 23 July 1921, the Chinese Communist Party was formed. A large upstairs exhibition area sets the historical context, displaying hated imperialist, Concession-era icons, such as the seat used by the chairman of the Shanghai Municipal Council. The centrepiece is a lifelike wax diorama immortalising the historic First Congress, with Mao centre stage. Then it's down to a small red-brick lane house to see where this gathering actually took place.

Shikumen Open House Museum

No.25, Lane 181, Taicang Lu, North Block, by Xingye Lu (3307 0337/www.xintiandi.com). Metro Huangpi Nan Lu. **Open** 10.30am-10.30pm Mon-Thur, Sun; 11am-11pm Fri, Sat. **Admission** RMB 20; RMB 10 under-12s & over-60s. **No credit cards. Map** p248 H7.

A small museum devoted to vernacular architecture of the kind seen around Xintiandi, with photographs and models that are labelled in Chinese and English. Its eight rooms recreate the house of a wealthy Shanghainese family, with a typewriter and abacus in the office, silk cushions in the living room and a chamber pot in the bedroom.

Dongtai Lu Antiques Market

Just a few twists south and east of Xintiandi's lake and park is one of Shanghai's best markets. Over 100 booths and shop-houses line Dongtai Lu and Liuhekou Lu, all filled with a mix of antiques (fresh-from-the-factory as well as the genuine article), kitsch and trash. Browse for Mao memorabilia, vintage furniture and locally printed Tintin books in Mandarin. It's popular with tourists and, although many of the pieces can be found across China, it's still a good place to hunt for fragments of Shanghai's past. Most stalls open between 10am and 5pm daily.

One block east of Dongtai Lu is the **Wanshang Bird & Flower Market** (open 7am-7pm daily), which is where locals come to buy pets – rabbits, hamsters, puppies, kittens and crickets. Be warned: the bought animals are dropped into plastic bags to be taken home, just like supermarket purchases.

At the southern end of the antiques market, where Ji'an Lu meets Fuxing Zhong Lu, is the **Fazangjiang Buddhist Temple** (Lanes 2-9, 271 Jian Lu, by Fuxing Zhong Lu, 6311 4971). Built in 1923, it boasts a huge main hall split into two levels. On the lower level worshippers join with monks in prayer, while the upper hall houses giant Buddhist statues and fine murals.

Sightseeing

French Concession

Shanghai turns on the charm.

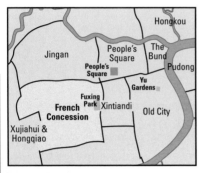

Maps p246 & p247

It lacks the monuments and majesty of the Bund and the photogenic Chinese scenes of the Old City, and it can't compete with People's Square for cultural institutions, but there's no question that the French Concession is the most enchanting part of Shanghai. Here you will find a more refined version of modern China: no Fortune 500 companies, no armies of sharply dressed office workers in a perpetual rush and certainly no unsightly factories.

As you stroll through this enchanting four-square mile section of old Shanghai, you'll want to take the pace down a notch or two and take in the views. The Concession's canvas is a preservationist's dream: tidy town houses, smart apartment blocks and compelling religious structures from the 1920s through to the 1940s, in just about all the styles that early 20th-century architects could dream up.

It is predominantly low-rise, thanks to an enlightened bit of colonial-era town planning that ruled buildings must not exceed a height of one-and-a-half times the width of the road, and so far it has escaped the worst excesses of China's 21st-century redevelopment. The streets are narrow, and loop and meander beneath canopies of closely planted trees. Reflecting the cosmopolitan nature of the district's former inhabitants, the architecture mixes elegant French-styled mansion blocks with Spanish villas; Germanic Bauhaus-style apartment buildings with English Tudor country houses, and onion-domed Russian cathedrals with Gothic fantasies.

It's all given flavour by a rich scattering of some of the city's best restaurants, markets and countless small boutiques. The constant push for the new and creative gives the neighbourhood some of the most palpable energy in Asia. Early mornings are soundtracked by shuffling street hawkers and the setting up of dawn markets; late nights echo with chattering revellers crawling from bar to bar. The French Concession is Shanghai's Marais, its Greenwich Village, its Soho even – but less crowded and prettier.

GETTING AROUND

The French Concession is easily the most pedestrian-friendly part of the city and it is possible to spend days indulging in nothing more structured than aimlessly wandering, nosing down alleys and peering into courtyards, window shopping, and taking lots of time out in cafés and bars.

Note that to the Chinese, there's no such thing as the 'French Concession' (it is part of the modern administrative districts of Luwan, Xuhui and Da Pu Qiao), but the term still has currency among the many foreign residents, who consider it to mean the area south of Yanan Lu, stretching from the Old City in the east to Xujiahui in the west. This area also includes **Xintiandi**, which, for the purposes of this guide, we have covered in its own chapter; *see pp73-75*.

For key sights and streets in the French Concession in **Chinese script**, *see pp252-255*.

Fuxing Park

The French municipality set aside the land for **Fuxing Park** ('foo-shing') in the early 20th century. The park's northern boundary was the Collège Français, one of the city's top public schools, while the central expanse was – and still is – a long rectangle delineated by arcades of tall plane trees. Turn up when the park gates open at 6am to watch the legions of tai chi enthusiasts perform their elegant exercises, or come later to observe games of chess or cards, or the gentle waltzing of the veterans and pensioners who gather here daily. Fellow observers include comrades Engels and Marx, or at least their granite-hewn likenesses. In the north-west corner of the park exit is a well-tended rose garden with a circular fountain, which is overlooked by several posh restaurants and nightclubs.

On the west side of the park is **Xiangshan Lu** (formerly rue Molière), spiffy address of the **Former Residence of Sun Yatsen** (*see below*). This is just one of several 'former residences' for the man considered the father of modern China; the house is open to visitors. Running north–south beside the house is **Sinan Lu** (née rue Massenet), one of the city's most attractive thoroughfares, which meanders between arcades of plane trees. Little surprise that several other dignitaries besides Sun Yatsen chose to make their homes here, including Yuan Shikai, the general who assumed the presidency and proclaimed himself emperor in 1912.

At no.73 is the **Former Residence of Zhou Enlai** (*see below*), Premier and Foreign Minister of China from 1949 to 1976, which is also open to visitors. As with most houses around here, from its external appearance this freestanding, stuccoed home could just as easily originate in northern Europe or America.

Returning north, Sinan Lu is crossed by Gaolan Lu, which is dominated by the golden dome of the former **Russian Orthodox Church of St Nicholas**, built in 1933 and dedicated to the murdered last Tsar and his family. There is a persistent story that during the Cultural Revolution the church was saved from destruction by a canny priest who added a Mao fresco above the doorway; the portrait is there but the tale is untrue. The church was once used as a washing-machine factory and more recently as a tapas bar and restaurant but, after complaints from the Moscow Patriarchate, the building has been closed and is to be used for something slightly less sacrilegious.

Former Residence of Sun Yatsen

7 Xiangshan Lu, by Sinan Lu (6437 2954). Metro Shanxi Nan Lu. **Open** 9am-4pm daily. **Admission** RMB 20. **No credit cards. Map** p247 G8.
Sun Yatsen (1866-1925), founder of the Kuomintang Party that sought to replace the ailing Qing Dynasty with democratic leadership, lived here with his wife, Soong Qingling, from 1919 to 1925. It's a fairly modest house with simple furnishings, but the place was witness to innumerable historic meetings, including that between Madame Sun's sister, Meiling, and her future husband, Chiang Kaishek. The place is stuffed full of memorabilia, from a fascinating library of over 2,700 volumes to family photos and a Suzhou embroidery of a cat. Recorded English commentaries play in the main rooms. *Photo p78.*

Former Residence of Zhou Enlai

73 Sinan Lu, by Fuxing Zhong Lu (6473 0420). Metro Shanxi Nan Lu. **Open** 9am-4pm daily. **Admission** free. **No credit cards. Map** p247 G9.
Precociously placed in an established Nationalist area, Zhou and his wife, Deng Yingchao, managed and promoted Shanghai's underground Communist movement from here in 1946-47. Meetings were held in the ground-floor reception room, while the upper floors contained Zhou's office (spartan but elegant, with his briefcase and black suit displayed in the corner) and dormitories for Party workers, including the bedroom of Dong Biwu, who went on to become a leading Party figure.

Taikang Lu

At its very southern end Sinan Lu intersects with Taikang Lu; part way along this busy street, an arch on the north side of the road gives access to a narrow lane known as the

Fuxing Park.

Sightseeing

The father of modern China's home: **Former Residence of Dr Sun Yatsen**. *See p77.*

Taikang Lu Art Street (lane 210). Since 1998, when a Chinese-Canadian entrepreneur turned a derelict sweets factory into low-rent studios for artists and designers, developers and aspiring creatives have seized space in neighbouring buildings with a mind to transform the area into some kind of alternative, low-rent Xintiandi. His original factory has some interesting tenants, including **Marion Carsten** (*see p139*), and there are all kinds of small boutiques, workshops, studios and cafés in the courts off this main alleyway. Although the area and its business concept took some time to catch on, the neighbourhood now draws crowds for its off-beat designers and alfresco cafés.

Five minutes' walk south of Taikang Lu is the morbid yet absorbing **Museum of Public Security** (*see below*), with a gun collection that's reputed to be the largest in the world.

Museum of Public Security

518 Ruijin Nan Lu, by Xietu Lu (6472 0256/www. policemuseum.com.cn). **Open** 9am-4pm Mon-Sat. **Admission** RMB 8. **No credit cards. Map** p247 F11. Opened in 1999 and housed in a concrete box of a building, the museum chronicles the history of the city's security services, going back to the first police department in 1854 – though the emphasis is on post-1949 achievements. Only the introductions to the exhibition areas are in English, but not much interpretation is required for the 3,000 items on display, which run from graphic photos of real-life murders to a huge armoury of weapons that includes fascinating period pieces, such as a cigarette-case weapon made for the mobster and police chief Huang Jinrong.

Huaihai Zhong Lu

Huaihai Zhong Lu, formerly avenue Joffre, is a great bisecting east–west slash across the French Concession. Its four lanes are always gridlocked, and its pavements every bit as crowded with shoppers. The easternmost end, around the Huangpi Nan Lu metro station, is a canyon of shopping malls of limited interest. To the west of the elevated Chongqing flyover, Huaihai is lined with pre-Liberation apartment blocks that rise above street-level boutiques catering predominantly to middle-class Chinese.

The busiest area is around the junction with **Ruijin Er Lu**, but there's also much of interest at the junctions further west: **Maoming Nan Lu, Shanxi Nan Lu** and **Fenyang Lu**. Beyond **Changshu Lu**, the commerce fades and several consulates occupy large villas. Finally, at its western extreme, Huaihai is home to local restaurants and small shops as it slides into the neighbouring municipality of Xuhui.

Ruijin Er Lu

The junction of Huaihai Zhong Lu and Ruijin Er Lu is all blaring 21st-century commerce, but you only have to walk a few minutes south to escape. On the west side of the street are the imposing gates of the **Ruijin Guesthouse**, a walled compound of several colonial-era buildings in a stately garden setting. This was formerly the town estate of HE Morriss Jr, whose father had made his money as founder and owner of the *North China Daily News*, at that time the second-largest English newspaper in Asia. The red-brick main residence became the Italian Consulate in 1938, before being sold to the Japanese. After 1950 it became government property and was used for hosting high-ranking Party leaders. It's now a hotel (*see p43*). Another building serves as the Shanghai offices for *The Economist*, while other tenants include the lovely **Art Deco Garden Café** (Building 3, 6472 5222 ext 3006), the fabulous **Face** bar (*see p124*) and Shanghainese restaurant **Xiao Nan Guo** (*see p112*). You're free to roam the immaculate grounds. Another gateway, on the west side, leads out to Maoming Nan Lu.

South again, Ruijin Er Lu connects with **Shaoxing Lu**, home of the Shanghai publishing world. Numerous publishers have their offices here, most of them with bookshops attached – and all, of course, selling books in Chinese. For reading matter in English, visit the unique and beautiful **Old China Hand Reading Room** (*see p108*) at no.27, which is a café, bookshop and museum of 1930s Shanghai memorabilia all in one. There are several other attractive cafés along this street too.

Just a few years ago, **Maoming Lu** was famed for its seedy bars and discos specialising in cheap booze, loud music and lairy behaviour but in 2005, after irate neighbours kicked up a fuss about the noise and the street brawling, the bars were shuttered and, in some cases, razed.

The junction with Huaihai Zhong Lu – somewhat in the middle of the Maoming – is signposted by the art deco spire and vertical lines of the **Cathay Theatre** (*see p160*), very obviously a 1930s creation. It remains a cinema, mixing Chinese-language movies with subtitled Hollywood blockbusters. South of here most of the street-front shops are tailors with a feel for the formal: the place to see more gorgeous *cheongsams* than you could possibly order. North of the Huaihai Lu, Maoming is a real treat, as it appears very much as it must have done in the days when this was rue Cardinal Mercier.

On the west side of the road is the former Cercle Sportif Français, one of the most prestigious clubs in Concession-era Shanghai. Ignore the distraction of the looming concrete tower block (added in the 1980s when the building became the **Okura Garden Hotel**, *see p41*) and take a walk around the gorgeous gardens, then go inside to view the ballroom and splendid staircase lobbies. Have a drink on the roof of the south-facing *porte cochère*, looking over the lawn – below it is a reinforced concrete bunker, a hidden reminder that the premises were used as a private guesthouse by Chairman Mao on his visits to Shanghai.

Old China Hand Reading Room.

On the opposite side of the road from the Okura is the **Jinjiang Hotel** (*see p42*), which was formerly Sir Victor Sassoon's **Cathay Mansions**. Built in 1928, this was the first high-rise to be constructed on Shanghai's unstable alluvial mud. It's best known now as the venue in which then-US President Richard Nixon and Chinese Foreign Minister Zhou Enlai signed the Shanghai Communiqué in 1972, the first step toward normalising US-China relations. Flanking the entrance to the hotel grounds is pop-chinoiserie boutique **Shanghai Tang** (*see p137*) and, in the small lane behind the store, highly regarded Shanghainese restaurant **Yin** (*see p113*).

Cathay Mansions was such a successful development that Sassoon built an even more luxurious block behind it, **Grosvenor House**, now apartments, with a central 21-storey tower flanked by two great batwings. You can access it by going in through the gate beside Shanghai Tang and following the drive round to the right. In recent years, contemporary local architects took on the challenge of creating a lobby befitting one of Asia's most domineering art deco buildings, with flashy but not especially authentic results.

Facing the Jinjiang across Changle Lu, the **Lyceum Theatre** (*see p187*) was built in the 1930s as the home of the British Amateur Dramatic Society. A young Margaret Hookham danced here, long before she changed her name and found fame as Margot Fonteyn. She was born in England but, at the age of eight, her father's work with the British Tobacco

Walk on Deco dawdling

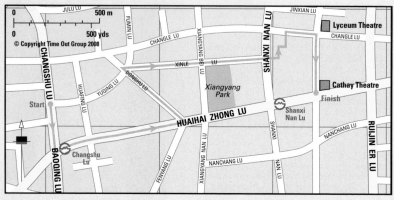

Sightseeing

Start Corner of Yuqing Lu & Changshu Lu
Finish Cathay Theatre (Huaihai Zhong Lu, by Maoming Nan Lu)
Time 90mins (with café stop)

Shanghai has the highest concentration of art deco buildings in the world – an impressive boast when you consider the heavy, and often indiscriminate, architectural losses of recent years. Although the city was late to follow the European design and architecture fad of the 1920s, the subsequent 1930s residential property boom allowed the city's creatives to more than compensate for the omission. On account of timing, Shanghai's art deco legacy is mostly of the sub-classification known as Streamline Moderne. As such, you will find the city full of horizontal linear elements – facing bricks and wide-paned windows – that owe more to the Bauhaus than to Paris of 1925.

The French Concession is without doubt art deco's home in China – and the most rewarding area for wandering. At 209 Changshu, at the corner of Yuqing Lu, is the lovely 1928 **Savoy Apartments** building, where you can gaze up at the beautiful and uncommonly well preserved plasterwork under the eaves, a trademark of the French architects Leonard, Veysseyre and Kruze. Walking south toward Huaihai Lu you will see the **Empire Mansions** on your left. Highlighting the rapid design switch from the elaborate detail of the Savoy of only three years previous, this Chinese-designed building is all about horizontal lines. The rare details are the sparingly used circular windows and the terrazzo entryway (at

1329 Huaihai Zhong Lu). Directly across the street is one of the city's few **art nouveau** structures, which was built as a police barracks for French officers.

Huaihai Zhong Lu is the home of the quintessential Shanghai art deco flat: some 20 examples line its plane-treed expanse. Take a peek at the tiny gem at **no.1274**, as well as the plaster detailing of **no.1252** and its cousin across the street. Sate chocolate cravings at **Whist**, Shanghai's choc-centric café at 1250 Huaihai Zhong Lu.

At laneway no.1200, turn left and gaze up at the **Gasgogne**, just 15 yards up the lane, one of Shanghai's most prized deco properties. Its roadfront walk-up units and off-the-street tower are coated in orange tiling, the signature colour of many buildings designed by Leonard, Veysseyre and Kruze. The Gasgogne tower was used by consular officials of many nations during the 1980s and 1990s, before China's military police decided in the noughties to posh up the property and turn it into high-end apartments. Sadly, the renovation showed precious little historical sensitivity – ceilings were lowered and floors raised to add extra bathrooms, while the lobby was coated in polished granite.

Keep walking east along Huaihai, passing the yellow-tiled **Hanray** at no.1162 – also designed by Leonard, Veysseyre and Kruze – to the corner of Donghu Lu. Take a left and proceed up the right side of the road. Walk deep into Lane 56 and you will discover a small estate of lost Moderne homes – few even appear inhabited these days. Their detailing – note the balcony railings – owes something to traditional Chinese motifs. Go back out in to the lane, and walk to no.70, the nostalgic **Donghu Hotel** (6415 8158, www.donghuhotel.com). This Gotham-style lair was built by the Al Capone of the French Concession, Du Yuesheng, or Big-Eared Du (*see p12* **City of sin**). The interior must have been quite something in its day, but today only the exterior is remarkable.

Passing the Donghu Hotel, turn right on to Xinle Lu. For refreshment, stop at no.167 for **One 1 Café**, which is attached to the Donghu and resplendent in traditional Chinese kitsch. Continue east on Xinle Lu; in the 1930s French Concession, there were some 35,000 Russians living here, many employed by Big-Eared Du as hired guns. **No.194 Xinle Lu** is an apartment block that shows strong Russian influence, in its Internationalist corner steel-framed windows and art nouveau penthouse balconies. It's also worth a detour to Lane 180 for a look at its three fantastically curvilinear detached homes. In their day they must have been extremely grand – though now they are slowly crumbling, like a Moderne-istic version of Miss Haversham's mansion.

Back on Xinle Lu, proceed east past the art deco flats on both sides of the road (most have been painted pale yellow due to a government scheme to 'promote a harmonious society') to the magnificent **Russian Mission Church** (no.55; *see p82*), where many a Russian immigrant would have come to search for relatives and friends from the old country. Thanks to improved relations between China and Russia, the Orthodox structure has recently been renovated and, whereas it has been a factory and disco in past decades, it may soon become a religious venue once again. For now, try to get in for a glimpse of the original ceiling murals.

Continue down the Xinle Lu, and cross Shanxi Lu in to one of the Concession's largest 1930s housing estates at **Lane 39**. Though far from art deco, these English cottage-style houses are worth a look; they were built at the same time as the Russian enclave you've just passed through. Walk to the end of the lane, take a left and keep walking until you leave the estate, coming out at Changle Lu, then take a right. On the first corner is the old Cercle Sportif Français, today's **Okura Garden Hotel** (*see p41*), also designed by Leonard, Veysseyre and Kruze. Although the exterior is a final throwback to the Italianate Renaissance style, the interior ground and first floors still maintain a deco feel. Just across the Maoming Lu from the hotel is Sir Victor Sassoon's **Cathay Estate**, whose strong Moderne lines on the street-front walk-ups, as well as the **Grosvenor House** tower, convey the building's power.

End your walk back on the Huaihai Zhong Lu at no.870 at the **Cathay Theatre** cinema (*see p160*), designed by one of Shanghai's great Central European architects, Gonda, in 1932. The interiors have been messed with but the exterior is still stunning.

● *Spencer Dodington of Luxury Concierge China (www.luxuryconciergechina.com) is an expert on Shanghai's architecture and culture.*

The Russian Orthodox church, **Cathedral of the Holy Mother of God**.

Company took the family to Shanghai. She studied ballet here before returning with her mother to the UK when she was 14. Her father stayed in Shanghai and was interned by the Japanese during World War II.

Shanxi Nan Lu

Shanxi Nan Lu lacks the charm of neighbouring streets. The junction with Huaihai is dominated by modern shopping plazas, where touts haunt the pavements delivering tugs and rapid-fire pitches of 'Bagwatchshoes-DVDlookalookalook!' For respite, veer north for the fairytale stylings of the **Hengshan Moller Villa** (30 Shanxi Nan Lu, by Yanan Zhong Lu); it's a guesthouse but the management doesn't mind non-guests taking a peek inside. As we went to press, it was closed for renovation but should reopen by late 2008. On the corner with Changle Lu is **Garden Books** (*see p133*), selling newspapers, magazines and English-language reading, as well as coffee, teas and ice-cream. **Xinle Lu**, running west off Shanxi, is one of the most appealing shopping streets, full of small, own-label fashion boutiques.

It runs by **Xianyang Park**, which is filled all day long with elderly Chinese indulging in 'slow exercises' and playing cards and mah-jong. Adjacent is Shanghai's other surviving Russian Orthodox church, the Byzantine-style **Cathedral of the Holy Mother of God** (55 Xinle Lu, by Xiangyang Lu). This 1931 church was also known as the Russian Mission Church,

as it was where many Russian newcomers came to search for friends and family among the refugees. A well-executed restoration was completed in 2008 – look out for the original holy frescos on the ceiling of the dome.

Fenyang Lu

An attractive old villa screened by tall trees is home to the Arts & Crafts Research Institute, a part of which is the **Museum of Arts & Crafts** (*see p83*). The building itself is in a neo-classical style and was designed by remarkable émigré Hungarian architect Ladislaus Hudec.

Fenyang Lu connects with **Taiyuan Lu**, which, back in the rum old days when it was known as rue Delastre, boasted not only a French-styled château but also a resident count and countess. The Count de Marsoulies was a lawyer who, along with several community leaders, had a falling out with local mobster Du Yuesheng when they asked him to remove his opium business from the Concession. To show that there were no hard feelings, Big Du invited the Frenchmen to dinner. Within the month, several of the dinner guests were dead of a mysterious illness; the rumour was that Big Du had poisoned the mushrooms. The widowed countess remained in the house until 1940. After the war, the US army rented the château and it's where General George Marshall stayed while attempting to broker a treaty between the Communists and the Nationalists. Today, the château is the **Taiyuan Villa** (*see p43*).

Back where Fenyang meets Yueyang is one of Shanghai's only monuments to a non-Chinese individual, a **statue of Pushkin** (Puxijin), erected in 1937 by the Russian community on the centenary of the poet's death.

Museum of Arts & Crafts

79 Fenyang Lu, by Taiyuan Lu (6437 2509). Metro Changshu Lu. **Open** *9am-4pm daily.* **Admission** RMB 8. **No credit cards. Map** p246 D8.

High-quality arts and crafts exhibits form only a small part of this museum. The villa in which the museum sits has been the home of an arts and crafts research institute since 1960 and visitors can observe artisans involved in carving, embroidery and paper-cutting. Much of the work is for sale and there is also an antique store in the basement. Before being a crafts museum, this wedding cake of a villa had several lives: originally it was built for the transport minister of the French Concession, and then housed parts of the UN relief organisation. From 1949 to 1952, Chen Yi, the first Communist mayor of Shanghai, lived in these spacious digs (not without a degree of irony, given the chandeliers, OTT showers with jets from all directions and marquetry floors).

Changshu Lu & west

As Huaihai dips into the westernmost part of the French Concession, the buildings become grander, with plenty of villas and mansions set in their own gardens. This was the 'country manor' part of town. Some of the properties now fly international flags as consulates, but many are bars and restaurants; places such as **Le Garçon Chinois** (*see p114*), **Sasha's** (*see p127*), **Face** (*see p124*) and **Yongfoo Elite** (*see p113*), once the British Embassy, should be visited for the settings alone.

A little out of the way but worth the effort is **Swire House** on Xinggou Lu. George Warren Swire was company chief of Butterfield & Swire, one of the first companies to set up operations in Shanghai. In 1934, he commissioned a new residence from celebrated Welsh architect Clough Williams-Ellis – creator of Portmeirion on the Welsh coast, immortalised as the setting for 1960s cult TV series *The Prisoner*. The architect never visited China, instead sending drawings and samples by post. The resulting property was sufficiently magnificent to earn it the nickname 'the Palace'. Post-1949, of course, it became a state guesthouse. Today the house is part of the **Radisson Plaza Xingguo Hotel** (78 Xingguo Lu, by Huashan Lu, 6212 9998, www.radisson.com).

Also in the neighbourhood, just north of the Dingxiang Garden and buried in the basement of one of a group of residential tower blocks, is the **Propaganda Poster Art Centre** (*see p84*) – a must for enthusiasts of political kitsch.

Back on Huaihai Zhong Lu is the **Shanghai Library** (corner of Gaoan Lu), which is Asia's largest book repository. It's not much use if you don't read Chinese, but pass by at around 8am to see the library staff out front doing their tai chi exercises before starting work. Further west is the striking red-brick **Normandie Apartments**, also known as the Intersavings Society Building, which is a dead-ringer for New York's Flatiron Building, only on a smaller scale. On the ground floor (enter from Wukang Lu) is café-bar-restaurant **Arch** (439 Wukang Lu, by Huaihai Zhong Lu, 6466 0807).

South across the busy intersection from the Normandie is the **Former Residence of Soong Qingling**, while a short walk further west it's commerce and industry that's celebrated at the **CY Tung Maritime Museum**, which is housed in a refurbished 19th-century dormitory on the campus of the prestigious Jiaotong University, China's second-oldest secular educational institution. Fans of JG Ballard's *Empire of the Sun* might like to stroll up Xinhua Lu, which angles off Huaihai Xi Lu north of the university; this is the former Amherst Road where both Ballard and his fictional alter ego Jim spent their childhood.

Cathay Theatre. *See p79.*

CY Tung Maritime Museum

Jiatong University Campus, 1954 Huashan Lu, by Huahai Xi Lu (6293 2403/www.cytungmaritime museum.com). Metro Xujiahui. **Open** 1.30-5pm Tue-Sun. **Admission** free. **Map** p246 A10.

The ground floor plots China's often-understated maritime history from Neolithic times to the present day. Exhibits highlight the maritime route of silk and porcelain during the Middle Ages and China's leading role in naval innovation during the 15th century. The first floor is dedicated to the activities and manifold interests of Shanghai-born shipping tycoon Mr Tung and includes the ship's bell from the ill-fated *Queen Elizabeth*; Tung acquired the old Cunard liner in 1970, only to see her destroyed by fire in Hong Kong two years later.

Former Residence of Soong Qingling

1843 Huaihai Zhong Lu, by Yuqing Lu (6474 7183). Metro Hengshan Lu. **Open** 9am-4.30pm daily. **Admission** RMB 20. **No credit cards. Map** p246 B9.

One of China's leading ladies, Soong (1893-1981) was the wife of Sun Yatsen, and a politician of some clout in her own right (for a while she was Vice-President of the People's Republic). This is the house in which she grew up and to which she returned to live following her husband's death in 1948. The sitting and dining rooms contain a photographic record of Mao's visit to the house and a large selection of gifts received from foreign dignitaries. Don't miss the garage and its two limousines, a Chinese 'Red Flag' and a Russian 'Jim' presented by Stalin in 1952. The displays include books, family photos and personal correspondence, as well as written exchanges with Mao, Nehru and Stalin.

Propaganda Poster Art Centre

Basement, Building B, 868 Huashan Lu, by Wukang Lu (6211 1845/www.shanghaipropagandaart.com). Metro Hengshan Lu. **Open** 10am-5pm daily. **Admission** RMB 20. **No credit cards. Map** p246 B7.

The brainchild of Yang Peiming, the PPAC is two basement rooms in a residential tower block hung floor to ceiling with a stunning collection of original posters from 1949 to 1979. Mr Yang delights in leading visitors through the collection (there are at least 200 pieces), explaining each piece of art. The fact that you may not understand Chinese and he has only four words of English is no impediment: when he comes to the images of ruddy-cheeked Chinese peasants crushing imperialist Uncle Sams underfoot, you worry that he's going to damage himself from laughing so hard. Some of the posters are also for sale.

Shaping the Concession

Shanghai's French community presented its claims for territory to the imperial Qing court in 1844, pressing for the same generous rights the British had gained the previous year in the aftermath of the First Opium War. The court allowed the French a muddy plot of less than one kilometre in breadth, south of the International Settlement (now the Bund area) and east between the old walled city of Shanghai and the river. Over the course of the next 70 years 'Frenchtown' expanded westward, eventually taking up about 7 square kilometres (four square miles).

The Frenchness of the Concession was far from absolute. By the 1930s there were fewer than 2,000 French nationals within its boundaries, compared to 12,000 English subjects and more than half a million Chinese. Main avenue Joffre (now Huaihai Lu) may have been named for Joseph Jacques Césaire Joffre, known as the 'Saviour of France' after his victory in the 1914 Battle of the Marne, but the street was more commonly known as 'Little Moscow' because of the 30,000 Russians who lived around it. Even so, there was a distinctly Gallic air about the place. The exclusively French municipal government (Conseil Municipal Français, or CMF) lined most streets with plane trees and enforced zoning regulations designed to make their part of the city more liveable. It's the legacy of these bits of localised legislation that gives today's French Concession a more bucolic air than much of the rest of the city.

There were, though, less attractive aspects of Frenchtown that contributed heavily to its character. By the beginning of the 20th century Anglo-Saxon sensitivities had largely forced the trades in opium and prostitution out of the International Settlement, so the criminal element, run by rival Chinese gangs, decamped to the more permissive sphere of French rule. The result was that the French Concession became the crime headquarters of Shanghai, if not all of China.

The gangsters are long gone, suppressed after the Communists took over in 1949. Neither has much of the Russian presence survived, save the two onion-domed Orthodox churches. However, the former Concession area retains an air of genteel sophistication absent from much of the rest of Shanghai. It's the part of town most associated with dining and drinking, and it's still where you'll find croissants (at the French Bakery on the corner of Ruijin Er Lu and Jianguo Xi Lu).

Xujiahui & Hongqiao

Pick through suburbia to find parks, gardens and Shanghai's oldest temple.

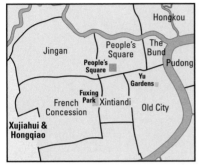

Map p246

Xujiahui (pronounced 'shoe-jeeah-way'), Gubei ('goo-bay') and Hongqiao ('hong-cheow') make up the suburban mass that is Shanghai's urban south-west. You'll have to work hard to find the charm in these areas but, with a little patience, there are fascinating sights to be found beyond the traffic congestion, soulless architecture, chain stores and super-sized restaurants.

Bordering the old French Concession, **Xujiahui** offers a veritable merry-go-round of light and sound, with its scores of neon-lit restaurants, office buildings and cheapy-cheap shops. Many young people think nothing of spending a whole day combing the crowded stalls for a cheap iPod or glittery fashion accessory. In contrast to high-end Nanjing Lu, Xujiahui's shops are decidedly mass market. Most of the activity is centred on the streets around Xujiahui metro station.

Hongqiao and Gubei to the west are where the upwardly mobile move to flaunt their wealth by purchasing gaudy neo-classical flats. **Hongqiao** begins where old Settlement-era Shanghai ends (roughly where Zhongshan Xi Lu runs today) and extends west to the city's domestic airport. South of Hongqiao and west of Xujiahui lies the relatively new district of **Gubei**.

Both neighbourhoods are home to large populations of Japanese, Koreans, Indians and Westerners, lured to China with housing allowances, personal drivers and maids. As a result, these areas boast some of the city's best supermarkets and a good selection of family restaurants, plus Japanese all-you-can-eat teppanyaki. But apart from eating and shopping there isn't a whole lot happening.

GETTING THERE

Many of the Hongqiao and Gubei folk are too wealthy to need public transport, so the network is patchy. Bus 911 from Huaihai Lu, corner of Shanxi Lu, runs all the way to the Zoo on Hongqiao Lu, as does the no.48 from Jingan Temple, via Yanan Xi Lu.

The most convenient way to get to Xujiahui is to take Line 1 of the metro to the stop of the same name. For Longhua Park and temple, get off at Caobao Lu and then a take a taxi. Metro Line 2 is being extended out to Gubei and Hongqiao but won't be completed until 2010. On foot, you can walk south down Hengshan Lu from the French Concession.

For key sights and streets in Xujiahui, Hongqiao and Gubei written in **Chinese script**, *see pp252-255*.

Xujiahui

Sitting quietly just a few hundred metres from the flashing lights and mall madness are the last remnants of Shanghai's oldest Western settlement – a Jesuit centre founded by a Chinese Catholic, Xu Guangqi (baptised Paul), in the early 17th century. Xu was a high-ranking

Shanghai South Railway Station. *See p86.*

Ming official and a committed scholar, who had converted to Catholicism. He donated some of his land in Xujiahui (meaning 'gathering place of the Xu family') to the Church and invited Jesuit missionaries to take up residence.

The nuns and priests held on to various mission buildings throughout the intervening centuries until the Cultural Revolution, at which time they were 'resettled' elsewhere. Some of the structures are still standing, but many are being pulled down to make way for new towers. One worth a visit is the Catholic Cathedral, **St Ignatius** (158 Puxi Lu, by Ziyang Lu, 6438 2595), built in 1910 on the site of earlier churches dating back to 1608. The more permissive political climate today allows the Chinese Catholic diocese to hold masses here for foreign and Chinese Catholics.

Next door is the fascinating Jesuit-built **Bibliotheca Zi-Ka-Wei** (6487 4095), established in 1847. Its Western hall was based on the layout of the Vatican Library and holds over 80,000 books in French, Latin and German. Tours are free and take place on Saturday (2-4pm; English available) but you can visit the adjacent reading room throughout the week (9am-4pm Mon-Sat). Take the opportunity to look at photos of Xujiahui dating back to the 1860s – the enthusiastic and friendly staff can help translate and explain the captions. Unfortunately, you can't touch the books inside the hall, but there are some interesting books in English and Chinese in the reading room that date back to the 1920s. Visitors are free to peruse these while sitting at one of the old wooden reading desks – topics range from history to philosophy to philology.

South-west Xujiahui now boasts the futuristic **Shanghai South Railway Station** (289 Laohumin Lu, by Liuzhou Lu, 5110 5110, www.nzdq.org; *photo p85*). Reopened in 2006, it is the first circular station in the world, and features a spectacular 50,000-square-metre (500,000-square-foot) transparent roof. This all-new station spelled the closure of Shanghai West Railway Station and Meilong Station, and it serves southern cities in China, including Hangzhou and Nanchang. The easiest way to get to the Shanghai South Railway Station is to hop on Line 1 of the metro to the stop of the same name. The Shanghai South Long Distance Bus Station is next door.

Longhua & south

South of central Xujiahui is the bold yellow **Longhua Temple** (*see p87*), Shanghai's oldest temple, named after the *longhua* tree under which Buddha attained enlightenment. Adjacent to the temple is urban Shanghai's only

Xujiahui.

Sightseeing

pagoda, standing an impressive 44 metres (145 feet) high, with delicate pointed eaves at each of its seven levels; the pagoda is not open to visitors.

As tranquil as it appears, the park in which the temple stands has witnessed much bloodshed. In 19th-century Shanghai, under the philosophy of 'kill the chicken to scare the monkeys', prisoners were led through the streets to be spat at and pummelled by spectators. Once at Longhua they would receive further gruesome and lengthy torture. During the 'White Terror' of 1927, when Kuomintang forces set about brutally exterminating their Communist rivals in Shanghai, thousands were led to Longhua where, out of sight of the general public, they were executed.

On the same site during World War II, the Japanese ran their largest civilian internment camp in China for British, American and other Allied nationals. The camp – and the pagoda – feature in JG Ballard's book *Empire of the Sun* (and in Spielberg's movie adaptation).

Nearby, **Longhua Martyrs Cemetery** (Lieshi Lingyuan) commemorates the lives of the murdered Chinese Communists. A graceful tree-lined walkway leads up to a pyramidal Memorial Hall, while landscaped gardens are dotted with bizarre statues, such as an enormous torso of a man, half-buried in the earth but with one arm reaching desperately for the sky. The park also has picnic-perfect lawns.

There's more greenery about two kilometres (1.2 miles) further south at the little-visited **Shanghai Botanical Garden** (*see below*) and also, to the south-west, in the lovely gardens of **Guilin Park** (*see below*).

Guilin Park

1 Guilin Lu, by Caobao Lu (6483 0915). **Open** 5am-6pm daily. **Admission** RMB 2. **No credit cards.**

For those who don't make it to Suzhou (*see p209*), the gardens of Guilin Park offer a little taste of the southern Yangtze style, with stark white walls and grey-tiled roofs. The garden walls create a fitting canvas for slender bamboo stalks and delicate magnolia buds. Don't miss the Shanghai Sweet-Scented Osmanthus festival (*see p152*) in late September and the beautifully designed teahouse at the rear gate.

Longhua Temple

2853 Longhua Lu, by Longhua Park (6456 6085). Metro Caobao Lu then taxi. **Open** 7am-4.30pm daily; 10am-4.30pm 1st & 15th of lunar calendar month & major Buddhist festivals. **Admission** RMB 10. **No credit cards.**

Shanghai's only fully functioning temple and monastery is also its largest and oldest. The star piece is a gargantuan 6,500kg (14,300lb) bell, which, legend has it, brings good fortune when struck three times (try your luck: RMB 10, RMB 300 on New

Year's Eve). Each New Year's Eve the bell is struck 108 times, to address the 108 troubles of Buddhist philosophy. The temple is also the venue for numerous other festivities, including the Birthday of the Queen of Heaven and the Longhua Temple Fair.

Shanghai Botanical Garden

1111 Longwu Lu, Baise Lu (5436 3369/www. shbg.org). Metro Shanghai South Railway Station. **Open** 7am-5pm daily. **Admission** RMB 15. **No credit cards.**

Whereas most of Shanghai's green spaces are filled with seasonal flowerbeds and rows of French-inspired plane trees, the Botanical Garden is lush and varied, with ponds, fields, bonsai gardens and greenhouses. Depending on the season, you can see beds brimming with heavy-headed peonies or curly-haired chrysanthemums. It makes for a wonderful picnic ground – arrive early to claim your spot. The only unfortunate aspect is its distance from Shanghai proper; it takes a longish cab ride to get here from a central location, costing around RMB 50.

Hongqiao Lu & around

Running directly west from central Xujiahui is **Hongqiao Lu**. In the Concession era, this street was lined with the country estates of the stinking rich. One of the most famous of these belonged to the wealthy businessman Sir Victor Sassoon. His Tudorbethan villa is now the **Cypress Hotel** (2419 Hongqiao Lu, by Huqingping Lu, 6268 8868), and sits out near to **Hongqiao Airport** (*see p216*) and **Shanghai Zoo** (*see p155*). Although the government has maintained this house and several dozen others as VIP accommodation, most such opulent reminders of the 1920s and 1930s have either been razed or left to deteriorate slowly. Some former residents have petitioned the government to return the properties to their original owners, but the development frenzy of the past decade has made the land too valuable to relinquish. Only a few villas will survive the next ten years. Apart from those that have been converted in to antique furniture shops, none are open to the public.

Just to the south of Hongqiao Lu is the **Soong Qingling Mausoleum** (*see p88*). The site was formerly the Wanguo (10,000 Countries) Cemetery, the resting place of many Shanghai notables. The revered Soong Qingling died in 1981; after her body was interred, the city changed the name of the cemetery in her honour. Her infamous sister Meiling, whose husband Chiang Kaishek was responsible for the massacre of Communists in 1937, declined to return to China for the funeral; she died in the USA in October 2003, aged 105. The park surrounding the mausoleum is popular as a social venue. Moon-gazing parties are held here during the **Mid Autumn Festival** (*see p152*).

For a lunch stop, it's worth heading a bit further west to **Hong Mei Lu**, known officially as the 'Hong Mei Leisure Pedestrian Street' (Lane 3338, off Hong Mei Lu), which has branches of some of the most popular Shanghai expat chains (Blue Frog, Baby Bamboo, Las Tapas), alongside a variety of independent and family-friendly international eateries, including **Bukhara** (*see p118*). This is a useful stop before heading to the nearby **Shanghai Zoo** (*see p155*), once the British Golf Club, which is home to rare tracts of green.

Further west lies **Gubei**, a largely residential area, which again is occupied for the most part by wealthy expatriates.

Soong Qingling Mausoleum

Soong Qingling Lingyuan, Wanguo Cemetery, 21 Songyuan Lu, by Hongqiao Lu (6275 8080 ext 541). Metro Hongqiao Lu. **Open** 8.30am-4.30pm daily. **Admission** RMB 3. **No credit cards.**

A green lung in the middle of one of Hongqiao's greyer areas, this cemetery is groomed almost to a fault, with razor sharp lawns and neatly trimmed bushes. On special occasions a flock of pigeons, said to be civil and women's rights activist Soong Qingling's favourite birds, are released as a symbol of peace. The park contains an exhibition hall and memorial statue to Soong Qingling, who was made an honorary president shortly before her death and was buried next to her parents in Wanguo Cemetery. The tomb of her beloved maid, Li Yane, lies alongside. Also lying here is Talitha Gerlach, an American Christian minister, whose bravery and devotion to Communist causes (and her anti-foot-binding campaign) earned her the respect of the Chinese government and one of the first green cards issued to a foreigner in Shanghai. Not far from Gerlach's grave are the prominent stones of notable Jewish families, the Kadoories and Sassoons; the original Jewish cemeteries in other parts of town were destroyed during the Cultural Revolution.

Little Britain

If you're looking for a corner of the Middle Kingdom that is forever middle England, look no further than Thames Town, a southern suburb of satellite city Song Jiang. Complete with chip shop, Churchill statue, cast-iron railings, neighbour-blocking hedges, lawns and pubs serving 'real ale', this weird but exclusive bolthole for Shanghai's nouveaux riches was completed in 2006 – and with it not a kerbstone out of place. The houses get 'older' as you approach the city centre; 1990s style mock-Tudor gives way to 1980s semi-detached, with a handful of Georgian-style townhouses flanking the Cathedral Square (distinguished old money types generally plump for the latter).

Congratulations go to Atkins, the British design firm behind the project, which has got the homogenised precinct-style town centre down to a tee. Costa Coffee sits next to the Cob Gate Fish Bar on Oxford Street. The blessed omission of a late-night kebab house, where fists may fly on a rainy Friday night in Blighty, lends an aura of calm to this model – in all senses of the word – community, where some of the 1,000 dwellings fetch up to RMB 6,000,000.

The really interesting thing about Thames Town is not so much that it looks and feels like a Phillip Larkin version of England but that it is representative of a Chinese urban planning fad that is considered contemporary and fashionable. The phenomenon of upwardly mobile couples and families buying repro-retro European-style residences is occurring all over greater Shanghai – look out for German New Town in Anting, with homes designed by Albert Speer Jr, son of the house architect of Hitler's Third Reich; Italian Town in Pujiang, with piazzas and canals; and Barcelona Town in Fencheng, with its very own Ramblas.

To visit Thames Town (www.thamestown. com), take Metro Line 9 from the Guilin Lu terminus (map p240 C5), close to Shanghai Stadium in Xujiahui.

Pudong

Shanghai's sky-high showstopper.

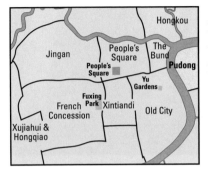

Maps p241 & p245

Modern Pudong is at the very heart of Shanghai's bid to become the most important economic and trading centre in east Asia. Visually, it's a staggering sci-fi landscape of spaceship-like towers, 88-storey pagodas, vast globes the size of rogue meteorites and golden skyscrapers where the sides of buildings act as giant video screens.

As construction continues to stretch further and further east, some of the streets, apartment blocks and parks are still waiting to be inhabited, meaning that, in contrast to the hustle and bustle of Puxi (the areas west of the river), there is an eerily quiet, clean and institutional feel to Pudong (meaning 'east of the river'). That said, Pudong's cultural life has developed substantially over the past few years, sprouting several key new cultural centres, such as the beautiful **Shanghai Oriental Art Centre** and the cutting-edge **Zendai Museum of Art**. In addition, a whole host of seriously wacky architecture is going up either side of the Huangpu in the build-up to Shanghai's **Expo 2010** (*see p23*). Some 70 million visitors are expected to visit the site from 1 May 2010.

Just 20 years ago, Pudong was little more than empty marshland with some shabby warehousing at the water's edge – and the distinct entity that was Shanghai stopped abruptly on the west bank of the Huangpu River. The development of these 530 square kilometres (205 square miles), stretching out to the East China Sea, has been so intense that the city is rumoured to be sinking under the weight of Pudong's towering new office blocks, hotels, apartment buildings and roads.

The pace of change in Pudong is head-spinning. When one hotel ceases to be the world's highest (the Grand Hyatt in the glittering Jin Mao tower), another takes its place (the Park Hyatt in the new World Financial Centre). The completion of the **Shanghai World Financial Centre** in October 2007 – one of the world's tallest buildings (*see p91* **Height matters**) and the tallest in mainland China – will serve to reassert the area's high-flying status. Inevitably, an array of other nearby building sites are poised to spring skyward. Among them, look out next for the twin-towered HSBC IFC building, set for completion in 2009, which will add two more glitzy hotels to Pudong's already smart accommodation selection. Still, nothing fades faster than visions of the future, and the area's original landmark, the pink-baubled **Oriental Pearl Tower**, looks decidedly dated, while the area's strips of newly inhabited apartment blocks can look and feel soulless.

CROSSING THE RIVER

Taking metro lines 2 or 4 is by far the quickest way of crossing the Huangpu River, although it's best to avoid the early morning rush hour when Shanghai's financial workers pour into Pudong. By taxi, the ride from People's Square, say, takes 15 to 20 minutes and costs RMB 20-25. Buses nos.3 and 584 (RMB 2) depart from opposite the Shanghai Museum (*see p60*) and drop off in front of the Jinmao Tower.

At the southern end of the Bund are the **ferries**, which cost as little as RMB 2 and depart from a terminal just south of the Meteorological Tower. Boats leave every 15 minutes and berth at the southern end of the Binjiang Dadao in Pudong.

The **Bund Tourist Tunnel** (5888 6000, 8am-10pm Mon-Fri, 8am-10.30pm Sat & Sun, tickets RMB 40) is certainly one of the more wacky ways of crossing the Huangpu. Clear-glass shuttles take you underground through a 647-metre (2,123-foot) tunnel, in which you're flanked by bright technicolour lights and lots of strobes. Local rumour suggests that this trippy journey may be phased out in favour of a more practical way for commuters to cross from the Bund to central Pudong, so enjoy it while you can. For an additional RMB 15, the tunnel includes an exhibition of rare deep-sea

Lujiazui. *See p92.*

creatures, Buddha statues and the infamous China Sex Culture Exhibition (*see p91*). The tunnel entrances are at 300 Zhongshan Dong Yi Lu/the Bund, by Nanjing Dong Lu, and 2789 Binjiang Dadao, by Fenghe Lu.

The riverfront

Stretching for 2.5 kilometres (1.5 miles) along Pudong's waterfront is **Binjiang Dadao**, a riverbank walkway lined with a plethora of cafés and bars, including German brewhouse **Paulaner Brauhaus** (*see p128*).

The Bund Tourist Tunnel surfaces by the wonderfully kitsch **Oriental Pearl Tower** (*see p91*), with its great pink spheres and florid 1980s music blaring out in every direction. At the base of the tower is the **Shanghai History Museum** (*see p92*).

West along Fenghe Lu is the **Natural Wild Insect Kingdom** (*see p155*), with over 200 different kinds of insects. East along Yincheng Xi Lu is the simple yet well-designed **Shanghai Ocean Aquarium** (*see p155*), home to sharks, penguins and an underwater glass tunnel.

Lujiazui metro station is on the intersection of Pudong's great Shiji Dadao (Century Boulevard) and Lujiazui Lu, and beside it is the ten-storey **Super Brand Mall**, jam-packed with big-brand shops and eateries. Next to it is the revamped **Pudong Shangri-La** (*see p44*), the last word in Bund views and high luxe. Enjoy a pre-dinner drink or dinner at the hotel's swanky **Jade on 36** bar-restaurant (*see p128*) with spectacular night views of the city.

Walk one block east on Century Boulevard for a close-up of Shanghai's iconic 370-metre-(1,200-foot) high **Jinmao Tower**. The building

incorporates oriental pagoda-like geometric detailing in its protruding eaves, stepped structure and delicate roof; the observation deck is on the 88th floor (5047 5101, open 8.30am-9.30pm daily, admission RMB 70). For an equally astonishing view, but without the throngs of tourists, try the restaurants and bars of the luxurious Grand Hyatt (*see p44*), which starts on the 53rd floor of the tower and finishes on the 87th. The interior of the Hyatt is a breathtaking sight in itself, one best viewed from the Patio Lounge on the 56th floor, at the base of the 33-storey atrium. Up on the 87th floor is the aptly named **Cloud 9** cocktail bar (*see p128*), a surreal but pricey option for a drink with an incredible view.

The **Jinmao Concert Hall** (5047 2612, www.jinmaoconcerthall.com, tickets from RMB 80), which hosts piano recitals, and jazz and classical performances, is located on the first floor of a square building, the JLife annexe, built adjacent to the tower. JLife also houses an extremely upmarket shopping plaza.

For still greater elevation, continue to the next block for the gleaming new 492-metre (1,614-foot) superstructure that is the **Shanghai World Financial Centre** (*see p91* **Height matters**), the second-highest structure in the world (an ever-mutating title). Along with its two vertigo-inducing observation decks, there are dizzying drinking and dining options from the 91st to the 93rd floors in the **Park Hyatt** (*see p44*).

Nearby is the **Lujiazui Development Museum** (15 Lujiazui Lu, by Shiji Dadao), just a few minutes' walk east of the Jinmao Tower. The museum has been closed to the public for several years, but the lovely red-and-black house (easily viewed from the outside), completed in 1917, was once one of the largest residences in Shanghai – and stands out in ultra-modern Pudong. A red cobblestone path at the back of the house leads right into the heart of **Lujiazui Central Green** (also known as Lujiazui Park), a huge expanse of green grass containing several shady spots for a coffee, plus fountains and a man-made lake.

China Sex Culture Exhibition

Next to the Bund Tourist Tunnel exit, 2789 Binjiang Dadao (5888 6000). Metro Lujiazui. **Open** *Summer* 8am-10.30pm daily. *Winter* 8am-10pm daily. **Admission** RMB 20. **No credit cards. Map** p245 N4.

Controversy has surrounded the exhibits in this collection of sexual antiquities since it first went on show in 1999. The museum showcases hundreds of pieces, including erotic statues and ancient sex symbols, and covers the subjects of sexual identity, ancient sex worship, marriage, the sexual oppression of women and sexual health. This saucy show is popular with young Chinese couples, who giggle their way around the exhibits arm in arm.

Oriental Pearl Tower

1 Shiji Dadao, by Lujiazui Xi Lu (5879 1888). Metro Lujiazui. **Open** 8am-9.30pm daily. **Admission** *1st Sphere & museum* RMB 85. *All spheres & museum* RMB 135. **No credit cards. Map** p245 O4.

Reaching 468 metres (1,535 feet) into the Pudong sky like a rocket waiting to launch, the tower's pink and purple lights and lasers light up the night sky, representing perfectly Shanghai's mania for everything kitsch. It was created back in 1994 by Shanghai civic

Height matters

The ambition to erect one of the world's tallest buildings may seem like macho nonsense. But there can be no denying the impact of the neck-craning 492 metres (1,614 feet) that make up the new **Shanghai World Financial Centre** (WFC), delivering unequivocally the pre-Expo ego boost that Shanghai so unashamedly covets.

The WFC offers visitors several ways to get high. An ear-popping selection of 91 elevators can whizz you up to the 94th floor observation deck. Better still is the 100th storey 'VIP observation aisle', a glass-bottomed tower-top walkway commanding stomach-churning views over Shanghai's previous entries into the 'my tower's bigger than yours' race – the Oriental Pearl and the Jinmao building next door. Other stylish perches from which to gaze down on Shanghai's 20 million lesser mortals are the 87th floor French restaurant, and the 92nd floor whisky cellar in the WFC's slick **Park Hyatt** hotel (*see p44*).

The progress of this glistening steel and glass behemoth hasn't always been onwards and upwards. The original skyscraper-topping design – an open circle over the city – was scuppered in favour of an open rectangle, as thoughts of a Japanese-style rising sun over Shanghai made the powers that be feel a little queasy. An elevator shaft fire in August 2007 may sound like a scary engineering snafu but, according to the authorities, was actually a good omen – the smoke pouring out of the building was deemed good feng shui. And the anti-seismic devices mean the half-kilometre high WFC can sway gently in dangerous typhoon conditions without the

merchant bankers on the 60th floor even noticing – or at least so they say.

The hype obscures a simple but startling truth: that China now has the financial and engineering wherewithal to out-build New York, Chicago and Toyko. The sky, it seems, is no longer the limit.
Shanghai World Financial Centre, 100 Century Avenue, by Haixin Lu (www.shanghaihills.com). Metro Lujiazui. **Admission** call for details. **Map** p245 P5.

Shanghai World Financial Centre.

Sightseeing

leaders eager to give the city a landmark that could be recognised the world over, as well as lead the city's new building explosion. Now surrounded by other towers, and the subject of thousands of tourist snaps every month, it's fair to say that it's done the trick.

The spheres contain various exhibitions, shops, restaurants and conference halls. Most tourists head to the observation deck in the central pink sphere/pearl, 263 metres (863 feet) off the ground and 45 metres (148 feet) in diameter. But to avoid getting a poke in the eye from the Chinese tour group leaders' flags and being deafened by their megaphones, head to the smaller Space Module situated at 350 metres (1,150 feet) for a higher and more relaxed view across the sprawling city.

Shanghai History Museum

Gate 4, Oriental Pearl Tower, 1 Shiji Dadao, by Lujiazui Xi Lu (5879 1888). Metro Lujiazui. **Open** 8am-9.30pm daily. **Admission** RMB 35. **No credit cards**. **Map** p245 O4.

Situated at the base of the Oriental Pearl Tower, this museum makes use of extraordinary memorabilia to illustrate the city's history, focusing on the colonial period (1860-1949). Stacked with artefacts, life-size dioramas, models, photos and paintings, the History Museum puts the spotlight on life in post-1840s Shanghai, from the city's cinema industry to its opium houses and curious forms of criminal justice. Even one of the bronze lions that guarded the Hongkong & Shanghai Bank on the Bund (*see p50*) is on display. Look out for 1920s limos used by local hotshots in the museum's foyer, and scale models of the city's ritziest colonial buildings, on the way out.

Lujiazui & Century Park

Shiji Dadao (Century Boulevard) is Pudong's vast eight-lane avenue, supposedly modelled on the Champs-Elysées in Paris. Starting at the Oriental Pearl Tower, it runs for four kilometres (2.5 miles) in a dead-straight line culminating at **Century Park**. This grassy parkland has trees, sculptures, lakes, an open-air theatre, a children's amusement park and a fishing area.

Before hitting the park, Century Boulevard is intercepted by the **Science & Technology Museum** (*see p93*). At weekends, small children gather in the big open areas in front of the museum and outside metro exits 1, 2, 7 and 8 to rollerskate and fly kites.

Opposite the Science & Technology Museum on Dingxiang Lu is the **Shanghai Oriental Art Centre**, one of the newest and most beautiful concert halls to grace the city. Shanghai's municipal government invested vast amounts of money in building the centre, which boasts a café, a French restaurant, state-of-the-art concert halls and the delightful **Shanghai Gallery of Antique Music Boxes**.

A 30-minute walk north-east of here is the **Zendai Thumb Plaza**. This outdoor mall contains a Carrefour, as well as upmarket home decor shops, bakeries, and Chinese, Japanese and Indian restaurants. More unusually, it also contains the **Immaculate Conception Church** (80 Zihuai Lu, by Dingxiang Lu, 6856 9852) and the excellent new **Zendai Museum of Modern Art** (*see p93*).

Science & Technology Museum.

Further down Metro Line 2 is Longyang Lu station. This is the terminus for Shanghai's super-slick train, the **Maglev**, which runs the 30 kilometres (19 miles) out to Pudong Airport in seven minutes. Although inconveniently located and linked to only one metro line, the RMB 80 return trip or RMB 50 one way (RMB 40 for air ticket holders) is worth it just to travel on the fastest train in the world, reaching speeds of up to 430km/h (that's nearly 270mph). Trains depart every 15 minutes from 7am to 9pm.

Century Park

Gate 1, 1001 Jinxiu Lu, by Fangdian Lu (3876 0588). Metro Century Park. **Open** *Summer* 7am-6pm daily. *Winter* 7am-5pm daily. **Admission** RMB 10. **No credit cards. Map** p241 H4.
The paths that zigzag across Shanghai's largest park make it ideal for rollerskating or cycling on the tandems that are available for hire. The 5.5km perimeter (3.5 miles) of the park is best jogged on the quieter footpaths. Small pedalos and slow motorised boats are also available for hire. Hawkers sell kites outside the entrance to the park, but, ironically, kite flying (along with football) is strictly prohibited within, as are animals.

Science & Technology Museum

2000 Shiji Dadao, by Yingchun Lu (6854 2000). Metro Shanghai Science & Technology Museum. **Open** 9am-5.15pm daily (last admission 4.30pm). **Admission** RMB 60. **Credit** MC, V. **Map** p241 G4.
This other-worldly glass-and-steel facility cost RMB 1.75 billion to build. It contains hundreds of high-tech, interactive attractions, focused on natural history, health, science and technology, and the earth's place within the galaxy. The complex also boasts a space theatre (tickets RMB 20), two IMAX 3D cinemas and an Iwerks '4D' theatre – incorporating regular 3D technology with the addition of effects such as moving seats, water-spray rain simulations, air blowing through the cinema like wind and even leg-ticklers in the seats.

Shanghai Gallery of Antique Music Boxes

3rd floor, Shanghai Oriental Art Centre, 425 Dingxiang Lu, by Shiji Dadao (6854 7647/www. shoac.com.cn). Metro Shanghai Science & Technology Museum. **Open** 10.30am-6pm daily. **Admission** RMB 50. **No credit cards. Map** p241 G4.
On the third floor of the impressive Shanghai Oriental Art Centre is this charming collection of European music boxes, with examples from the 19th and 20th centuries. English titles and explanations are provided.

Shanghai Oriental Art Centre

425 Dingxiang Lu, by Shiji Dadao (6854 1234/ www.shoac.com.cn). Metro Shanghai Science & Technology Museum. **Map** p241 G4.
This spectacular 'blossoming flower' concert hall was designed by French architect Paul Andreu. Opened in 2005, it houses a state-of-the-art performance hall, concert hall and opera theatre, as well as the music-box collection on the third floor. You can wander into the

Shanghai Oriental Art Centre.

lobby at will, but the place really comes into its own for concerts, during which more than 880 inlaid lights decorating the roof change colour in response to the music being played. The dress code strictly stipulates 'no slippers'. *See also p188.*

Zendai Museum of Modern Art (Zendai MoMA)

Zendai Thumb Plaza, No.28, Lane 199, Fangdian Lu (5033 9801/www.zendaiart.com). Metro Century Park. **Open** 10am-8pm Tue-Sun. **Admission** RMB 20; free Wed. **No credit cards. Map** p241 H3.
Robert Indiana's famed *LOVE* sculpture marks the entrance to this small but very contemporary art museum. Under the directorship of Shen Qibin, who is also head of Shanghai's better-known Doland: Shanghai MoMA (aka Duolun, *see p96*), the Zendai hosts a range of international modern art exhibitions, aiming to attract and involve young people through ever-present interactive displays. Young Chinese artists get prominent exhibition space, and are encouraged to weave ideas on politics, society and the environment into their sculptures and installations. Recent exhibitions include Li Xiaosong's electronic *Brain-quake*, featuring a low-tech white brain with pop-up thought boxes, plus a solo show from internationally renowned Wang Jianwei, one of China's best-known conceptual artists. The museum also hosts jazz concerts, film screenings, debates, and lectures by foreign and local artists. Check the website for the exhibition schedule.

Hongkou

Neighbourhood charm and a cleaned-up creek just north of the Bund.

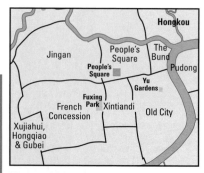

Hongkou

Jingan · People's Square · The Bund · Pudong

People's Square

Yu Gardens

Fuxing Park

French Concession · Xintiandi · Old City

Xujiahui, Hongqiao & Gubei

Maps p241, p244 & p245

Most visitors spend their time exploring the Bund, while residential Hongkou – across the creek to the north – remains a relatively unknown part of old Shanghai. The grey view across to Hongkou may not inspire much enthusiasm but don't let that put you off – the area has an intriguing history, with interwar remnants of Chinese, Japanese and Jewish settlements, and a major regeneration project that is cleaning up and transforming Suzhou Creek (*see p95* **Liquid refreshment**).

Hongkou's known history is quite brief. In 1853, the Americans founded the American Concession on the then-swampy Hongkou waterfront and, a decade later, this merged with the British Concession to form the International Settlement. By the beginning of the 20th century, the district had gained 30,000 Japanese residents, earning it the nickname 'Little Tokyo'. After the Japanese invaded Manchuria, Chinese unrest in Hongkou led Japanese troops to occupy this part of the city. A few years later, upheavals in fascist Europe saw Ashkenazi Jews flee to this remote safe haven, with several thousand remaining here for the duration of the war.

GETTING THERE

Most of what's interesting lies in the vicinity of Duolun Lu (which is just off Sichuan Bei Lu) and Lu Xun Park; to get here take Metro Line 3 from Shanghai Railway Station to Dong Baoxing Lu. Alternatively, bus no.21 runs by Duolun Lu from Sichuan Zhong Lu, one block in from the Bund. A taxi to Duolun Lu picked up near People's Square will cost around RMB 15.

Duolun Lu & Lu Xun Park

L-shaped **Duolun Lu** (officially called 'Duolun Culture Street') has been spruced up since it provided a home for various famous writers, most notably Lu Xun, the 'father of modern Chinese literature'. The street forms a quaint pedestrianised thoroughfare, cobblestoned and lined with *shikumen* lane housing, jade and wood carving shops, cafés and small galleries. The street furniture includes gleaming bronze statues of famous Chinese writers.

At the eastern end of Duolun is the **Doland: Shanghai Duolun Museum of Modern Art**, known to locals as 'Duolun'. Although the institutional grey cubist architecture is rather incongruous, the exhibits always generate enough buzz to draw people over from the other side of town. At the point where the street curves north are two fine old mansions, both of which are now cafés: the **Old Film Café**, at no.123, is quirky and cosy, the walls covered with black and white photos of movie stars, and nearby **Reading Room Café**, at no.195, is also worth a visit.

The ground floors of many of Duolun's houses have been turned into art and antique stores, heaped high with collections of old magazines, crockery, watches, posters and assorted aged miscellanea. At **nos.179-181 Duolun Lu** is one of the city's finest collections of memorabilia from early 20th-century Shanghai and the Cultural Revolution years. Duolun Lu also has several **mini museums** devoted variously to chopsticks (no.191), porcelain (no.185) and most intriguing of all, at no.183, Huand Miaoxin's incredible collection of over 18,000 Mao badges (from RMB 50), which some zealous revolutionaries wore pierced into their skin as proof of their loyalty.

Down a turning towards the north-east of Duolun is the **Former Residence of Lu Xun**, often referred to as the father of modern Chinese literature. It is in this elegant 1924 mansion that the Chinese League of Left-wing Writers was founded in March 1930. Walk out into the courtyard garden to see a quintet of statues of young writers, looking very earnest and revolutionary among the bushes.

A short walk from Duolun is **Lu Xun Park**, also known as Hongkou Park, one of the city's most pleasant green spaces. It's a great

Liquid refreshment

The Suzhou Creek regeneration project, started in 1998, finally gets the finishing touches.

Suzhou Creek played a crucial role in shaping Shanghai's identity. Stretching 125 kilometres (78 miles) inland to its source at Tai Lake, the zig-zagging creek served as a vital trade link between Suzhou, in Jiangsu province, and the mouth of the Yangzte River, via what was then the small fishing town of Shanghai. The link served to strengthen Shanghai's position, and ultimately power shifted downstream.

In 1842, when the Treaty of Nanjing opened Shanghai up for trade, Suzhou Creek adapted again. International trade poured in, warehouses were built, and cargo docks crowded the river. More than just a waterway ferrying food downriver and opium up, the creek by now also marked the boundary between the British Concession to the south and the American Concession to the north. Later, in 1937, when the Japanese invaded, the Americans retreated to the Brits' area and the newly dubbed International Concession, while the Japanese took over the north.

Following World War II, Suzhou Creek saw a period of harmful stagnation. Polluted and abused, the creek had to wait until the start of the 1990s – when plans for a new city centre were taking shape – for Shanghai's government to give it a future. Remaining industry was removed, residential space developed and warehouses were taken over by artistic communities. In particular, the area around **50 Moganshan Lu** (*see p163*), previously a textile mill compound, helped turn Shanghai into one of the centres of the Chinese art boom. The river was once again mirroring the city's progress, though any real reflection would have been hard to fathom: the creek's industrial past, and subsequent neglect, had turned the water pitch-black, and the river was one of the most fetid in China.

Realising an open sewer running through its centre would do nothing for Shanghai's reputation, the city authorities launched the Suzhou Creek Rehabilitation Project in 1998. The overhaul began with vital sewage treatment plants and water oxygenation programmes, but the blueprint also included a queue of promenades, riverside retail developments, ecological education parks, several new museums, an entertainment centre and even pleasure boat rides.

As we went to press, it was unclear how many of the plans would materialise by the time the Expo raises the curtain on the all-new Shanghai. Open and worth a look if you're at Moganshan 50 is **Menqing Gardens** (on the south side of the river at Yichang Lu & Jiangning Lu, or over Changhua Lu from Moganshan Lu; Metro Zhangtan Lu), an eco-park with shops on the site of the old Shanghai Brewery. Two museums are also being built: the first dedicated to yachts, the second to matches (and housed in an old match factory).

Squeaky-clean tourist attractions aside, the Rehabilitation Project has seen the return of fish and the removal of the pervading stench, even if the gentrification process has not been without controversy. The project cleared out many longstanding communities (check out the beautiful 2001 film *Suzhou River* for a vision, albeit a fantastical one, of the Creek's underworld), while increasing rents at Moganshan 50 are already jeopardising the original artist studios and galleries that contributed so extensively to the area's new lease of cultural life. As with so many of the city's showcase projects, it remains to be seen what will survive the clean-up.

Sightseeing

Doland: Shanghai Duolun MoMA.

community spot where groups of people gather to sing traditional songs and dance, particularly on sunny Sunday afternoons. In addition to a couple of lovely lakes, it contains the tomb of Lu Xun, fronted by a giant seated bronze of the writer with memorial calligraphy inscribed by Chairman Mao himself. There's also a museum, the **Lu Xun Memorial Hall** and, flanking the north-west corner of the park, the contemporary art museum **Zhu Qizhan**.

Doland: Shanghai Duolun Museum of Modern Art

27 Duolun Lu, by Sichuan Bei Lu (6587 2530/ www.duolunart.com). Metro East Baoxing Lu. **Open** 9am-5.30pm daily. **Admission** RMB 10; RMB 5 reductions. **No credit cards.** **Map** p241 E2.
The first state-owned museum in China devoted entirely to modern art is an impressive seven-storey affair. Run by the culture bureau of the Hongkou district, it opened in 2003 but has already become one of the city's most active cultural institutions. It has brought in several big-name shows, including such artists as Jean-Michel Basquiat, and frequently collaborates with other Asian museums. It boasts an active artist-in-residence programme; visitors are encouraged to pop in to the artists' studios on the fifth floor. There are regularly changing temporary shows, screenings and music events and some well thought out and creative workshops for children.

Former Residence of Lu Xun

No.9, Lane 132, Shanying Lu, by Duolun Lu (5666 2608). Metro East Baoxing Lu. **Open** 9am-4pm daily. **Admission** RMB 8. **No credit cards.** **Map** p241 E1.
Full of original furniture and a collection of Lu Xun's belongings, but with his books conspicuous by their absence: the writer's secret library was housed elsewhere and found its final home in Beijing.

Lu Xun Memorial Hall

200 Tianai Lu, by Sichuan Bei Lu (6540 2288). Metro East Baoxing Lu. **Open** 9am-4pm daily. **Admission** free. **No credit cards.** **Map** p241 E2.
This spacious museum opened in 1999. The second level displays a voluminous collection of Lu Xun's books, letters, hand-scripted essays and personal artefacts, including his hawk's bill-rimmed glasses and a plaster-cast death mask still embedded with a few strands of his facial hair.

Zhu Qizhan Art Museum

580 Ouyang Lu, by Dalian Xi Lu (5671 0741/ www.zmuseum.org). Metro Dalian Xi Lu/Hongkou Stadium. **Open** 10am-4.30pm Tue-Sun. **Admission** RMB 10. **No credit cards.** **Map** p241 E1.
Originally named after the renowned ink-brush painter, Zhu Qizhan has since remodelled itself as a contemporary art museum. Directed by former Duolun staffers, it offers some similar material while promoting art education.

Huoshan Lu

Huoshan Lu – not to be confused with Huashan Lu – is the heart of Jewish Shanghai. Get here by crossing Waibaidu Bridge (or Garden Bridge) then walking east along Dongdaming Lu or take a taxi from the Bund. Note that the bridge is closed for repairs until March 2009.

At 65 Huoshan Lu is what once was the **Broadway Theatre**, which boasted a Jewish-owned roof garden called the Vienna Café. Now the big neon sign in Chinese reads 'Broadway Disco'. East along the street are some charming brick almshouse-like townhouses with small gardens at the front; this was formerly Jewish housing during the war. **Huoshan Park** (open 6am-6pm daily), an unexpected leafy area, has the distinction of bearing the city's one public monument to the area's historic role as a Jewish haven; the inconspicuous stone engraved in English, Chinese and Hebrew alludes to the Hongkou neighbourhood as a 'designated area for stateless refugees'.

Follow Zhoushan Lu north to Changyang Lu and track back west for the **Ohel Moshe Synagogue** (62 Changyang Lu, 6512 0229). Built in 1927, Ohel Moshe was run by Meir Ashkenazi, the spiritual leader of the Russian Jewish community and chief rabbi of Shanghai from 1926 to 1949. The hollow ground floor has a small display of grainy photos of Jewish buildings from China's past. The third floor is now the tiny **Jewish Refugee Museum** (62 Changyang Lu, by Zhoushan Lu, 6537 1238), the only Jewish museum in China.

For further insight take a tour with renowned Israeli journalist and historian Divr Bar-Gal of **Shanghai Jewish** tours (www.shanghai-jews.com).

Eat, Drink, Shop

Song Fang Maison de Thé.
See p145.

Restaurants

One of the world's most exciting places to fuel up.

Eat, Drink, Shop

Beijing can keep its temples and Peking duck haunts, for there's no better city for eating in all of China than Shanghai. OK, so Hong Kong does Cantonese (while silently seething at their lack of local hairy crabs) and Beijing has a slight edge on duck (though a few great ones escaped to **Xindalu**), but nowhere else in China is there such a diverse mix of provincial cuisines and so dynamic a fine dining scene. Long gone are the days of being restricted to a hotel restaurant in Shanghai – though if you have the good fortune to be lodging at the Pudong Shangri-La or Hyatt on the Bund, that wouldn't be a bad thing at all these days.

Shanghai's restaurant scene has everything in today's culinary spectrum, from upscale Hunanese restaurants (**Guyi**) to raucous Middle Eastern-accented Uighur cooking (**Afanti**), to Shanghainese and European fine dining institutions that are bound to be contenders whenever Michelin starts to pay serious attention to the city (which, rumour has it, will be in the very near future). In fact, many of the red book's chefs already are paying attention – either on unannounced recon missions or in special one-off shows – and talk swirls constantly about who will be the next major chef to land in Shanghai.

In the meanwhile, there's great eating to be done across the board. **Whampoa Club** and **Jean-Georges** (both at Three on the Bund), **Jade on 36**, **Sens & Bund**, **Allure**, **Family Li Imperial Cuisine** and **Fu 1088** fit the bill for a big night out, for everything from Asian-inflected fine dining and refined Shanghainese to a formal romp through recipes straight from the Forbidden City's kitchens. Mid-market Western restaurants that could play in any city are a recent development in Shanghai, and they ply their wares with a host of backdrops. Art deco? **Hamilton House**, just off the Bund. Mod bistro? **Franck**, hidden off a leafy French Concession street.

But if you didn't come to China to nibble on *pains au chocolate* or pizza, you could easily spend months jumping from home-style Shanghainese to Taiwanese, dipping in to the cuisine of the fiery interior, without ever seeing a white tablecloth or a slice of bread. Start at **Ding Tai Fung**, a sparkling Taiwanese chain (the heresy!), for the best Shanghainese soup dumpling in town (but *see p118* **Dumplings** first for instructions on how to eat it). Reserve a table at **Jishi** for a home-style, red-braised Shanghai dinner, or pop over to **Crystal Jade** for a shatteringly crisp pork belly. Don't balk at the fact that they are all chains – in Shanghai, 'independent' and 'cheap' aren't words that signify good or authentic. This becomes abundantly clear with Shanghai street food, which can't compare to that of Bangkok or Singapore. A quick trip to Wujiang Lu for **Yang's Fry Dumpling**, and that basket of *xiaolongbao* from **Ding Tai Fung**, and you can comfortably consider yourself schooled in Shanghainese street food.

That's not to say cheap food in Shanghai can't be good. A rolling hot pot with enough plates of lamb to make your head spin (and

The best Restaurants

For cheap eats
Afanti (see p117); **Bao Luo** (see p109) and **Jishi** (see p112) for Shanghainese classics; **Bi Feng Tang** (see p104) for dim sum; **Charmant** (see p109) for Taiwanese; **Di Shui Dong** for Hunanese dishes (see p110); **Xiao Fei Yang** (see p117) for hot pot.

For design fireworks
Jade on 36 (see p118); **Shintori** (see p115); **South Beauty** (see p112); **Whampoa Club** (see p100); **Yongfoo Elite** (see p113).

For dim sum
Crystal Jade (see p107).

For flexing your plastic
Jade on 36 (see p118); **Jean-Georges** (see p101); **Laris** (see p101); **Sens & Bund** (see p101).

For Shanghai dumplings
Ding Tai Fung (see p107); **Nan Xiang** (see p106); **Yang's Fry Dumpling** (see p106).

For a taste of old Shanghai
Fu 1088 (see p105); **Jishi** (see p112); **Whampoa Club** (see p100); **Yin** (see p113); **Yongfoo Elite** (see p113).

Crystal Jade. *See p107.*

bottles of ice-cold beer to help keep it spinning) at **Xiao Fei Yang** (*see p117*), or a checkered tablecloth full of spicy Hunan dishes at **Di Shui Dong** (*see p110*), will set you back about the same price as a Tokyo taxi. A minor jump in price, and the atmosphee increases dramatically. Witness this at **Lynn** (*see p105*), **Pin Chuan** (*see p112*), **South Beauty** (*see p112*) and **Yin** (*see p113*), or take it one step further to **Fu 1088** (*see p105*), an unmarked villa decked out in 1930s antiques and with quite possibly the best food Shanghai has to offer right now.

For a round-up of Shanghai's best one-room, family-run eateries, *see p110* **Family feast**.

The Bund

The Bund is home to many of the city's top restaurants, and a dinner at **Jean-Georges**, or brunch at **M on the Bund**, is worth every penny of their considerable cost. While most of the hot spots are by the water, with prices to match the unforgettable views, new options are starting to pop up in the grid of streets just behind the famous neoclassical façades. For the moment, the best of the bunch is the art deco revival and bistro food at **Hamilton House**.

Chinese

Family Li Imperial Cuisine

Huangpu Park, 1/F, 500 Zhongshan Dong Yi Lu, by Beijing Dong Lu (5308 1919). **Open** 11.30am-2pm, 5.30pm-late daily. **Set menu** RMB 400-2,000/person. **Credit** AmEx, DC, MC, V. **Map** p245 M4 ❶ Dongbei

Family Li's über-refined, multi-course approach to Chinese cooking might seem reminiscent of European fine dining. But, in fact, the dishes date back to the labour-intensive kitchens of Beijing's Forbidden City, from where a Li family relative smuggled the recipes long ago. Cooking emphasises beauty in presentation and luxury in gluttony, as well as rare ingredients like bird's nest and shark fin. The original is in a charming courtyard house hidden deep in Beijing's alleys; Shanghai's version is – naturally – flashier and more expensive. There's no communal dining room, just nine glitzy private rooms; menus are set and prices start at RMB 600 per person.

Tan Wai Lou

5th floor, Bund 18, 18 Zhongshan Dong Yi Lu, by Nanjing Dong Lu (6339 1188/www.bund18.com). Metro Nanjing Dong Lu. **Open** 11.30am-2.30pm, 5-10pm daily. **Main courses** RMB 68-3,580. **Credit** AmEx, DC, MC, V. **Map** p245 M4 ❷ Cantonese

Tan Wai Lou, one of the city's most elegant Chinese restaurants, was designed by Italian architect Filippo Gabbiano to capture the spirit of the city's meteoric rise. The menu, which incorporates

Taiwanese and Cantonese classics, demonstrates a flair for fusion (think foie gras and sashimi), and reflects the tastes of the big spenders in its midst, who finish off a business banquet set to Bund views with a cognac and a Cohiba. *Photo p104.*

Whampoa Club

5th floor, Three on the Bund, 3 Zhongshan Dong Yi Lu, by Guangdong Lu (6321 3737/www.threeonthe bund.com). Metro Nanjing Dong Lu. **Open** 11.30am-2.30pm, 5.30-10pm daily. **Main courses** RMB 168-200. **Credit** AmEx, DC, MC, V. **Map** p245 M5 ❸ Shanghainese

One of Asia's pre-eminent chefs, Jereme Leung has breathed new life into traditional Shanghainese cuisine in this dazzling modern deco setting created by celebrated Hong Kong designer Alan Chan. The extensive menu features everything from soups and seafood to shark's fin and Leung's signature slow-cooked Australian abalone. His adaptations of classic dishes include drunken chicken with Shaoxing wine, shaved ice and house-smoked tea eggs, plus a dollop of caviar. Leung also innovates with dishes such as almond and cocoa-fried spare ribs, and seared foie gras on red glaze. If you can stretch to it, the six-course tasting menu (RMB 588) is superb. Diners can also choose from a special tea menu for a traditional ceremony served at the table or in one of the opulent private tearooms. Reservations are recommended for dinner. *Photo p108.*

Xindalu

1/F, Hyatt on the Bund, 199 Huangpu Lu, by Wuchang Lu (6393 1234 ext 6318/www. shanghai.bund.hyatt.cn). **Open** 11.30am-2.30pm, 5.30pm-10.30pm daily. **Main courses** RMB 160-1,688. **Credit** AmEx, DC, MC, V. **Map** p245 N3 ❹ Dongbei

Xindalu is a Chinese restaurant every bit as understated but professional as its host, the new Hyatt on the Bund (*see p29*). A glassed-in kitchen affords a view of the flaming woks, misty bamboo steamers and imported Peking duck oven. The menu plays up the food of neighbouring Zhejiang and Jiangsu provinces, though it has quickly become known as a destination for its crispy-skinned Peking ducks. Glistening birds are carved tableside, divided up into platefuls of crunchy skin (dip them in sugar); tender breast meat and skin-on dark meat, to be wrapped up in pancakes with cucumber, spring onion and plum sauce. You'd be remiss in thinking that's all it does, though – the clay-wrapped beggar's chicken is just as good, as is most of the menu, and Xindalu has the only cocktail list in town that makes use of Maotai, a fiery, floral rice wine.

European

Hamilton House

137 Fuzhou Lu, by Jiangxi Lu (6321 0586/www. hamiltonhouse.com.cn). Metro Nanjing Dong Lu. **Open** noon-1am daily. **Main courses** RMB 120-230. **Credit** AmEx, DC, MC, V. **Map** p245 M5 ❺

The streets just behind the Bund have long been an architectural treasure trove but a dining wasteland. In late 2007, Hamilton House was the first to join the dots together. It revamped the first floor of its namesake art deco building and turned it into an exceptional French restaurant overlooking perhaps the most beautiful intersection in the city. Stylishly retro, it manages to be classy without resorting to heavy-handed nostalgia. Period tables, plush scalloped chairs, and a unisex powder room all figure in the elegant space, and unpretentious bistro dishes grace your plate. Go straight for the poached egg on a thick slab of brioche with spinach, pork belly, shallots and a red wine butter, or a braised, stuffed pork trotter with a sweet onion soubise.

Sens & Bund

6th floor, Bund 18, 18 Zhongshan Dong Yi Lu, by Nanjing Dong Lu (6323 9898/www.bund18.com). Metro Nanjing Dong Lu. **Open** 11.30am-10.30pm daily. **Main courses** RMB 238-598. **Credit** AmEx, DC, MC, V. **Map** p245 M5 ❻

The Pourcel Brothers – those silent, determined twins of Jardin de Sens fame – churn out fine dining restaurants like plates of seared foie gras. And this sleek white space, the flagship restaurant at the restored neo-classical Bund 18 building, is their Shanghai entrant. Expect a refined Michelin-style French menu (the brothers' Montpellier flagship has two Michelin stars), from which Shanghai's Frenchmen and local fashionistas select beautifully presented dishes with a refined Mediterranean flair, while sipping wines from one of Shanghai's strongest list of Gallic grapes. Try the lobster terrine with duck breast and vanilla oil, black truffle soup with artichoke and butternut squash, or roast pigeon with curry pastilla and bitter cacao *jus*. Finish with a raspberry soufflé with green tea ice-cream and lemongrass foam. Set menus of signature dishes are also available. Reservations necessary.

Fusion

Jean-Georges

4th floor, Three on the Bund, 3 Zhongshan Dong Yi Lu, by Guangdong Lu (6321 7733/www.threeonthe bund.com). Metro Nanjing Dong Lu. **Open** 11.30am-2.30pm, 6-11pm daily. **Main courses** RMB 238-330. **Credit** AmEx, DC, MC, V. **Map** p245 M5 ❼

The Jean-Georges in question is, of course, Jean-Georges Vongerichten, the Alsace-born chef lauded for his New York restaurants Vong, Perry St and the eponymous three-Michelin-starred original. Long a fan of Shanghai cuisine, he put his money where his mouth was nearly four years ago, and introduced the city to his Asian-infused take on traditional French cuisine at this Bund-side location. Decorated with eel-skin sofas and pony leather armchairs, the restaurant is part Gothic Shanghai gentlemen's club, part Manhattan martini bar. Diners can order à la carte or select one of two seven-course tasting menus. Start with the foie gras brûlée with dried

sour cherries or scallops with caper-raisin emulsion and caramelised cauliflower, before moving on to mains like the sea bass with parsnips and fragrant coconut juice. Desserts are perhaps the best in town. The RMB 188 weekend brunch menu, a merciful introduction to the cream of Shanghai's restaurant crop, is an unbeatable deal, and the bar (*see p120*) is a favourite of local chefs, as much for its separate menu as the outstanding cocktails. Reservations required for both lunch and dinner.

Laris

6th floor, Three on the Bund, 3 Zhongshan Dong Yi Lu, by Guangdong Lu (6321 9922/www.threeonthe bund. com). Metro Nanjing Dong Lu. **Open** 11.30am-2.30pm, 6-10.30pm daily. **Average** RMB 450-500. **Credit** AmEx, MC, V. **Map** p245 M5 ❽

The prevailing trend in restaurant decor is retro-chic Old Shanghai, but not at Laris – this place is all about 'new Shanghai' and the money that goes with it. It's the first signature restaurant of self-styled celebrity chef David Laris, once upon a time the executive chef of Terence Conran's London restaurant Mezzo, and taps into the nouveau Shanghainese love of luxe: cue bright marble interiors and fat velvet couches, and cocktails in the sexy Vault Bar (*see p121*), followed by fresh oysters, lobster and Russian caviar at the marble Claws, Wings & Fins bar. The menu dresses up Asian flavours in nouvelle fine dining fashion: crab with avocado salsa and lemongrass gazpacho, or cod fillet with mono miso emulsion, sea urchin and braised daikon. Reservations necessary.

M on the Bund

7th floor, 20 Guangdong Lu, by Zhongshan Dong Yi Lu (6350 9988/www.m-onthebund.com). Metro Nanjing Dong Lu. **Open** 11.30am-2.30pm, 6-10.30pm daily. **Main courses** RMB 182-288. **Credit** AmEx, DC, MC, V. **Map** p245 M5 ❾

Before Jean-Georges (*see above*), there was M on the Bund. Named after the city's networking tour de force Michelle Garnaut, M has been a bellwether for Shanghai's headlong bout of economic growth since it opened in 1999. The art deco revival venue is striking, with sweeping views of the historic Bund and across the Huangpu River to the mighty skyscrapers of Pudong. The North African-meets-Mediterranean menu feels like a personal collection of favourites, as does much of the menu. Staples include the crispy-skinned suckling pig, a Fez-style couscous royale, salt-baked lamb and delicious pavlova. It's all very good, but if you're a gastronome pining for a dégustation menu you might be happier across the street at Three on the Bund. That said, it does have the best service in town, a fantastic wine list and is a marvellous spot for brunch, a bargain at RMB 258 for three courses. Toast the Shanghai skyline with a glass of champagne or raise a pinky at Sunday high tea, and then head down a floor to another M venture, the Glamour Bar (*see p120*) for cocktails. Reservations are required for lunch and dinner.

New Heights

7th floor, Three on the Bund, 3 Zhongshan Dong Yi Lu, by Guangdong Lu (6321 0909/www.threeon thebund. com). Metro Nanjing Dong Lu. **Open** 11am-2.30pm, 6-10.30pm daily. **Main courses** RMB 110-150. **Credit** AmEx, DC, MC, V. **Map** p245 M5 ⑩

In what seems an almost socialist gesture for such an unreservedly fat-cat capitalistic city, New Heights – the cheapest of the quartet of eateries situated in Three on the Bund – actually occupies the top floor of the development, bagging the best views and a wonderful roof terrace complete with 180° panorama of the river and Pudong. The menu is please-every-one Western, with a few Asian concessions, and New Heights draws crowds like they passed out flyers at passport control. That said, the food is usually well executed, and goes beyond its descriptions of burgers, fish and chips, and pasta by using high-quality ingredients and big bold flavours. The menu is slated to have a long-overdue shake-up, but that won't, and shouldn't, stop the hordes. The view is still fantastic, service is great and a drink at the bar (*see p121*) is an essential part of anyone's Shanghai stay.

People's Square

As a main bus and metro terminus, People's Square has a clutch of cheap noodle joints, Western fast-food outlets and Japanese or Chinese chain restaurants plus, in season, some prime crab outlets; *see p113* **Hairy crabs**. **Huanghe Lu**, beside the Park Hotel,

Chinese cuisines

Chinese people have a well-deserved reputation for eating practically anything. But each region is different. The Cantonese certainly aren't picky (civet cat, anyone?), while northerners do, in fact, eat dog, believing that it keeps them warm in winter. Shanghainese diners, meanwhile, are notoriously fussy, and do not like to be thought of as indiscriminate eaters. Still, it's all relative: delicacies such as live shrimp, king snake and turtle are considered Shanghainese specialities, and are served at many restaurants.

Just as in the West nobody would say 'Let's go eat European', the Shanghainese don't go out for a Chinese – they eat Cantonese, Shanghainese or Sichuan. Cuisines from most provinces of China are available in Shanghai, although some are more popular than others.

Shanghainese

As you'd expect, this is the most popular cuisine in town, rich both in flavour and texture. Heavy, unctuous brown sauces are used for braising meat such as pork shanks or knuckle, or to simmer fatty pork balls with vegetables. Dumplings are popular, and very different from the lighter Cantonese variety. The most famous Shanghainese dumplings are *xiaolongbao* (*see p116* **Dumplings**), which are dipped in a sauce made with Shanghainese brown vinegar and shreds of ginger. This unusual vinegar is an essential flavouring in many other dishes as well – it's an ingredient in some braising sauces and stir-fries, and is drizzled over seafood, including delicate freshwater shrimp.

While the main starch of Chinese food from the south is rice, the Shanghainese prefer bread. The poetically named 'silver threads' bread (so-called because the interior dough is formed into long, thin strands and then wrapped in a flat sheet of dough) is subtly sweet and comes either steamed or fried; the former is better for sopping up juices.

Shanghainese also specialise in so-called 'cold dishes', which are actually served tepid or at room temperature. They're most often eaten as an appetiser but are so delicious and varied it's easy to make an entire meal of them. They include jellyfish flavoured with sesame oil, mashed soybeans with preserved vegetables, sweet and crispy fried eel, and 'drunken' chicken or pigeon, which has been marinated in rice wine until the flavour permeates the meat.

Shanghai means 'by the sea' and the region's own peculiar sea cucumber is served braised with shrimp roe. Similarly, shark's fin soup is usually served with braised chicken and ham, giving it a curious taste (one not enjoyed by all).

Cantonese

Cantonese is the cuisine of the south, exported worldwide via Hong Kong. In this type of cooking, the freshness of ingredients is paramount and cooking techniques (especially steaming) highlight this freshness. Because subtlety of flavours is so important, Cantonese cooks use a delicate hand with seasonings. To those who prefer more robust flavours, Cantonese food might seem bland.

Traditional Cantonese cooking techniques include steaming and stir-frying – which seals has plenty of Shanghainese eateries big and small, as does **Yunnan Nan Lu**. People's Square is very low on chic restaurants but for more refined surrounds, try **Kathleen's 5** (*see p122*) or the branch of **Xiao Nan Guo** (*see p112*) just to the north of the square.

Jingan

Jingan is the bustling, downtown section of the city, and restaurants are crammed into every street, lane and glass-walled shopping mall. The choice is staggering, and you could spend a week eating without ever leaving the area. Stop at Wujiang Lu for cheap meat skewers, pulled noodles and mediocre hot pot.

Cafés & snacks

Element Fresh

Shanghai Centre, 1376 Nanjing Xi Lu, by Xikang Lu (6279 8682/www.elementfresh.com). Metro Jingan Temple. **Open** 7am-11pm Mon-Thur, Sun; 7am-midnight Fri, Sat. **Main courses** RMB 38-138. **Credit** AmEx, DC, MC, V. **Map** p243 E5 ⑪

A smart, bright and informal Californian-style deli attached to the Shanghai Centre, this is just as popular for Western-style breakfasts as for its lunchtime smoothies, gourmet sandwiches (think grilled chicken with miso-yogurt dressing) and healthy global dishes. Juices are fresh, service is quick and there's a dinner menu full of pastas, Asian sets and dishes like a roast chicken or miso mirin-rubbed tuna.

in the flavour of food by cooking it quickly over high heat for no more than a minute – producing dishes such as delicate rice noodles, dumplings and a variety of deep-fried savoury pastries.

Dongbei

Dongbei is the name of the cuisine from Beijing and the north-east region of China. It is rich and oily, with plenty of meat, vegetable and aubergine dishes, all flavoured with lashings of spring onions and garlic. Lamb and mutton are popular, and stir-fried slivers of meat and vegetables are frequently served stuffed into pockets of sesame-coated baked breads. The cuisine's most famous dish is Peking duck. It is always served with great ceremony by a white-gloved waiter carving off the deep, mahogany-coloured skin, wrapping the pieces in a thin pancake with a dab of plum sauce and a sliver of spring onion. When it's good, the skin is the best part of the duck – it should be crisp, flavourful and with just a hint of fat.

Hunanese & Sichuan

China's western spice-belt provinces of Hunan and Sichuan have similar base ingredients, but the source of the spice is different. Hunanese dishes use chilli, but Sichuan mixes dried chillies with gum-numbing, metallic-tasting pink peppercorns harvested from prickly ash trees. Sichuan food is hearty and rich, with sauces that ideally blend sweet, sour and spicy flavours. Hot and sour soup is probably the Sichuanese dish best known in the West – it combines vinegar, pepper and chillies to

make a powerful, sinus-clearing broth. Dumplings and breads are also popular. Steamed buns are usually served with tea-smoked duck; meat dumplings look similar to Cantonese won ton, but instead of being served in a subtle broth, they're smothered in a sauce of soy, garlic and chillies.

Xinjiang

The autonomous region of Xinjiang is situated south-east of Kazakstan and Afghanistan, thus the influences in the Xinjiang cuisine are more Central Asian than Chinese. Lamb stews and skewers are combined with naan bread, spicy salads, dark beer and live entertainment.

Nevertheless, the breezy menu is best perused when looking for breakfast or lunch; better dinner options abound in the area, although it's true that not many of them have terraces with a view of bustling Nanjing Xi Lu. The main drawback is Element Fresh's popularity, which a recently added second floor has failed to completely solve. If it's just a bright sandwich you're after, its new online ordering system will get you around the wait. No smoking indoors during the day. **Other locations** throughout the city.

New York Style Pizza

Shop J16, 1699 Nanjing Xi Lu, by Huashan Lu (3214 0024). Metro Jingan Temple. **Open** 10am-11pm daily. **Pizzas** RMB 88 (RMB 10 per slice). **No credit cards. Map** p242 D6 ⑫

Hungry for a wide slice of New York-style pizza, dripping with greasy cheese and pepperoni? The kind of slice you fold in half to fit in your mouth, divine after a night out and perfect for lunch on the run? Check out this pizza joint just next to the subway entrance at Jingan Temple, which has become a favourite for homesick Americans. With its bright orange decor, NYSP isn't the place for a date but for a greasy pie and slices it can't be beat. Free toppings are another bonus, as is delivery until 10.30pm, free within 6km (3.7 miles). **Other locations** 1272 Beijing Xi Lu, by Xikang Lu (3222 0150); Rm 101, No.24, Lane 728 Anyuan Lu, by Yejiazhai Lu (2958 8809).

Wagas

Room LG12A, Underground Floor 1, CITIC Square, 1168 Nanjing Xi Lu, by Shanxi Bei Lu (5292 5228/www.wagas.com.cn). Metro Nanjing Xi Lu. **Open** 7.30am-10.30pm daily. **Mains** RMB 45-48. **Credit** AmEx, DC, MC, V. **Map** p243 E5 ⑬

A prime venue for snack lunches, Wagas is a big hit with office workers. The fare is healthy – fresh salads, great pastas, soups and sandwiches, plus daily blackboard specials, as well as fresh juices and smoothies. The coffee's excellent, and there's always a good selection of cakes and muffins. After a shake-up at the mall, the location has moved inward, and given up its outdoor terrace to Starbucks, though this has allowed for a redesign of the interior. It now looks like a hip living room, and from the lack of empty seats, you'd think they were giving sandwich wraps away. To find it, look for the bench Ronald McDonald occupies on Nanjing Lu, and head down the flight of stairs to his right. It's just inside the mall. **Other locations** throughout the city.

Chinese

Bi Feng Tang

1333 Nanjing Xi Lu, by Tongren Lu (6279 0738/ www.bifengtang.com.cn). Metro Jingan Temple. **Open** 10am-5am Mon-Fri; 8am-5am Sat, Sun. **Dim sum** RMB 10-20. **Credit** AmEx, DC, MC, V. **Map** p243 D5 ⑭ Cantonese

Tan Wai Lou. *See p100.*

The local answer to McDonald's, Bi Feng Tang (or, inevitably, BFT) is a city-wide chain that draws round-the-clock crowds with cheap Cantonese dim sum and savoury snacks. This branch is hugely convenient for guests at the Ritz-Carlton just over the road. It's kitted out like a traditional fishing village, with an outdoor seating area of small wooden huts draped with nets and festive lights. Expect the usual dough-wrapped suspects from steamed shrimp and pork dumplings to barbecue pork buns, as well as various congees and, for dessert, baked egg-custard tart. Hungry late-night clubbers make up a significant portion of the custom at the 24-hour French Concession branch (175 Changle Lu, by Ruijin Yi Lu, French Concession, 6467 0628).
Other locations throughout the city.

Fu 1088

375 Zhenning Lu, by Yuyuan Lu (5239 7878). Metro Jiangsu Lu. **Open** 11.30am-2.30pm, 5pm-midnight daily. **Credit** MC, V. **Map** p242 B5 ⑮ Shanghainese

One of the few old villas of Shanghai to survive the wrecking ball of progress has been duly rewarded with an appropriately stylish restaurant. Moneyed Shanghainese refinement fills all 17 rooms at this private house turned restaurant, proprietress Fu Yafen's second venture, outclassing her already classy Fu 1039. Old English wallpaper and Yafen's extensive collection of turn-of-the-century antiques decorate the rooms. White-gloved service staff watch over a room each and executive chef Tony Lu presides over a careful kitchen. The weight of oil and soy normally associated with the city's cuisine is feather-light here, evidenced in Shanghai's best rendition of smoked fish (*xunyu*) or a plate of tiny peeled 'crystal' river shrimp sweetened only with the addition of freshly shelled peas. Reservations comes with a polite reminder of a RMB 300 per person minimum, but it hardly concerns the rarefied diners here; money can't buy better Shanghainese cooking – and for the moment, it's still a bit of a secret.

Lynn

99-1 Xikang Lu, by Nanjing Xi Lu (6247 0101). Metro Jingan Temple. **Open** 11.30am-2.30pm, 5.30-10.30pm daily. **Main courses** RMB 48-860. **Credit** MC, V. **Map** p243 E5 ⑯ Shanghainese

Fancy Shanghainese restaurants tend to err on the side of glitz, gold chandeliers and gargantuan spaces, but Lynn does not fall prey to ersatz glamour. Its long dining room could sneak right into the coolest districts of Manhattan, and if the kitchen followed along, it would undoubtedly be a hit. A Rothko-like duotone hangs at the end of the subdued space, and waiters in stylish black uniforms flit back and forth dropping off plates of smoky, deboned duck or flash-fried river shrimp. The kitchen is as sophisticated as the mixed local and foreign clientele, and has made Lynn a prime choice for hip business dinners and stylish dates. Reserve, even on weekdays, and skip the fusion dishes.

Eat, Drink, Shop

Meilongzhen

No.22, 1081 Nanjing Xi Lu, by Jiangning Lu (6253 5353). Metro Nanjing Xi Lu. **Open** 11am-1.30pm, 5-9pm daily. **Main courses** RMB 25-880. **Credit** AmEx, DC, MC, V. **Map** p243 F5 ⑰ Shanghainese

The kitchens at Shanghai's most famous local restaurant have been churning out dishes since 1938. The building was once home to the Chinese Communist Party and the restaurant remains state-run. The classic decor consists of mahogany and marble furniture, carved wood panels and paper lanterns. Sichuan and Shanghainese dishes both figure on the menu. It's a touristy place, to be sure, and the service can be apathetic, but the cooking rises well above both of those slights. Especially good are a simply poached cold chicken dish (*bai zhan ji*) and Sichuan twice-cooked pork (*hui guo rou*). It's a bit hard to find, in a lane off bustling and bright Nanjing Xi Lu. Look for the massive wooden posts next to Swarovski.

Other locations Westgate Mall, 77 Jiangning Lu, by Nanjing Xi Lu, Jingan (6255 6688); 2nd floor, 2550 Zhongshan Bei Lu, by Wuning Lu, Putuo (6245 7777).

Yang's Fry Dumpling

54-60 Wujiang Lu, by Shimen Yi Lu (6267 6025). Metro Nanjing Xi Lu. **Open** 10.30am-11.30pm daily. **Cost** RMB 1 per fry dumpling. **No credit cards.** **Map** p243 F5 ⑱ Dumplings

Snack street Wujiang Lu took a hit in 2007, with the city cracking down on the crowded road's unlicensed vendors. The effect has been negligible, except that it's easier to spot Yang's Fry Dumpling, and the snaking lines in front of it at all hours. To say it's a Shanghai institution is an understatement. Shanghainese living abroad often cite Yang's *shengjian bao*, a shallow-fried dumpling stuffed with pork unique to the city, as the food they most long for. They're crisp on the bottom, fluffy on top and essentially made to order, with a furious blur of hands stuffing and wrapping the dumplings before they go off to be crisped up on a large black pan, and topped with sesame seeds. Inside lies ginger-tinged ground pork and flavourful soup, the best in town. Be careful not to spill any of the scalding liquid on your shirt, and pack some napkins.

Other locations throughout the city.

Fusion

roomtwentyeight

urbn Hotel, 1/F, 183 Jiaozhou Lu, by Xinzha Lu (5172 1300). Metro Jingan Temple. **Open** 6am-11pm. **Main courses** RMB 150-200. **Credit** AmEx, DC, MC, V. **Map** p242 C5 ⑲

The hip quotient at this small eco-conscious hotel has been carried over into the attached restaurant, run by the management of local sandwich-and-smoothie chain Wagas. It's an understated space with a gorgeous Zen courtyard, tucked away in the heart of downtown, just behind Jingan Temple, and the food is unfussy Western accented with Asian and Mediterranean influences (suckling pig with

mustard and apples, for example). They call it 'mod Oz' and 'mod' is certainly the correct adjective, but where most places in Shanghai choose between style and substance, the group's experience has taught them how to balance both. Reservations are best for weekend nights and, when the sun is shining, the courtyard is a gem for lunch.

South-east Asian

Thai House

Room 205, 2/F, Bldg 12, Lane 657 Wuding Lu, by Xikang Lu (5169 9217). Metro Jingan Temple. **Open** 10am-midnight daily. **Main courses** RMB 30-40. **Credit** AmEx, DC, MC, V. **Map** p242 D4 ⑳ Thai

Hands down the best Thai food in Shanghai. Get past the grungy alleyway (yes, the address is right; no, you're not lost), around the corner, and up the first flight of stairs in an apartment building to this literally named, unlikely location. Protective locals won't tell you that it's one of the very few Thai places that doesn't cave in to Shanghai's demands to tone down and sweeten up Thai food. The balance of sweet, sour and fiery flavours is intact, as is the no-frills, tourism poster decor. Prices are cheap, so there's no need to be stingy in the ordering. Sour fish soup, a fishy papaya salad, nahm prik with fresh vegetables and Issan-style sausage should all be on your table.

Other locations 518 Jiashan Lu, by Zhaojiabang Lu, French Concession (6431 5607).

Old City

The Old City is being rapidly pulled down, and much of what's left is street food you'd be better off without. **Nan Xiang**'s location in the Temple of the City God, near Yu Gardens, keeps it safe, but absolutely rammed. **Lu Bo Lang** (inside temple, 115 Yuyuan Lu, 6328 0602), the teahouse smack in the middle of the central pond, has pricy food but if you want to linger, it's better to go for the ceremony and then cab it out of there.

Chinese

Nan Xiang

85 Yuyuan Lu, Yu Gardens (6355 4206). **Open** 10am-9pm daily (1st floor); 6.30am-8pm daily (2nd floor); 10.45am-6.30pm (3rd floor). **Dumplings** RMB 12/16 takeaway dumplings (min spend RMB 60 per person for eat in). **Credit** AmEx, DC, MC, V. **Map** p245 M7 ㉑ Dumplings

In the heart of the Yu Gardens, this three-storey shrine to Shanghai's famous soup dumpling (*xiaolongbao, see p118* **Dumplings**) is one of the city's most famous eateries. It features on every tourist itinerary, as evidenced by the permanent, lengthy queues. The basic dumpling varieties are steamed pork and pork with crabmeat, but the higher the floor, the more elaborate the offerings; the third floor is where to go for the crab roe filling. We prefer the second floor, which boasts the best views of the nearby lake and its zigzag bridge.

Xintiandi

The fantasy of old Shanghai is alive and kicking at this recreated Disney-esque district of cultural gawking and overexcited consumption. It doesn't keep local foodies away, though, as it has the best branches of **Crystal Jade** and **Ding Tai Fung**; high-class Italian at **Va Bene** (House 7, North Block, Lane 181, 6311 2211), and recent prime-rib-slinging newcomer **Lawry's** (House 22-23, Unit 1, North Block, Lane 181, 6387 0097).

Cafés & snacks

KABB

House 5, North Block, Lane 181, Huangpi Nan Lu, by Taicang Lu (3307 0798/www.bluefrog.com.cn). Metro Huangpi Nan Lu. **Open** 7am-late daily. **Main courses** RMB 40-120. **Credit** AmEx, DC, MC, V. **Map** p248 H7 ❷❷
KABB is a popular American spot for luxe comfort food. The outdoor seating is busy all day – you'll spot the mix of lunching ladies and sore-footed tourists before you realise what it is. Breakfasts are huge American affairs, lunches stick to burgers (RMB 70-85), sandwiches (such as a Reuben on rye or a juicy steak version) and grilled chicken salads. Dinner has a simple but tasty menu of pastas (RMB 100-125), steaks and mains you'd find in any American town. Come dinner, plenty of people pop in for a drink, and in between, others bring laptops to take advantage of the Wi-Fi.

Chinese

Crystal Jade

Unit 12A & 12B, 2nd floor, House 6-7, Lane 123, Xingye Lu, South Block, by Zizhong Lu, Xintiandi Plaza (6385 8752). Metro Huangpi Nan Lu. **Open** 11.30am-3pm, 5-11pm Mon-Sat; 10.30am-3pm, 5.30-11pm Sun. **Main courses** RMB 46-580. **Credit** AmEx, DC, MC, V. **Map** p248 H8 ❷❸ Cantonese
Part of a Singaporean chain with restaurants also in Hong Kong, Jakarta and Saigon, Crystal Jade is popular for its inexpensive but incredibly good Cantonese and Shanghainese dim sum. The top picks are the baked barbecue pork bun, the steamed shrimp dumplings and the spicy Sichuan noodles. The regular menu features superb Hong Kong barbecue fare, especially the suckling pig and roast duck. Break off from eating to watch the mesmerising performance of kitchen staff making noodles by hand (it's all in the wrist action, apparently), seen through a slot window near the entrance, and then

come back for dessert. Booking is essential for lunch and dinner, although at busy times you may have to wait even if you have a booking. *Photo p99.*
Other locations B110, Hong Kong New World Plaza, 300 Huaihai Zhong Lu, by Madang Lu, Xintiandi (6335 4188); 7th floor, Westgate Mall, 1038 Nanjing Xi Lu, by Jiangning Lu, Jingan (5228 1133).

Ding Tai Fung

11A (under Alexander Health Club), F2, No.6, South Block, Xintiandi, 123 Xingye Lu (6385 8378). Metro Huangpi Nan Lu. **Open** 11am-3pm, 5pm-midnight daily. **Main courses** RMB 38-158. **Credit** AmEx, DC, MC, V. **Map** p248 H8 ❷❹ Taiwanese
This Taiwanese restaurant, whose Taipei branch was once voted one of the 'World's Ten Best Restaurants' by the *New York Times*, serves chic street food in pristine bamboo steamers. In this branch, decorated with cartoon caricatures of Chinese celebrities, well-off locals munch on an upscale take on Shanghai's venerable *xiaolongbao* (soup dumplings), indisputably the best version in their hometown. These unctuous pork and crab dumplings, filled with a mouth-watering broth of pork juice and tender meat, accented with garlic and ginger and encased in an impossibly thin wrapper, are dipped in strong black vinegar. The place also offers a great double boiled chicken soup, with the rich intensity of a consommé, and refreshing cold salads. It all makes a perfect lunchtime repast after browsing Xintiandi's boutiques, and is a safe foray into Shanghainese street food that will have you wishing they'd open a branch in a city near you.
Other locations 1st floor, 12 Shuicheng Lu, by Hongqiao Lu, Gubei (6208 4188); Unit 24, 3rd floor, 168 Lujiazui Xi Lu, by Lujiazui Huan Lu, Pudong (5047 8882); Unit 2001, 2nd floor, 168 Fangbang Zhong Lu, by Guangqi Lu, Old City (6334 1008).

Lan Ting

107 Songshan Lu, by Xingan Lu (5036 9650). Metro Huangpi Nan Lu. **Average** RMB 50-80. **No credit cards. Map** p248 J7 ❷❺ Shanghainese
See p110 **Family feast**.

Yè Shanghai

Unit 1, House 6, North Block, Lane 181, Taicang Lu, by Huangpi Nan Lu (6311 2323). Metro Huangpi Nan Lu. **Open** 11.30am-2.30pm, 5.30-11pm Mon-Thur, Sun; 11.30am-2.30pm, 5.30pm-midnight Fri, Sat. **Main courses** RMB 46-580. **Credit** AmEx, DC, MC, V. **Map** p248 H7 ❷❻ Shanghainese
Named after a hit song of the 1940s recorded by popular local songstress Zhou Xuan, Yè Shanghai ('Shanghai Night') is a nostalgic trip of red lanterns, antique furniture and sepia-toned images of old Bubbling Well Road and the pre-war racecourse. The menu, of course, features such typical Shanghainese dishes as stir-fried river shrimp and the hometown soup dumpling, as well as chef's specials such as a luxe pork 'lion's head' meatball or king prawns with chilli sauce. Reserve to get a window seat, and use the kitchen's skill as a benchmark for other Shanghainese meals.

Fusion

T8

House 8, Lane 181, Taicang Lu, North Block, by Huangpi Nan Lu (6355 8999/www.t8shanghai.com). Metro Huangpi Nan Lu. **Open** 11.30am-2.30pm, 6.30pm-midnight Mon, Wed-Fri; 6.30pm-midnight Tue; 11.30am-4pm, 6.30pm-midnight Sat, Sun. **Main courses** RMB 208-428. **Credit** AmEx, DC, MC, V. **Map** p248 H7 ㉗

T8 looks South-east Asian, has a Hungarian chef and tastes Mediterranean. Hefty slate slabs laid over fish-filled pools make for a striking entrance, while the main dining area has sleek lacquered furniture with a warm, Thai touch. Central to the action is the large open kitchen, where half a dozen young chefs sear, sauté and flash-fry in front of diners seated at counter tables. On the beautifully presented dégustation menus, the punchy food is worthy of all the superlatives it gets, and the Asian-slanted à la carte menu doesn't disappoint either. Roasted duck consommé with enoki mushrooms and marinated beef sashimi with soy jelly are just two recent additions. Accompany with something from the fine Australian-accented wine list and be sure to reserve for dinner.

French Concession

Inevitably, you will eat in the French Concession. If not for one of the joints below, then perhaps for the US prime steaks at discreet **Roosevelt Steakhouse** (160 Taiyuan Lu, by Yongjia Lu, 6433 8240), the fancy teppanyaki at **Ambrosia** (150 Fenyang Lu, by Taojiang Lu, 6431 3935), or Brittany's most famous export at **La Crêperie** (1 Taojiang Lu, by Yueyang Lu, 5465 9055).

Cafés & snacks

Citizen Bar & Café

222 Jinxian Lu, by Shanxi Nan Lu (6258 1620). Metro Shanxi Nan Lu. **Open** 11am-1am Mon-Fri; 10am-1am Sat, Sun. **Main courses** RMB 80-180. **No credit cards. Map** p247 F7 ㉘

Come to this artsy little spot for a bit of European style at affordable Shanghai prices. Downstairs is a swanky bar with claret velvet sofas, walnut tables, panelled walls and bracing martinis; the upstairs dining room serves classic bar snacks, simple brunches and tasty sandwiches. Citizen, with its gentrified neighbourhood vibe, is where the city's hipsters nibble on tuna tartare with citrus dressing, or dig in their heels for some quality time with their MacBooks. On week nights, it's great for a relaxed drink, but on the weekends, it spills over with hipsters.

Old China Hand Reading Room

27 Shaoxing Lu, by Shanxi Nan Lu (6473 2526/www.han-yuan.com). Metro Shanxi Nan Lu. **Open** 10am-midnight daily. **Snacks** RMB 25. **Credit** MC, V. **Map** p247 F9 ㉙

Whampoa Club. *See p100*.

A beautiful space owned by the Old China Hand Press, the Reading Room is a joint venture between photographer/collector Deke Erh and the writer/historian Tess Johnston. They specialise in the architectural heritage of the Concession-era, documented in a series of self-published coffee-table volumes (sold here). The café is decorated in Ming Dynasty fashion with salvaged bits of wood latticing, period furniture, antiques and, naturally, bookcases. Far from musty, the place is light and airy courtesy of big picture windows overlooking the street, although the atmosphere is hushed with tables typically taken by studious types, heads buried in books. The menu is limited to beverages of flower teas, coffees and soft drinks, with not much food beyond a few sandwiches and cheesecake.

Paul

G/F, The Village, 6 Dongping Lu, by Hengshan Lu, (5465 9131/www.paul.fr). Metro Changshu Lu. **Open** 7.30am-10.30pm daily. **Bread & pâtisserie** RMB 5-87. **Credit** AmEx, DC, MC, V. **Map** p246 D9 ㉚
Hold on, aren't they just a commercial, European bakery? Yes, they are and a damn good one at that. When the Paul franchise came to Shanghai last year, snapping up prime locations and turning out crusty, chewy baguettes, the long-standing lament about the quality of bread in China became obsolete. The rapidly expanding franchise (six stores at press time, and growing) is hands-down the best place to go for a loaf of bread or an apricot tart, and are just

as good for a brie sandwich or hot chocolate. All locations have seating, and this, the largest branch, even has a simple French restaurant.
Other locations throughout the city.

Chinese

Bao Luo

271 Fumin Lu, by Changle Lu (5403 7239). Metro Changshu Lu. **Open** 11am-6am daily. **Main courses** RMB 16-158. **No credit cards.** **Map** p246 D7 ㉛ Shanghainese
Packed day and night, Bao Luo is brash, loud, smoky Shanghai dining at its best. A tiny frontage of a single room and reception desk leads to a cavernous dining hall and a grand staircase leading to a warren of tiny rooms above. This landmark restaurant might be intimidating for non-Mandarin speakers at first, but they quickly settle in. Classics are red-braised pork belly (*hongshao rou*), baby eel in sweet sauce, and chopped vegetables wrapped in thin sheets of dried tofu, but the menu is large and made for exploring. Take a few chances; prices are cheap. And pity the waitresses, who have to wear red dresses with a funny pleat that makes it look like they've got the backs caught in their knickers.

Charmant

1414 Huaihai Zhong Lu, by Fuxing Xi Lu (6431 8107). Metro Changshu Lu. **Open** 11am-4am daily. **Main courses** RMB 30-138. **Credit** AmEx, DC, MC, V. **Map** p246 C8 ㉜ Taiwanese

Family feast

Let's face it, you're not going to get invited into anyone's home for dinner. Not in China, and particularly not in Shanghai. Urban Chinese tend to be very private about their homes. This, in part, stems from the diminutive size of the average Shanghai home (few people have a dining room big enough to accommodate dinner guests), and also from a culture of entertaining at restaurants (hence the ubiquitous private rooms at most Chinese restaurants). The good news is that with an open mind and a sense of adventure, you can get surprisingly close to a home-style experience at a handful of minuscule city eateries, doubling as living rooms and serving down-home Chinese food.

These mini eateries won't suit everyone, however. For a start, some spoken Mandarin is a must (either that or advanced charades skills and/or a very helpful concierge) – and interested parties should come expecting the interior decor to fall somewhere between basic and non-existent. Still, your efforts will be repaid in plentiful and authentic portions of local food and more than enough atmosphere to make up for any aesthetic shortcomings. Mum will be taking your order (or, in the case of menu-less Chun, *telling* you what you're going to have), and another family member will be cooking out back.

At **A Shan** (*see p117*), it's the old man that dishes up plates of fatty, braised fish tails with soy and spring onions, slabs of pork belly, and the house-fermented green plums – a rare dish these days, and something of an acquired taste – that draw as many childhood-chasing, nouveaux riches as it does local workers. The family at **Lan Ting** (*see p107*), a grimy storefront around the corner from Xintiandi, turns out delicious plates of sweet chicken thighs and tiny river shrimp tossed in rice wine and sugar. At **Mao Longs** (*see p112*), the resident mum presides over dishes of morning glory (also called water spinach or convulvus) with a bright-pink fermented tofu sauce and a fantastic *hongshao rou* (red-braised pork belly), unusually spicy in a city with such a sweet tooth.

But it is the tiniest four-table dining room that has the biggest reputation. After a nod from *The New York Times*, and a series of other international write-ups, tiny **Chun** (*see p111*) has seen its popularity mushroom, with punters pouring in for a taste of its pork-stuffed snails and whatever else the *maitre d'* decides you're having (there's no menu). It wasn't exactly easy to bag one of the four tables before; now it takes even more wrangling. Show up unannounced, and you'll be out of luck. Call ahead, or get your concierge to, and tell mum very nicely how much you want to eat her food and how punctual you'll be, and she might just save you a table. Bring cash.

Eat, Drink, Shop

Mao Longs.

Casual Taiwanese eaterie Charmant is a bit of a mystery. Why do all the waitresses have the same haircut? How do they make the sesame smoothie, an ice-cream-like dessert that looks something like wet concrete, taste so good? And why can't other restaurants seem to copy their formula? They take a menu of Taiwanese favourites like a creamy, cold tofu with preserved eggs or three-cup chicken, add improved versions of dishes from across the continent, like Sichuan shredded chicken in peanut sauce and Chongqing-style spicy chicken, and serve it all with smiling faces until 4am. Don't be a lunch martyr by trying to brave the midday crowds; instead, come for a late dinner, and don't neglect the 'smoothies', labelled 'choua bin' (black sesame and mango are the most popular).
Other locations 2nd floor, 560 Songtao Lu, by Chunxiao Lu, Pudong (5027 3736); Rm 102, Building 2, 3000 Longdao Avenue, by Zhangdong Lu, Pudong (6879 0972).

Chun
124 Jinxian Lu, by Maoming Lu (6256 0301). Metro Shanxi Nan Lu. **Open** 11.15am-1.30pm, 5-8pm daily. **Average** RMB 50-70 per person. **No credit cards.** **Map** p247 F6 ⑬ Shanghainese
See p110 **Family feast.**

Di Shui Dong
2nd floor, 56 Maoming Nan Lu, by Changle Lu (6253 2689). Metro Shanxi Nan Lu. **Open** 11.30am-12.30am daily. **Main courses** RMB 20-158. **No credit cards.** **Map** p247 F7 ⑭ Hunanese
A Shanghai veteran, Di Shui Dong is a throwback to dining in the days before 'design' wrecked many a perfectly good restaurant. It does rustic Hunan cooking in a space designed to mimic a rustic farmhouse – expect oily floors, checkered tablecloths and menu items written in big characters on streamers tacked to the wall. The menu is almost bilingual, with curious translations (human pickles?), and a host of home-style goodies. Skewered shrimp, stir-fried pickled beans with smoky bacon, bullfrog, and just about anything that combines pork and chilli are all winners – the cumin-crusted ribs (*ziran paigu*) go head to head with Guyi (*see p111*) for best in the city. A menu of fresh fruit juices is a good idea to temper the spice – opt for a pitcher of chunky apple juice if ice-cold beer, the true soulmate of Hunanese food, isn't your thing.
Other locations Unit B, 5 Dongping Lu, by Yueyang Lu, French Concession (6415 9448); 626 Xianxia Lu, by Shuicheng Lu, Gubei (3207 0213).

Dongbei Ren
1 Shanxi Nan Lu, by Yanan Zhong Lu (5228 9898/www.dongbeiren.com.cn). Metro Shanxi Nan Lu. **Open** 11am-10pm daily. **Main courses** RMB 20-98. **No credit cards.** **Map** p243 F6 ⑮ North-eastern
Much is made of the stereotypical directness of the folks hailing from North-eastern China, the *dongbei ren* (north-eastern people). They're not shy, and neither are the waitresses here, who shout as you come in, sing as you eat and engage in as much banter as you allow. The food follows suit – big, hardy flavours that stick to your ribs and weigh you down when you leave. *Jiaozi*, boiled dumplings, are the region's speciality, though the fresh tofu and sweet-and-sour fish are just as much a reason to come to this gaudy, floral-printed chain. For the more adventurous, there's donkey meat or penis wine.

Guyi
87 Fumin Lu, by Julu Lu (6247 0758). Metro Jingan Temple. **Open** 10.30am-2pm, 5.30-10.30pm daily. **Main courses** RMB 38-160. **Credit** AmEx, DC, MC, V. **Map** p246 D6 ⑯ Hunanese
Hunan, as natives like to point out, was Chairman Mao's home province. Inevitably, after informing you of that, people will ask if you know what his favourite food was. The answer is *hongshao rou*, red-braised pork belly, but that's only because when he was around, Guyi wasn't. They show off a much better side to Hunanese food (the Shanghainese do *hongshao rou* better anyway), which is a cousin to Sichuan – heavy on chillies, cumin and pickled vegetables, but not on those pesky, numbing Sichuan peppercorns. Hunanese places tend to be home-style and rustic, but Guyi has become enormously popular by moving the cuisine into an upmarket environment, packed with locals and expats in equal parts, and keeping both the soul and the burn in the food. Preserved eggs with roasted peppers, incendiary skewered shrimp covered with pickled chilli (eat the shell), cumin-crusted ribs, stir-fried pickled beans with smoky bacon and an iron pot of tea-tree mushrooms are essential. For dessert, there's a unique fried banana dessert, covered in hot caramel. Dunk the pieces in the bowl of water to harden the sugar, and eat quickly. Expect to wait half an hour or more for a table as bookings aren't taken; pass the time with a drink at nearby Manifesto (*see p126*).
Other locations 2nd floor, No.66, Lane 999 Changshou Lu, by Yuyao Lu, Jingan (6232 8377).

Hengshan Café
308 Hengshan Lu, by Wuxing Lu (6471 7127). Metro Hengshan Lu. **Open** 10am-3.30am daily. **Main courses** RMB 40-688. **Credit** MC, V. **Map** p246 B10 ⑰ Cantonese
Less a café and more a Cantonese restaurant, Hengshan Café might be on a seedy stretch of street, but the only flesh for sale here is extra fatty and strung up on meat hooks in the fluorescent-lit windows: golden roast goose and syrupy roast pork. It's a step-up from your workaday Hong Kong roast duck restaurant – literally. As you enter, make a quick right and head upstairs to the stylish dining room where the ever-present, ever-friendly Hong Kongnese owner awaits. Take his recommendation for a black chicken soup with ginseng (the Cantonese are China's broth masters) and roast goose, and wash it down with a glass of salted-lemon Sprite. If you're coming at prime time (6-9pm), you'll need to reserve, but from 9pm until the late, late close, dropping in should be fine.

Eat, Drink, Shop

Other locations 1417 Huashan Lu, by Hunan Lu, French Concession (6283 2282); 719 Yanan Xi Lu, by Jiangsu Lu, Changning (6226 0525); 2428 Xietu Lu, by Wanping Nan Lu, Xuhui (6468 5177)

Jishi

41 Tianping Lu, by Huaihai Xi Lu (6282 9260).
Metro Hengshan Lu. **Open** 11am-midnight daily.
Main courses RMB 22-368. **Credit** AmEx, DC, MC, V. **Map** p246 B9 ❸ Shanghainese

Dishing up superb home-style Shanghainese cuisine, this no-frills, two-storey shack and side annex has been packing in lively locals for years. It has spread all over the city with Xin Jishi (the 'new' Jishi), but this, the original, is still the best. Chatty diners sit elbow to elbow, while the waiting staff shout out orders as they stomp up and down the narrow rickety staircase. No oil, sugar or MSG is spared and must-eats include drunken chicken marinated in mild Shaoxing wine; deep-fried bamboo shoots; braised pomfret draped with deep-fried spring onions and cloaked in a thick, Shanghai-style soy sauce; and the house special, a monstrous pork shoulder, with more delicious fat than any one person could (or should) ever eat. Eat it anyway; Shanghainese girls claim it's the secret to their complexion. Reservations are required for dinner.
Other locations throughout the city.

Mao Longs

134 Jinxian Lu, by Maoming Lu (6256 1167).
Metro Shanxi.Nan Lu. **Open** 11am-9.30pm daily.
Average RMB 100 per person. **No credit cards.**
Map p247 F7 ❸ Shanghainese
See p110 **Family feast.**

Pin Chuan

47 Taojiang Lu, by Wulumuqi Nan Lu (6437 9361).
Metro Changshu Lu. **Open** 11am-2pm, 5-11pm daily.
Main courses RMB 40-168. **Credit** AmEx, DC, MC, V. **Map** p246 C8 ❹ Sichuan

The Dongping Lu/Taojiang Lu area is fast becoming one of Shanghai's most happening restaurant scenes, with South Beauty, Haiku, Azul/Viva and plenty of upstarts within quick walking distance of each other. But Pin Chuan has been around longer than any of them, lighting diners' mouths on fire with fiery red chillies, or numbing them with Sichuan peppercorns. The upscale Sichuan restaurant sits beside a small green park opposite the US Consulate in an old Shanghai home, recently given a makeover. The new owners have added Shanghainese dishes to the spicy menu, but haven't done away with classics like *shui zhu yu* (slices of raw fish cooked tableside in a bowl of hot oil, chillies and Sichuan peppercorns); cold noodles given crunch with peanuts, chillies and spring onion; and *lazi ji*, small knuckles of golden deep-fried chicken on the bone buried in a bowl of glistening dried chillies. Friendly waiters, some of whom speak enough English to guide novices through the menu, may make helpful suggestions, like pointing out that it's not a good idea to eat the dried chillies or large slices of ginger – they're for flavour only.

Shu Di Lazi Yu Guan

187 Anfu Lu, by Wulumuqi Zhong Lu (5403 7684).
Metro Changsu Lu. **Open** 11am-2pm, 5-10.30pm daily. **Main courses** RMB 20-68. **No credit cards.**
Map p246 C7 ❹ Sichuan

A Shanghai restaurant that is innovative yet serves spicy, home-style Sichuan food is more than rare; it's almost unheard of. Some claim this isn't an authentic Sichuan restaurant, which is probably true – it's much more than that. The chain is owned by famous Sichuan actor Ren Quan, a foodie who has picked his favourite dishes from his home province, as well as a collection of classics from the north-east and other regions – expect downhome Chinese cooking as inexpensive as it is delicious. The speciality dish, spicy fish (*lazi yu*), comes in large crocks that are set to simmer on the table, teasing your tastebuds as they emit wafts of ginger, peppercorns and chillies (ask the waitress to scoop out the chillies if you struggle with fiery food). Try the *zhu xiang ji*, meaty spring chickens that are diced, marinated and deep-fried, then combined with crunchy leeks, young green onions, fennel seeds and chillies in a bamboo basket, and fried once more. It's just one of a slew of fabulous dishes at this run-down place, its greasy-looking floors overshadowed by great food.
Other locations 53 Fengxian Lu, by Nanjing Xi Lu, Jingan (6267 0097); 1 Shuangfeng Bei Lu, by Xietu Lu, Xuhui (5424 5485); 82 Fushan Lu, by Shangcheng Lu, Pudong (5081 2700).

South Beauty

28 Taojiang Lu, by Baoqing Lu (6445 2581). Metro Changshu Lu. **Open** 11am-10.30pm daily. **Main courses** RMB 38-888. **Credit** AmEx, DC, MC, V.
Map p246 D8 ❹ Sichuan

Shanghai restaurateurs really go a bundle for design gimmicks. At this branch of the respected Sichuan spice vendor South Beauty, diners have to parade down a long, water-fringed catwalk towards a large mirror that slides back to reveal itself as a door. The restaurant is a little more straightforward than the approach route, with an airy main dining area downstairs and light-filled private rooms upstairs, both of which overlook a street-side bamboo garden. Despite Shanghai's reputation for being spice-shy, there is no holding back on the heat here: dishes such as chicken with spring onions and vinegar, and a caveman-like bridge of a cumin and garlic-laced beef rib have a high singe factor. When it's time for dessert, the 'Chinese calligraphy set' is so visually magnificent you'll hesitate to eat it!
Other locations throughout the city.

Xiao Nan Guo

2nd floor, Ruijin Guesthouse, 118 Ruijin Er Lu, by Yongjia Lu (6466 2277). Metro Shanxi Nan Lu.
Open 10.45am-2pm, 4.45-10pm daily. **Average** RMB 150-200 per person. **No credit cards.**
Map p247 F8 ❹ Shanghainese

This is the flagship branch of a city-wide chain known for terrific food and efficient service. It's an airy hangar of a dining hall in a gorgeous garden

Eat, Drink, Shop

setting. Tables are huge and designed for sharing. Some of the exemplary cold dishes include drunken chicken and chopped wild herbs with diced tofu, while of the hot fare we recommend spring onion pancakes, roasted pigeon, soft tofu with rich crab roe and crabmeat, and sautéed pea shoots. Intrepid diners can test their mettle against dishes such as turtle with sticky rice, salt-and-pepper snake or marinated snake skin. You'll need to make a reservation if you're coming for dinner.

Other locations throughout the city.

Yin

1st floor, Jinjiang Gourmet Street, 59 Maoming Nan Lu, by Changle Lu (5466 5070). Metro Shanxi Nan Lu. **Open** noon-3pm, 6-10pm daily. **Main courses** RMB 30-150. **Credit** AmEx, DC, MC, V. **Map** p247 F7 ❹ Shanghainese

Part of the 1929 Jinjiang Hotel complex (*see p42*), Yin riffs on an 'Old Shanghai' theme, with decor of cherrywood floors and antique screens, a stage and unused piano at one end of the room and a long bar at the other, which is staffed by *qipao*-clad girls who know their way round a cocktail list. But Japanese-born restaurateur Takashi is also canny enough to bring the place into the 21st century with warm lighting and splashes of colour, courtesy of pop artist Zeng Fanzhi. The food is superb, with a menu that roams through the best of China's regional cuisine, from the far west's Xinjiang-style lamb with cumin to eastern seafood dishes, such as fat Shanghainese-style shrimp. Food is served on the restaurant's own flatware, which colourfully updates traditional Asian square-cut plates and tea beakers. Japanese restaurant Zen (*see p115*) is just upstairs.

Yongfoo Elite

200 Yongfu Lu, by Hunan Lu (5466 2727/www.yongfooelite.com). Metro Changshu Lu. **Open** 11am-midnight daily (last order 10pm). **Average** RMB 500 per person. **Credit** AmEx, MC, DC, V. **Map** p246 B8 ❹ Shanghainese

Yongfoo Elite says a lot about Shanghai: for the most part it's style over substance, but when the style is this stunning, it merits a visit. A former British consulate caught the eye of eccentric Wang Xingzheng, who promptly mixed and matched styles for the renovated interior and over-the-top gardens. A vintage Gucci couch here, a few Ming antiques there, some token tchotckes scattered about, and a price tag perfectly suited for China's nouveaux riches, quickly made it the kind of place *Wallpaper** nods at. And, they did, in 2004, as the restaurant is quick to point out, in a nomination for best club. Technically, the members-only stipulation has been dropped for the restaurant, though anyone willing to pay these prices for decidedly average Shanghainese dishes, belongs to a de facto elite 'club' of their own. Food purists would be better off elsewhere, but for its atmosphere, East-Westiness and endearing decor, it merits a stop (for afternoon tea if nothing else). The entrance isn't all that clear; look for the nightly meeting of Bentleys, BMWs and bored drivers on sleepy Yongfu Lu.

Hairy crabs

As the autumn winds begin to blow, crab connoisseurs from across Asia descend on Shanghai to feast on the region's most famous delicacy: hairy crabs. The season runs from the ninth through the tenth lunar month (roughly early October through November). Early on, it's the roe-filled females to look for, towards the end of the season, males are best. You'll see these hairy-clawed crustaceans pop up all over Asia, but Shanghai is their ancestral home. They're highly prized, and the best crabs, from Yangcheng Lake, are even subject to rampant counterfeiting (they tried laser-printing numbers on the shells once; it didn't work). To all but the most discerning, it's a non-issue.

They aren't the meatiest crabs, but there is a way to maximise returns on your labour. First, remove all the legs and claws. Flip the crab over, twist off the hinged flap, and then open the crab by firmly grabbing the shell near the eyes and at the back. The top will pop off. Once you remove the grey 'lungs', the rest is edible. Don't forget about the orange roe inside the top of the shell – it's the most prized part. Break the ends off the legs, and force the meat out with your chopstick. Don't be shy. Eating hairy crabs is a messy business, but when it's all over, the restaurant should provide a small bowl of fragrant water to clean your hands.

The meat is dipped in black vinegar with ginger, and warm Shaoxing wine is the traditional drink. The better restaurants will handle the dirty work for you, if you like. **Wangbaohe** (555 Jiujiang Lu, by Fujian Zhong Lu, 5396 5000), the most famous crab restaurant, even has a specialised eight-piece hairy crab tool set. Otherwise, hairy crabs are available most places. Five-star hotels are always a good bet.

European

Casa 13

No.13, 1100 Huashan Lu, by Fuxing Xi Lu (5238 2782/www.casa13.cn). Metro Changsu Lu then 20mins walk. **Open** 11am-11pm daily. **Main courses** RMB 120-190. **No credit cards.** **Map** p246 A7 ❻

As in 'home', and specifically the home of busybody restaurateur Eduardo Vargas. He's moved around, building other mid-market houses over the years (*see below* Viva/Azul, for instance), to the delight of Shanghai diners, but with this, one of his latest ventures, he's really hit the nail on the head. It's a cosy, hidden lane gem of a building (as almost all of Shanghai's best houses are) with a pared-down pan-Med menu and a varied and interesting wine list. It's the kind of home cooking you might get if your mother were a chef with a taste for all things tasting of the Mediterranean: a generous charcuterie board, wonderful house olive oil or braised beef cheeks with beets. Dishes are simple and made to be shared, and the intimate, unfussy atmosphere is made for dates. The enclosed patio is a summer gem, making you feel like you have a charming French Concession residence for the price of lunch.

Franck

376 Wukang Lu, by Hunan Lu (6437 6465/ www.franck.com.cn). Metro Xujiahui. **Open** 7-10.30pm Tue; noon-2.30pm, 7-10.30pm Wed-Sat; noon-2.30pm Sun. **Average** RMB 300-400 per person. **Credit** AmEx, DC, MC, V. **Map** p246 B8 ㊼
This eponymous French bistro from French chef Frank Pecol is a modern, slender space hidden away in a French Concession lane complex, its zinc bar lit by spare lightbulbs, and its desirably chewy baguettes replenished by attentive staff. When it opened in summer 2007, the short, rotating menu emphasising just a few quality ingredients made it an instant success, and the varied, predominantly French wine list didn't hurt its prospects either. Changing dishes like *oeuef mayonnaise* and veal liver rotate around a short blackboard, with a few stable staples, like the house-smoked salmon and *terrine de campagne*, served with a crock of mustard, a bowl of cornichons and as many baguettes as you can spread it on. Don't just turn up, as reservations are absolutely essential.

Le Garçon Chinois

No.3, Lane 9, Hengshan Lu, by Dongping Lu (6445 7970). Metro Changshu Lu. **Open** 6pm-2am daily. **Main courses** RMB 70-168. **Credit** AmEx, DC, MC, V. **Map** p246 C9 ㊽
Still the most romantic little eaterie in town, Le Garçon is in an old French villa secreted down a winding, leafy alleyway. Sparsely decorated with commissioned murals painted by local artists, it boasts a delightful, pocket-sized bar, invariably packed with devotees of owner Takashi's throwback style, where old jazz, great service and traditional takes on Shanghainese and Spanish cuisine are the order of the day. Its kitchen once turned out classy Northern Vietnamese dishes, but recently made the shift to Shanghainese, which it does with just as much skill. Order the *xiang su ya*, a steamed, chilled, and fried duck dish that could compete with confit as the most delicious thing ever done to a duck. Downstairs, expect wonderful tapas, accented simply with sea salt, garlic and olive oil, and squid served in squid ink sauce with crusty slices of bread. Le Garçon Chinois is everything a villa restaurant should be (except well-known).

El Willy

20 Donghu Lu, by Huaihai Zhong Lu, French Concession (5404 5757). Metro Shanxi Nan Lu. **Open** 11am-2am daily (last orders 10pm). **Main courses** RMB 200-300. **Credit** AmEx, DC, MC, V. **Map** p247 E7 ㊾
'Who is the Willy?', you may ask. The answer: a tornado of a Spanish chef who whirled into Shanghai in 2008, partnered with the Japanese owners of the house/lifestyle centre/'small, small museum' that the restaurant is housed in, and was immediately swarmed for his modern Spanish menu. In a town of mediocre Spanish food, El Willy's adventurous cooking – lots of low-temperature cooked eggs, paellas that incorporate everything from bone marrow to local crabs, savoury sorbets and *granitas* all over the place – coupled with the homely atmosphere, made him immediately stand out. It's not all about dinner – lunch here is one of the best deals in town – but if you're doing dinner, reserve.

Fusion

Mesa

748 Julu Lu, by Fumin Lu (6289 9108/www.mesa-manifesto.com). Metro Changshu Lu. **Open** 11am-late daily. **Main courses** RMB 130-250. **Credit** AmEx, DC, MC, V. **Map** p243 D6 ㊿
Mesa is a former factory warehouse that has been beautifully reappointed as a chic, airy and light-filled dining room, although the original function of the building is still apparent in the high ceilings, deco picture windows and unusual explosion-proof hanging lights, once common in the city's factories. It's a striking space, and one that provides the setting for some of the best Western cuisine in town. Visit for classy, well-executed Mediterranean-style dishes occasionally touched with Asian flavours (as with the tuna tataki with fresh mint). Desserts are comfort classics, like a bread and butter pudding with almond ice-cream. Mesa's all-day weekend brunch is excellent and ace bar Manifesto (*see p126*), a sibling venture, is upstairs.

Viva/Azul

18 Dongping Lu, by Wulumuqi Nan Lu (6433 1172). Metro Changshu Lu. **Open** 11am-11pm daily. **Average** RMB 150-200. **Credit** AmEx, DC, MC, V. **Map** p246 C9 ⓛ
Peruvian chef Eduardo Vargas is unstoppable, opening mid-market success after mid-market success (*see also p113* **Casa 13**). His formula, as it is here, is simple cooking with bold flavours (Latin in this case), a reasonably priced, interesting wine list and friendly service. Azul/Viva turned five this year, and is going strong. Azul is the drinking part of the operation, with tapas to nibble on, while upstairs Viva is a soft-focus affair featuring couches and throw cushions. Dishes play on sweet and sour flavours – spicy duck breast with chilli-honey glaze, say – and the mocha tart makes for a sinful finale. Reservations required for dinner.

Indian

Vedas

550 Jianguo Xi Lu, by Wulumuqi Lu (6445 8100/ www.vedascuisine.com). **Open** 11am-3pm, 6-11.30pm daily. **Main courses** RMB 45-145. **Credit** AmEx, DC, MC, V. **Map** p246 D10 ❷

Vedas caters to a loyal clientele of upmarket Indian families and fashionable French Concession expats in a simple space where the open kitchen is the main attraction. As the heady scent rising from an array of copper pot curries surrounds you, watch the team of five-star chefs from Delhi pick spears of the succulent Kesari chicken out of the tandoor – these other-worldly boneless chunks of yogurt-marinated chicken are not to be missed. Richly spicy lamb rogan josh, creamy *dal makhani* (slow-cooked black lentils topped with a pat of salty butter) and a cooling dessert of frozen yogurt kulfi round out some of the best Indian cuisine you'll find.

Japanese

Haiku

28B Taojiang Lu, by Baoqing Lu (6445 0021). Metro Changshu Lu. **Open** 11.30am-2pm, 5.30-10pm daily. **Main courses** RMB 68-700. **Credit** MC, V. **Map** p246 C8 ❸

Haiku's modern, minimalist Japanese look means the restaurant is as much of a scene as a sushi destination, though fans of the overloaded rolls might argue otherwise. An army of chefs, necessary to keep up with both busy floors, put anything and everything and heaps of mayonnaise into the rolls. Purists might cringe, but the crowds love it, and truth be told, fat rolls like the moto-roll-ah (a mix of spicy tuna, crab salad, avocado, tuna loin and chilli-mayo sauce) and the butterfly roll (tempura shrimp, crab salad, avocado, eel and regular shrimp) are pretty tasty. The roll list is as big as the rolls themselves, but there's more. Steak 'butteryaki', a sirloin cooked teppanyaki-style in butter is also popular. Reservations recommended.

Shintori

803 Julu Lu, by Fumin Lu (5404 5252). Metro Changshu Lu or Shanxi Nan Lu. **Open** 5.30-10.30pm Mon-Fri; 11.30am-2pm, 5.30-10.30pm Sat, Sun. **Main courses** RMB 50-300. **Credit** AmEx, DC, MC, V. **Map** p246 D6 ❹

As good as the food is, it's not what you remember from a visit to Shintori. Instead, what you take away is a mental slide show of impressions of one of the city's most laughably wonderful interiors. It's all mod secrecy, starting with a pathway that snakes through a thicket of slender bamboo. The restaurant itself is like one of Ken Adams' designs for a James Bond submarine hangar – a sunken pool-like main space with steps up to side galleries and a vast open stainless-steel kitchen, with a surrounding upper gallery – and everything is done out in polished concrete. When it opened, several years ago, it was the talk of the town, and though it's faded a bit (the result of being such a trendy restaurant in such a trendy town), it's still worth a visit. The cuisine is primarily Japanese, though not the most traditional, but it's the presentations that get you: sashimi on granite platters, cold noodles in a bowl of sculpted ice.

Tian Jia

2/F, Lane 1520, 15 Huashan Lu, by Tai'an Lu (6281 4918). Metro Hengshan Lu then walk. **Open** 11.30am-2.30pm, 6-11pm daily. **No credit cards.** **Map** p246 A8 ❺

Tian Jia has built a mini-empire on the belly of the tuna. Toro, fatty belly found only on the larger specimens of tuna, is the king of the sashimi world for its melt-in-the-mouth texture, and is priced accordingly. So when Tian Jia quietly started its first restaurant offering a multi-course toro tasting menu at the relatively inexpensive price of RMB 250, Japanese residents and visitors packed the place. In there you get thick slices of chu-toro, thin slices of fatty, pink o-toro, regular toro marinated in lemon and salt, more thin slices of toro to dip into a simmering pot of dashi, a few king crab legs, and a bowl of chopped tuna, spring onion and shredded nori over rice. The secret soon got out, and they had no choice but to expand. All the same, the first, and most difficult to find, location is still the best. If you're already well-versed in the ways of the tuna belly, you might be skeptical of the quality at this price, but don't be put off. The secret to Tian Jia's pricing? They're a wholesale importer.

Other locations 105 Changliu Lu, by Dingxiang Lu, Pudong (6854 5687); 3rd floor, 1166 Yanan Xi Lu, by Panyu Lu, Changning (6115 9649); 68 Taicang Lu, by Songshan Lu, Xintiandi (5383 6886).

Zen

1-2/F, 2nd floor, Jinjiang Gourmet Street, 59 Maoming Nan Lu, by Changle Lu (5466 5070). Metro Shanxi Nan Lu. **Open** noon-3pm, 6-11pm daily. **Main courses** RMB 28-88. **Credit** AmEx, DC, MC, V. **Map** p247 F7 ❻

Situated upstairs from the Shanghainese eaterie Yin (*see p113*) is Japanese restaurant Zen. The design isn't Zen at all: it's much warmer – a mix of art deco, Shanghai style and sympathetic modern additions, including lovely pendant light fittings. Dishes are classic Japanese – sushi, sashimi, tempura, yakitori and noodles – consumed in the company of discerning locals, Westerners and Japanese. Service is impeccable and prices are very reasonable. Reservations required.

South-east Asian

Coconut Paradise

38 Fumin Lu, by Julu Lu (6248 1998). Metro Changshu Lu. **Open** noon-2pm, 5pm-midnight daily. **Main courses** RMB 50-170. **Credit** AmEx, DC, MC, V. **Map** p246 D7 ❼ Thai

Tucked away in a tastefully restored villa, this is an effortlessly elegant Thai restaurant, from the careful wine list to the lemongrass scent that washes over you as you step through the teak doors. With an old Chiang Mai lady pounding curry pastes in the kitchen, expect fiery, authentic and affordable Thai fare, including a perfectly complex red curry and a fragrant stir-fry of shrimp with 'asparagus beans' brightened by threads of kaffir lime leaf. It's as romantic and dimly lit as a date place could be, and the service problems that once plagued it seem to have been ironed out.

Lan Na Thai

Bldg 4, Ruijin Guesthouse,118 Ruijin Erlu, by Fuxing Zhong Lu (6466 4328/www.facebars.com/ sh/lannathai.asp). Metro Shanxi Nan Lu. **Open** noon-2.30pm, 5.30-10.30pm Mon-Thur, Sun; noon-2.30pm, 5.30-11pm Fri, Sat. **Main courses** RMB 70-198. **Credit** AmEx, DC, MC, V. **Map** p247 F8 **59** Thai

Opened in 1999, Lan Na Thai is decked out with elegant Ming Dynasty furniture and serene Buddhist sculptures, and boasts gorgeous views of the guesthouse gardens. No wonder Shanghai first-timers find the languid, colonial air of the place irresistible. Some long-termers get sniffy, take umbrage at the high prices and stay downstairs in the splendid Face Bar (*see p124*), but everyone has to do Lan Na at least once. The food is Thai Thai, as opposed to the Chinese Thai that is the norm around here. Even so, if you like your chicken larb spicy or your green curry hot, then you still need to ask for it to be prepared that way. Reservations required for dinner.

Lost Heaven

38 Gaoyou Lu, by Fuxing Xi Lu (6433 5126). Metro Changsu Lu. **Open** 11.30am-1.30pm, 5.30-11.30pm daily. **Main courses** RMB 30-160. **Credit** AmEx, DC, MC, V. **Map** p246 B8 **59** Yunnanese

The Yunnan borderland, touching Burma and Laos, might balk at being represented in such posh, dark-wood exoticism. Lost Heaven evokes a Golden Triangle fantasy of copious carved wood, dark lighting, and statuettes bathed in red light, but who minds getting lost in it when it looks this good? Shanghai certainly doesn't, and this upmarket, large-scale adaptation of the southern border's cooking is a popular one. It's tagged 'Yunnan folk cuisine', meaning many of the dishes are only politically Chinese, their vibrant use of herbs, mushrooms and wild spices a clear sign of the ethnic minorities they've been borrowed from.

Naam Thai

Unit 1107-1108 High Street Loft, 1/F, 508 Jiashan Lu, by Jianguo Lu (5465 6005). Metro Shanxi Nan Lu then 20mins walk. **Open** 11am-10pm daily. **Main courses** RMB 60-108. **Credit** MC, V. **Map** p247 E8 **60** Thai

Open a ghetto of hipness (the High Street Loft), and a Thai restaurant becomes de rigueur – a licence for fancy over form if ever there was one. But in the capable hands of Walter Zahner (he also of T8's management team and many years in Bangkok), it means a minimalist Thai setting of sleek, light

Dumplings

The *xiaolongbao*, literally the 'little basket bun', is a key feature of Shanghainese street food. This tiny bun, whose delicate skin cradles a juicy filling of pork and a fragrant, rich soup, is found everywhere – from delicious but dingy roadside stalls to fancy dim sum joints. It takes practice to fold these tiny packets, which are about an inch in diameter and filled with pork or a mixture of pork and crab. The soup in the buns is actually gelatin, which is in the meat filling and melts during the steaming process. The result is a broth of incredible richness, which should be eaten with caution (fresh off the steamer, *xiaolongbao* are scaldingly hot).

Etiquette is an exercise in taste-bud preservation: first, carefully peel the bun off the steamer and place it in a spoon. Then gently dip the dumpling in a bit of vinegar, and bite a hole in the wrapper to allow steam and a bit of soup to escape. Drink the soup, then gobble down the tender pork filling and wrapper.

While the *xiaolongbao* is the best known of the Shanghai dumplings, *shengjianbao* is equally revered in the city; it's the sturdy and filling cousin of the steamed bun. *Shengjianbao* falls somewhere between a fried pot sticker and a steamed bun; cooked over a high heat in huge, flat pans, they're topped with a large wood lid that allows the bun to steam during the frying process. Golden brown and crisp on the bottom, with fluffy dough and a topping of sesame seeds and chives, the buns are also filled with a rich, meaty soup and an unctuous mix of pork, garlic and ginger.

For good, safe *xiaolongbao*, try **Ding Tai Fung** (*see p107*) – or look for the nearest street stall. The best *shengjianbao* can be found at **Yang's Fry Dumpling** (*see p106*).

woods and a thoughtfully edited menu, with hardly a Buddha statue in sight. The menu is compact, and set a bit sweet by default, but the cooking is spot-on. The jumble that is usually a Thai beef salad has been rethought as a whole, with sliced steak rubbed with dried chilies and dressed in lime juice and fish sauce, and the rest of the menu follows suit. The foodies will even spot a rarity or two, like betel leaves with savoury toppings or a coconut-less jungle curry of bamboo shoots. A short but sweet wine list holds a few gems, and there are plenty of healthy fruit juices and blends for non-drinkers.

Simply Thai

5 Dongping Lu, by Hengshan Lu (6445 9551). Metro Changshu Lu or Hengshan Lu. **Open** 11am-11pm daily. **Main courses** RMB 45-108. **Credit** AmEx, DC, MC, V. **Map** p246 D9 **61** Thai

The ever-expanding 'Simply Thai' group now includes flower and lifestyle stores, but what it did first – and still does best – is Thai food. The menu at its restaurants covers all the staples: curries in red, green and yellow flavours, tom yam dishes and plenty of seafood. Spicing is light, and a touch sweet, but flavours are abundant. The surroundings at Dongping Lu are lovely – a cosy two-storey house decorated in a minimalist fashion with some courtyard seating looks out on a picturesque tree-lined street. It's perfect for quiet, candlelit dinners; the Xintiandi branch is more business-like and better suited to lunch. Consistent cooking, reasonable prices and a decent wine list make this a regular favourite with the city's expats.

Hongkou

Hongkou isn't really a fine-dining destination, but more a home to the fluorescent-lit, workaday kind of restaurant concerned with value, not memories. These three are notable exceptions, and it'd be difficult to forget the moment they bring out the live viper in a see-through bag at the **Jin Long Snake Hot Pot** restaurant (183 Wujin Lu, by Wusong Lu, 6324 4303), open till 4am, or the amount of neon on the Zhapu Lu food street, but otherwise, Hongkou is best for a walk.

Chinese

Afanti

B-1/F, Tianshan Hotel, 775 Quyang Lu, by Zhongshan Bei Er Lu (6555 9604). **Open** 9am-midnight daily. **Main courses** RMB 20-80. **No credit cards. Map** p241 F1 **62** Uighur

Fine dining this is not. Afanti is a riotous affair featuring the hardy food of western China's Xinjiang province. Occasionally, around 9pm, the kitsch dining room of painted pastoral scenes and gold accents turns into an impromptu techno-boom-boom party that could be mistaken for an outtake from a Borat movie. But before all that, there's a hearty feast of the region's food, unmistakable for its focus on lamb, and heavy use of garlic and cumin. Thick-skinned dumplings stuffed with ground lamb, a rich stew (*da pan ji*) of tomato, potato, garlic, chicken, cardamom, star anise and green pepper, as well as dense, unleavened breads, can be found on every table, along with the region's Sinkiang Black Beer. After it's all over, head upstairs (the main event is in the basement) to the informal streetside part of Afanti's operation for grilled lamb everything, from testicle to neck to kidney, and then pop next door into the attached market for a fresh pomegranate juice (in season).

Xujiahui & Gubei

Technology and electronics are big in Xujiahui, as are middle-class eateries, but there's not a tremendous amount of places you'd want to make a special trip for. For a shopping stop, **Prima Taste** (1111 Zhaojiabang Lu, by Tianyaoqiao Lu, 6426 8898), in the Metro City mall, is a safe bet for Singaporean.

Chinese

A Shan

2378 Hongqiao Lu, by Hongjing Lu, Gubei (6268 6583). **Open** 11.30am-1.30pm, 5.30-9pm daily. **Average** RMB 100. **No credit cards. Map** p240 A4 **63** Shanghainese
See p110 **Family feast**.

Shanghai Lao Zhan (Old Station)

201 Caoxi Beilu, by Nandan Dong Lu, Xujiahui (6427 2233). Metro Xujiahui. **Open** 11.15am-2pm, 5-9.30pm daily. **Main courses** RMB 40-280. **Credit** AmEx, DC, MC, V. **Map** p246 A11 **64** Shanghainese

Housed in an ex-convent that dates back to the 1920s, the dining rooms here have been given a classic look of dark wood, whitewashed walls, tiled floors and ornate light fixtures. Waiters dressed in traditional jackets deliver typical Shanghainese fare, the best of which includes smoked fish, asparagus soup and 'eight treasure' duck. Request a table by the window for a view out over the garden with its two antique train carriages, one of which was previously used by the Empress Dowager, and the other by the influential Soong Qingling.

Xiao Fei Yang

169 Nandan Lu, by Wending Lu, Xujiahui (6438 1717/www.xfy.com.cn). Metro Shanghai Indoor Stadium. **Open** 10am-4am daily. **Main courses** RMB 5-58. **No credit cards. Map** p240 C4 **65** Hot pot

People make a lot of excuses for hot pot. In summer, they'll tell you the steaming broth and the fatty lamb dunked in it will cool you down. In winter, it'll heat you up. In truth, it's a practical rationalisation – no one wants to give up the communal, raucous pastime of sitting around a table with plates of sliced meats and vegetables for something as trivial as the seasons. Hot pot restaurants abound, but this Mongolian style chain (as opposed to the tongue-searing variety favoured in Sichuan) is the cream of the crop. The lamb is the fattiest (a good thing) and the broth is brimming with flavour, but there's one rule even Xiao Fei Yang won't break: hot pot is resolutely casual. Warm beverages are skipped in favour of ice-cold beer.

Xinjiang Fengwei Restaurant

280 Yishan Lu, by Nandan Lu, Xujiahui (6468 9198). Metro Yishan Lu. **Open** 10am-2am daily. **Main courses** RMB 50-60. **No credit cards. Map** p240 C4 **66** Uighur

Xinjiang cuisine is one of China's best-kept secrets, a Middle Kingdom meets Middle East blend of flavours and techniques. The Uighurs , who live in the western deserts bordering Pakistan and Afghanistan, cook complex stews like *da pan ji* (chicken in a heady tomato braise accented with star anise, tsaoko cardamom, tomatoes, onions and peppers) and huge hunks of roasted mutton, which pair perfectly with the region's dense, unleavened breads. This is the best place in town to eat these dishes, washed down with a malty black beer, in delightfully tacky surroundings. You'll need to bring your dancing shoes as well: dinner is a riotous affair with waiters breaking into song and frequently dragging diners on to the dancefloor. Reservations required for dinner.

Bukhara is a classy North Indian restaurant, way out in the city's western suburbs. Dosa freaks and idli lovers might be out of luck, but they'll quickly be hypnotised by Bukhara's ways with a tandoor oven. A glass window in the earthy, wood-heavy dining room affords a view of the chefs plucking sikh kebabs, golden roast chicken and kashmiri naan from the hot ovens, with plenty of people watching. The food has the most subcontinental clout around, the service is polished and it's one of the few places that pull the notoriously myopic downtown diners out of their central comfort zone. Reservations suggested, particularly on the weekends. Otherwise, spend a while downstairs in the lounge nursing a Kingfisher.

Changning

This is the suburbs, but the dining out here is getting better all the time. For everything smoked, there's **Bubba's Texas BBQ** (2262 Hongqiao Lu, by Jianhe Lu, 6242 2612), but much of the population out here is Japanese, as are the restaurants. There's a cluster on Shuicheng Lu, near Maotai Lu, and another strip on Guyang Lu. **Daikichi** (435 Guyang Lu, by Songyuan Lu, 5477 5084), a brightly lit yakitori joint, is the pick of the litter.

Chinese

1221

1221 Yanan Xi Lu, by Panyu Lu (6213 6585). Metro Yanan Xi Lu. **Open** 11am-2pm, 5-11pm daily. **Main courses** RMB 25-1,680. **Credit** AmEx, DC, MC, V. **Map** p240 C3 ⓺ *Shanghainese*
Owner Michelle Liu was raised by Shanghainese parents in Hong Kong, and her mixed background is expressed in diverse local and Cantonese dishes, with a few other regional specialities thrown in. The menu is very Western-friendly and the cooking isn't as heavy on the oil as elsewhere, so the bulk of the clientele are expats. The food is consistently excellent so it's hard to go wrong, but we particularly like shredded chicken with peanut sauce and sautéed beef with fried dough sticks. It's a classy looking place with white starched tablecloths, chalkboardblack floor and modern art for colour. It's also a little difficult to find, being located some way from central Jingan; look for the Howard Johnson Apartment Hotel on the north side of Yanan Xi Lu, and the restaurant is just a tiny bit further, slotted down at the end of a small alleyway.

Indian

Bukhara

3729 Hongmei Lu, by Yan'an Xi Lu (6446 8800). **Open** 11am-2pm, 5.30-11pm daily. **Main courses** RMB 75-380. **Credit** AmEx, DC, MC, V. **Map** p240 A4 ⓺

Pudong

It's sad to say, but for all Pudong's marvellous spikes of skyscrapers, finding a decent meal can be tough. If you're close enough to see the base of the Oriental Pearl Tower, head to either the Pudong Shangri-La's **Gui Hua Lou** (6882 8888) for excellent regional Chinese or its **Nadaman** (6882 8888) for outstanding Japanese. For something a bit more affordable, there's a host of restaurants in the Super Brand Mall, with a branch of **South Beauty**, good Sichuan at **Yu Xiang Ren Jia** (5049 1977), and decent Shanghainese at **Lang Yi Fang** (5047 1266), or in the glass Citigroup Tower, a branch of Haiku dubbed **Sushi, Inc.** (2/F, 33 Huayuan Shiqiao Lu, by Fucheng Lu, 5877 6551).

Fusion

Jade on 36

36/F, Tower Two, Pudong Shangri-La Hotel, 33 Fucheng Lu (6882 8888/www.shangri-la.com). Metro Lujiazui. **Open** 6-10.30pm daily. **Set menu** RMB 480-888. **Credit** AmEx, DC, MC, V. **Map** p245 O5 ⓺
The gleaming restaurant jewel of the Pudong Shangri-La (*see p44*) is this 36th floor stunner, with sweeping views and a dining room by Adam Tihany. Next door is the jewel box-like bar (*see p128*), and both are nearly as breathtaking as the view: a private elevator whistles you to the top of the tower and you disembark in a hallway with ornate Venetian marble floors and eccentric design accents. Chef Paul Pairet's unique food is the ideal complement to such rarified surroundings, and has been garnering attention worldwide; expect nouveau fine dining with a deft, playful touch. The foie gras lollipop, a creamy foie gras terrine coated in crunchy caramel and served on the end of a chopstick, melts in your mouth, served with a shot of hot spiced tea that is then cooled by a final layer of fluffy champagne foam. The lemon tart, a whole candied lemon stuffed with lemon curd, sorbet and citrus sections with a precarious sliver of sablée for a crust, makes a beautiful finale to one of the four degustation menus.

Bars & Pubs

Drinks with attitude (and often altitude).

Gone are the days when two or three designated 'leisure' zones represented the best of Shanghai's drinking scene. The inadequacies of those neon-lit disco bars were plain to see, however loud their hostesses screamed, 'Hey, handsome man, come inside!' Although a few are still digging in with their long fake nails, most have been silenced by a new orchestra of boozy sirens – microbreweries at one end, cocktail-twirling style stages at the other. But what has really shaken things up is the proliferation of everything in between.

Not so long ago, a neighbourhood bar meant a dive at best, or a hostess joint at worst. All that has changed. Now, Shanghai has its wine bars, whisky bars and DJ bars, as well as intimate just-round-the-corner bars. This new-found variety means you no longer have to shuffle over to the Bund to enjoy a decent glass of wine or a properly mixed cocktail. Neighbourhood newcomers **Enoteca**, for wine, and **Tara 57** for cocktails, are leading the new school, and every month Shanghai's entrepreneurial spirit manifests itself not just

in the proliferation of armchair stock traders but also in a flourish of new bars.

All the same, the Bund is still the arena for the real posing, pouting and showing off. The champagne-fuelled fireworks at **Bar Rouge**, the fashion parade at **Glamour Bar** and the deployment of cologne-soaked bounty hunters all along remind you that Shanghai is in the midst of some serious money-making. Of course, the real millionaires are celebrating deals in private dining rooms. But the young Shanghainese, egged on by the expat party crowd, have learned that their new-found wealth can buy far more than a night in a karaoke bar.

As well as the venues listed below, many of the venues described in the **Music** and **Nightlife** chapters double as drinking dens.

The Bund

The ongoing work along the Bund to move traffic underground – and to improve the pedestrian experience in time for the magic year, 2010 – is causing heavy disruption on Shanghai's premier strip of real estate, and throwing dust up where the couture-clad would really rather it wasn't. Still, the effort going into the project is testament to the authorities' appreciation of just how vital the Bund is to new Shanghai. Slowly but surely the whole area is benefiting, as new retro chic outpost **Hamilton House** (*see p100*) and the new **Lan Club** (at the corner of Sichuan Lu and Guangdong Lu; due to open summer 2008) start the reach back into what has already started to be known as the 'Back Bund'.

Bar Rouge
7th floor, Bund 18, 18 Zhongshan Dong Yi Lu, by Nanjing Dong Lu (6339 1199/www.bar-rouge-shanghai.com). Metro Nanjing Dong Lu. **Open** 6.30pm-1.30am Mon-Thur, Sun; 6.30pm-4am Fri, Sat. **Credit** AmEx, DC, MC, V. **Map** p245 M4 ❶
Several years in, bordello-chic Bar Rouge – up on the seventh floor of the high-end commercial complex Bund 18 (*see p48*) – is still the favoured stomping ground for the brasher branch of the Bund

▶ ❶ Pink numbers given in this chapter correspond to the location of each bar or pub as marked on the street maps. *See pp240-249.*

Glamour Bar. *See p120.*

Bars

Enoteca

A new wine bar with a winning formula: simple style, tasty tapas and exceptionally cheap wine (a rarity in Shanghai). Join the after-work crowd as they play the Enoteca version of Risk. Two bottles? Why don't we order a third? *See p124.*

Glamour Bar

Glamour Bar manages to drape all its guests – young and old, suits and hipsters – in a cloak of elegance and then tickle them with a good-time blend of gorgeous drinks and even better music. *See below.*

JG Bar

The best mixed drinks on the Bund, surrounded by the dark and sensuous embrace of Jean-Georges. Who needs a

view when you've got a glimpse of 1930s decadence staring back at you right out of your martini. *See below.*

Tara 57

The attractions at this French Concession haunt are simple but effective: no need to dress up; music you probably own yourself; and signature absinthe cocktails that laugh at most of what's being concocted by Bund bartenders. *See p127.*

YY's (Yin Yang)

While all around it hysterical bar owners fight for Shanghai's fickle crowds with ladies' nights, costume nights, two-for-one deals and open bars, YY's has glided into its second decade on a smoke cloud of personality and alternative cool. *See p127.*

---

drinking scene. Money is dropped at an eye-popping rate here, with seemingly no end of cocktails (prepared by show mixologists), sparkler-decorated champagne bottles and credit-card slips being ferried out of the bar area. Bar Rouge is certainly spendy (expect to part with upwards of RMB 80 for a cocktail) and showy (a string of red chandeliers light the bar; sleek, lipstick-red furniture), but whether it is classy is, shall we say, a matter of varying opinions. It has legions of detractors, for whom the blazer and jeans uniform for the boys and skimpy outfits for the girls get a touch predictable. Still, for a taste of the Shanghai high life, the Bar Rouge spectacle may well be worth the cost of one of its exotic cocktails. Plus, you can always escape the wafts of perfume by going on the stellar terrace, undoubtedly one of the city's premier vantage points for Pudong gazing. Expect thumping music, an elite pick-up atmosphere and plenty of attitude – for a quiet beer, head elsewhere.

Captain Bar

6th floor, 37 Fuzhou Lu, by Sichuan Zhong Lu (6323 7869/www.captainhostel.com.cn). Metro Nanjing Dong Lu. **Open** 11am-2am daily. **Credit** AmEx, DC, MC, V. **Map** p245 M5 ②

With hardwood floors, wicker chairs and sampan theming, Captain Bar has the appearance of a three-star hotel bar, but one that is, in fact, attached to a backpackers' hostel (*see p32*) – with the curious result that boarders can enjoy a cocktail at their lodgings that costs almost as much as their bed for the night. Non-residents should visit for the scenery: although set back off the Bund, the bar terrace boasts an uninterrupted view of the Huangpu and river traffic. It's not as good as the view at any of

the other highfalutin Bund frontrunners, but the almost exclusively tourist crowd is less likely to curl a lip at your saggy jeans and yellowing T-shirt.

Glamour Bar

6th floor, M on the Bund, 20 Guangdong Lu, by Zhongshan Dong Yi Lu (6329 3751/www.m-onthebund.com). Metro Nanjing Dong Lu. **Open** 5pm-2am daily. **Credit** AmEx, DC, MC, V. **Map** p245 M4 ③

Of all the jewels in the Bund crown, the art deco-accented Glamour Bar wins in the style stakes, with carefully mismatched upholstered furniture, low lamps, gorgeous 1930s-inspired coloured glassware and retractable painted screens dividing up the huge room. The older corporate moneyspinners are here, but you're just as likely to spot the city's manicured It crowd too, sporting couture. It's all fuelled by other-worldly cocktail creations (from RMB 78) – don't miss the kumquat mojito or the clear chocolate martini – and inspired musical direction, with multifarious DJs making sure anything from dubstep to Studio 54-era disco sound just right for the occasion. Check the website for Glamour's programme of talks, concerts and readings on weekend afternoons. *Photo p119.*

JG Bar

4/F, Three on the Bund, 3 Zhongshan Dong Yi Lu, by Guangdong Lu (6323 7733/www.threeonthe bund.com). Metro Nanjing Dong Lu. **Open** 11.30am-1.30am daily. **Credit** AmEx, DC, MC, V. **Map** p245 M5 ④

Once a rather wasted space where diners would occasionally pause for an aperitif or digestif, but more likely just walk past on their way to the toilets, the bar at culinary temple Jean-Georges (*see p101*) has been reworked into a destination in its own right

– with one of the city's best bartenders on board and a new cocktail list of reworked classics (employing the likes of cumin-infused rums and rare absinthes). The space is as dark, handsome and brooding as the adjoining dining room and, while you can't see the river, we wager you won't be complaining: the exceptional bar menu gives you the chance to taste the famed Jean-Georges kitchen without hocking your air fare home.

Lounge 18

5th floor, Bund 18, 18 Zhongshan Dong Yi Lu, by Nanjing Dong Lu (6323 8399/www.bund18.com). Metro Nanjing Dong Lu. **Open** 2pm-2am daily. **Credit** AmEx, DC, MC, V. **Map** p245 M4 ❺
This welcome addition to Bund 18 provides what other bars on the strip categorically don't: restrained elegance. The demure, airy marble interior with green foliage harks back to days gone by, without resorting to the usual dark leather-heavy deco furniture. DJs and a dancefloor keep Lounge 18 in the present day, albeit with a suitably loungey and soulful house playlist. There is no terrace, but windows look out on to the river, and there is a de rigeur 'creative space' (*see p164*) with art exhibitions.

New Heights

7th floor, Three on the Bund, 3 Zhongshan Dong Yi Lu, by Guangdong Lu (6321 0909/www.three onthebund.com). Metro Nanjing Dong Lu. **Open** 10am-2am daily. **Credit** AmEx, DC, MC, V. **Map** p245 M5 ❻
New Heights hasn't got the monopoly on Bund-side views these days, but it has certainly still got one of the best. At night, when the Pearl Tower is threatening to take off like a Bond villain's space rocket, and the Aurora building has transformed itself into a giant TV screening swimming fish on loop, the deck offers one of the best seats in town for letting the ridiculous charm of Pudong wash over you, along with a strong G&T. New Heights is more restaurant (*see p102*) than bar, and those that do come are not the high-energy, high-spending revellers dancing away down the rest of the strip. Instead they're here for the scaled-back bar version of the restaurant menu, decently priced drinks and a calmer opportunity for appreciating the Huangpu river, with its own parade of twinkly dinner cruises and stealthy river barges. Quintessential Shanghai. *Photo p122.*

Vault Bar

6th floor, Three on the Bund, 3 Zhongshan Dong Yi Lu, by Guangdong Lu (6321 9922/www.threeonthe bund.com). Metro Nanjing Dong Lu. **Open** 6pm-midnight Mon-Wed, Sun; 6pm-2am Thur-Sat. **Credit** AmEx, DC, MC, V. **Map** p245 M5 ❼
Despite being a rather awkward room that has neither space nor view, the classy bar at Laris (*see p101*) features plenty of marble and leather sofas, and attracts a dressy crowd – especially for the two-for-one martini night on Thursdays. That's when the party set rolls by, though you're more likely to overhear real estate gossip or expats whining about

factories in Shenzhen than rub shoulders with the native movers and shakers. Cocktails are big and bold and, despite a Dom Perignon foam here and a flamboyant fruit display there, are seemingly still macho enough for the bankers to be drinking them. Don't miss the chocolate and raspberry martini created with chocolate liqueur made in the Laris kitchen. A DJ provides music, but this is a stage for holding court not dancing. Bar snacks (after 10pm) are, as you might expect with Laris at the helm, exemplary; try sardines in olive oil (RMB 78), lobster soup (RMB 88) or chocolate fondant (RMB 75).

Vue

33rd floor, West Tower, Hyatt on the Bund, 199 Huangpu Lu, by Wuchang Lu (6393 1234/www. shanghai.bund.hyatt.com). Taxi or bus. **Open** 5pm-1am Mon-Thur, Sun; 5pm-2am Fri, Sat. **Credit** AmEx, DC, MC, V. **Map** p245 N3 ❽
The Super Potato-designed bar at the top of the Hyatt on the Bund (*see p29*) doesn't work for us decor-wise – rustic touches don't exactly chime with future-blue mood lighting – but it has something no one else has got: a view of both the Bund and Pudong skylines. From the (newly dubbed) North Bund, you can sip your cosmo (RMB 70) and look south down the main drag of the Huangpu, with the Pearl Tower seemingly in touching distance on the left and the new Peninsula hotel (*see p31*) and the rest of the Bund twinkling on the right. The other attraction is the outdoor hot tub surrounded by day beds on the terrace upstairs. Let's face it, five-star hotel guests are unlikely to strip off, but it does see a bit of action during parties.

People's Square

People's Square has never really taken off as a social hub. Perhaps it's the space, open and lacking in mystery, or the dominance of imposing art institutions, or perhaps it's the fact that Shanghai's Communist Party Headquarters sits right in the middle. Whatever, the bars here are islands only; convenient havens after shopping and sightseeing. For the highest views, take an elevator up to **789** at Le Royal Meridien (*see p35*) or the **JW Bar** at the JW Marriott (*see p33*). For something closer to ground, try the recently opened **Art Lab** (6327 9900) on the 2nd floor of the MoCA (*see p57*).

Barbarossa

231 Nanjing Xi Lu, by Huangpi Bei Lu (6318 0220/ www.barbarossa.com.cn). Metro People's Square. **Open** 11am-2am Mon-Thur, Sun; 11am-3am Fri, Sat. **Credit** AmEx, DC, MC, V. **Map** p244 H5 ❾
This being fast-paced Shanghai, this fantastical three-floored Moroccan-styled bar and restaurant, overlooking an ornamental lake in the leafier half of People's Square, has inevitably lost some of its thrill. The in crowd has moved on, the hedonistic drinking

subsided, but in the process more room has been made for those tuning in more to the relaxed cushions and hookah pipes theme. Music is a strong hand at Barbarossa, with downtempo, soul and house playing throughout the week. Throw in the bonus of a daily happy hour (5-8pm), a super-central location, and close proximity to the MoCA (*see p57*) and Shanghai Art Museum (*see p60*), and you have several reasons to visit. Take the path to MoCA next to the Nanjing Lu entrance to Shanghai Art Museum, then almost immediately take another path on your left instead of carrying on to MoCA. You will see the lake ahead of you. *Photo p126.*

Kathleen's 5

5th floor, Shanghai Art Museum, 325 Nanjing Xi Lu, by Huangpi Bei Lu (6327 2221/www.kathleens5. com.cn). Metro People's Square. **Open** 11.30am-midnight daily. **Credit** AmEx, DC, MC, V. **Map** p244 H5 ⑩

You rarely hear anyone planning their night out around a visit to Kathleen's 5 (located atop the Shanghai Art Museum), where the bar has been moved to a smaller space at the back, and the (covered) outdoor areas are given over to the restaurant. Still, it survives and has plenty of fans, precisely because of its intimate size, the views and, less reassuringly, the fact that, with the exception of hotel bars and the noisier Barbarossa (*see p121*), there still isn't anything else in the area in which to escape the city-centre chaos. There is a globe-trotting menu and the strong wine list is a big plus, as is the view from the restaurant overlooking the greenery of People's Park and the glittering skyscrapers.

Jingan

Drinking dens around Jingan Temple are still characterised in the main by American-style sports bars. These much-loved expat haunts, such as **Malone's** (255 Tongren Lu, by Nanjing Xi Lu, 6247 2400) and **Big Bamboo** (123 Nanyang Lu, by Shanxi Bei Lu, 6256 2265), don't however offer the visitor much more than a place to catch up on matches from home and gobble, if you must, nachos and wings.

The **Tongren Lu** bar strip (south of Nanjing Xi Lu) became the city's action station a few years back, but the arrival of style, know-how and sophistication to Shanghai's nightlife elsewhere has left it looking very sorry for itself. It is a rather pathetic gaggle of girlie bars and beggars still trying to cash in on a clientele too drunk to move on. There are exceptions – the exuberant cool of the lounge bar at **Issimo** (*see p36*) or the wholesome fun of **Blue Frog** (*see p124*) on the Tongren strip itself.

Mokkos

Room 103, 1245 Wuding Xi Lu, by Wanchuandu Lu (6212 1114). Metro Jiangsu Lu. **Open** 7pm-2am Mon, Wed-Sun. **No credit cards. Map** p242 A5 ⑪

Several blocks away from Jingan Temple and a world away from the area's other bars, this secretive hangout is run by a young Japanese couple and specialises in *shochu*, the Japanese (or Korean) spirit distilled from, among other raw materials, rice, wheat, sugar cane or sweet potato. There are around 150

beautifully decorated bottles to choose from, most hovering around the 25% proof mark, and served, simply, over an oversized ice ball (RMB 25-55). Sit at the tree-trunk bar: the owners are charming and the regulars friendly. You may even get involved in an impromptu drumming and singing session.

The Spot

331 Tongren Lu, by Beijing Xi Lu (6247 3579). Metro Jingan Temple. **Open** 10am-2am Mon-Thur, Sun; 11am-3am Fri, Sat. **Credit** MC, V. **Map** p242 D5 ⑫

Located on the northern end of Tongren Lu, away from the mess further south, the Spot sits somewhere between a pub, bar and live music venue. Though nothing cool, it pulls in crowds at the weekend for cover bands and every other night of the week for its lack of pretension. The drinks are cheap (RMB 30 for a Tsingdao beer), there is a small terrace at the front, and the crowd is friendly and mixed. Handy for the Portman Ritz-Carlton (*see p36*) and the Shanghai Centre (*see p65*).

Xintiandi

As well as those listed below, check out **KABB** (*see p107*) for American comfort food par excellence.

DR Bar

No.15, North Lane, Lane 181, Taicang Lu, by Huangpi Nan Lu (6311 0358). Metro Huangpi Nan Lu. **Open** 4pm-1am Mon-Thur, Sun; 4pm-2am Fri, Sat. **Credit** AmEx, DC, MC, V. **Map** p248 H7 ⑬

New Heights. *See p121.*

Not 'Doctor Bar' (so, alas, no chesty barmaids in white-rubber nurse outfits) but DR Bar, which stands, we are reliably informed, for 'Design Resources'. This is the bar of Xintiandi's American architect Ben Wood, and appropriately enough, tables are furnished with copies of *Wallpaper** and other similar cred-enhancing reads. The bar is a stylish little assemblage of dark wood, black lounge sofas and subdued lighting. It's a smart-date sort of venue, intended as a setting for beautiful bartenders and good-looking guests comfortable with the concise list of classic cocktails (from RMB 55) – try the unsweetened Hemingway daiquiri.

The Fountain

No.4 North Lane, Lane 181, Taicang Lu, by Huangpi Nan Lu (6326 8800). Metro Huangpi Nan Lu. **Open** 10am-1.30am daily. **Credit** AmEx, DC, MC, V. **Map** p248 H7 ⑭

For somewhere so inundated with tourists, it's surprising that Xintiandi still has its quieter spots – upstairs at this two-floor restaurant is one of them. Avoid the soulless, bright and overdesigned ground floor, and head for the small wine lounge upstairs – a far more comfy affair – where you can still order retro food (such as warm prawn salads), while keeping yourself up, just, in low-slung armchairs. It's romantic, soporific even, and a perfect tonic to the hordes outside. Note that there's a minimum charge of RMB 100 per person upstairs.

Racks

5th floor, No.7, South Block, Lane 181, Taicang Lu, by Huangpi Nan Lu (6384 2718/www.racksmdb. com). **Open** 5pm-5am Mon-Fri; 2pm-5am Sat, Sun. **Credit** AmEx, DC, MC, V. **Map** p248 H8 ⑮

Racks is a pool hall, but not like the one you used to go to as a teenager. Here tables come in every shade from purple to yellow, leather sofas surround them, and eager waitresses are on hand to re-rack the second the black goes down. In fact, it's more like a club with pool tables – and, perhaps on account of the general Chinese indifference towards dancing, Racks has proved an instant hit from day one. Predictably, renting a table is pricey on weekends, when DJs belt out hip hop anthems, rich kids knock back whisky and green tea, and minimum spends of at least RMB 2,500 apply. During the rest of the week, it's more than affordable (RMB 100 per hour) and will have you cursing the ripped-up table at your local boozer in no time.

Sugar

No.2, North Block, Xintiandi, Lane 181, Taicang Lu, by Huangpi Nan Lu (5351 0007/www.thecollectionsh. com). Metro Huangpi Nan Lu. **Open** noon-1am daily. **Credit** AmEx, DC, MC, V. **Map** p248 H7 ⑯

Occupying the top floor of the ambitious multi-venue confection known as the Collection, this candy-themed joint is one side red-and-white-striped dessert parlour with white sofas, one side dark wood cocktail bar. Both treats can be taken in either, and

Eat, Drink, Shop

there's even some imaginative crossover: think superb sweet-influenced cocktails (from RMB 68), such as the Dickens, featuring own-made lemon curd, or the Skittles cocktail. While high-concept sushi restaurant Pure downstairs is still finding its feet, the sweet-toothed Shanghai youths – at least those with money – love Sugar, and there's every chance you'll wander in on the high jinks of a ladies' night complete with lingerie show or *Alice In Wonderland* fancy dress. *Photo p127.*

TMSK

House 11, North Block, Lane 181, Taicang Lu, by Huangpi Nan Lu (6326 2227). Metro Huangpi Nan Lu. **Open** 1.30pm-1am daily. **Credit** AmEx, DC, MC, V. **Map** p248 H7 ⓱

Dreamt up by Taiwanese actress Yang Hui Shan and her husband, TMSK is two parts tack to one part delirium. The couple are both 'glass artists', which means their joint has oversized glass sculptures and a multicoloured bar that's like stained glass on acid; far-out, but also quite beautiful and definitely worth a look. The martinis are served in glasses that were inspired by ancient Chinese symbols. Come after 8.30pm any night for the house band, who play techno-inspired Chinese folk music while wearing cast-off outfits from *Star Trek*. We're not making this up.

French Concession

It might not have the concentration or the attitude of the Bund bar scene, but the French Concession is home to some of Shanghai's best bars and has a good deal more variety. The leafy streets harbour everything from cosy pubs and dive bars to concept bars and secret cocktail lounges, with a few hostess bars hanging on beside.

Blue Frog

207-206 Maoming Nan Lu, by Yongjia Lu (6445 6634/www.kabbsh.com). Metro Shanxi Nan Lu. **Open** 11am-late daily. **Credit** AmEx, DC, MC, V. **Map** p247 F9 ⓲

Since Maoming Lu shed its girlie bar image (or rather had it bulldozed), the original Blue Frog has matured. There's still a roll of honour on the wall of those crazy chaps who have drunk every one of the 100 shooters on offer, but you're more likely to find girlfriends catching up for a gossip than scrums of revellers launching themselves into a night out. The daily happy hour (4-8pm) is a good time to get settled. Staff are cheerful and the food (burgers, sandwiches, pasta), is consistently good.
Other locations throughout the city.

Constellation

96 Xinle Lu, by Xiangyang Bei Lu (5404 0970/www. seiza-bar.com.cn). Metro Shanxi Nan Lu. **Open** 7pm-2am daily. **Credit** MC, V. **Map** p247 E7 ⓳

This narrow Japanese-run cocktail and whisky bar operated quietly for some months before it got picked

up by the after-work drinking set as a sought-after backdrop for their show-off whisky talk. The hype was fanned by the small number of highly-prized seats – and, it must be said, a very strong selection of Japanese and Scottish malt whiskies and myriad other spirits with which to interpret the classically-leaning cocktail list (prices from RMB 50). The UV lights create a surreptitious air, contrasted by the neat, waistcoated and bow-tied bartenders – perfect for after-work business types wanting something smart and a little bit furtive. Note that if there's no seat available you won't be allowed to stand, and for the lack of room, you wouldn't want to anyway. Book to avoid disappointment.

Cotton's

132 Anting Lu, by Jianguo Xi Lu (6433 7995/www. cottons-shanghai.com). Metro Hengshan Lu. **Open** 11.30am-2am. **No credit cards.** **Map** p246 C10 ⓴

A great place to beat the blistering summer heat or the damp winter, this laid-back bar features four fireplaces and quite possibly the best garden for outdoor drinks in town. At Cotton's, located in a beautifully restored old villa on a quiet street, the friendly proprietor Cotton and her well-drilled staff serve deliciously stiff concoctions. Try the espresso martini, or the spicy Chairman Mao shot, which has become the bar's trademark. Utterly lacking in pretension, and with character to spare, this is a bar you'll want to make your own.

Enoteca

53-57 Anfu Lu, by Changshu Lu (5404 0050/www.enoteca.com.cn). Metro Changshu Lu. **Open** 9.30am-2am daily. **Credit** AmEx, DC, MC, V. **Map** p246 C7 ㉑

In the business cut and thrust of Shanghai, a set of wine importers decided to do something radical: open a wine bar, treat it as a shop window for their wholesale arm, and sell their wares at cost price. Considering good wine is a relatively expensive commodity in Shanghai, and that cheap Chinese wine makes you pay in other ways, the result, neighbourhood bar Enoteca, has been rammed from day one. Bottles, not glasses, start at about RMB 90, inoffensive contemporary styling provides the backdrop, and a young, after-work crowd of locals and expats tuck into sharing plates while moving swiftly on to their second and third bottles. *See also p125* **Enological evolution.**
Other locations 58 Taicang Lu, by Ji'nan Lu, Xintiandi (5306 3400).

Face

Building 4, Ruijin Guesthouse, 118 Ruijin Er Lu, by Fuxing Zhong Lu (6466 4328). Metro Shanxi Nan Lu. **Open** noon-1.30am Mon-Thur, Sun; noon-2am Fri, Sat. **Credit** AmEx, DC, MC, V. **Map** p247 F8 ㉒

A tad jaded in the face of so much young blood in the city's bar scene, Face still manages to pull in a mix of local drinkers and tourists who come for its location in a French Concession villa, next to the immaculate lawns of the state-owned 1920s Ruijin

Eat, Drink, Shop

Enological evolution

Traditionally, the Shanghainese are thought of as enthusiastic but wholely unfussy drinkers. The image of a room full of wedding guests, or a table of celebrating business men, clinking their glasses with a hearty 'gan bei' (literally 'dry glass', or 'bottoms up'), is nothing new. What's changing is the contents of the glasses: where the tipple of choice was once invariably *baijiu*, a sorghum-based spirit with a mean kick and mouth-twisting taste, now it's just as likely to be red wine.

As China prospers and horizons broaden, consumer tastes are changing, and wine imports, particularly of red wine, have been rising with double-digit yearly growth over the past decade. Wine lists are expanding, high-end wine import businesses are booming and the Shanghainese are filling their glasses with unprecendented zeal.

Still, enophiles are quick to point out that wine culture has been adopted with Chinese characteristics – the wedding banquet might be serving its red wine with Sprite and an ice cube, and a Bund sommelier relates how a RMB 20,000 bottle of Bordeaux was mixed with coke before his very eyes. Consumption of good-quality wine is still low, and restricted almost entirely to expats and the business elite in wealthy cities. Convincing even middle-class Chinese to fork out RMB 300 for a vintage from France is a battle that has not yet been won, and what is mostly drunk nationally is poorly made domestic plonk.

However, China's potential for wine production is huge. Its geography offers just about every wine-growing climate, but few vines have been planted. Much of 'Chinese' wine is, therefore, made with low-grade grape juice imported from South America, with quite terrifying results. Still, these bottles are extraordinarily cheap, and they are the most accessible entry for young aspirational consumers looking to buy into the good life.

Enological insensitivities aside, the new wine scene has meant a much-needed diversification of the Shanghai drinking scene, which not so long ago was dominated by dive bars and beer. No wonder the global wine industry is eyeing the Chinese market.

If you do want to taste something local, choose carefully. **Grace Vineyard** is one pioneering Shanxi producer that produces consistently impressive wines. Other big producers like **Great Wall**, **Changyu** and **Dynasty** are beloved of patriotic politicians, but flit between drinkable but highly priced vintages and cheap plonk.

Of Shanghai's multiplying wine bars, our top picks are **Enoteca** (*see p124*), for affordable quoffing; the **Wine Residence** (57 Jiangyin Lu, by Huangpi Bei Lu, People's Square, 6318 0857), part of a chic restaurant, bar and wine cellar partnership in a restored villa tucked behind the JW Marriott; and **Just Grapes** (462 Dagu Lu, by Shimen Yi Lu, Jingan, 3311 3205), which has a wine shop attached.

Enoteca.

Guesthouse (*see p43*). On a summer evening there are few finer places to be than at a table on the forecourt, beside immaculately manicured lawn. It's even better if you're there between 5pm and 8pm for half-price drinks. Inside, the red-leather couches, opium beds and lounge chairs allow patrons to indulge in colonial fantasies. Still, the drinks are nothing special and if it's a cutting edge you want, the city's cool-hunting clique has long since moved on. Upstairs is restaurant Lan Na Thai (*see p116*).

Manifesto

748 Julu Lu, by Fumin Lu (6289 9108/www.mesa-manifesto.com). Metro Changshu Lu. **Open** 6pm-midnight Mon-Thur, Sun; 6pm-2am Fri, Sat. **Credit** AmEx, DC, MC, V. **Map** p243 D6 ㉓

A refit last year has given fresh legs to Manifesto, something you'll be needing too if you've spent the afternoon boutique-hopping around Julu and Changle Lu. A cocktail on the terrace here should do the trick, thanks to an innovative list that goes beyond the classics (try the Dr Zhivago, with whisky and vanilla vodka; RMB 58). Industrial light fittings hang from the high ceilings, while wooden floors, peachy walls and floral patterned mirrors soften the room. The position, near the sought-after Fumin and Julu intersection, ensures you won't be alone. Enter through Mesa (*see p114*) and head up the spiral staircase.

O'Malley's

42 Taojiang Lu, by Wulumuqi Lu (6474 4533/ www.omalleys-shanghai.com). Metro Changshu Lu. **Open** 11am-2am daily. **Credit** AmEx, DC, MC, V. **Map** p246 C8 ㉔

An Irish pub, but with a huge front room kitted out with a screen that consistently draws the best crowd in the city for watching major sporting events. Chinese Premiership fans swap stats with expats and waiters keep everyone watered with (rather expensive) Guinness. Inside is quite lovely too: the 19th-century building was once an infant school and, although not entirely free of the occasional bit of juvenile behaviour, is an enchanting collection of tiny rooms, corners and coves over two floors. Real fires burn in winter, folkies busk in side rooms and there is the unmistakable olfactory underscore of beer and cigarettes (something now lacking even in Ireland). Outside, the walled beer garden has a play area and a lawn, making this popular with expat families at the weekend.

People 7

805 Julu Lu, by Fumin Lu (5404 0707). Metro Changshu Lu. **Open** 11.30am-1am daily. **Credit** AmEx, DC, MC, V. **Map** p246 D6 ㉕

People 6 has long gone, but People 7 has kept hold of its hip image – and crowds. The secret door-release gimmick is baffling, with two sliding doors to guess at before you can work your way in (slip your hand into the centre of the nine round holes, twice). The interior has plenty of wow: a shell of a two-storey building, with the raw concrete beams and exposed walls, and a corrugated steel ceiling. The bar counter is one immensely long and eerily glowing light box. The drink to go for is the Spring Water saké cocktail or the 'tube wine' (RMB 185), a fruit bowl heaped with ice embedded with two dozen

Barbarossa. *See p121.*

test-tube shots of booze (designed to be shared). The toilets also seem designed to perplex the alcohol-addled mind: the doors are hinged in the opposite fashion to how they appear and there's no light switch to be found… just close the door behind you and ta-da! What a lark.

Sasha's
House 11, 9 Dongping Lu, by Hengshan Lu (6474 6167/www.sashas-shanghai.com). Metro Changshu Lu. **Open** 10am-1am Mon-Thur, Sun; 10am-2am Fri, Sat. **Credit** AmEx, DC, MC, V. **Map** p246 C9 ㉖
Sasha's combines the laid-back nonchalance of a neighbourhood bar with all the classy stylings appropriate to its setting – in an old Concession-era villa that is said to have belonged to TV Soong, at one time the richest man in the world. Thankfully, the lurid red paint job is confined to the exterior and the interior is feet-up comfortable with hardwood floors, wicker chairs and a nice long bar counter with stools for singletons and sofas for groups. Given the prices, it's a good idea to turn up for the daily 5-7pm happy hour. There's a bar menu and a good lunch set with assorted Med and Asian standards, plus a more formal steak restaurant upstairs. The large beer garden patio is a big plus on summer nights.

Tara 57
2nd floor, 57 Fuxing Xi Lu, by Yongfu Lu (6431 7027). Metro Changshu Lu. **Open** 7.30pm-3am daily. **Credit** MC, V. **Map** p246 C8 ㉗
Trust us, this cocktail lounge, despite being sandwiched less than glamorously between Boona Too café and a KTV joint up top, consistently mixes some of the most delicious drinks in the city. Named after the plantation in *Gone With The Wind*, it's opposite JZ Club and round the corner from the Shelter (*see p185*), so treated by many as an indulgent stop before heading on. The room is tiny, but try grabbing one of the small booths screened off with chiffon, then order one of the signature absinthe cocktails and kick back. These are served in over-sized martini glasses, and are delicious and potent; after two you'll probably decide there's really no need to move on after all.

Velvet Lounge
1st floor, Bldg 3-4, 913 Julu Lu, by Changshu Lu (5403 2976/www.cosmogroup.cn/velvet). Metro Changshu Lu. **Open** 6pm-3am Mon-Thur; 6pm-5am Fri-Sun. **Credit** AmEx, DC, MC, V. **Map** p246 D7 ㉘
One of the city's best-loved after-hours hangouts, Velvet Lounge is an attractive bar, lounge and diminutive club rolled into one. Early evening it steps out as a lounge, with its low-slung coloured sofas populated by a mixed crowd getting in a few before moving on to clubs. By midnight, the three rooms are busy with a rowdier crowd of entrepreneurs, off-work chefs and hipsters, the seats taken and punters (willingly) forced on to the disco- and soul-soaked dancefloor. It doesn't calm down again until very, very, late. Thankfully, Velvet also serves its highly prized pizzas until 3am.

YY's (Yin Yang)
125 Nanchang Lu, by Maoming Nan Lu (6466 4098). Metro Shanxi Nan Lu. **Open** 2pm-4am daily. **Credit** AmEx, DC, MC, V. **Map** p247 F8 ㉙
Around the end of the 1990s, YY's was *the* place. It was the haunt of subculturals, artists and radicals – characters like Mian Mian (author of banned sex 'n' drugs novel *Candy*) and Wei Hui (author of *Shanghai Baby*, who was once gloriously condemned by Chinese state media as 'decadent, debauched and a slave of foreign culture'). It's no longer quite so essential, but ten years on the sparse and well-worn ground-floor bar still serves as a sort of common room for the city's young and not-so-young chain-smoking, creative set. The steep prices mean it's more gallery owner than struggling artist. Drinking continues into the early hours, and it remains ideal for a post-club snifter or even early morning dumplings ordered in from next door.

Pudong

As we went to press, the Hyatt family was adding the finishing touches to the latest outpost of its Shanghai triumvirate – the **Park Hyatt** (*see p44*), covering the top 14 floors of the new 492-metre (1,614-foot) World Financial Center. This means they can still claim to have the highest bar in the world – after trumping their own **Cloud 9** in the next-door Jin Mao tower. Pudong does altitude bars like nowhere else on the planet, but this doesn't mean that they have atmosphere. Most people whizz up

Sugar. *See p123.*

Eat, Drink, Shop

Cloud 9.

for one drink and a good look at the view before taking their night elsewhere.

At ground level, the drinking choices in Pudong are even more sparse. The **Wall** nightclub (*see p185*) opens its doors early for the lounge crowd and **Blue Frog** sits at the front of the Super Brand Mall.

Cloud 9

87th floor, Grand Hyatt, Jinmao Tower, 88 Shiji Dadao (5049 1234/www.shanghai.grand.hyatt.com). Metro Lujiazui. **Open** 6pm-1am Mon-Thur, Sun; 6pm-2am Fri, Sat. **Credit** AmEx, DC, MC, V. **Map** p245 O5 ③⓪

Until its taller Hyatt sibling arrived at the top of the World Financial Center next door, Cloud 9, at 420m (1,386ft) above sea level, was reputedly the highest place to go drinking on earth – apart, of course from mountain bars. Be warned, though, the heavenly views that its height suggests can often be obscured by clouds. It's spectacular all the same – and the dark and steely interior is a sight in itself. Prices match the altitude, with an imposed minimum spend of RMB 120 per person after 8.30pm.

Jade on 36

36 floor, Pudong Shangri-La, 33 Fucheng Lu, by Lujiazui Xi Lu (6882 3636/www.shangri-la.com). Metro Lujiazui. **Open** 6pm-1am Mon-Thur, Sun; 6pm-2am Fri, Sat. **Credit** AmEx, DC, MC, V. **Map** p245 O5 ③①

It might not be as high as the Hyatt boys, but the Shangri-La's Jade on 36 bar gets closest to a destination bar classification of all the hotel drinking offerings in town. The interior, designed by Adam D Tihany, features shocking pink and green geometric boxes over a central bar, crazy carpet on the wall and space-age washrooms. Prices are steep but at least the Bund views are gobsmacking and the cocktails excellent – our advice is to avoid the garish tini-this tini-that creations the place has become famous for and select instead one of the East-meets-West updated classics, such as Oriental Plum Sour, a whisky sour with plum brandy (RMB 68). For a review of the fine dining restaurant next door, *see p118*.

Paulaner

Riverside Promenade, Binjiang Da Dao (6888 3935/ www.bln.com.cn). Metro Lujiazui. **Open** 10am-1am Mon-Thur, Sun; 10am-2am Fri, Sat. **Credit** AmEx, DC, MC, V. **Map** p245 N5 ③②

The original German brewhouse in the French Concession is never short of expat businessmen and rich families happy to pay over the odds for plates of sausage and own-brewed beer. This outpost is better equipped for the weary sightseer: a front row seat on the Huangpu and far fewer screaming kids. Beer isn't cheap (small glasses go for RMB 60) but there is an early evening half-price happy hour on Monday (4-7pm).
Other locations 150 Fenyang Lu, by Fuxing Lu, French Concession (6474 5700); House 19-20, North Block, Xintiandi, Lane 181, Taicang Lu, near Madang Lu, Xintiandi (6320 3935).

Shops & Services

The big Shanghai spend.

Highstreet Loft. *See p130.*

Shopping in Shanghai is a unique experience: thrilling, overwhelming, at times extremely frustrating – but never boring. The city streets are packed with a potent mix of street markets, poky pavement stalls, designer flagships, pristine malls and edgy independent boutiques. Modest boutiques turn out to be dens of designer factory overruns; budget houseware stores become treasure troves for quirky fashion accessories (who could resist high-heeled, pointed Wellington boots for just RMB 10?). Even the least passionate shoppers will find themselves tempted by rows of miniature tea sets, piles of sequinned slippers, stacks of bamboo steamers, yards of pashminas and the odd repro Buddha head. In short, Shanghai will pack your present drawer for years.

Outside of well established stores, prices are cheap and often negotiable. The Chinese even bargain in high-street shops, so always try for something off the asking price. Haggling techniques vary but it is generally accepted that good humour is essential; pooh-poohing the vendor's wares will get you nowhere. Decide on how much you want to pay before you begin

haggling, and if you aren't getting your desired price, remember to walk away – you may find the price instantly drops.

Although credit cards are increasingly accepted, cash is king. Be sure to try before you buy as refunds or exchanges will rarely be given, with or without a receipt. If it's clothes you're after, bear in mind that Chinese sizes are minuscule. XL is equivalent to a UK size 12 or US size 10. And the shop assistant will look at you as though you truly are extra large.

THE RISE OF LUXURY GOODS

China has a booming market for luxury goods, and Shanghai is firmly at the helm. China's most fashionable city is quickly becoming the big-brand testing ground for the rest of the country. As a result, scruffy Beijing misses out on a good proportion of the top international brand launch parties and must wait longer for the stores to open. High-end brands continue to want in on Shanghai, competing to make their mark with extravagant champagne launch parties and fashion shows, and cashing in on some of the most stunning historical sites and viewpoints.

Luxury emporiums, from old and new labels, dominate the Bund. At **Three on the Bund**, there's Giorgio Armani and Hugo Boss. Next door, no.5 is home to avant-garde home interior showroom **Design Republic** (www.thedesignrepublic.com), more like an art gallery than a furniture warehouse. At **Bund 6**, D&G has taken over the first floor with a flashy gold and black flagship store (with the Martini Bar). A few blocks down, Cartier and Ermenegildo Zegna have fancy spaces in the upscale retail complex **Bund 18**. The shopping malls along the western strip of **Nanjing Lu** are packed with designer boutiques. You'll find fashion darlings Louis Vuitton, Gucci and Prada, as well as edgier brands such as Anna Sui, Diesel and John Galliano.

The city is a magnet for creative types and entrepreneurs – and a lively boutique scene reflects this. But, despite the burgeoning economy, they live in difficult times: ruthless price wars, rising rents and an obsession with big-name foreign brands make it tough for small – and even medium-sized – shops to stay in business. Even high-end Chinese designers struggle to establish themselves in the luxury game. Taiwanese brand **Shiatzy Chen** (*see p137*) is one notable exception – its beautifully tailored, Asian-inspired men's and women's garments occupy an ornate retail space on the Bund. Bund 18 also showcases homegrown talents **Zhang Da** and **Han Feng** at the Younik boutique.

SHOPPING AREAS

For the highest concentration of cool per metre, head straight to the tree-lined streets of the **French Concession**. You're likely to find treasure wherever you go but we recommend scouring the myriad boutiques on **Nanchang Lu**, **Shanxi Nan Lu**, **Xinle Lu**, **Changle Lu**, **Maoming Lu**, **Jinxian Lu**, **Fuxing Lu** (Middle and West side) and **Julu Lu**. Here you can get your hands on a mix of the latest trends, some local brands and international designer labels at low prices. For international high-street labels, stick to the area's main shopping artery **Huaihai Zhong Lu** (between Shanxi Lu and Xizang Lu) where you'll find H&M, Zara, Mango, Uniqlo and Japanese-inspired Chinese fashion store Y by Codes Combine.

Lane 210 off **Taikang Lu** (aka Tianzifang; *photo p135*) has mushroomed from a dinky art street into a trendy maze of boutique- and café-filled alleys. Several local designers have located here and the rest of the boutiques do their best to fit in with the creative vibe. This rather quaint area is quiet during the week, which can be a relief. Following in its footsteps, trendy shopping enclaves are springing up all over town. Ones to watch are **Ferguson Lane** (376 Wukang Lu), the **Village** (6 Dongping Lu) and **Highstreet Loft** (*see p130*).

The most visitor-friendly place to commence your shopping is **Xintiandi** – a cluster of traditional *shikumen* tenement housing converted into upmarket shops, bars and restaurants. You can do lunch, catch a movie, purchase high-end souvenirs and pick up a new outfit ready for alfresco sundowners.

For pure luxe, it has to be the **Bund**, where you can splurge to your heart's content on fashion, high-end restaurants and contemporary Chinese art while taking in the breathtaking Pudong skyline. Real-deal Jimmy Choo heels, Hermès scarves and Dior shades can be found at the western end of the **Nanjing Xi Lu** thoroughfare. Most of the biggest designers on the international circuit have opened up shops there. Start your spree at City Plaza next to Jingan Temple and head west.

If you can handle the concrete and the crowds, mall-rich **Xujiahui** could be worth a visit. The concentration of shopping malls and stores must have been designed with monsoons in mind. Metro Line One delivers its passengers directly into the major shopping destinations of the Pacific Department Store and Grand Gateway Mall.

General

Malls

As in most countries, malls in Shanghai don't measure high on the creativity meter, though they will probably come as a welcome relief in the rainy season (mid June to mid July). Nanjing Xi Lu in Jingan is home to the big three: **CITIC Square**, **Plaza 66** and **Westgate**. Standing proud at the end of Huaihai Zhong Lu (by Xizang Lu) is **Shanghai Times Square** and **Infiniti**. In the western district of Xujiahui, four malls square up to each other at the junction of Hengshan Lu and Zhaojiabang Lu (of which **Grand Gateway** has the most to offer). Pudong side, the biggest contender is the super-sized **Super Brand Mall** (168 Lujiazui Xi Lu, by Yincheng Xi Lu), with an H&M, Zara, Sephora and Toys R Us.

Highstreet Loft

508 Jiashan Lu, by Jianguo Xi Lu, French Concession (5466 6675/www.highstreetloft.com). Metro Shanxi Lu, then taxi. **Open** 11am-10.30pm daily. **Credit** varies. **Map** p247 E9.

This shopping complex is an interesting new platform for local and lesser-known overseas designers. While the lack of interest shown by locals may in

The art of the T-shirt

As well as stocking up on fake Fendi totes, designer factory seconds and Cartier watches, it's well worth turning your attentions to the local design crowd. Even though the Shanghainese generally show little interest in local fashion design, there's a burgeoning scene to be discovered and for many of the city's local creatives, the T-shirt is their preferred canvas.

The trend began with **Shirt Flag** (330 Nanchang Lu, by Maoming Nan Lu, French Concession, 5465 3011, www.shirtflag.com), the city's veteran T-shirt designers, who specialise in quirky Communist propaganda-inspired graphics splashed across T-shirts (around RMB 180) and bags.

Shirt Flag is now joined by a whole crowd of hip T-shirt designers, including nearby **Eblis Hungi** (Shop 18, 139 Changle Lu, by Ruijin Er Lu, French Concession, 5382 6807), one of the most promising local labels, with a coveted collection of denims and T-shirts. His signature is a bandaged mummy face illustration that's printed on a range of T-shirts (starting at around RMB 180), along with other playful, and often eerie, images. A few doors down, **eno** (139-23 Changle Lu, by Ruijin Er Lu, French Concession, 6386 0120,

www.eno.cn) has garnered a cult following among the younger fashion crowd. The concept brand invites local designers to create graphics for their T-shirts – available in various colours for men and women (from RMB 200). The pièce de resistance at eno's flagship is a giant conveyor belt which is used to display T-shirts in motion.

Popular local design company **insh** (200 Taikang Lu, by Sinan Lu, French Concession, 6466 5249, www.insh.com.cn), headed by Helen Lee, sells T-shirts with playful designs inspired by local city life and Chinese emblems and traditions; pick up your 'I heart Shanghai' here.

For edgier T-shirts from just RMB 100, stop by concrete den **the Thing** (276 Changle Lu, by Ruijin Er Lu, French Concession, 6384 9229, www.thething.cn), founded by a local design duo. They take their inspiration from music, film, art, technology and modern-day China, making for a set of hip and wearable works of art. Leader of street fashion, **the Source** (see p137) also stocks T-shirts from Japan's touted manga cartoon artist Santa Inoue and is the only place to stock them in China. Images from his cult Tokyo Tribe 1 comic are pasted across the collection.

eno.

the end prove a problem, it's definitely worth taking a look. A particular favourite is the snazzy Latino styles at Pampa showcasing select pieces from ten Argentinian designers (Room 101, Building 2, 5465 9329). There are also a number of no-name outlets selling well-priced factory overruns from the likes of D&G, Chloé and Kenzo. *Photo p129.*

Plaza 66

1266 Nanjing Xi Lu, by Shanxi Bei Lu, Jingan (6279 0910/www.plaza66.com). Metro Nanjing Xi Lu. **Open** 10am-10pm daily. **Credit** varies. **Map** p243 E5.

There are few faster ways to blow the holiday budget than taking your plastic for a spin here. Stores include Fendi, Louis Vuitton, Marni and Tiffany. In addition to multibrand boutiques I.T and Joyce (on the second and third floors), Plaza 66 keeps fashion junkies up-to-date with the latest from Yohji Yamamoto, Galliano and Philip Lim. Recommended dining options include conveyor-belt soup noodles at Red Door, aka Xiamien Guan, and dim sum at Zen. The Atrium café is good for people-watching, if not so hot for the actual food.

Raffles City

268 Xizang Zhong Lu, by Fuzhou Lu, People's Square (6340 3600/www.rafflescity-shanghai.com). Metro People's Square. **Open** 10am-10pm daily. **Credit** varies. **Map** p244 J5.

Raffles City is Shanghai's busiest mall. Its most successful outlet is the multibrand store Novo Concept, which carries Miss Sixty, Quiksilver and a handful of Hong Kong brands. There's also a Uniqlo, Kookaï, Red Earth and Mango – all under one gargantuan roof. When you're all spent, head down to the basement for a delicious cream-filled puff pastry from Japanese chain Beard Papa.

Markets

Stockpiling everything from fashion and fabrics to antiques and live animals, Shanghai's markets are a paradise for the determined haggler. Food and flowers excluded, the starting price is generally four times the local, and ultimately acceptable, price.

Even if you're not self-catering, it's worth checking out one of the city's **wet markets**. They're usually teeming with fresh vegetables, live animals and even livelier vendors. It's best to eat before you venture in, though, as a wink from a freshly chopped fish head or a pile of skinned frogs may turn the stomach. There is a good wet market on the corner of Jianguo Xi Lu and Taiyuan Lu in the French Concession and another on Zhenning Lu and Yuyuan Lu.

In an effort to clean up Shanghai's fake products, officials closed the infamous Xiangyang Lu fakes market in 2006, but replacements have since sprung up at 580 Nanjing Xi Lu (by Chengdu Lu) and

Plaza 66.

underground at the Shanghai Science & Technology Museum Metro station. And there's still a band of vendors lurking around Xiangyang Lu and Shanxi Lu tempting you down side alleys with the promise of Rolex watches and Louis Vuitton bags.

For antiques markets, *see p146*.

D Mall
Renmin Dadao, by Xizang Zhong Lu, People's Square. Metro People's Square. **Open** 10am-9pm daily. **No credit cards. Map** p244 J5.
Beneath the grass and concrete parades of People's Square lies a warren of passageways packed with low-cost fashion, cosmetics and accessory stores. Best buys are the colourful wigs (roughly RMB 50), hair extensions and blinging jewellery, which can be found just off the row of cheap manicure stalls. Locals call this market 'Dimei'.

Fabric Market
399 Lujiabang Lu, by Lishui Lu, Old City. Metro Lujiabang Lu. **Open** 8am-5pm daily. **No credit cards. Map** p249 M10.
If you're disheartened by the minuscule sizing in the city, make a beeline for the fabric market where you can get a whole new wardrobe made to measure, from formal suits to cashmere coats and silk *qipaos*. It houses over 100 stalls carrying a wide range of natural and synthetic fabrics, domestic and imported (for tips, *see p136* **Made to measure**). Nearly all stalls have tailors on hand (at an extra fee of RMB 30) but the quality varies considerably. Note that the lesser-known Shanghai Shiliupu Clothing Material Market, on the corner of Dongmen Lu and Zhonghua Lu (map p249 N7), is equally good for amassing fabrics and slightly less stressful on the weekends.

Qipu Lu Market
168 & 183 Qipu Lu, by Henan Bei Lu, Hongkou. **Open** 9am-5pm daily. **No credit cards. Map** p244 L2.
Getting round Qipu Lu requires a fair amount of stamina, but the dizzying choice and silly prices make it worthwhile. There are numerous multi-storey buildings, crammed with clothing, shoes, accessories and plenty of fake goods, most priced between RMB 30 and RMB 100. When you've pushed, elbowed and bargained enough, take a breather on the streets around the market, which are full of life and sizzling food stalls.

Yuyuan Bazaar (Yuyuan Shangsha)
288 Fuyou Lu, Jiujiachang Lu, Old City. **Open** 8.30am-8.30pm daily. **No credit cards. Map** p249 M7.
If you can bear the crowds, the inflated prices and the cloying stench of tofu, then this is a great place to stock up on Chinese souvenirs. Stalls are crammed with embroidered silk jackets (RMB 100) and dressing gowns (RMB 60), freshwater pearls (RMB 10-60 per string), ceramic tea sets (RMB 40), imitation Cultural Revolution posters (RMB 10),

wooden fans (RMB 30) and painted scrolls (RMB 50). Shops along Fangbang Lu offer more of the same. Persistent souls have been known to unearth the odd dusty treasure at the Fuyou Antiques Bazaar (no.459), which is also the location of multi-storey jewellery enterprises Lao Miao and First Asia.

Specialist

Books & magazines

Most high-end hotels carry a basic selection of international press; the best is offered at the newsstand at the Portman Ritz-Carlton (*see p36*). But for a massive range of magazines and books **Chaterhouse** is your best bet. People may direct you to the traditional booksellers' street, Fuzhou Lu, which runs between People's Square and the Bund, but note there's little material there for English-language readers.

Chaterhouse
Shop B1-E, Shanghai Times Square, 93 Huaihai Zhong Lu, by Liulin Lu, Xintiandi (6391 8237/ www.chaterhouse.com.cn). Metro Huangpi Nan Lu. **Open** 10am-10pm daily. **Credit** AmEx, DC, MC, V. **Map** p248 J7.
Although small, this bookshop offers Shanghai's best range of newly published fiction and non-fiction titles. There's even a stock of Biggles books from around 1940, and a vast selection of magazines on more contemporary topics (starting at RMB 80). **Other locations** Unit 68, 6th floor, Super Brand Mall, 168 Lujiazui Xi Lu, by Yincheng Xi Lu, Pudong (5049 0668).

China National Publications Import-Export Corporation (CNPIEC)
5th floor, CITIC Square, 1168 Nanjing Xi Lu, by Jiangning Lu, Jingan (5292 5214). Metro Nanjing Xi Lu. **Open** 10am-10pm daily. **Credit** AmEx, DC, MC, V. **Map** p243 E5.
This minuscule foreign-language bookstore, located on the fifth floor of the CITIC Square mall, majors in non-fiction English titles. It also stocks a selection of international press, including *The Economist*, *Newsweek*, the *Wall Street Journal* and *Wallpaper**.

Foreign Languages Bookstore
390 Fuzhou Lu, by Fujian Zhong Lu, People's Square (6322 3200). Metro Nanjing Dong Lu. **Open** 9.30am-6pm daily. **Credit** V. **Map** p244 L5.
Come here for maps and books about Shanghai. There are also Chinese-language learning materials on the ground floor and English-language fiction, with a focus on the classics, up on the fourth.

Garden Books
325 Changle Lu, by Shanxi Bei Lu, French Concession (5404 8728/www.bookzines.com). Metro Changshu Lu. **Open** 10am-10pm daily. **Credit** AmEx, DC, MC, V. **Map** p247 E7.

AMYLIN' S PEARLS & JEWELRY
艾 敏 林 氏 珠 宝

1.*More than 13 years of expertise in jewelry design and sales with happy repeat customers around the world.*
2.*Extensive selection of classic and creative designs.*
3.*Premium quality pearls with reasonable price.*
4.*All major credit cards accepted.*
5.*Free exchange or full refund within 30days with Original receipt.*

Shanghai Downtown Store
Room 30 3rd floor 580 NanJing West Road
Tel: +86-21-5228-2372

Shanghai GuBei Store
39 Yi Li South Road
Tel: + 86-21-6275-3954

Shanghai Pudong Store
A2002 Century Avenue
Tel:+86-21-6862-2226

BeiJing Store
4311 4th floor Hong Qiao pearl Market
Tel: +86-10-6711-7528

Open everyday:10:00AM-7:00PM
www.amylinspearls.com Email:amylinpearls@gmail.com Mobile:0086-139-163-134-66 Fax: 0086-21-6446-6649

A friendly place to sit and browse while sipping a coffee or tucking into a bowl of Italian ice-cream. General-interest books on Shanghai are well represented, and there's also a decent fiction section upstairs, as well as more art and architecture titles displayed on the ground floor.

Shanghai's City of Books

465 Fuzhou Lu, by Fujian Zhong Lu, People's Square (6391 4848). Metro People's Square. **Open** 9.30am-8pm daily. **Credit** AmEx, DC, MC, V. **Map** p244 K5.

Given that it covers seven storeys, it's no surprise that this place scores points for its fantastic range of subjects (even if the foreign section is small), with more than 200,000 books, video and audio products.

Electronics & photography

While still not as cheap as Hong Kong, prices for electronics have fallen dramatically here in recent years, thanks to a proliferation of good local brands. You can score good deals on home-grown DVD and MP3 players, portable CD players and digital cameras. Even international brands can be got for around 10 per cent less than in the UK. In addition to the places below, try the electronics market at Fuxing Zhong Lu and Xiangyang Nan Lu. Word of advice: always ask to see the original boxes.

Film processing is cheap in China, costing around RMB 30 for a 24-exposure film. A good bet is Guanlong (*see below*), but Kodak has outposts at Xintiandi and on Huaihai Zhong Lu near the Shanghai Library. There's also a market dedicated to cameras and equipment on the corner of Luban Lu and Xietu Lu, including second-hand gear in good condition on the fourth and sixth floors.

Baoshan market

Qiujiang Lu, between Baoshan Lu & Sichuan Bei Lu, Hongkou. Metro Baoshan Lu. **Open** 9am-5.30pm daily. **No credit cards. Map** p244 L1.

Tiny stalls sprawl over several streets and cluster in indoor nooks – even if you aren't a techie, this market is fun to wander round. There's a ton of second-hand (and potentially stolen) appliances to sift through, and plenty of local and fake brands, but the best buys are the little gadgets, such as MP3 players, which go for a fraction of the price elsewhere.

Cybermart

282 Huaihai Zhong Lu, by Huangpi Nan Lu, Xintiandi (6390 8008/www.cybermart.com.cn). Metro Huangpi Nan Lu. **Open** 10am-8pm daily. **Credit** V. **Map** p248 H7.

Impossible to miss with its deafening music booming from massive speakers outside, Cybermart is one of the best places for good-quality electronic and digital devices. Computers, printers, memory sticks and digital music players occupy the first floor, while mobile phones, blank CDs, webcams and computer components for techie DIYers are on the second and third. The place is ISO 9001-certified, signalling that it meets high quality standards overall.

Guanlong Photographic Equipment Company

180 Nanjing Dong Lu, by Jiangxi Zhong Lu, the Bund (6323 8681). Metro Nanjing Dong Lu. **Open** 9am-9pm daily. **Credit** AmEx, DC, MC, V. **Map** p244 L4.

A shutterbug paradise, this massive electronics store has everything from high-end digital and point-and-shoot cameras to MP3 players and camcorders. Prices aren't especially low, but you're paying for reputable brands such as Sony and Nikon. On-site photo processing is available, as are other professional photographic services.

Metro City

1111 Zhaojiabang Lu, by Caoxi Bei Lu, Xujiahui (6426 8380/www.shmetrocity.com). Metro Xujiahui. **Open** 10am-10pm daily. **Credit** AmEx, DC, MC, V. **Map** p246 A11.

Hidden in the basement of this futuristic mall (look for the giant glass sphere) is a buzzing, bleeping electronics market offering the latest advances in technology. Make sure you do the rounds before purchasing, and remember to bargain.

Taikang Lu. *See p130.*

Eat, Drink, Shop

Made to measure

Half the fun of being in Shanghai is ordering a brand new wardrobe of tailor-made clothes. The city is famed for its tailors, and you'll spot them tucked away down the side streets, beavering away at their antique sewing machines. The best place to kick-start the creative process is the city's **Fabric Market** (see p133), one of the most colourful places in Shanghai. You can find anything here, from formal suit cloth to disco-sequinned chiffon. But, before you get lost in the kaleidoscope, there are a few things to remember that will help ensure you end up with the real deal.

● Don't be fooled by vendors lighting the fibres to prove they are selling real **wool** (RMB 80-150 per metre). That old trick only signals the presence of natural hair (remember the last time you singed your fringe?), it doesn't actually show the percentage of wool in the fabric. A better test is to roll the material between your fingers: if little bobbles start to form then you can be pretty sure it's not pure.

● **Silk** (around RMB 60 to 80 per metre) should be ultra-thin and fine, but still weighty. When you scrunch the silk up in your hand, if it doesn't wrinkle, it's a polyester blend.

● When you go shopping for **cashmere** (approximately RMB 150 per metre), beware of hairy/furry weaves. If you can't stroke the furry fibres in the opposite direction, then you know it's not real.

● Stall holders will try to sell you excessive amounts of cloth. Remember that a pair of trousers requires roughly 2.5 metres (8 feet), a jacket 2 metres (6.5 feet) and a shirt 1.5 metres (5 feet).

TAILORS

While every stall markets a nifty tailor, not all of them are gifted. **Xiao Li** (13 0416 73841 mobile) works in the market and can come to your home or hotel for fittings (add RMB 30). Expect to pay around RMB 40 for a pair of trousers and RMB 80 for a shirt, but keep it simple with copies.

Otherwise, stick to the local English-speaking heroes Danielle, XiaoYu and Silk King. For conservative tastes, **Danielle** (99 Fahuazhen Lu, by Panyu Lu, Changning, 6282 0925) can make a two-piece suit in two days for RMB 2,000. Her tiny store is towards the west of town and has a selection of formal-wear fabrics; prices include the material.

Silk King (588 Nanjing Dong Lu, by Zhejiang Zhong Lu, the Bund, 6352 2398) is the best place for *qipaos* and other traditional Chinese designs; expect to pay around RMB 1,000 for a *qipao*, excluding fabric (silk from RMB 198 per metre). For the city's fashionistas, **XiaoYu** (Room 101, 88 Fengxian Lu, by Shimen Yi Lu, Jingan, 13 0021 95532 mobile, appointment only) can recreate a designer item in seven to ten days; a two-piece suit with fabric costs around RMB 1,000 (RMB 700 for tailoring only) – less for consecutive sets.

Another popular spot with the expat community is **Tony the Tailor** (684 Changle Lu, by Fumin Lu, French Concession, 5403 0335). Tony has been in the business for 31 years and has suited the likes of Clint Eastwood and Sylvester Stallone.

Useful Phrases

copy exactly *qing anzhao yuanyang fuzhi*
too big/too small *tai da le/tai xiao le*
Can I have the leftover fabric? *Wo keyi ba sheng xia de buliao na zou ma?*
Please deliver to my hotel *Qing songdao wo de jiudian*
Please come to my hotel *Qing dao wo de jiudian lai*

Fashion

Most of the biggest names in the fashion industry have landed in Shanghai, but high taxes on imported goods mean that you'll end up paying more than you would back home. If you must feed your label addiction, head to Plaza 66 (see p132) and, just next door, Citic Square. There has also been an influx of high-street brands in recent years, namely H&M, Zara, Mango and soon-to-arrive American Apparel.

Shanghai's best deals, however, are to be found among the designer surplus items and seconds of the boutiques that line the streets of the French Concession – and a blossoming bunch of local fashion designers. In addition to a string of edgy streetwear dens (see p131 **The art of the T-shirt**), mainstays include: **Qiu Hao** for slinky designs (158 Jinxian Lu, by Maoming Nan Lu, French Concession, 6256 0134); **Jenny Ji** for feminine finery; the minimalist aesthetics of **Shion by Choichangho** (13 Taikang Lu, by Sinan Lu, French Concession, 6467 1866); and the understated conceptual shapes in **Wang Yi Yang**'s Cha Gang and Zuczug lines (299 Fuxing

Xi Lu, by Huashan Lu, Xujiahui, 6466 1089; 2/F, South Block, 123 Xingye Lu, Xintiandi).

If you're on the Changle Lu strip, be sure to stop in one of the three **One By One** outlets, run by a trio of local designers (Qiu Hao, Chocho and Da Xiong). **Unreplaceable** also offers a good mix of own designs and label overruns (no.15, 339 Changle Lu, by Xiangyang Nan Lu, French Concession, 5404 7787, www.unreplaceable.com).

Estune

139-19 Changle Lu, by Ruijin Er Lu, French Concession (5306 9973). Metro Shanxi Nan Lu. **Open** 10am-8.30pm daily. **Credit** AmEx, DC, MC, V. **Map** p247 F7.

In a minimalist concrete space dominated by a large cluster of light bulbs hanging from the ceiling, designer Yin Jianxia displays his mainly black and white women's collection. A standout from the local designer set, he cleverly experiments with asymmetry and structure, while keeping his pieces ultra covetable. His silk mini dresses are a winner. *Photo p140.*

I.T

Lane 123, Xingye Lu, by Madang Lu, Xintiandi (6336 5131). Metro Huangpi Nan Lu. **Open** 11.30am-11pm daily. **Credit** AmEx, DC, MC, V. **Map** p248 H8.

Although the city is home to many multi-designer brand stores, successful Hong Kong retail group I.T still offers some of the most fashion-forward collections in town (including names such as Costume National, DSquared2, Stella McCartney, Tsumori Chisato and Martin Margiela). More affordable urban brands, such 5cm, Izzue and b+ab, also feature.
Other locations 3rd floor, Plaza 66, 1266 Nanjing Xi Lu, by Shanxi Bei Lu, Jingan (6288 4270).

Nest

Studio 201, Lane 210, Taikang Lu, by Sinan Lu, French Concession (6466 2416/www.nestshanghai. com). Metro Shanxi Nan Lu. **Open** 10am-7pm daily. **Credit** AmEx, DC, MC, V. **Map** p247 G10.

A collective of designers with an eco conscience inhabit this airy space, including Danish design company Jooi, which adapts traditional Chinese detailing with fun, modern sensibilities. Check out the stylish silk evening bags and scarves with delicate hand-embroidered butterflies and playful animal-design shoulder bags (from RMB 200 up to RMB 1,000). There's also a range of natural bamboo lifestyle products and clothing, and organic cotton baby gear from Wobabybasics (www.wobabybasics.com).

Shanghai Tang

59 Maoming Nan Lu, by Changle Lu, French Concession (5466 3006/www.shanghaitang.com). Metro Shanxi Nan Lu. **Open** 10am-10pm daily. **Credit** AmEx, DC, MC, V. **Map** p247 F7.

The famous Hong Kong brand (with outlets in New York, London, Paris, Tokyo et al) excels in traditional China with a kitsch twist. The shop itself is a sultry space of dark wood, bright chinoiserie and delicate wafts of ginger flower essence. Wares range from leather coats to silk-covered diaries, but the most popular buys are the signature reversible 'double fish' motif velvet Tang jackets and custom-made *qipaos* from the Imperial Tailor department. The labels may read 'Made by Chinese' but, be warned, prices are wholly Fifth Avenue.
Other locations No.15, North Block, 181 Taicang Lu, by Xingye Lu, Xintiandi (6384 1601).

Shiatzy Chen

Nine on the Bund, 9 Zhongshan Dong Yi Lu, by Guangdong Lu, the Bund (6321 9155/www.shiatzy chen.com). Metro Nanjing Dong Lu. **Open** 10am-10pm daily. **Credit** AmEx, DC, MC, V. **Map** p247 F7.

This Taiwanese-born designer takes Qing Dynasty collars and intricately embroidered silk one step further with very traditional, yet elegant and stylish attire straight out of a modern-day Forbidden City. Perfect for that high-class costume party, men's jackets go for around RMB 5,000.
Other locations Unit D, 59 Maoming Nan Lu, by Changle Lu, French Concession (5466 1266).

Source

158 Xinle Lu, by Fumin Lu, French Concession (5404 3808/www.thesource.cn). Metro Shanxi Nan Lu. **Open** 10am-10pm daily. **Credit** AmEx, DC, MC, V. **Map** p246 D7.

For sneaker junkies and shoppers looking for edgy urban gear, this two-floor industrial-style store-cum-gallery space has the goods. Find such trendy international brands as Addict, Onitsuka Tiger and Insight on the rails. There's also an in-house denim factory where you can get a pair of bespoke jeans in 24 hours for around RMB 900.

Fashion accessories & services

The city's markets are a good place to stock up on low-cost pashminas, fun jewellery, belts, bags and tights. For genuine pashminas, cashmere and silk scarves, and shawls in an array of colours and patterns, try **Woo** (Room 316, Building 1, Highstreet Loft, 508 Jianguo Xi Lu, French Concession, 5465 9325, www.wooscarf.com). Family-run **Tree** (90 Shaoxing Lu, by Ruijin Er Lu, French Concession, 6433 2795; 74 Fuxing Xi Lu, 126 Wulumuqi Nan Lu, French Concession, 6467 1758) is also a favourite for soft natural leather bags, belts, wallets and accessories in a palette of earthy tones.

Dry cleaning

With Shanghai being China's premier city of business, one of the city's boom industries is dry cleaning – someone has to wash all those suits, after all. So if you keep an eye out, you'll probably find one within walking distance of where you are staying. Prices are low, around

Where To Find World's Top Bespoke?

In the market for a custom-made suit? Be preparde to drop some dough. Depending on the location, size and materials used, your bespoke suit can run you several thousand dollars. Here are some of the world's best.

Milan	*Brioni Bespoke*	London	*Kilgour*
Paris	*Galeries Lafayette*	Hong Kong	*Custom Tailoring by Hemrajant*
Shanghai	***Dave K.C. SHIUNG***	Dubai	*Royal Fashions*
Los Angeles	*Anto Distinctive Shirtmaker*	Sydney	*J.H. Cutler*
New York, Beverly Hills	*Turnbull and Asser*	Atlanta	*Custom Clothing of Atlanta*

Shanghai Tailoring History

Full Circle

In 2003, *Dave K.C. Shiung*, originally an apprentice to one of those long-gone master tailors of old Shanghai, brought his shop back the source of his master's training. With his little shop on Wuyuan road in the old French Concession, Dave keeps the tradition of those old masters alive today and continues to pass on the same techniques and values to the next generation of Shanghai tailors.

Suit Yourself

There is a simple explanation why Shanghai, once synonymous with custom tailoring, now has far fewer tailors than Hong Kong: the Mao suit (or the Sun Yat-sen suit, as it's known in China).

Things quickly turned sour for Shanghai's famed custom tailors in the late 1940s. According to China's most celebrated tailor, *Dave KC Shiung*, the golden age of the Shanghai tailor began to unravel with the occupation of Shanghai by the Japanese in 1937, and ended once and for all in the following decade. The city's traditonally trained custom tailors, shorn of custom and inspiration, left to seek more fashion conscious pastures. Most ended up in Hong Kong, giving the city its modern-day reputation as Asia's tailoring capital...

by Christian Edwards (China International Business Magazine), Sep 2007
For more information, please check www.tailordave.com

The Only, Original, Authentic Dave

Is this man really the world's best tailor?

SHANGHAI – Officially this is the Xuhui District, but things don't seem to have changed much since it was part of the French Concession. From this stretch of Wuyuan Road you dom't see showy skyscrapers or shopping malls. Only walled lanes and leafy trees and those vaguely Mediterranean villas thatlook like they belong in Beverly Hills. There are a lot of foreign consulates around here, and a lot of businesses that cater to them...

by Marilise Gavenas (DNR Textile Report), Jan 2006
For more information, please check www.tailordave.com

RMB 30 per item, and the time taken can vary from one day to five. Well-known chains to look for are Meifeng (often located in the corner of the local Lianhua or Hualian supermarket chains) and Elephant King.

Elephant King

107 Nandan Dong Lu, by Tianyaoqiao Lu, Xujiahui (6469 9773/www.xiangwang.com.cn). Metro Xujiahui. **Open** 8.30am-9pm daily. **No credit cards.** **Map** p246 B12.
This Taiwanese chain is well established and trustworthy. Expect to pay around RMB 35 for your items, with service requiring up to five days. **Other locations** throughout the city.

Shanghai Jazz Cleaner

Unit 203A, Shanghai Centre, 1376 Nanjing Xi Lu, by Xikang Lu, Jingan (1333 193 5332 mobile). Metro Jingan Temple. **Open** 7.30am-9.30pm daily. **No credit cards.** **Map** p243 E5.
Shanghai Jazz Cleaner is an established favourite of the expat community, who are more than happy to hand over their cherished evening gowns and dinner jackets. Service takes three days, and the average price is RMB 35 per item.
Other locations Carrefour, 269 Shuicheng Nan Lu, by Yanan Xi Lu, Gubei; 1500 Huaihai Zhong Lu, by Huashan Lu, French Concession (6437 4862).

Jewellery

The Old City and the pedestrianised section of Nanjing Dong Lu that runs inland of the Bund are home to several multi-storey, state-run jewellery operations. Unfortunately, the counters in these places are typically tended by surly and unhelpful staff. If you want to brave it, try **Lao Miao** (462 Nanjing Dong Lu, by Shanxi Nan Lu, the Bund, 6352 7768, www.laomiao.com.cn) and **Chow Tai Fook** (300 Huaihai Zhong Lu, by Madang Lu, Xintiandi, 6335 3570, www.ctf.com.cn), both of which have heaps of precious metals, diamonds, jade and pearls.

For smoother service and concomitantly higher prices, visit **Tiffany & Co** (D116, City Plaza, 1618 Nanjing Xi Lu, by Jiaozhou Lu, Jingan, 6288 2748, www.tiffany.com); the **Cartier** flagship on the ground floor of Bund 18 (18 Zhongshan Dong Yi Lu, by Nanjing Dong Lu, the Bund, 6323 5577) or the multitude of pearl stalls that throng **Pearl City** (2-3/F, Shanghai Travelling Building, 558 Nanjing Dong Lu, by Fujian Zhong Lu, the Bund, 6322 3911, www.shanghaipearlscity.com). For more unusual designs, browse the various boutiques around Taikang Lu – men may even find something that pleases among the chunky stainless steel and titanium pieces at **JIP** (no.51, Lane 210 Taikang Lu, by Sinan Lu, French Concession, 6445 4479).

AmyLin's Pearls & Jewellery

3rd floor, 580 Nanjing Xi Lu, by Chengdu Lu, Jingan (5228 2372/www.amy-pearl.com). Metro Nanjing Xi Lu. **Open** 9am-8.30pm daily. **Credit** AmEx, DC, MC, V. **Map** p243 G5.
Graced by pictures of the foreign dignitaries, celebrities and VIPs – Bill Clinton, and Tony and Cherie Blair among them – who have shopped at AmyLin's, this is Shanghai's foremost pearl dealer. Here you'll find natural pink, white and lilac varieties or, for those with more adventurous tastes, dyed green, yellow and black Zhejiang freshwater strands. Amy's prices (around RMB 80 to RMB 250) include custom stringing and the staff speak good English.
Other locations 2002 Century Avenue, inside Metro Stop Science & Technology Museum, Pudong (6862 2226); 39 Yili Nan Lu, by Guyang Lu, Minhang (6275 3954).

Marion Carsten Silver Jewellery

Suite 106, Building 3, 210 Taikang Lu, by Ruijin Er Lu, French Concession (6415 3098). Metro Shanxi Nan Lu then walk/taxi. **Open** 10am-6pm daily. **Credit** AmEx, DC, MC, V. **Map** p247 F10.
German expat Marion Carsten spent four years studying the art of the goldsmith in Dusseldorf. Her chokers and matching bracelets are hand-assembled and finished, using inventive combinations of silver mixed with suede, leather and fresh-water pearls.

NoD

Unit 3, no.25, North Block, 181 Taicang Lu, by Huangpi Nan Lu, Xintiandi (6326 2140). Metro Huangpi Nan Lu. **Open** 10.30am-10.30pm daily. **Credit** AmEx, DC, MC, V. **Map** p248 H7.
Shanghainese designer Jiang Qiong Er says that her aim is to 'bridge the abyss separating the commonplace and the extraordinary'. Quite right too. What that means in practice is bold, striking necklaces and earrings fashioned out of such mundane elements as stainless steel, screw nuts and even washers. You'll be able to find a different collection from the same designer at the Younik boutique in the Bund 18 building (18 Zhongshan Dong Yi Lu, by Nanjing Dong Lu).

Shoes

Shanghai's affordable and dazzling footwear is enough to bring out the Imelda Marcos in all of us – although sizes can be a problem. Chinese have dinky feet, so even if a size 39 is in stock it's going to feel like a 38. Quality is also variable. Don't be fooled by upmarket-looking boutiques: they'll take your RMB 300 and your shoes will still fall apart in a few months. The best tip is to bargain hard and remember the same shoes can be got for RMB 60 a pair in the markets (there's an entire basement devoted to cheap trendy shoes at Qipu Lu Market, *see p133*). For cheap shoes (RMB 70) and sizes up to 41 (UK: 7; US: 912), head to the shoe stall at Shanxi Nan Lu metro station (exit 2) at the entrance to the Parkson department store's

supermarket. More refined fashion-conscious feet should make an appointment with local designer **Mary Ching** for a pair of killer heels (www.marychingshanghai.com).

100 Change & Insect

318 Nanchang Lu, by Maoming Nan Lu, French Concession (6467 3677). Metro Shanxi Nan Lu. **Open** 10.30am-10.30pm daily. **No credit cards.** **Map** p247 F8.
This Hong Kong chain has fresh styles for guys and gals. Don't be put off by the name: the designs are fashion-streets ahead of the rest of the city's offerings. You can expect to pay around RMB 400 for some funky footwear, double that for boots.
Other locations 380 Changle Lu (6267 0789); 76 Xinle Lu (5404 0767).

Gloss

Unit 5, 1/F, 123 Xingye Lu, Xintiandi (6384 1066/www.thegloss.ch). Metro Huangpi Nan Lu. **Open** 11am-10pm daily. **Credit** AmEx, DC, MC, V. **Map** p247 H7.
For the real McCoy limited-edition Nikes, Adidas and other hip sneaker brands, head to Gloss in Xintiandi.

Hot Wind

108 Shanxi Nan Lu, by Changle Lu, French Concession (5403 6909/www.hotwind.net). Metro Shanxi Nan Lu. **Open** 10am-10pm daily. **No credit cards.** **Map** p247 E7.

Hot Wind stocks a broad assortment of discounted men's and ladies' footwear from such international favourites as Nine West, Timberland, Merrell, Prada and Fendi. The crowded store also stocks a decent selection of outdoor and camping gear.
Other locations throughout the city.

Suzhou Cobblers

Room 101, 17 Fuzhou Lu, by Zhongshan Dong Yi Lu, the Bund (6321 7087/www.suzhou-cobblers.com). Metro Nanjing Dong Lu. **Open** 10am-6pm daily. **Credit** AmEx, DC, MC, V. **Map** p245 M5.
Suzhou Cobblers is an emporium of exquisite hand-made silk slippers, which can be worn both at home and around town. Mary Janes and mules feature Suzhou embroidery, including 'double fish', floral and vegetal designs with charming bags to match. Like their stuff but run out of suitcase space? Purchases can also be made at the online store.

Wang Hand Craft

11 Xianxia Lu, by Yan'an Xi Lu, Changning (6229 3916). Metro Loushanguan Lu. **Open** 10.30am-10pm daily. **Credit** MC, V.
For fine leather shoes, take your imaginings to Wang Hand Craft. The meticulous cobblers who staff the place will mould footwear to your exact specifications – copying existing shoes or reproducing them from magazine cuttings. Expect to pay RMB 1,000-plus for a solid, sturdy pair of shoes.

Estune. *See p137.*

Food & drink

Shanghai No.1 Foodstore (*see below*), **Shanghai Changchun Foodstore** (*see below*) and **Shanghai No.2 Foodstuff Shop** (955-965 Huaihai Zhong Lu, by Shanxi Nan Lu, French Concession) are as much sightseeing experiences as shops – the same goes for the city's many wet markets (*see p132*). For Western foodstuffs, try **City Shop**, which has outlets at the Shanghai Centre (map p243 E5) and in Printemps department store (939-947 Huaihai Zhong Lu, by Shanxi Nan Lu, French Concession, 6431 0118), or French hypermarché **Carrefour**, which has a large branch in Gubei (269 Shuicheng Nan Lu, by Yanan Xi Lu, Gubei, 6209 8899).

There are now also numerous smaller Western-style delis and convenience stores to satisfy expat cravings – one of the most popular being **Fei Dan** (382 Dagu Lu, by Chongqing Nan Lu, 6340 6547). The delicious meat pies from **Slice** (1/F, Shanghai Times Square, 99 Huaihai Lu, by Xizang Nan Lu, Xintiandi, 6386 8588) will also fill a hole. For freshly baked baguettes, tarts and other mouth-watering French treats, get a take away or eat in at **Paul** (*see p109*). *See also p145* **Tea-time**.

Cheese & Fizz
Unit 105, North Block, 119 Madang Lu, by Taicang Lu, Xintiandi (6336 5823). Metro Huangpi Nan Lu. **Open** 10am-12.30am daily. **Credit** AmEx, DC, MC, V. **Map** p248 H7.
Pick up imported and pricey delicacies (RMB 60-80 for 100g of cheese) ranging from over three dozen French cow, goat and ewe-milk cheeses to Italian artichoke hearts, olives and biscuits. Pair them up with a bottle of French, New World or Italian vino. French/Chinese duo Clarence and Glendy also sell freshly baked quiches, rustic pâté and crusty baguettes to eat in or take away.

Epicvre
98 Xinle Lu, by Fumin Lu, French Concession (5404 7719/www.epicvre.com). Metro Shanxi Lu. **Open** 10am-11pm daily. **Credit** AmEx, DC, MC, V. **Map** p246 D7.
One of many fine-wine retailers to have appeared on the scene in recent years, Epicvre offers an impressive handpicked collection of French wines. There's also a menu of gourmet sweets and snacks that will nicely complement the grape.
Other locations 116 Nanchang Lu, by Yandang Lu, French Concession (5306 8365).

Huangshan Tea Company
605 Huaihai Zhong Lu, by Gusi Nan Lu, Xintiandi (5306 2974). Metro Huangpi Nan Lu. **Open** 9am-10pm daily. **Credit** AmEx, DC, MC, V. **Map** p248 H7.
Specialists in high-grade Chinese teas, sold by weight. The store also carries an assortment of classic teapots, made in the town of Yixing, 193km (120 miles) north-west of Shanghai. After a few years' use you can supposedly brew tea just by pouring water into the pot, such is their ability to absorb flavour.

Shanghai Changchun Foodstore
619-625 Huaihai Zhong Lu, by Sinan Lu, French Concession (5386 4940). Metro Shanxi Nan Lu. **Open** 9am-10pm daily. **No credit cards**. **Map** p247 G7.
This local classic is a good place to check out favourites like dried meats (often spicy) or supersweet sesame or mixed nut cakes. It usually offers tastings, but beware, what looks like chocolate may turn out to be red bean or, worse, sweetened meat.

Shanghai No.1 Foodstore
720 Nanjing Dong Lu, by Guizhou Lu, People's Square (6322 2777). Metro Renmin Park or People's Square. **Open** 9.30am-10pm daily. **Credit** AmEx, DC, MC, V. **Map** p244 K4.
Operating since 1954, this massive food store on the pedestrian stretch of Nanjing Dong Lu west of the square sells domestic and imported products. The ground-floor sprawl stocks everything from freshbaked goods and dried fungus to salted fish and Dove chocolate bars. Pay-by-weight nuts and preserved fruits are particularly popular. Tobacco and spirits are available, in addition to supplies of Eastern and Western health remedies.

Eat, Drink, Shop

Gifts & souvenirs

Decorative chopsticks, mini tea sets, fans, embroidered textiles... with such a wealth of trinkets, gift shopping should prove no problem for even the most unimaginative of tourists in Shanghai. Markets aside, the place to browse for presents, and home accents, is the French Concession, particularly along Fuxing Xi Lu and Julu Lu, not forgetting the characterful shops at arty Taikang Lu.

Arts & handicrafts

China is famed for its production of fine silk, embroidery and ceramics, not forgetting traditional scroll paintings, batik, carpets and rattan. There's heaps to choose from at the **Yuyuan Bazaar** (*see p133*), but the goods are mainly mass-produced on the cheap so be sure to bargain hard. Also check out **Ju Roshine Life Art Space** (56 Maoming Nan Lu, by Changle Lu, French Concession). If chintz is not your style, Taikang Lu is full of more tasteful handicrafts at higher prices. The contemporary art scene is also taking off in a big way – roam the network of independent galleries that fill the warehouses along Moganshan Lu.

See also p144 **House & home**.

Brocade Country

616 Julu Lu, by Xiangyang Lu, French Concession (6279 2677/www.brocadecountry.com). Metro Shanxi Nan Lu. **Open** 10am-7pm daily. **No credit cards**. **Map** p243 E6.

Liu Xiaolan has filled this store with handicrafts from her minority community, the Miao, who inhabit the southern province of Guizhou. Pick up intricate tapestries or second-hand embroidered jackets, even some antique items for RMB 100-1,000.

Calico Cat

597-9 Fuxing Zhong Lu, by Shanxi Nan Lu, French Concession (6433 6638/www.calicocat.cn). Metro Shanxi Nan Lu. **Open** 10.30am-8.30pm daily. **Credit** AmEx, DC, MC, V. **Map** p246 A7.

As the name rightly suggests, this is a quirky little place. Using the blue and white fabric that is characteristic of Jiangsu province, designer Xing Xiuping has created a whole range of playful designs on bags, purses, tablecloths and clothing. Tailor-made outfits can be prepared within a week for around RMB 600 a set.

Other locations No.2, Lane 248, Taikang Lu, by Sinan Lu, French Concession (5465 7120).

Chinese Ink Painting Shop

134 Nanchang Lu, by Sinan Lu, French Concession (5386 3997). Metro Huangpi Nan Lu, then 15mins taxi/walk. **Open** 11.30am-5.30pm daily. **No credit cards**. **Map** p247 G7.

For a special China memento, pay a visit to local artist Liu Duojia whose beautiful calligraphy scrolls (which sell for between RMB 50 and RMB 100) have a more personal touch than the same old stuff that you'll find for sale at the markets.

Eddy Tam's Gallery

20 Maoming Nan Lu, by Jinxian Lu, French Concession (6253 6715). Metro Shanxi Nan Lu. **Open** 9am-9pm daily. **Credit** AmEx, DC, MC, V. **Map** p247 F7.

Specialising in the acquisition and custom framing of Chinese art, Eddy Tam's is the pick of the numerous galleries that make their homes along this stretch of Maoming Nan Lu. It carries lots of hand-painted Jinshan stencils (brightly coloured folk images) and is also the exclusive agent for local artist Xie Weimin, whose oeuvre includes watercolours of Shanghai buildings.

Shanghai Harvest Studio

Room 118, Building 3, Lane 210, Taikang Lu, by Zhaojiabang Lu, French Concession (6473 4566). Metro Shanxi Lu, then taxi/walk. **Open** 10am-6pm daily. **No credit cards**. **Map** p247 G12.

This quaint studio space sells a vibrant collection of Miao-embroidered home and fashion accessories, and traditional dress. Adding an element of authenticity, true Miao-minority girls sit busily sewing away in the background.

Spin

Building 3, Lane 758, Julu Lu, by Fumin Lu, French Concession (6279 2545). Metro Changshu Lu. **Open** 11.30am-10.30pm daily. **Credit** AmEx, DC, MC, V. **Map** p246 D6.

Spin capitalises on the rich ceramic heritage of China's clay capital Jingdezhen in Jiangxi province. The cool open interior stocks China Blue and other hand painted pieces crafted by a collective of designers, including Gary Wang (USA), Langshen Li and May Zhao (both Shanghainese). Their works incorporate Chinese themes in a sophisticated and subtle way. Prices are, for the most part, reasonable: salt and pepper shakers, say, for RMB 50 each or an abstract vase for around RMB 300.

Urban Tribe

133 Fuxing Xi Lu, by Wukang Lu, French Concession (6433 5366/www.urbantribe.cn). Metro Changshu Lu. **Open** 10am-10pm daily. **Credit** MC, V. **Map** p246 B8.

Run by local Shanghainese folk, this is a tranquil eco-friendly boutique-cum-gallery showcasing simple yet elegant home accents, boho clothing, jewellery and accessories. There are also striking photographic works for sale.

Other locations No.14, Lane 248, Taikang Lu, by Sinan Lu, French Concession (5465 1668).

Health & beauty

Parkson and **Carrefour** both stock decent selections of branded Western beauty and personal-care products. Otherwise, try one of Shanghai's several outlets of Sephora (*see p144*), Watson's (*see below*) or the department stores in malls (*see p130*). **Ba Yan Ka La** (Suite B1-b, 376 Wukang Lu, by Hunan Lu, French Concession, 6126 7600) also offers deliciously fragrant hair and body products, formulated from natural elements using the principles of Chinese herbal science.

Hairdressing

If you dare to brave one of the numerous local barbers, you can get a cut for around RMB 10 to RMB 30. But, unless you speak the language, you'll likely have difficulty communicating your requirements (plus staff won't be trained in handling Western hair types). Settle for a *xi tou* instead – a relaxing head massage and shampoo session. For those after familiar care and attention, there's a **Vidal Sassoon** (Building 16, 181 Taicang Lu, Xintiandi, 6311 2201) and two **Toni & Guy** salons (Shanghai Times Square, 98 Huaihai Zhong Lu, by Liulin Lu, Xintiandi, 5351 3606; and in the Shanghai Centre, map p243 E5).

Eric Paris Hairdressing & Beauty

4 Hengshan Lu, by Wulumuqi Lu, French Concession (6473 0900). Metro Hengshan Lu. **Open** 10am-8pm daily. **Credit** AmEx, DC, MC, V. **Map** p246 C9.
A refuge for expat ladies who've experienced far too many bad China-hair days to take any more risks. Relax in the safe hands of Eric and his well-trained, English-speaking staff. A cut and blow-dry goes for around RMB 400.
Other locations 3N 4-5, J-Life Mall, Jinmao Tower, 88 Shiji Dadao, by Yincheng Lu, Pudong (1376 139 0706 mobile).

Esprit Salon

301B CITIC Square, 1168 Nanjing Xi Lu, by Jiangning Lu, Jingan (5292 8800). Metro Nanjing Xi Lu. **Open** 10am-10pm daily. **Credit** AmEx, DC, MC, V. **Map** p243 E5.
Favoured by in-the-know expats for its affordable yet cutting-edge hairstyles. All the stylists have trained at Esprit in Hong Kong and most can speak English. Even better, discontented customers can return to the salon within seven days for the same service free of charge. Women's haircuts start from RMB 300.
Other locations Super Brand Mall, 168 Lujiazui Xi Lu, by Yincheng Xi Lu, Pudong (5049 3988); 4/F, 336 Xizang Zhong Lu, by Nanjing Dong Lu, People's Square (3330 3399).

ID Hair

274 Nanchang Lu, by Ruijin Er Lu, French Concession (3406 0490). Metro Shanxi Nan Lu. **Open** 10am-10pm. **Credit** MC, V. **Map** p247 F7.
This team of well-coiffed hairdressers, with English-speakers on board, will chop and style your tresses to perfection from just RMB 100. At the same time, flick through their selection of Western glossy mags and get your nails done.

Nanjing Cosmetology & Haircut Co Ltd

784 Nanjing Xi Lu, by Nanjing Xi Lu, Jingan (6253 2958). Metro Nanjing Xi Lu. **Open** 9am-9pm daily. **No credit cards**. **Map** p243 F5.
In business for more than 70 years, the Nanjing Cosmetology & Haircut Company is considered by locals to be the best in men's and women's hairdressing. The place has more than a whiff of history about it, with traditional barber stations on the ground floor, and ladies' cuts and colouring on the second, up a sweeping, balustraded staircase. Apart from the RMB 50 cut/wash/shave for men, prices are steep – a hairwash/massage (*toubu anmo*) will set you back RMB 75, but the price includes a 15-minute head and upper body massage. The list of services is available in English.

Pharmacies

Shanghai is packed with pharmacies, most of which sell both Western and Chinese medicine. They are also often open 24 hours, but **Shanghai No.1 Pharmacy** (616 Nanjing Dong Lu, by People's Square, 6322 4567) is an especially safe all-night bet. For medicinal herbal teas, try the **Herb Store** (152 Fumin Lu, by Julu Lu, French Concession, 5403 4458).
For **opticians**, *see p222*.

Fulintang Xinyidai

Unit 3, Suite 1A, South Block, 123 Xingye Lu, by Madang Lu, Xintiandi (6384 5987/www.fulintang. com). Metro Huangpi Nan Lu. **Open** 10am-midnight daily. **Credit** AmEx, DC, MC, V. **Map** p248 H8.
Although it has been around since the days of the Qing Dynasty, this venerable institution has these days adopted a modern approach to Chinese herbal medicine. Healthy ingredients are administered in the form of convenient snacks and floral teas. You could go for liver-relieving osmanthus tea, perhaps, or buy some soup packs and Chinese mushrooms coated with sweet sesame.

Tong Hang Chun Traditional Chinese Medicine Store

20 Yuyuan Xin Lu, by Jiuxiao Lu, Old City (6355 0308). **Open** 8.30am-9pm daily. **Credit** AmEx, DC, MC, V. **Map** p249 M7.
Established in 1783, Tong Hang Chun is the city's oldest medicine store. Large glass jars containing sea horses, antlers and placentas share space with modern-day over-the-counter medication. With everything labelled in Chinese and no English-speaking staff, you're best bringing someone who can translate or just browse through the bear bile powder and gnarly ginseng.

Watson's

787-789 Huaihai Zhong Lu, by Ruijin Yi Lu, French Concession (6431 8650/www.watsons.com.cn). Metro Shanxi Nan Lu. **Open** 9.30am-10.30pm daily. **Credit** AmEx, DC, MC, V. **Map** p247 F7.

Born in Hong Kong, this Western-style chain drugstore is a one-stop shop for toiletry and personal-care. In addition to everyday items like deodorants and razors, it also carries affordable make-up brands, Chinese and Western health remedies and teas, basic first-aid supplies, and the Scholl footcare line. **Other locations** throughout the city.

Shops

Face Shop

131 Maoming Lu, by Huaihai Lu, French Concession (6466 3756/www.thefaceshop.com). Metro Shanxi Nan Lu. **Open** 10am-10pm Mon-Sun. **Credit** MC, V. **Map** p247 F7.
This sweet-smelling South-Korean beauty chain is the Orient's answer to the Body Shop. In addition to its own-brand skin and hair care products, made with all-natural ingredients, there's a selection of well-priced cosmetics.
Other locations throughout the city.

Sephora

629 Huaihai Zhong Lu, by Ruijin Lu, French Concession (5306 6198/www.sephora.cn). Metro Shanxi Nan Lu. **Open** 10am-10pm Mon-Thur; 10am-11pm Fri, Sat. **Credit** AmEx, DC, MC, V. **Map** p247 F7.
The French beauty giant wholly satisfies the appetites of the beauty-driven masses, stocking top-of-the-range cosmetics, fragrances, and other beauty and skincare essentials. The choice here is far greater than in any of the department stores and it's always up-to-date with the latest names on the market.
Other locations throughout the city.

House & home

Annabel Lee

No.1, Lane 8, Zhongshan Dong Yi Lu, by Fuzhou Lu, the Bund (6445 8218/www.annabel-lee.com). Metro Nanjing Dong Lu. **Open** 10am-10.30pm daily. **Credit** AmEx, DC, MC, V. **Map** p245 M5.
Local designer and owner Feng Bo has spent a lot of time in Japan, and it shows in her smart, minimalist approach. Her simple yet elegant embroidered designs include fine linen place settings, raw silk travel pockets, cushions and business card holders, and sleek, silky pyjamas with jade buttons.
Other locations Unit 3, North Block, Lane 181, Taicang Lu, by Huangpi Nan Lu, Xintiandi (6320 0045); Okura Garden Hotel; Portman Ritz-Carlton; Four Seasons Hotel.

Blue Shanghai White

Unit 103, 17-103 Fuzhou Lu, by Zhongshan Dong Yi Lu, the Bund (6323 0856/www.blue shanghaiwhite.com). Metro Nanjing Dong Lu. **Open** 10.30am-6.30pm daily. **No credit cards**. **Map** p245 M5.
This is the sales space for Shanghai native Wang Hai Chen's distinctive furnishings, which combine blue and white porcelain with hand-polished antique pear wood. Fine celadon tea cups with handwoven

tassles are popular, as is the crockery with painted images of *shikumen*, the celebrated but quickly vanishing architecture of old Shanghai.

Casa Pagoda

15 Taikang Lu, by Sinan Lu, French Concession (6466 7521/www.casapagoda.com). Metro Shanxi Lu, then taxi/walk. **Open** 10am-8pm daily. **Credit** AmEx, DC, MC, V. **Map** p247 G10.
This slick home furnishings boutique gets the 'East Meets West' aesthetic just right. Combining chic European flavours with Asian traditions, there's a stylish mix of home furnishings to suit a range of modern and old-style interiors.

Jin

614 Julu Lu, by Xiangyang Lu, French Concession (6247 2964). Metro Shanxi Nan Lu. **Open** 11.30am-8pm daily. **Credit** MC, V. **Map** p243 E6.
There's a jumble of larger furniture pieces and dinky Chinese trinkets in this charming boutique. Between the travelling chests (RMB 600) and refined wood and rattan emperors' chairs (RMB 2,000), you'll find silk bags and delicate blue and white ceramics (RMB 100-300), plus cushions and little notebooks (RMB 40-60).

Madame Mao's Dowry

207 Fumin Lu, by Julu Lu, French Concession (5403 3551/www.madame-maos-dowry.com). Metro Changshu Lu. **Open** 10am-7pm daily. **Credit** AmEx, DC, MC, V. **Map** p246 C8.
Its English and Chinese owners conceived this as the kind of store in which Madame Mao – head of art and culture during the Cultural Revolution – might have shopped with her daughters. Two floors are filled with vintage posters, paintings and industrial propaganda, plus antique furniture and lifestyle products.

Shanghai Trio

House 6, 37 Fuxing Xi Lu, by Wulumuqi Nan Lu, French Concession (6433 8901/www.shanghai trio.com.cn). Metro Changshu Lu. **Open** 9am-6pm Mon-Fri. **Credit** AmEx, DC, MC, V. **Map** p246 C8.
Located in a charming old residence, this showroom is a sublime setting for the innovative creations of French owner/designer Virginie Fournier. Favourites include Fournier's silk pouches and her small silk cases in the shape of rice baskets. These – as well as other products such as the tablecloths (RMB 1,300), cushion covers (RMB 300) and baby clothes (RMB 200-500) – are fashioned from all-natural Chinese fabrics such as cashmere, linen, silk and cotton.
Other locations Unit 5, Building 1, Lane 181, Taicang Road, by Huangpi Nan Lu, Xintiandi (6355 2974).

Simply Life

Unit 101, 159 Madang Lu, by Taicang Lu, Xintiandi (6387 5100/www.simplylife-sh.com). Metro Huangpi Nan Lu. **Open** 10.30am-11.30pm daily. **Credit** AmEx, DC, MC, V. **Map** p248 H7.
A city-wide chain that provides one-stop shops for pricey but high-quality Chinese-style home decor products and gifts. Choice items include house-brand

Tea-time

Served endlessly with every meal, used in traditional ceremonies, and touted for its medicinal properties and health benefits, tea drinking is an integral part of the Chinese way of life – and has been for millennia. To get properly acquainted with the national drink, your first port of call should be **Shanghai Dabutong Tianshan Tea City** (518 Zhongshan Xi Lu, by Yuping Nan Lu, Changning, 6259 9999, www.dabutong.com), a labyrinth of stalls selling tea leaves of every imaginable variety – green, red, black, wulong, or one of countless aromatic brews. Vendors are friendly and happy to let you try before you buy; you might even want to snap up a cute tea set to complement your newfound taste.

Tea houses and stalls crowd the area around **Yu Gardens** (see p67) but for fine teas in more stylish packaging, stock up at **Song Fang Maison de Thé** (227 Yongjia Lu, by Shanxi Lu, French Concession, 6433 8283; pictured), which sells high-end tea leaves in cool turquoise tins, decorated with the shop's pseudo-Communist logo. Look out for the fine black keemun tea, a cavity-fighter packed with fluoride. **Huangshan Tea Company** (see p141) in Xintiandi, another purveyor of high-quality leaves, is renowned for its traditional teapots from Yixing.

The city's oldest and most famous teahouse is the **Huxinting Teahouse** (see p68), picturesquely planted in the middle of a lake by the Yu Gardens. All manner of VIPs (including Queen Elizabeth II, Bill Clinton and Gerhard Schröder) have had a brew here. Order a pot of jasmine (considered an antidepressant), and watch the flower of this soothing tea slowly unfold in the hot water. A cuppa in more peaceful surrounds can be had at the lovely **Old China Hand Reading Room** (see p108); slurp your way to smooth skin and slim limbs with a cup of metabolism-increasing oolong tea.

Tea aficionados from around the world unite for ceremonies, seminars and exhibits at the annual **International Tea Culture Festival** (see p150), held around the end of April in the Zhabei district. Enthusiasts wanting to get close to the source should book a room near the tea plantations in the Hangzhou Hills (home to China's most famous green tea, long jing, thought to work wonders for your kidneys) at the luxurious **Fuchun Resort** (Hangfu Yangjiang Road, Hangzhou, 0571 6346 1111, www.fuchunresort.com).

A word of warning: don't accept invites to tea ceremonies, most common around touristy areas like the Yu Gardens. It may appear innocent but it's likely to be a big fat scam. Some unlucky foreigners have been whacked with bills for thousands of RMB at the end of the ceremony.

Eat, Drink, Shop

silk boxes, place settings, appliqué greeting cards, embroidered pillows and glazed ceramic crockery sets and vases. The flagship store is in Xintiandi; on top of the usual range it also stocks hot local fashion brand insh, as well as high-end imports from the likes of Alessi and Bodum.

Other locations 9 Dongping Lu, by Hengshan Lu, French Concession (3406 0509).

Antiques

Genuine antiques are hard to come by in Shanghai – the city is better known for the restoration of old furniture. The Chinese also have a knack for making things look old and weathered even when they're not. Along Hongqiao Lu and Wuzhong Lu in the far-western Hongqiao/Gubei district are a number of reputable dealers with immense warehouses of furniture both old and new. Government-owned **Shanghai Antique & Curio Store** (192-240 Guangdong Lu, by Henan Zhong Lu, the Bund, 6321 5868) is also a safe bet for the real thing, and will provide insurance and shipping services. For antiques of a smaller and more portable nature, it's worth scouring the junkier stalls and shops of **Dongtai Lu Antiques Market** (*see below*). Note that foreigners are not allowed to take anything out of the country that's more than 200 years old; it is thus essential that you ensure your piece carries the official red seal of authenticity and you have the right export documentation.

Annly's Antique Warehouse

No.68, Lane 7611, Zhongchun Lu, by Husong Lu, Hongqiao (6406 0242/www.annlyschina.com). **Open** 9am-6pm daily. **Credit** AmEx, DC, MC, V.
If you are good at bargaining, there are plenty of deals to be had here. There's a wide choice of pieces from the close of the 19th century, and fewer reproductions than in the other warehouses along this stretch.

Dongtai Lu Antiques Market

Dongtai Lu & Liuhekou Lu, by Xizang Nan Lu, Xintiandi. Metro Huangpi Nan Lu. **Open** 9am-6pm daily. **No credit cards. Map** p248 J7.
Only a fraction of what you see here could qualify as antique, but this is still a great place to pick up Mao memorabilia, fake propaganda posters, imitation porcelain, little Buddhas, snuff bottles and other interesting curios. Reputable dealer Chine Antiques has an outlet at 38 Liuhekou Lu.

Henry's Studio & Antiques

359 Hongzhong Lu, by Wuzhong Lu, Hongqiao (6401 0831/www.antique-designer.com). **Open** 9am-6pm daily. **Credit** AmEx, DC, MC, V.
If it's choice you want, take a trip out to this furniture emporium. We're talking 4,000sq m (43,000sq ft) of warehouse, displaying over 2,000 pieces of beautiful antique and new-design furniture. A local favourite for its good after-sales service.

Hu & Hu Antiques

No.8, Lane 1885, Caobao Lu, by Hongxin Lu, Hongqiao (3431 1212/www.hu-hu.com). Metro Xingzhong Lu (line 9). **Open** 9am-6pm daily. **Credit** AmEx, DC, MC, V.
Since 1998, sisters-in-law Lin and Marybelle Hu have been combing the countryside for stylish bits of antiquity to fill their large showroom and warehouse. There's a wide selection of furniture, from Anhui wedding beds to Shandong wine cabinets. Pieces are tastefully restored to customer specifications.

Music & entertainment

You're spoilt for choice for DVDs and CDs on Shanghai's streets. Of course, it's all fake and the quality varies wildly, so never pay more than around RMB 8. Serious music lovers will also be disappointed as there's little beyond the mainstream and the newest releases take time to appear. You can also stock up on cheap TV box sets and better quality films (RMB 10-RMB 15) at Movie World on Dagu Lu (by Chongqing Lu, Xintiandi) and the pointedly named Even Better than Movie World which is right opposite on Dagu Lu, or try Hollywood (25 Taikang Lu, by Sinan Lu, French Concession, 6467 3098).

Sport & fitness

Many malls reserve an entire floor for sporting gear, notably **Grand Gateway** (*see p130*) and **Raffles City** (*see p132*). **Hot Wind** (*see p140*) is good for outdoor and camping gear, as is **Wild Camel** (340 Changle Lu, by Ruijin Er Lu French Concession, 6258 6997).

Decathlon

393 Yinxiao Lu, by Longyang Lu, Pudong (5045 3888). Metro Longyang Lu. **Open** 9am-9pm daily. **Credit** AmEx, DC, MC, V.
It's a bit of a trek to Decathlon, but well worth it for the best choice of sportswear and sports equipment in the city, at reasonable prices.
Other locations 88 Xianxia Xi Lu, by Jianhe Lu, Hongqiao (6238 5511); 600 Lantian Lu, by Yunshan Lu, Pudong (5030 7558); 2 Shenbei Lu, by Humin Lu, Hongqiao (5442 5585).

Ye Huo

296 Changle Lu, by Ruijin Yi Lu, French Concession (5386 0591/www.yehuo.com). Metro Shanxi Nan Lu. **Open** 10.30am-10pm daily. **Credit** AmEx, DC, MC, V. **Map** p247 F7.
A camping store that stocks all the goods necessary for a weekend with Mother Nature. Good local brands – of which the best are Backpackers, Zealwood and Zebra – are cheap, and flawed or last-season foreign brands are also reasonably priced. English-speaking staff can suggest the best places in China to pitch your tent.

Arts & Entertainment

Features

Zendai Museum Of Modern Art.
See p163.

Festivals & Events

Get in on some messy merrymaking as Shanghai experiments with new events and fresh formats.

For the festival fanatic, Shanghai may prove to be a little disappointing. Fancying itself as a modern metropolis, the city pays little heed to traditional Chinese festivals; these occasions are marked by half-hearted celebrations, executed more out of duty than enthusiasm. Outside temple walls, religious holidays pass unnoticed by the largely secular Shanghainese.

Yet for a 'global city', Shanghai lacks the variety and quality of cultural goings-on enjoyed by other great cities – a weakness the municipal government is determined to put right. With the Expo 2010 on the horizon, Shanghai is on a mission to prove itself as hip and culturally rich as other international metropolises. The government has put its support (read: massive funding) behind new events such as the **ShContemporary** art fair and the **World Music Expo** – with impressive results. All the same, inexperienced organisers and ill-defined themes – the number of new festivals purporting to 'showcase Chinese contemporary culture' is dizzying – mean that many events offer no more than a glimpse of the city's huge potential. Gala openings attended by socialites fuelled on free champagne go with a bang, of course, while the barely marketed main-draw ends with a whimper.

Still, things are changing and there are festival gems to be found. Leading writers and thinkers are now coming through town thanks to the **Shanghai International Literary Festival**; large-scale music jamborees such as the **Yue Festival** are starting to take shape; and the **eArts Festival** is putting Shanghai on the international digital art radar. The city has also recently played host to some interesting experiments. **Nuit Blanche**, the all-night culture jam hosted by over a dozen cities worldwide, experimented with a Shanghai edition in 2007, as did pro tennis organisation ATP, which held its prestigious **Masters Cup** tournament here until 2008 – a symbolic vote of confidence in the up-and-coming Chinese sports market.

As of 2008, China changed its public holiday schedule, making national holidays of three traditional festivals – **Qingming Jie**, the **Dragon Boat Festival** and the **Mid-Autumn Festival** – and shortening the May 'Golden Week' holiday to one day. Though the government cited respect for tradition as a key reason for the changes, the real spur was undoubtedly the need to ease burdens on China's tourism infrastructure. Citizens generally take advantage of Golden Weeks to travel, and the transport system, hotels and roads become overwhelmed by the masses. It is hoped that now, with only Chinese New Year and National Day as week-long breaks, the situation may improve. With three traditional festivals as new holidays, some hope more resources will be spent on them, resulting in better organised celebrations.

PRACTICALITIES

Traditional Chinese holidays follow a lunar calendar, meaning the dates change year by year and, though Chinese New Year and National Week are predictable, business hours during the celebrations vary, with many places closing for the whole week. Make travel plans well in advance: tickets sell out, prices can increase by as much as 50 per cent and many travel agents are closed. It's best to avoid tourist destinations altogether unless you enjoy the company of megaphone-wielding tour guides. For a list of **national public holidays**, *see p229.*

Up-to-date and accurate information on forthcoming events is hard to find, but the *Shanghai Daily* and *Shanghai Star* newspapers are good sources, as are the English-language magazines such as *City Weekend* (www.cityweekend.com.cn), *that's Shanghai* (www.thatssh.com) and *Shanghai Talk* (www.talkmagazines.cn). All can be found in the major hotels, as well cafés and restaurants catering to foreigners. Websites such as www.smartshanghai.com and www.shanghaiexpat.com are also good sources of information, the former covers entertainment happenings, the latter practicalities.

Concierge staff at high-end hotels usually speak English and keep a 'what's on' list. Purchasing tickets in advance may require sleuthing around. **MyPiao** (6126 0710, www.mypiao.com) and **Emma** (6481 2938, www.emma.cn) are good sources for major events, including big-name concerts and high-profile sporting events (both sites have English translations).

Spring

Lantern Festival

Yu Gardens, 218 Anren Jie, Old City (6355 9999).
Taxi or bus. **Admission** RMB 10. **No credit cards.**
Date 9 Feb 2009; 28 Feb 2010. **Map** p249 M7.
The Lantern Festival marks the end of winter and
is the last day of the Chinese New Year. It is custom-
ary to display a red lantern outside the home so that
the Taoist Lord of Heaven will visit to bestow luck
and happiness. The tradition of wandering the
streets with paper lanterns has largely died out but
Yu Gardens (Yuyuan; *see p67*) has a wonderful
selection of exquisitely crafted creations on display.
The festival is also known as Yuanxiao Jie, from
yuanxiao, which are dumplings filled with anything
from rose petals to bean paste to, our favourite,
zhima (black sesame paste). Families gather to eat
these round sweets symbolising reunion, harmony
and happiness. Make sure you try some. Note:
Yuyuan fills up quickly and the doors are shut to
prevent overcrowding, so arrive by late afternoon.

Shanghai International Literary Festival

Glamour Bar, 6th floor, 20 Guangdong Lu, by
Zhongshan Dong Yi Lu, the Bund (6350 9988/www.
m-restaurantgroup.com). Metro Nanjing Dong Lu.
Admission RMB 65 (incl 1 drink) per session. **No**
credit cards. **Date** 3 wknds Mar. **Map** p245 M5.
One of the city's most professionally executed and
best-loved festivals, Shanghai's Lit Fest, held in
Glamour Bar (*see p120*), has been gaining momen-
tum year after year, and now attracts boldface
names from around the globe. The last two editions
have seen the likes of Booker Prize winners
Arundhati Roy and Kiran Desai, as well as Gore
Vidal, Amy Tan, John Ralston Saul and James
Fallows. The festival also serves as a platform for
local and locally based authors such as Lijia Zhang,
Duncan Hewitt and Lynn Pan, making for lively dis-
cussions with diverse voices.

Shanghai Fashion Week/ Fashion Culture Festival

Various venues (6386 5748/www.sifc.org.cn/en).
Date mid-late Mar; late Oct-early Nov.
See p153.

Nanhui Peach Blossom Festival

289 Beimen Lu, Huinan Town, Nanhui (6802
9770/www.taohuajie.com). No.2 bus from Shanghai
Stadium. **Date** late Mar-early Apr.
The Nanhui district is home to hundreds of hectares
of peach trees, which come into full bloom in April.
People flock here to enjoy the pink blossom and take
in folksy festivities, including singing, dancing and
a 'Farmer's Wedding Performance'. The posh city
folk also like to marvel at quaint peasants tending
the trees and engaging in manual labour, inspiring
many of them to roll up their sleeves and head to the
Nongjia Le ('Peasant Happiness Home'), a kind of
model farm where city slickers can pick fruit and

Shanghai Fashion Week/
Fashion Culture Festival.

sample home-cooked pumpkin cakes and green
onion pastries. Nearby Shanghai Flower Port boasts
a version of Dutch tulip garden, Keukenhof.

Qingming Jie

Various temples & graveyards (6972 0010).
Date 4 Apr 2009; 5 Apr 2010.
Qingming has two meanings in Chinese: 'clear and
bright', and 'tomb sweeping'. The festival thus refers
both to enjoying springtime, as well as doing some
spring cleaning at the graves of the deceased. The
day is spent honouring ancestors by laying flowers,
and offering food and drink at their graves. Joss
paper is folded into shapes that are burned for the
dead as 'hell bank notes', providing a yearly 'living
allowance' for the deceased. As of 2008, Qingming
Jie is an official national holiday, and many businesses shut for the day (it is considered inauspicious
for commerce with so many spirits wandering the
earth). Traffic jams can cause acute gridlock on the
city's outer roads, so many families celebrate before
or after the actual date.

Longhua Temple Fair

Longhua Temple, 2853 Longhua Lu, by Longhua
Park, Xuhui (6456 6085). Metro Caobao Lu then
taxi. **Admission** free (outside the temple).
Date 2wks Apr. **Map** p240 C5.
This fair dates back to the Ming Dynasty and is the
largest of its kind in Shanghai. For two weeks –

Arts & Entertainment

Dragon Boat Festival.

starting on the third day of the third lunar month – rites are performed for Maitreya (the future and final Buddha) and grand Buddhist ceremonies are held at Longhua Temple (*see p87*), the largest and most well-preserved ancient temple in Shanghai. The fair includes street theatre, paper cutting, calligraphy, Chinese opera and a parade of mythological figures.

International Tea Culture Festival

Various venues (3303 0071/www.tea-sh.cn).
Date mid-late Apr.
Tea fanatics from around the world pour into Shanghai to attend tea ceremonies, seminars and exhibits. The activity centres around Zhabei Park in the northern Zhabei District of Shanghai, which is transformed into a tea appreciation zone, with various tasting opportunities and folk performances, plus tours of nearby tea fields.

BMW Asia Open

Tomson Golf Club, 1 Longdong Dadao, by Luoshan Lu, Pudong (5833 8888/www.bmw-golfsport.com/ www.tomson-golf.com). Taxi or bus. **Date** mid Apr.
Golf is increasingly popular in China, and this tournament hopes to establish itself as the region's major event. It's the first of BMW's four international competitions; the other ones are held in England, Germany and the USA. US$2.3 million in prize money attracts the big hitters: Tiger Woods, David Howell, John Daly and Zhang Lianwei have all competed.

World Music Expo

Shanghai Concert Hall, 523 Yanan Dong Lu, by Longmen Lu, People's Square (6466 8660/www. worldmusic.blogbus.com). Metro People's Square.
Admission varies. **Date** late Apr-early May.
Map p244 J6.

Launched in 2008, this government-sponsored event is part of Shanghai's promotional amp-up for Expo 2010, which sadly means the last edition will be in 2010. Still, the Expo committee's eagerness to hype up Shanghai translates into some decent offerings. The 2008 edition focused on traditional music forms and brought ensembles from all corners of the Middle Kingdom to perform alongside the Royal Drummers of Burundi and Huun-Huur-Tu from Tuva. Organisers say more contemporary groups will enter the mix in the next two incarnations.

Birthday of Sakyamuni Buddha

Jingan Temple, 1686 Nanjing Lu, by Wanghangdu Lu, Jingan (6256 6366). Metro Jingan Temple.
Admission free. **Date** 2 May 2009; 21 May 2010.
Map p242 D5.
Public displays of faith are rare in Shanghai but the birthday of Sakyamuni Buddha ('Shijiamuni' in Mandarin) is an exception. Monks chant prayers and perform a ritual cleaning of their Buddhas.

KIA X Games

KIC Jiangwan Sports Centre, 346 Guohe Lu, by Zhengli Lu, Yangpu (962 388/www.kiaxgamesasia. com). Metro Jiangwan Zhen. **Admission** RMB 120; RMB 50 students. **No credit cards. Date** early May 2009.
BMX gets your blood pumping? Moto X puts your knickers in a knot? Then check out Asia's largest action sport event where pro adrenaline junkies ride, skate, jump and climb their daredevil way through the KIA X Games. The BMX stunt riding and flash bouldering events are especially nail-biting. KIA's title sponsorship expires after the 2009 Games, but insiders say the event is likely to continue, perhaps with a different backer. *Photo p152.*

Summer

Dragon Boat Festival

Suzhou Creek. **Date** 28 May 2009; 16 June 2010.
This national holiday celebrates poet Qu Yuan, who drowned himself in 278 BC to protest at government corruption. Legend has it that a fisherman threw small packets of rice wrapped in bamboo leaves into the water to prevent the fish eating his body. These glutinous rice snacks, *zongzi*, are still served as a reminder of Qu Yuan's noble sacrifice; bean paste, egg or pork varieties can be found steaming in little crock-pots at convenience stores. Exhilarating dragon boat races are held on the Huangpu River and Suzhou Creek. To join in the fun (no previous experience necessary) visit www.shanghaiexpat.com.

Shanghai International Film Festival (SIFF)

Various venues (6253 7115/www.siff.com).
Date mid June.
According to the International Federation of Film Producers Associations, the SIFF is the only 'A-grade' film festival in Asia. Though it isn't in the same league as Cannes or Berlin, the festival is starting to lure some big Western names to its red carpet. The event features a good mix of Chinese, Hollywood and independent international offerings. Be sure to check the programme's fine print: foreign films may be dubbed into Chinese and Chinese films may not have English subtitles. Premières can sell out quickly but nabbing last-minute tickets for regular screenings is often relatively easy.

Founding of the Chinese Communist Party

Museum of the First National Congress of the Chinese Communist Party, 374 Huangpi Nan Lu, by Xingye Lu, Xintiandi (5383 2171). Metro Huangpi Lu. **Date** 1 July. **Map** p248 H8.
Government newspapers run front-page editorials extolling the supreme glory of the People's Party, and old stagers organise ceremonies around the city, centred on the Museum of the First National Congress of the Chinese Communist Party (*see p75*).

Autumn

Kunshan Beer Festival

Kunshan Stadium, Kuntai Lu, by Dayang Qiao, Kunshan. Bus from Jinjiang Hotel (see p42).
Admission RMB 10. **Date** early Sept.
A rather sterile canal town, Kunshan rarely sees as much fun as during the Beer Festival. Expats from Shanghai flood the town for a weekend drowning themselves in suds. The festival features several biergarten, which come complete with Chinese waitresses in lederhosen. This is about as authentic as it gets: the food is passable (sauerkraut and spaetzle are served alongside Chinese fried rice and meat sticks), the beer selection limited and the antics fairly tame. Still, the kitsch is worth the journey. Prost!

ShContemporary

Shanghai Exhibition Centre, 1333 Nanjing Xi Lu, by Tongren Lu, Jingan (3222 0381/www.shcontemporary.info). Metro People's Square.
Date mid Sept. **Map** p243 E6.
In recent years, countless new art fairs and exhibitions have cropped up across the Middle Kingdom, all attempting to ride the Chinese contemporary art wave, and Shanghai is certainly no stranger to the trend. While the relatively young ShContemporary art fair (est. 2007) may belong to this group, it does boast significant government and corporate backers and, as such, puts together an impressive show, both organisationally and artistically. The 2008 edition saw artists and curators from 130 galleries and over 20 countries gather to rub shoulders, sip champagne, exchange *mingpian* (name cards) and, if all else failed, discuss art.

Formula 1 Grand Prix

Shanghai International Circuit, Anting, Jiading (9682 6999/www.icsh.sh.cn/www.f1china.com.cn). Taxi or bus. **Admission** RMB 380-3,980. **Credit** MC, V. **Date** 3 days late Sept.
The latest and most high-profile addition to the city's sporting calendar brings with it heaps of glamorous events and Chinese celebs. The US$450 million circuit itself has been the focus of much international attention – it is the most expensive motorsport circuit ever constructed and, what's more, seven-time world champion Michael Schumacher claimed it to be the best racetrack he's ever seen. Those without VIP invitations can catch a blurred glimpse of Hamilton, Massa et al at the circuit, a 40-minute drive north-west of the city centre. Shuttle buses are available (see website for details).

Yue Music Festival

Zhongshan Park (Zhongshan Gongyuan), Changning (www.yuefestival.com). Metro Zhongshan Park.
Admission RMB 100-360. **No credit cards.**
Date late Sept/early Oct. **Map** p240 B3.
When it comes to big music festivals, China still has a way to go. But as long as you're not expecting a Glastonbury or a Bonnaroo – but, rather, the equivalent of one or two of their stages – you'll be just fine. Beijing generally puts on the best audio ragers – Midi in May and Modern Sky in October are solid bets – but the Yue Festival (started in 2007) is getting Shanghai into the spirit. Faithless, Talib Kweli and Ozomatli have all played along with up-and-coming Chinese bands. The organisers are known for bringing over some of the best non-bubblegum Western pop you'll see in China, including the Infadels and Bugz in the Attic. Expect a largely expat crowd though – the locals are more likely to queue up for Maroon 5 and Avril Lavigne.

Shanghai Sweet-Scented Osmanthus Festival

Guilin Park, Caobao Lu, by Guilin Lu, Caohejing (6483 0910). Taxi or bus. **Date** late Sept-early Oct. **Map** p240 B5.

Arts & Entertainment

Unleash your free radicals at the **Kia X Games**. *See p150.*

Around the time of the Mid-Autumn Festival (*see below*), thousands of trees bloom in Guilin Park in the south-west of the city, releasing a heady, blissful fragrance. The former pleasure garden of gangster Du Yuesheng becomes the stage for film screenings, martial arts demonstrations, acrobatics and fashion shows.

Shanghai Biennale

Shanghai Art Museum, 325 Nanjing Xi Lu, People's Square (6327 2829 ext 257/258/www.shanghai biennale.com). Metro People's Square. **Admission** RMB 20. **No credit cards**. **Date** Sept-Nov 2010 (even yrs).** Map** p244 H5.

The Shanghai Biennale was launched in 1996 as a showcase for Chinese art, but since 2000 it has become an international affair. Its curatorial team, and its content, has diversified over the years, and recent themes include 'Techniques of the Visible' (2004) and 'Hyper-Design' (2006). The latter was a breakthrough for the event, featuring accessible interactive works that had people queuing hours in the hot September sun. Among the standout works was Liu Jianhua's *Yiwu Survey*, a large shipping container jutting out of the wall disgorging a flow of cheap plastic manufactured goods from Yiwu, the Yangtze River Delta's manufacturing centre. The 2008 theme 'Translocalmotion' promises to be of great relevance to Shanghai, which is a city of both immigrants and migrants. The 2008 Biennale will also commemorate the social history of People's Square (once the city racecourse), where it is held, with an exhibition composed of photos and stories supplied by local residents; and the square's parks and metro stations will host public art, as will other transport hubs such as the Shanghai Railway Station and Pudong Airport.

Mid-Autumn Festival

Yu Gardens, 218 Anren Lu, Old City (6355 9999). Taxi or bus. **Admission** free. **Date** 3 Oct 2009; 22 Sept 2010. **Map** p249 M7.

The Moon Festival (Zhongqiu Jie) is one of the most important dates on the Chinese lunar calendar, a time for family gatherings, moon-gazing and eating mooncakes, a rich, dense pastry stamped with pretty designs and filled with lotus seed paste, egg yolks or other sweet fillings (warning: mooncakes aren't to everyone's taste). Children are told the traditional myth: a fairy, who lives alone on the moon with her jade rabbit, is visited by a celestial general for whom she dances. Shadows visible on the moon during the festival are thought to be their silhouettes. It's generally a time to gather with families; but anyone can join in the welcoming of the harvest moon at the Yu Gardens, where seas of lanterns are on display.

National Week

The Bund, by Nanjing Dong Lu. Metro Henan Lu. **Date** 1-5 Oct. **Map** p245 M4.

National Week triggers an exodus from Shanghai as locals take advantage of the holiday to travel. Those who stay behind roam Nanjing Lu or Huaihai Lu assaulting each other with giant inflatable plastic hammers and setting off firecrackers.

Shanghai eArts Festival

Various venues (3226 0502/www.shearts.org). **Date** mid-late Oct.

The Shanghai eArts Festival means business. At its inception, it was China's first electronic arts festival; now it's the world's largest, proving the 'go big or go home' Shanghai attitude. Art installations are scattered around the city, parks host open-air film screenings, the Shanghai Oriental Arts Centre (*see p188*) showcases Chinese opera and digital media crossover performances, and giant LED screens on the Bund feature avant-garde works by foreign artists. The project has already attracted some heavyweight partners, with MIT, Pompidou Centre and Ars Electronica all in on the action.

Shanghai Fashion Week/ Fashion Culture Festival
Various venues (6386 5748/www.sifc.org.cn/en).
Date mid-late Mar; late Oct-early Nov.
Glamour-pusses and fashionistas strut around town in full regalia on their way to fashion shows and – more importantly – parties. Of course, unless you're an industry insider you're unlikely to get near any of the real movers and shakers. This is a government event and, fashion-wise, it's hardly a New York, Paris or Milan. On the plus side, the small-scale means that scoring a seat at local designers' shows or attending trade exhibitions can be as easy as calling the organisers.

Shanghai International Arts Festival
Various venues (6272 0702/0455/www.artsbird. com). **Date** mid Oct-mid Nov.
When compared to Hong Kong's world-class arts festival, Shanghai's seems a bit shabby. Classical music is the main draw (with big names like Yo-Yo Ma and Sir Simon Rattle), with miscellaneous Chinese opera, big-name Canto-pop stars, little-known international dance and theatre troupes, and obscure off-off-Broadway groups thrown in for fun.

Shanghai Art Fair
Shanghai Mart, 2299 Yanan Xi Lu, by Gubei Lu, Changning (6468 2778/www.cnarts.net/sartfair).
Taxi or bus. **Admission** RMB 30. **No credit cards.**
Date mid Nov. **Map** p240 B4.
The grand dame of Asian art gatherings, the Shanghai Art Fair draws crowds of over 50,000 that ooh and ahh at international contemporary pieces. The supermarket-style showing may offend purists, but there is an excellent selection of art on hand. And the shopping-aisle format is rather fitting for the Shanghai show, as all goods on display can be yours to take home – at a price, of course.

Toray Cup Shanghai International Marathon
The Bund (6629 8808/www.shmarathon.com).
Metro Nanjing Dong Lu. **Date** last Wed of Nov.
Map p245 M4.
In conjunction with the Health Promotion Festival, die-hard runners risk their lungs in the city's biggest street marathon. The event includes a less intense 21km (13-mile) half-marathon – plus a 4km (2.5-mile) fun run – for those not up to the long haul. Expect congested traffic, as many roads, including the Bund, are closed to accommodate the racers. In recent years, the Toray Cup has drawn 20,000 runners.

Winter

Chinese New Year
Various locations. **Date** 26 Jan 2009; 14 Feb 2010.
See below **Chinese New Year.**

Chinese New Year

Yuandan or Chunjie (Spring Festival), **Chinese New Year** is the biggest fixture on the Chinese calendar. Officially it lasts three days, and on the first day, families gather to eat special meals symbolising good fortune, prosperity and health. Typical dishes include dumplings (for luck), blood clams (wealth) and fish balls (family harmony).

For many foreigners, the thought of Chinese New Year conjures up festive images of red and gold dragons gaily wagging their heads to the sound of clanging cymbals. A quaint picture, certainly, but hardly representative of Chinese New Year (CNY) in modern Shanghai. Traditions have been gradually abandoned, with home-cooked dinners replaced by huge banquets in gilded seafood restaurants – and the soundtrack is provided less by cymbals than by the cacophonous Chujie Lianhua Wanhui, or Spring Festival variety show. It features garishly dressed Canto-pop crooners, obnoxious child performers and full-on song

and dance numbers extolling the exemplary virtues of the Chinese military.

China's new-found prosperity has – for better or worse – played a part in altering the traditions of CNY. In the past, when people said *nian nian you yu* ('may there be fish to eat every year') they really meant it. *Yu* ('fish') is a homophone for abundance and, during Mao's Great Leap Forward, CNY was the only time many families ate meat of any kind. Families began to prepare months in advance, travelling miles back to their *jiaxiang* ('home town'), painting New Year poems to hang either side of the front door, buying food, wrapping dumplings and rolling *tangyuan* (doughy dumplings served in soup).

At CNY, fireworks are set off to scare away evil spirits. To experience the pyrotechnic blowout get a window seat in a tall building or hotel – spots on the Bund afford good views, though think twice about heading that way if heaving crowds aren't your thing.

Arts & Entertainment

Children

Release your little emperor.

At first glance, Shanghai's imposing skyline threatens to dwarf everyone, especially tots. But this lack of dedicated children's attractions – can spring pleasant surprises on both parents and kids. The biggest attraction is without doubt the city itself: bustling markets, urban parks and fantastical skylines are scenes children will remember.

The low crime rate and efficient transport system help to make Shanghai family-friendly, although the climate can be a challenge – the oppressive humidity in summer and the chilling dampness in winter can drive tourists with children back into their climate-controlled hotel rooms. Fight the urge to cocoon. Instead, make the most of Shanghai's excellent shopping scene (with kids' bargains galore), markets, few but well-executed museums, river cruises and awe-inspiring acrobat troupes – not to mention the mountains of dazzling projects slated for the World Expo in 2010 (see pp23-25 **Expo 2010**).

PRACTICALITIES

Be sure to give your children a copy of the hotel address written in Chinese characters and the hotel phone number, just in case you get separated while out – English isn't widely spoken. The standards of public toilets range from revolting to reasonable, so carry pocket tissues and hand sanitiser, and aim for bathroom breaks in major hotels, chain restaurants or upscale shopping centres.

Prepare your children for the likelihood of being stared at by locals. Foreign children, especially those with blond hair and blue eyes, are still curiosities for many Chinese, particularly the older generations. It's a harmless fascination, but still a bit alarming when a stranger closes in to get a better look.

Where to stay

Shanghai's hotels primarily serve business travellers, and most hotels are configured accordingly. With advance notice, most high-end hotels can provide cribs, cots and highchairs. Babysitting is provided at some major hotels, however availability changes often. Be sure to confirm whether babysitting is offered before you make your reservation. Few hotels have play areas, and some may refuse to admit children to their swimming pools if there is no shallow end. Others, like the **Hilton** (250 Huashan Lu, by

Changshu Lu, French Concession, 6248 0000, www.hilton.com), admit children with parental supervision into the pool area.

The **Portman Ritz-Carlton** (see p36) and the **Westin** (see p31) are both accommodating towards young travellers. Both have children's menus, offer activity kits upon check-in and allow youngsters in the pool area (with adult supervision). In addition, the Westin has the best children's brunch in town. The Portman has a playroom on the eighth floor, and its Tea Garden restaurant has healthy mains for children.

The **Radisson Plaza Xing Guo** (78 Xing Guo Lu, by Hunan Lu, French Concession, 6212 9998, www.radisson.com), set among extensive grounds, is a quiet, amenity-rich hotel set in a peaceful, yet central, neighbourhood. The **Novotel Atlantis** (728 Pudong Avenue, by Fushan Lu, Pudong, 5036 6666, www.novotel. com) is the best child-friendly choice in Pudong. Its pool is open to children, and its brunch offers half-price grub for six- to 12-year-olds (free for under-sixes), along with a play area.

For families staying five days or more, a better bet may be a serviced apartment. Try the **Shanghai Centre Serviced Apartments** (Shanghai Centre, 1376 Nanjing Xi Lu, by Tongren Lu, Jingan, 6279 8502), which are in the heart of downtown and offer many child-friendly services.

Sightseeing

For child-friendly activities in Shanghai, go with the flow: the Huangpu River and the Bund and Pudong riverfronts hold the greatest concentration of attractions with child appeal. There are **riverboat tours** (see p47) and the surreal sound and light show of the **Bund Tourist Tunnel** (see p89) under the river. Once on the other side of the water in Pudong, there's the **Oriental Pearl Tower** (see p91), with its fantastic views and sci-fi looks, as well as the **Natural Wild Insect Kingdom** and **Shanghai Ocean Aquarium** (for both, see p155). Underneath the Pearl Tower is the **Shanghai History Museum** (see p92), which contains numerous interesting reconstructions of Old Shanghai streets. Another museum that justifies a trip to Pudong is the interactive **Science & Technology Museum** (see p93), three stops past the Oriental Pearl Tower on

Changfeng Ocean World.

Metro Line 2. It boasts IMAX theatres, sound and light displays, an indoor rainforest, a robot theatre and a hands-on children's 'technoland'.

On People's Square, the **Urban Planning Centre** (*see p60*) has a huge model of what city planners envisage for Shanghai by 2020.

Changfeng Ocean World

Gate 4, 21 Changfeng Park, 451 Daduhe Lu, by Jingshajiang Lu, Putuo (6223 8888/www.ocean world.com.cn). No.6 Tour Bus Line from Shanghai Stadium/Metro Zhongshan Park. **Open** 8.30am-5pm daily. **Admission** RMB 120; RMB 90 children; free children under 1m. **Credit** AmEx, DC, MC, V. **Map** p240 A3.

Still waters run deep at Changfeng Park, located a half-hour drive north-west of the city centre. Beneath its boating lake lies Ocean World (formerly Aquaria 21), an impressive Australian-owned aquarium with more than 10,000sq m (107,500sq ft) of tanks filled with fish, penguins and sharks, plus an adjoining 2,000-seat stadium with daily beluga whale shows. The foyer is designed like an aircraft cabin, and the aquarium's galleries take visitors on a flight of fancy to South America, through Inca temples, past waterfalls and across the Amazon basin before reaching fresh- and salt-water tanks. The park offers fine entertainment for all ages and is more interactive than its competitor, Shanghai Ocean Aquarium (*see below*). Visitors can take a glass-bottom boat tour or a simulator ride on an underwater rollercoaster, and older guests (over-tens) can arrange to swim with the whales or dive with the sharks. There is limited English signage, but exhibits speak for themselves.

Natural Wild Insect Kingdom

1 Fenghe Lu, by Binjiang Avenue, Pudong (5840 5921/www.shinsect.com). Metro Lujiazui. **Open** 9am-5pm Mon-Fri; 9am-5.30pm Sat, Sun. **Admission** RMB 40; RMB 25 children; free children under 0.8m. **No credit cards. Map** p245 O4.

Slithering snakes, leaping lizards and snapping turtles fill the cages at the Insect Kingdom, which boasts 200-plus species of insects from as far afield as Africa and South America. Creepy crawlies are joined by monkeys, ferrets and cuddly rabbits.

Shanghai Ocean Aquarium

158 Yincheng Bei Lu, by Dongyuan Lu, Pudong (5877 9988/www.aquarium.sh.cn). Metro Lujiazui. **Open** 9am-5.30pm daily (until 8.30pm during summer holidays). **Admission** RMB 120; RMB 80 children 0.8m-1.4m; free for children under 0.8m. *Audioguide rental* RMB 15 with RMB 200 deposit. **Credit** MC, V. **Map** p245 P4.

Shanghai Ocean Aquarium has what you might call tunnel vision. The highlight of this state-of-the-art Chinese-Singaporean venture, one of the largest attractions of its kind in Asia, is a 155m (509ft) underwater clear viewing tunnel, which offers 270-degree views of sharks, turtles and exotic fish. The surrounding nine galleries plumb the depths of four oceans and five continents, and feature 15,000 fish representing 360 species, with a special section devoted to species from China's own Yangtze River.

Shanghai Zoo

2381 Hongqiao Lu, by Hami Lu, Hongqiao (6268 7775/www.shanghaizoo.cn). Bus 925 from People's Square/No.4 Tour Bus Line from Shanghai Stadium. **Open** *Nov-Feb* 7am-5pm daily. *Apr-Sept* 6.30am-

5.30pm daily. *Mar, Oct* 7am-5.30pm daily.
Admission RMB 30; free admission for children under 1.2m with paying adult; admission with elephant show RMB 40. **No credit cards**. **Map** p240 A4.

Compared to its snazzy Western counterparts, the atmosphere of Shanghai's zoo is drab and institutional. Even star attractions among its 600-plus species, like the giraffes and giant pandas, occupy enclosures that resemble World War II bunkers. Fortunately, the extensive green grounds and flower gardens help to compensate. Once a British golf club, the former fairways now make pleasant picnic spots, and the water features provide a quaint home for geese, swans and other birds. While the children's zoo is lacklustre, the elephant and sea lion shows are entertaining, and a Ferris wheel provides a bird's-eye view of the park. By 2010, a new metro station will open on-site, providing easy connections to the city centre.

Parks & playgrounds

Because Shanghai is an unremittingly urban city, the relatively scarce public parks and squares are popular gathering spaces for all the generations and thus great for people-watching. Head with the kids to the **Bund** (*see pp48-55*) to watch the sword- and fan-wielding tai chi groups in the morning and to **People's Square** (*see pp56-62*) for kite flyers in the afternoon. These activities are not staged for tourists' benefit; they are poignant glimpses of life in the 'real China' that both children and parents will long remember.

Century Park
1001 Jinxiu Lu, by Shiji Dadao, Pudong (5833 5621/www.centurypark.com.cn). Metro Century Park. **Open** 16 Mar-15 Nov 7am-6pm daily. *16 Nov-15 Mar* 7am-5pm daily. **Admission** RMB 10; free children under 1.2m. **No credit cards. Map** p241 H4.

A veritable triathlon of fun awaits children at Shanghai's largest park. They can pedal their way through the park's 1.4sq km (0.5sq miles) on rented bicycles, covered pedal cars and tandems (RMB 30-80/hr), navigate the park's canals by electric boat (RMB 30-50), and soar through the skies on the kiddie rollercoaster in the amusement park (rides RMB 5-20). You can also engage in more traditional pursuits in a variety of designated areas, including fishing and picnicking.

Fuxing Park
2 Gaolan Lu, by Sinan Lu, French Concession (5386 0540 ext 0). Metro Huangpi Nan Lu. **Open** 6am-6pm daily. **Admission** free. **Map** p247 G8.

This park's broad promenades remain virtually unchanged since families from the surrounding French Concession pushed their prams under the same towering plane trees a century ago. More modern additions include a rose garden, amusement rides and remote-controlled model boats.

Zhongshan Park
780 Changning Lu, by Yuyuan Lu, Changning (6210 5806). Metro Zhongshan Park. **Open** Oct-Mar 6am-6pm daily. *Apr-June* 5am-6pm daily. *July-Sept* 5am-7pm daily. **Admission** free.

This park offers good year-round entertainment for children. Its spectacular indoor playground, Fun Dazzle (open 9am-5pm), with tunnels, mazes and slides galore, is a great fallback when it's too cold to wander the park's meandering paths or ride the outdoor carousel, motor boats and dodgem cars.

Eating & drinking

Shanghai has plenty to appease small, grumbling stomachs – and knives and forks are available more often than not. When it comes to fast food, Chinese children are just as crazy for McDonald's, KFC and Pizza Hut as their Western peers. If you're visiting the child-friendly sights of Pudong, check out the neighbouring **Super Brand Mall** (Lujiazui Xi Lu, by Yincheng Xi Lu), which houses fast-food standbys, Asian fare and a branch of the reliable expat favourite **Blue Frog** (*see p124*). For a snack with a view, you can stroll along the riverside promenade for ice-cream at **Häagen-Dazs** (Binjiang Avenue, by Pudong Nan Lu) or hot pretzels and other German food at the **Paulaner Brauhaus** (2967 Binjiang Avenue, by Fenghe Lu).

Back over the river in downtown Shanghai, expat magnet the **Shanghai Centre** (*see p141*) houses familiar chains such as Tony Roma's (6279 7129), a barbecue restaurant with a children's menu; California Pizza Kitchen (6279 8032), whose children's menu doubles as an activity book; and a branch of Element Fresh (*see p103*), purveyor of healthy pan-Asian and European food.

Put your chopstick skills to the test at family-friendly Chinese chains like **Bi Feng Tang** (*see p104*); its English and photo menu makes it the ideal stop for an easy-to-assemble dim sum meal, and the few boat-shaped tables are a hit with children. Perennial expat favourite **1221** (*see p118*) is used to accommodating families; it has highchairs on hand and a vast English-language menu of basic Chinese dishes. **City Diner** (149 Tongren Lu, by Nanjing Xi Lu, Jingan, 6289 3699) offers American-style diner fare for when little tummies crave Western-style breakfast.

Many upscale hotels and restaurants direct their mammoth Sunday brunches towards families by offering supervised children's play clubs and junior menus. The **Westin**'s (*see p31*) brunch is the current favourite among expats. Its free, nanny-supervised kids' corner has its own menu, cartoons and activities, plus half-price grub for the six- to 12-year-olds (and the food is free for under-sixes). The Yi Café at the **Pudong Shangri-La** (*see p44*) is a huge hit with children for its extensive dessert bar, with candy floss, ice-cream and takeaway boxes of sweets. The **Novotel Atlantis** (*see p29*) and the **Portman Ritz-Carlton** (*see p36*) are worth checking out, as is the panoramic **M on the Bund** (*see p101*), which offers an abbreviated children's brunch menu, and **Mesa** (*see p114*), which has a nanny-supervised play area.

Elsewhere, the Irish pub **O'Malley's** (*see p126*) has a huge sunny garden with a play area, and baby-changing facilities in the (clean) toilets, plus lots of sport on the screens. **Park 97** (2 Gaolan Lu, by Sinan Lu, French Concession, 5383 2328), inside Fuxing Park, serves Italian and Japanese fare, as well as a Western-style brunch at the weekend with a kids' table and activity packs. A few tables outside overlook the park, where children can let off steam while parents linger over coffee. The open-air mall that is **Xintiandi** is usually a big hit with youngsters for its myriad fast-food outlets, cafés and ice-cream.

To put together a picnic, stock up at the **Westin** (*see p31*). In the basement of Parkson Department Store, on the corner of Huaihai Zhong Lu and Shanxi Nan Lu (connected to the Shanxi Nan Lu metro station), you'll find a good, cheap supermarket, which also carries a decent variety of baby food and supplies. For a splurge, stop at **City Shop** (www.cityshop.com.cn), which has a wide range of imported food items; it also has a convenient branch in the Shanghai Centre, among other locations.

Shops

Good things really do come in small packages in Shanghai; discounted children's gear goes for a song. Most of the world's biggest children's brands for clothes and shoes, plus some toys, are made in factories outside Shanghai. As a result, you'll find samples, overruns, fakes and plenty of the real thing in the wealth of small shops around the French Concession (try Changle Lu by Shanxi Nan Lu for a concentration of kids and maternity clothes stores) and in the markets. English-language children's books can be picked up at the **Foreign Languages Bookstore** (*see p133*) on Fuzhou Lu. For a cornucopia of art supplies, check out the numerous shops on Fuzhou Lu by Fujian Lu.

The huge **Decathlon** store (*see p146*) in Pudong is a good place to stock up on cheap trainers and sportswear for children.

Bao Da Xiang
685 Nanjing Dong Lu, by Zhejiang Zhong Lu, People's Square (6322 5122). Metro Nanjing Dong Lu. **Open** 9.30am-10pm daily. **Credit** MC, V. **Map** p244 K4.
Tucked between department stores on the tourist-packed Nanjing Pedestrian Road, this children's emporium has an arcade in the basement and five more storeys filled with goods for infants to teens. It sells a mix of imported toys and clothes.

Ni Hong Children's Plaza
10 Puan Lu, by Yanan Dong Lu, Xintiandi (5383 6218/www.shnhgc.com). Metro Huangpi Nan Lu. **Open** 9.30am-8pm daily. **No credit cards.** **Map** p244 J6.
There is much buried treasure to be found in this underground children's market. Nearly 200 shops sell cheap, brand-name shoes and clothes for new-borns up to eight-year-olds, as well as toys, costumes and accessories. Prices are negotiable, especially when buying multiple items from one store. Enter by the stairway near the corner of Jinling Lu and Puan Lu, by the bus station.

Orient Shopping Centre
8 Caoxi Bei Lu, by Zhaojiabang Lu, Xujiahui (6487 0000). Metro Xujiahui. **Open** 10am-9.30pm Mon-Thur; 10am-10pm Fri-Sun. **Credit** MC, V. **Map** p246 A11.
Now dwarfed by the newer, bigger neighbouring malls of Xujiahui, the Orient remains a top destination for foreign-brand toys and baby supplies. Finds range from Gameboys to strollers to art supplies.

Services

Childminding
Temporary childcare can be difficult to arrange at short notice; check with your hotel before you book an evening out. The more upscale hotels will generally offer babysitting services in-house for RMB 30-120 per hour, plus a taxi surcharge if the session lasts past 10pm.

Health
Shanghai has two special children's hospitals, both good. Generally, some English-speaking staff will be on hand. For more general information on healthcare, *see p220*.

Children's Hospital of Fudan University
Opposite Zhongshan Hospital, 183 Fenglin Lu, by Qingzhen Lu, French Concession (5452 4666/www.ch.shmu.edu.cn). **Credit** MC, V. **Map** p246 D11.

Shanghai Children's Medical Center
1678 Dongfang Lu, by Pujian Lu, Pudong (5839 5238/5873 2020 ext 6172). Metro Dongfang Lu. **Credit** MC, V. **Map** p241 G4.

Film

Backing into the future.

Tony Leung and Wei Tang in Ang Lee's *Lust, Caution.*

Once upon a time, Shanghai wasn't just the Paris of the East, it was also its Hollywood. China's first full-length feature was produced in Shanghai in 1923 and by the 1930s the city had a studio system cranking out scores of silent melodramas, acted out by its own pantheon of tragic starlets. The glamour travelled and the city's filmic fame was perpetuated worldwide by such vehicles as 1932's *Shanghai Express* and 1947's *The Lady from Shanghai* – never mind that the two corresponding stars, Marlene Dietrich and Rita Hayworth, barely ventured beyond California. In fact, a quick search on the Internet Movie Database (www.imdb.com) reveals that there are over 130 films with Shanghai in the title, few of which will have been set in the city but all of them wanting a piece of the image.

Things went dark under the Communists, during which time film had to serve the party – and in many ways the Shanghai film industry is still struggling to recover, suffering from a serious lack of commercial investors and no dedicated film academy (Tongji University offers a BA in film production but is low on equipment). In addition, Shanghai Film Studios, the city's only studio, invests largely in films

possessing the necessary ideological quotient, or works with foreign productions shooting in Shanghai (*see p159* **Set in Shanghai**), often profiting handsomely from such collaborations. But film buffs should not despair – creative local gems can be found, you'll just need to dig a little deeper.

CINEMAS, SUBTITLES & CENSORSHIP

Though Shanghai has a number of spanking new multiplexes – most of them located in shopping malls – the bulk of these comfy theatres play the same three to four films (China's movie laws restrict foreign film imports to 20 a year, and most of those are Hollywood blockbusters). The rest of the screens are devoted to commercial Chinese films – costume epics such as Zhang Yimou's *Curse of the Golden Flower* and Chen Kaige's *The Promise* – films that pull so much weight that they can sometimes monopolise all of the screens in a given theatre.

Films that probe too deeply under China's veneer of prosperity – such as Li Yu's *Lost in Beijing*, which shows the lives of two couples becoming entwined through a drunken sexual liaison – tend to steam up the glasses of censors at China's rather prudish regulatory body. *Lost in Beijing* was prohibited in theatres and its producers banned from filmmaking for two years. Foreign films are also subject to trimming; *Lust, Caution* lost nine minutes to the cutting-room floor.

Chinese dubbing is widespread for foreign films, though the cinemas listed below regularly play original-language versions. It pays to call ahead and check. Note that the majority of Chinese films are not subtitled in English.

One unfortunate byproduct of Shanghai's adoption of multiplexes is price rises: they have brought with them international multiplex prices, so expect to pay RMB 50 and upwards for a ticket, more during opening week and at the weekend. Online and phone bookings are usually possible – though service in most places is in Chinese only. Credit cards aren't accepted.

FILM FESTIVAL

In business since 1993, the **Shanghai International Film Festival** (6253 7115, www.siff.com, mid-late June) is China's only recognised film festival, and it usually attracts a few stars. The SIFF devotes a bit too much space to commercial films, but it nonetheless offers a rare chance to see a wide selection of Chinese films, which are properly subtitled for the benefit of the judges. It's worth noting that films shown during SIFF are outside the official import quota and thus largely uncut by the censors.

Set in Shanghai

After China opened up to the world in 1980, it was only a matter of time before foreign film productions started to want a slice of Shanghai. Steven Spielberg led the way in 1987 with what is arguably his best film, *Empire of the Sun* (1987), sections of which were shot on the Bund. Where Spielberg went, many more have followed, attracted by the city's colonial mystique and, more recently, by its futuristic skyline.

Notable productions in recent years include Merchant Ivory's *The White Countess* (2005), starring Ralph Fiennes; John Curran's *The Painted Veil* (2006), a romantic drama set in Concession-era Shanghai; Ang Lee's spy drama *Lust, Caution* (2007), set in a Japanese-occupied Shanghai and starring Tony Leung Chiu Wai; and Florian Gallenberger's *John Rabe* (2008), starring Steve Buscemi, a film about China's Schindler, a German businessman who saved the lives of countless Chinese during the Nanjing Massacre. *Shanghai*, a Weinstein endeavour to star John Cusack and Gong Li, was slated to be shot in Shanghai during 2008, but at the time of writing the producers were struggling to secure the necessary permits from the Chinese government.

Though the city's colourful past continues to sell, modernisation is changing its face at an unrelenting pace, throwing up neon signage and pink shiny apartment buildings in its wake. The result is that many filmmakers now head to the backlots of Shanghai Film Studios, located south of Shanghai in Songjiang, which feature a stretch of 1930s Nanjing Lu complete with trams and cobblestones. Catch a glimpse of this set in *The White Countess*, *Jasmine Flower*, starring Joan Chen, and Steven Chow's *Kung Fu Hustle*. When shooting *Lust, Caution*, Ang Lee chose not to use this hackneyed old strip, instead constructing his own stretch of Nanjing Lu complete with 100 storefronts.

As Shanghai discards its past to make way for a shiny future, the giddy vision of the 21st century that is Pudong is also starting to snare starring roles – as the futurescape in Michael Winterbottom's dystopian sci-fi chiller *Code 46* (2003) and the glittering backdrop for Tom Cruise's skyscraper-diving antics in *Mission: Impossible III* (2006). For 21st-century Shanghai playing, unusually, 21st-century Shanghai, look out for David Veerbeek's *Shanghai Trance* (2008), a series of three interwoven love stories set against the Shanghai skyline.

For more intimate portraits of the city, you'll need to look to local independent directors, such as **Peng Xiaolian** (*see p160*) – known for her humanistic family dramas portraying different social groups in Chinese society coping with the cyclone of change – or Lou Ye for his moody noir, *Suzhou River* (2000), and Shu Haolun for his experimental 2006 documentary *Nostalgia*, which records Shanghai's disappearing lane life.

Resident expats are also making a strong contribution: Christine Choy with *Ha Ha Shanghai*, a doc about the director's struggle to reclaim her family home; and French documentary maker Sylvie Levey, known for her probing documentaries such as *Shanghai Waiting for Paradise* about lane life and family relationships and *High Crimes in Shanghai*, which looks inside a women's prison.

Cinemas

For more adventurous programming, you'll have to look beyond the cinema chains. The **German Consulate** (102A Pidemco Tower, 318 Fuzhou Lu, by Shandong Zhong Lu, People's Square, 6391 2068 ext 602, www. goethe.de/shanghai) organises screenings of German films; **Ciné-Club de l'Alliance** (5-6/F, 297 Wusong Lu, by Tanggu Lu, Putuo, 6357 5388, www.alliancefrancaise.org.cn/shanghai) does the same for Francophiles. For experimental local (often subtitled) films, check the programme at **Image Tunnel** (*see p161*). **Maria's Choice** film club meets monthly at Kodak Cinema World (*see p161*) to watch screenings of Chinese movies subtitled in English and also features director talks; email mariaschoice-subscribe@topica.com to get on the mailing list.

Cathay Theatre

870 Huaihai Zhong Lu, by Maoming Nan Lu, French Concession (5404 0415/www.guotaifilm.com). Metro Shanxi Nan Lu. **Tickets** RMB 30-70. **No credit cards. Map** p247 F7.

Known in Chinese as the Guotai, the Cathay has a long and rich history. Built in 1930 by a Cantonese merchant, it bears a characteristic art deco vertical brick façade and once attracted filmgoers from as far away as Japan. It showed mostly American films

Peng Xiaolian

Though Shanghai-born filmmakers such as Lou Ye (*Suzhou River*), Wang Xiaoxiao (*Beijing Bicycle*) and Wong Kar-wai (*Happy Together*) have made names for themselves abroad, few have remained in the city and even fewer have taken on the challenge of engaging with the socio-economic enigma that is 21st-century Shanghai. **Peng Xiaolian** is the exception. Unlike most Shanghainese alumni of the Beijing Film Academy, Peng returned to her home town, initially eking out an existence as an independent filmmaker. Against the odds, she managed not only to survive but also to get nominated for awards at the Shanghai and Cairo international film festivals – and to win a Golden Rooster, China's equivalent of an Oscar, for *Shanghai Story* (2003; pictured).

One of Peng's strengths is her clear-eyed vision of the city, which she describes as a 'character' in her films. Peng's *oeuvre*, which mostly comprises realist family dramas, has remained firmly rooted in her home city, conveying beautiful vignettes of Shanghai life – everything from the ubiquitous hot water thermoses to the city's thrusting skyscrapers – and sophisticated portraits of everyone from old bourgeois families to struggling young migrants.

In a sense, her films serve as a social record, commemorating the city's history and personalities. *Shanghai Women* (2002), the first film in Peng's 'Shanghai trilogy', tells of a woman searching for stability after a divorce, who is forced to move in with her matronly mother. *Shanghai Story* (2004) depicts a middle-class family struggling with a Cultural Revolution hangover. *Shanghai Rumba* (2006), the third and most nostalgic pic, weaves together film, literature and political history in an atmospheric love story.

Peng's most recent film, *Shanghai Kids* (2008), while probably not her best piece of cinema, is a penetrating critique of the social and economic inequalities that persist in a city much hyped for its high living and conspicuous consumption. It is essential viewing for anyone wanting to take a look under the glittering surface of city glitz.

It does what it says on the façade: **Shanghai Film Art Center**.

until the Revolution, at which point both the sign and the films on offer switched to Chinese. During the Cultural Revolution, it became the People's Theatre, and accordingly showed a mix of Soviet, Chinese and North Korean films. Today it shows big-budget Chinese and Hollywood films with the occasional screening of something more unusual.

Image Tunnel

2F, Building 19, 50 Moganshan Lu, by Changhua Lu, Jingan (2813 0548/www.imagetunnel.com). Metro Zhenping Lu. **Tickets** RMB 15-20 members (membership RMB 10); RMB 25 non-members. **No credit cards. Map** p242 D1.

Image Tunnel shows an unusual variety of underground films, such as a documentary about strays called *Rain Cats* and *In the Mood for Shenhua*, an experimental piece about the Shanghai Shenhua football team. Housed in a crumbling Moganshan Lu house, it scores highly on atmosphere, even if the wooden seating leaves a lot to be desired.

Kodak Cinema World

5th floor, Metro City, 1111 Zhaojiabang Lu, by Caoxi Bei Lu, Xujiahui (6426 8181/http://cinemaworld. kodak.com/english.htm). Metro Xujiahui. **Tickets** RMB 60-80. **No credit cards. Map** p246 A11.

One of Shanghai's better-established multiplexes, Kodak Cinema World does its best to show a decent mix of local and international fare, as well as hosting special film events, including Maria's Choice nights (*see p160*). English-language films are played almost exclusively in their original version. The cinema's website is in English, providing profiles of forthcoming releases and listing show times.

Peace Cinema

290 Xizang Zhong Lu, by Hankou Lu, People's Square (6322 5252/www.shdgm.com). Metro People's Square. **Tickets** RMB 60-80. **No credit cards. Map** p244 J5.

Located at the junction of metro lines 1 and 2, the Peace is convenient for just about everyone. You'll often see young couples flocking here to see the lat-est Hollywood offerings. There are five screens, including a vast IMAX screen, which makes it an ideal place to take in a big-budget kung fu flick.

Shanghai Film Art Centre

160 Xinhua Lu, by Huahai Xi Lu, Changning (6281 7017/www.filmcenter.com.cn). Metro Xujiahui. **Tickets** RMB 80. **No credit cards. Map** p246 A9.

About as close to an arts cinema as you'll get in this city, the Film Art Centre is home to most of the major screenings during the Shanghai International Film Festival (*see p159*) in June, when it gets its fair share of VIPs. Great tides of reporters rush from press screenings in the Film Art Centre to directors' talks at the neighbouring Crowne Plaza hotel and, if you look confident enough, you sometimes can waltz right in like the big-shot critics and directors.

UME International Cineplex

5th floor, No.6, Lane 123, Xingye Lu, by Madang Lu, Xintiandi (6373 3333/www.ume.com.cn). Metro Huangpi Nan Lu. **Tickets** RMB 70-80. **No credit cards. Map** p248 H8.

One of Shanghai's newest multiplexes, UME is also located in one of its trendiest areas, Xintiandi, fitting in perfectly among the hip boutiques, bars and nightclubs. With mainly moneyed local and international customers, the cinema plays foreign films in their original versions, as well as screening most current Chinese films.

Yonghua Cinema City

6th floor, Grand Gateway, 1 Hongqiao Lu, by Huashan Lu, Xujiahui (6407 6622/http://test. okticket.cn). Metro Xujiahui. **Tickets** RMB 60-80. **No credit cards. Map** p246 A11.

This looks and feels like a top-notch multiplex. Nestled on the sixth floor of a mall, it's gaining in popularity, with screenings often close to capacity. All the trimmings are here: thick carpets, lots of screens, popcorn by the bucketful and foreign films screened alternately in English and dubbed Mandarin.

Galleries

The buzz is out – Chinese art is in.

Zendai Museum of Modern Art.

Shanghai's contemporary art scene is, by any measure, a youngster – its most established contemporary art gallery, **ShanghART**, run by Swiss gallerist Lorenz Helbling, celebrated its tenth anniversary in 2007. The early days were hard-going and Helbling apparently even considered giving up at one point. What a difference ten years can make: ShanghART now has three spaces in Shanghai (plus a new Beijing outpost), and contemporary Chinese art is booming beyond all possible prediction. It was recently declared the third-biggest art market in the world, after New York and London.

With the market exploding, and hefty sums changing hands for Chinese art, every gallerist and their dog is rushing in to get a piece of the action. As a result, the Shanghai gallery scene finds itself in a state of continual flux – and the creative energy is tangible. The past few years saw the opening of numerous spaces, among them **m97**, **140sqm Gallery**, **Beaugeste Photo Gallery**, **Fei Art Centre**, **IFA**, **ISLAND6**, as well as the reopening of **Creek Art** and **Bund 18 Creative Centre**. Along the way, several have given up on Shanghai (such as M.S.G. Art, which retreated to LA),

but many more continue to flood in. New York's **James Cohan Gallery** has a space lined up in Jingan and the **Pompidou Centre**, though still stuck in tedious government negotiations, has managed to secure a space.

Though a highly market-oriented scene has to some extent created a distorted output – where works reflect the desires of collectors rather than Chinese artists – on the whole, the artists are gaining from the boom. A number of installation artists have made impressive names for themselves in recent years, including **Xu Zhen**, who staged a mockumentary about sawing off the top of Mount Everest; **Gu Wenda**, who produced ink sticks out of hair; and **Zhang Huan**, who paraded in front of the Whitney with meat strapped to his body. Video artist **Yang Fudong**, acclaimed for his contemplative work, has also made waves internationally. Even no-name artists, fresh out of college, seem able to pull off sell-out shows.

Under the pretence of fuelling creativity, the government has been on a building spree, throwing up 'creative clusters' all over. These developments often seem to be more about real estate then creativity, typically old factories with a new coat of paint and significant rises in rent. Spaces such as the beautifully converted abattoir **1933** (29 Shajing Lu, by Liyang Lu, Hongkou, 6501 1933, www.1933-shanghai.com) – co-created by Paul Liu, former CFO of the Three on the Bund, and celeb chef David Laris – and **Red Town** (containing Shanghai Sculpture Space) match stunning design with astronomical rents that few seem able to afford. Meanwhile, other more affordable art spaces – such as the vast **800 Wujiaochang** complex, out in the north-east of the city – are just too far away to attract a crowd.

Outside of the commercial art scene, Shanghai is also developing. In 2008, the city saw a flowering of public art during the 366 Intrude Art & Life exhibition (www.intrude 366.com), featuring public art projects by over 360 international and Chinese artists. Projects included art vending machines, a sound performance conducted completely in the dark and angel sculptures hanging precariously off buildings around the city. An archival show in 2009-10 will document the event.

For more traditional collections, visit the **Shanghai Art Museum** (see p60) at People's Square, **Zendai Museum of Modern Art** (see p89) in Pudong and the **Doulun** (see p94) in Hongkou. For details of what's on where, check the listings in that's Shanghai (www.urbanatomy.com).

MOGANSHAN LU – ART ENCLAVE
While New York has the Meatpacking District and London Hoxton, Shanghai has Moganshan Lu. In a grim industrial park beside the once-fetid Suzhou Creek, **Moganshan Lu**'s chill warehouses at one time offered a solution to the high rents and cramped spaces faced by artists elsewhere in the city – and it was here that Shanghai's underground art scene took root. The artists moved in towards the end of the 1990s and around 30 now have studios in the area.

These studios and galleries used to host some of the most edgy art in Shanghai but as rents – and hype – rocket skyward, it is increasingly filled with galleries of a more commercial bent, and many emerging artists are now heading across the creek to the nicely groomed Brilliant City. In this grove of pink apartment buildings a stone's throw away, they can rent an unfinished apartment for often a lot less than a grungy warehouse. Nonetheless, Moganshan still offers great one-stop shopping for art initiates.

The easiest way to get to Moganshan Lu, which lies just north of the Jade Buddha Temple (see p66), is by taxi. It's best to visit in the afternoon and, given the erratic hours of many galleries, it also pays to call ahead.

Those inclined to scratch a bit deeper should stop at the more underground **696 Weihai Lu** (by Maoming Lu, map p243 F5/6), home to about 30 artists (including Ma Liang and Zhang Yong) and a few galleries, interspersed with fashion designers and car-parts dealers.

Neither Weihai nor Moganshan are polished enclaves, as few want to invest in renovations with the wrecking ball lurking constantly in the background. Word has it that the fate of these arty communities won't be decided until after the Expo in 2010, when real estate markets are expected to stabilise.

Fairs & festivals

In 2007, the city was inundated with rather self-important arty types for the city's first international-calibre annual contemporary art fair, **SHContemporary** (see p151). Though Shanghai already had several of her own art fairs – the **Shanghai Art Fair** (see p153), the biggest in Asia, and the **Shanghai Spring Art Salon** in May (www.cnarts.net/artsalon) – both were blown out of the water by this high-end, foreign-run spectacle, held in the Shanghai Exhibition Centre. The fair attracted big names in Asian and international contemporary art, including Korean artist Nam June Paik with a sculpture made up of television screens and Indian artist Sharmila Samant with a sari made out of bottle caps.

As part of its mission to convince the world of its modernity, the Shanghai government also launched the first ever **Shanghai eArts Festival** (see p153) in 2007, which it claims to be the largest electronic art festival in the world. Superlative chasing aside, it was a laudable effort that saw a variety of innovative projects such as a giant motion-sensitive ink brush crafted out of a Wii joystick, and a musical installation of umbrellas that opened and closed in formation to the tune of Singin' in the Rain.

For something younger, and a chance to get a glimpse of the stars of the future, check out **Get It Louder** (www.getitlouder.com), a new nationwide design show launched with the emphasis on youth culture, with everything from fashion design to animation. It succeeds in capturing the spirit of under-30 artists, and is steeped in a culture of manga and emoticons.

The state-run **Shanghai Biennale** (see p152) was launched in 1996 as a showcase for Chinese art, but since 2000 it has been an international affair. Recent themes have revolved around the interconnections of technology, urbanisation and art. Arty jet-setters will be pleased to hear that the **Art Compass** programme (www.artcompass 2008.com) has coordinated for the five major

Arts & Entertainment

Asia-Pacific art fairs (the Biennale of Sydney, the Gwangju Biennale, Singapore Biennale, Shanghai Biennale and Yokohama Triennale) to run at around the same time.

Galleries

Beaugeste Photo Gallery

Rm 519-520, Lane 210, Taikang Lu, by Sinan Lu, French Concession (6466 9012/www.beaugeste design.com). Open 10am-6pm daily. Map p247 G10.
Though tiny, Beaugeste – opened on Taikang Lu in 2007 by long-time photo enthusiast Jean Loh – manages to feature an extraordinary selection of both documentary and conceptual photography. To get in, knock on the door of the design studio.

BizArt

4/F floor, Building 7, 50 Moganshan Lu, by Changhua Lu, Putuo (6277 5358/www.biz-art.com). Metro Shanghai Railway Station or Zhongtan Lu. Open 11am-6pm Mon-Sat. Map p242 C1.
Founded in 1998, BizArt has developed a strong reputation for conceptual art over the years. Run by one of Shanghai's top conceptual artists, Xu Zhen, it is always seeking to push the envelope and, despite the corporate-sounding moniker, it is much more about nurturing young artists than selling paintings. It's a bit like a training camp for young artists, many of whom graduate to bigger galleries, and as you might expect, the quality is variable, with the notable exception of artists such as Jin Feng and Zhou Xiaohu.

Bund 18 Creative Centre

4/F, 18 Zhongshan Dong Yi Lu, by Nanjing Dong Lu, the Bund (6323 7066/www.bund18.com). Metro Nanjing Dong Lu. Open 11am-7pm Tue-Sun. Map p245 M4.
The Creative Centre – part of Bund 18, the multilevel dining and retail complex that occupies the former Chartered Bank of India and Australia – is one of Shanghai's most interesting new spaces, relaunched in 2007 with a renewed focus on Asian contemporary art. Fronted by Korean curator Kim Sunhee, it shows mainly Korean and Japanese conceptual art, along with a well-edited selection of local artists, such as Qiu Anxiong, whose pensive black and video work *Nostalgia* depicted factories billowing smoke into the Chinese landscape. Though Lounge 18 bar (*see p121*) now occupies a large percentage of the space, its design is so classy – and the Bund views so good – that we gladly forgive the imposition.

Eastlink

5th floor, Building 6, 50 Moganshan Lu, by Changhua Lu, Putuo (6276 9932/www.eastlink gallery.cn). Metro Shanghai Railway Station or Zhongtan Lu. Open 10am-6pm daily. Map p242 C1.
Founded by a local returnee who lived for 12 years in Sydney, Eastlink used to be the most avant-garde of the city's galleries, but it has been a little more hit-or-miss of late – in part because of its admirable dedication to showing young artists. The strongest

recent show was Body Talk, which featured conceptual artists, including Huang Yan, who paints Chinese landscapes on his body.

epSITE

Rm 106, Building 7, M50, 50 Moganshan Lu, by Changhua Lu, Putuo (6266 9191/www.epson.com.cn/ epsite). Metro Shanghai Railway Station or Zhongtan Lu. Open 10am-6pm Tue-Sun. Map p242 D1.
epSITE hosts a range of shows by local photojournalists and documentary photographers, presenting a rich panorama of life in China; Zeng Li's grey industrial landscapes were a recent highlight.

IFA

2nd Floor, Building 6, M50, 50 Moganshan Lu, by Changhua Lu, Putuo (6277 7856/www.ifa-gallery. com). Metro Shanghai Railway Station or Zhongtan Lu. Open 10am-7pm Tue-Sun. Map p242 D1.
Spacious IFA on Moganshan Lu often hosts shows from the ISLAND6 (*see below*) crowd, along with conceptual photography by artists such as Liu Bolin, who paints himself in camouflage blending almost seamlessly into his drab urban surroundings.

ISLAND6

Bldg 6, 120 Moganshan Lu, by Changhua Lu, Putuo (no phone/www.island6.org). Metro Shanghai Railway Station or Zhongtan Lu. Open 10am-7pm daily. Map p242 D1.
Not-for-profit artist collective ISLAND6, housed in a handsome old flour mill dating back to the early 20th century, deals mainly in experimental and electronic mediums: LED, motion sensors, sound, light, neon, projection and video. At the time of writing, there were rumours of a venue change; check the website before you set out. There's a small display space, ISLAND6 Shack, on Moganshan Lu (115 Moganshan Lu, by Changhua Lu); visits are by appointment but you can always take a look through the windows.

M97

2/F, 97 Moganshan Lu, by Changhua Lu, Putuo (6266 1597/www.m97gallery.com). Metro Shanghai Railway Station or Zhongtan Lu. Open 10.30am-6.30pm Tue-Sun. Map p242 D1.
Shanghai's most professional photography gallery features both foreign and local works, well printed and displayed, and with informative accompanying literature (in English). American owner Steve Harris has a keen eye for new artists, such as Michael Wolf with his Hong Kong urban landscapes.

140sqm

Rm 26, Lane 1331 Fuxing Zhong Lu, by Fenyang Lu, French Concession (6431 6216/www.140sqm. com). Metro Shaanxi Nan Lu. Open 11am-7pm Tue-Sun. Map p246 D8.
This little gallery, tucked away in an historic building on Fuxing Lu, features a well-edited selection of local painters, with an emphasis on young talent, plus local and international photographers. Highlights of 2007 included the Tian Yibin exhibition of photographs taken during the Korean Mass Games.

Shanghai Gallery of Art

*3rd floor, Three on the Bund, 3 Zhongshan Dong Yi
Lu, by Guangdong Lu, the Bund (6321 5757/www.
threeonthebund.com). Metro Nanjing Dong Lu.*
Open 11am-11pm daily. **Map** p245 M5.

The city's ritziest gallery, the SGA is part of the
Three on the Bund complex and boasts 1000sq m
(10,750sq ft) of floor space, and a staggering ziggu-
rat-like atrium designed by Brit architect Michael
Graves. The gallery prides itself on staging site-spe-
cific works that interact with the venue. Notable
examples include Gu Dexin's *2007.4.14*, in which the
artist created a blue silicone pool covered with flies
in the atrium and sewers running with silicone blood
– a disturbing meditation on corruption in China.

Shanghai Sculpture Space

*Red Town, 570 Huaihai Xi Lu, by Kaixuan Lu,
Changning (6280 7844/www.sss570.com). Metro
Hongqiao Lu.* **Open** 10am-5pm Tue-Sun.

This huge, attractively converted warehouse presents a range of modern Chinese sculpture, as well
as more classical works and an outdoor sculpture
garden, all about a ten-minute taxi ride from the infamous and now closed Xiangyang market. Although
the shows tend to be infrequent, and of varying quality, the space is nonetheless atmospheric and occasionally hosts excellent travelling exhibitions, such
as *Body Media*, an interactive multimedia exhibition
cura-ted by Richard Castelli.

ShanghART H-Space

*Building 18, 50 Moganshan Lu, by Changhua Lu,
Putuo (6359 3923/www.shanghartgallery.com).
Metro Shanghai Railway Station or Zhongtan Lu.*
Open 1-6pm Tue-Sun. **Map** p242 C1.

Here, at ShanghART's exhibition space, you'll see the
best and usually the newest work from its formidable stable of artists. Standouts in 2008 included Zhao
Bandi's Panda fashion show for 'ShanghART Night',
featuring Panda-inspired designs based on different
Chinese types such as the corrupt official and the
migrant worker; and Yang Fudong's video installation *No Snow under the Broken Bridge*, a pensive
black and white piece featuring costumed youths
parading by Hangzhou's West Lake.

ShanghART Warehouse

*Building 16, 50 Moganshan Lu, by Changhua Lu,
Putuo (6359 3923/www.shanghartgallery.com).
Metro Shanghai Railway Station or Zhongtan Lu.*
Open 10am-6pm Tue-Sun. **Map** p242 C1.

Lorenz Helbling, Shanghai's Swiss godfather of contemporary art, founded ShanghART in 1995.
Despite being a little disorganised, his warehouse is
the closest thing Shanghai has to a permanent collection of contemporary Chinese art. It has an excellent website, with some 3,000 images from its stable
of artists. Though the Warehouse lacks the curatorial focus of its H-Space, it occasionally features
interesting installations such as the Pumpkin
Project, by Li Shan and Zhang Pingjie, an exhibition
of bio art projects involving real gourds.

Smart art. **Shanghai Gallery of Art**.

of print media, gay groups have been able to exchange information freely on the internet. **Shanghai LGBT** is a vibrant community of gay, lesbian, bisexual and transgendered individuals that hosts fortnightly happy hours at selected gay venues. Its Yahoo! group (http://groups.yahoo.com/group/shanghailgbt) currently boasts of over 700 members, a mix of young expats and locals. For a lesbian-only list, sign up with **LesinShanghai** (http://groups.yahoo.com/group/lesinshanghai). Sports buffs might want to log on to **Sunhomo.com**, an online community of gay sports groups that meet informally on a weekly basis. The only caveat: while many of the members can speak English, the website is completely in Chinese. Email the moderator, Rio (rio_2008@126.com) and he will be happy to help.

To make connections before or during a visit to Shanghai, try out **Fridae.com**, Asia's largest gay portal, with member profiles in English. Other personals websites popular among locals and Shanghai expats include **Gaydar.co.uk** and **Gayromeo.com**. The Shanghai chatroom of **Gay.com** is usually packed most evenings, but as always, do be on your guard against 'moneyboys'.

The Shanghai listings on **Utopia-asia.com** are by far the most current and updated of any gay listings on the internet. Shanghai's favourite city blog **Shanghaiist.com** also has the latest news and gossip on the scene (shanghaiist.com/tags/gay).

Bars, cafés & clubs

The Shanghai scene may seem to have few dedicated gay nightspots by comparison to other world cities, but bear in mind that just a few years ago, it was all underground. Most bars are a pleasing mix of Chinese, Western and Asian expats, plus, of course, the ever-present rent boys. Previously, each bar would have its own tightly knit crowd and new visitors would find themselves receiving plenty of curious attention, but that's no longer the case. There are a few mixed bars in town, but discretion is still advised – if you fancy a gay night out, it's best to stick to the gay venues. Lesbian haunts are few and far between, although the scene is eclectic, with girls more than welcome at predominantly male gay bars. On the last Saturday of the month, Shanghai LGBT hosts 'Girls Rule the Studio' at **Shanghai Studio**.

The queer dynasties

It's easy to forget that homosexuals weren't persecuted in China before Communism – in fact, there is a very long and open history of Chinese same-sex relationships. On the formation of the People's Republic in 1949, however, homosexuality was condemned as contributing to the decadent capitalist lifestyle, and during the Cultural Revolution gays and lesbians were actively persecuted. They were not only publicly criticised, they also received jail sentences for fictional crimes.

In China's long and colourful history, more than a few major episodes are shaded pink. Homosexual love has been portrayed extensively in Chinese art – many explicit paintings and prints survived the Cultural Revolution – and literature. Indeed, 19th-century Chinese attitudes to sexual behaviour shocked the early European settlers; while Christianity denounced homosexuality as a sin, this was never the case with Taoism and Confucianism, China's major religions.

In ancient times the 'Yellow Emperor' Huang Di (2697-2597 BC), the disputed founder of Chinese culture, was thought to have kept male lovers. More widely acknowledged, and testified to in official literature from the period, is the series of openly bisexual emperors who ruled over two centuries of the Han Dynasty. Emperor Ai, for instance, was evidently enamoured of his male concubine, Dong Xian. One night, while slumbering in the arms of his lover, Dong Xian lay on the emperor's sleeve. Emperor Ai needed to get up – things to do, people to see – but, not wanting to wake Dong Xian, he cut his sleeve to free himself from the embrace. Terribly sweet… if a little costly in tailoring bills. This story created the phrase *duanxiu* ('the cut sleeve'), which is a term meaning gay love, now commonly known as 'the passion of the cut sleeve'.

Still more famous is the earlier story of Duke Ling of Wei and his handsome male favourite Mi Zixia. One fine day, when they were in an orchard, Mi Zixia was so struck by the sweetness of a peach that he insisted on giving the other half to the duke. The phrase 'to be fond of the left-over peach' became a euphemism for same-sex love.

Nowadays, the preferred slang term for homosexuals is *tongzhi* (which literally means 'comrade') while *tongxinglian* is the formal term meaning same-sex relations.

MANifesto. *See p170.*

Arch

439 Wukang Lu, by Huaihai Zhong Lu, French Concession (6466 0807/www.archcafe.com.cn). Metro Xujiahui, then 20-min walk. **Open** 7.30am-1am Mon-Fri; 9am-1am Sat, Sun. **Credit** MC, V. **Map** p246 B9.

Housed in the old 1930s Normandie Apartments building, Shanghai's version of the Flatiron building, Arch is a restaurant, café and bar popular among architects, designers and various media folk. It serves a great selection of pastas, sandwiches and steaks at prices that are nicely affordable. The laid-back atmosphere makes this a great spot to wine and dine before you hit the bars later in the evening. Chances are you'll meet the friendly Filipino manager, Angelo, who will be happy to share with you what's going on in town.

Bobos

307 Shanxi Nan Lu, in clubhouse of Bugaoyuan complex, by Jianguo Lu, French Concession (6471 2887). Metro Shanxi Nan Lu, then 20min walk. **Open** 7pm-late daily. **Admission** free. **No credit cards**. **Map** p247 F10.

If you think the Shanghai gay scene is too small for cliques, think again: Bobos is a bear bar – or should that be a panda bar? Relocated a few years back from Suzhou Creek, this funky little bar, with giant bear paws on the walls, has a mix of high stools and comfy sofas, and boasts an impressive dancefloor complete with bear cage. Bobos-goers are mainly bears and bear hunters, but everyone is warmly welcomed. Music is eclectic, jumping from 1960s-style retro Chinese pop to the latest Western dance tunes. The bar is located in a residential complex; walk

past the security guard at 307 Shanxi Lu, cross the lake bridge, enter the glass building, descend the stairs and head behind the black curtain. Then belly up to the bar and discover your inner panda.

Eddy's

1877 Huaihai Zhong Lu, by Tianping Lu, French Concession (6282 0521/www.eddys-bar.com). Metro Hengshan Lu. **Open** 7pm-2am daily. **Admission** free. **No credit cards**. **Map** p246 A9.

Just across the street from Shanghai Studio, beloved Eddy's has been around for over a decade. From its humble beginnings as the first gay bar in town, it has changed location no fewer than six times on the way to becoming the stylish watering hole it is today. The red under-lit bar, high stools and Chinese-style interiors are impressive, but the atmosphere is the real draw. The waiters here can be a bit pushy with the drinks at times, but the ever-present Eddy is always on hand to make sure that everyone is happy.

Frangipani Bar & Café

399 Dagu Lu, by Shimen Yi Lu, Jingan (5375 0084/ www.gay399.com). Metro Shimen Xi Lu. **Open** 6pm-late daily. **Admission** free. **No credit cards**. **Map** p243 G6.

Frangipani opened in 2006 bang in the city centre, with a fresh and relaxed feel, a cool, industrial look (think ample space and exposed concrete), and a mixed clientele of locals and expats. But – and this could turn out to be a big 'but' – it sits on a strip that has seen many a new bar die a cold, lonely customerless death. The last Saturday we stopped by, Frangipani was less than kicking – so we'd better keep our fingers crossed that it can dig itself a niche.

Lai Lai Dance Hall

2F, 235 Anguo Lu, by Zhoujiazui Lu, Hongkou (6546 1218). **Open** 6.30-9.30pm Fri-Sun. **Admission** RMB 5. **No credit cards.**

For a slice of the local scene, head to Lai Lai Dance Hall, tucked away in a run-down neighbourhood in the north-east, with cracked wooden floors and a primitive sound system. This is arguably the city's only entertainment venue for older gay Chinese gentlemen, who congregate here each weekend to dance ballroom and socialise. Many of the men you'll meet here are over 40, and most are married with children, living a double life to conform with social requirements. This peculiar gay meeting ground has been covered with great interest by the media, including CNN, but don't come toting your camera as many an onlooker has been unceremoniously ejected when arriving with Nikon in hand.

PinkHome

18 Gaolan Lu, by Ruijin Er Lu, French Concession (7002 102 1038/www.pinkhome.cn). Metro Shanxi Nan Lu. **Open** 9pm-late Fri, Sat. **Admission** RMB 60 Fri; RMB 80 Sat. **Credit** MC, V. **Map** p247 F8.

In an unlikely location next to a beautiful Russian Orthodox church, PinkHome is currently Shanghai's only gay dance club. 2007 saw a massive rebranding and expansion exercise that didn't entirely fly due to the launch of another bigger, better club in town. With that club raided and shut down, PinkHome is once again enjoying a resurgence and is particularly popular among the younger (read: below 25) crowd. Expect an up-for-it atmosphere, and high-octane house. The pretty little garden outside the club is one of the only places in Shanghai where you can sit on the grass. *Photo p166.*

Shanghai Studio

No.4, 1950 Huaihai Zhong Lu, by Xingguo Lu, French Concession (6283 1043/www.shanghai-studio.com). Metro Xujiahui, then 20min walk. **Open** 9pm-2am daily. **Admission** free. **Credit** MC, V. **Map** p246 A9.

This underground gallery and bar housed in a former bomb shelter has really taken off in the past year or so. Take the large red doorway at the end of the lane and follow a subterranean labyrinth of art-filled corridors until you reach the basement. The bar's cosy and intimate setting creates a friendly and unpretentious environment, attracting an enjoyable mix of young and trendy locals, creative types and expats. It's relaxed on weekdays (and heaving on weekends), and you'll never be alone here for too long as Jack, the owner, always makes a point of introducing newbies to his friends. Lesbians and fag hags also love this joint.

Transit Lounge

141 Tai'an Lu, by Huashan Lu, French Concession (6283 3051/www.h5.dion.ne.jp/~pizzi5/tl-top.html). Metro Hengshan Lu. **Open** 8.30pm-2am daily. **Admission** free. **No credit cards. Map** p246 A9.

Cosy Transit Lounge has moved from the building right above Shanghai Studio to a brand new location just five minutes away. The new lounge boasts the same homely feel as its previous location – but is bigger, brighter and more sophisticated. We think this new venue holds great promise as the ideal spot for a quiet drink in a neighbourhood of busy bars. It attracts a mainly Japanese clientele.

Sauna/massage

Jumpmale Men's Body Care & Lounge

879 Fahuazhen Lu, by Yan'an Lu, Changning (6282 8656/www.jumpmalespa.com). Metro Yanan Xi Lu. **Open** noon-midnight daily. **Treatments** *Oil massage* RMB 380-780/60mins. **No credit cards.**

Jumpmale offers a package of massage, aromatherapy and beauty treatments in nine clean and beautifully appointed therapy rooms. While the treatments here are slightly more expensive than those you'll find elsewhere, Jumpmale is also much cleaner than many of the older and, let's be honest, dingier massage centres you generally find in gay listings. There are English-speaking staff at the counter and you needn't worry about getting ripped off, even when you've asked for an outcall massage. Tipping is appreciated, but not necessary.

Lianbang

228 Zhizaoju Lu, by Xietu Lu, Huangpu (6312 5567). Metro Xizang Nan Lu. **Open** 24hrs daily. **Admission** RMB 38-78. **No credit cards. Map** p248 K10.

China has a tradition of public bathhouses but Lianbang goes well beyond the naked camaraderie of the average local scrubbing spot. Look for the red door, hidden down an alley that serves as entrance to a neighbouring hotel and massage complex. Pay the admission (RMB 40 gives you access to all floors) and switch your shoes for slippers, then explore the three floors of dingy corridors and rooms filled with languid pyjama-clad locals of all ages, lounging, smoking, napping or getting it on. The sauna attracts few foreigners, so your every move will be scrutinised, and be mindful that you need to keep your jammies on once you're out of the bath.

Shops

MANifesto

B1, No.4, 1950 Huaihai Zhong Lu, by Xingguo Lu, French Concession (6294 6880/www.manifesto. com.cn). **Open** 2pm-midnight daily. **Admission** free. **Credit** AmEx, DC, MC, V. **Map** p246 A9.

Housed within Shanghai Studio (*see above*), MANifesto boasts a wide collection of designer menswear and fitness gear, and is the first store of its kind in China. Nurse a cocktail while you and your boyfriend decide which tanktop and swimming trunk combo to wear to the next circuit party. Should you want to browse before you arrive MANifesto also accepts online orders, and ships throughout China and worldwide. *Photo p169.*

Mind & Body

Treat yourself.

Shanghai's sumptuous spas and traditional therapies are the perfect antidote to the city's pollutants and partying ways. Right up there with streetside dumplings and tailor-made clothes, thorough and affordable massage is one of the great privileges of life in Shanghai. Plunge into a hot spring pool in a suburban bathhouse, stretch out on a divan in one of the city's ubiquitous neighbourhood massage parlours, or purge city-scourged skin with a relaxing facial in a French Concession villa. And with many establishments open long hours, locals unwind on the massage table after a hectic day at work or even a night on the town.

Chinese philosophy has long valued the balancing power of touch. For more than 5,000 years, the Chinese have made use of acupressure on the body's energy channels (meridians) to promote the flow of energy (*qi*). Acupressure has been proven effective in treating headaches, sinus problems, muscle tension, insomnia, menstrual cramps, digestive disorders, anxiety and even addiction.

Traditional massage, known as *tuina* (literally 'push and grasp'), is accomplished by pressing and kneading acupoints to release muscle tension and stimulate circulation. Although it's possible to find all schools of massage in Shanghai – from Swedish, with its emphasis on essential oils, to Thai with its acrobatical stretching exercises – *tuina* remains the most widely sought out and practised form in town.

For a very Shanghai evening, enjoy *tuina* at one of the city's mid-level retreats, where the scent of sandalwood and the sparse melodies of ancient Chinese instrumentation envelop the senses. Local spots like Jade Massage and Green offer additional Chinese acupressure services, including *guasha*, which involves vigorous scraping along the spine's meridians with a blunt instrument such as a piece of jade; and fire cupping, which applies pressure to the acupoints through the placing of a hot glass or plastic cup on the skin, thus creating a vacuum. Although you might look a little beat up afterwards – both treatments leave bruises that fade within a few days – the process isn't painful and most patients report feeling looser and lighter following a session.

If you'd prefer to remain unmarked and want international standards with Chinese characteristics, visit the swanky **Mandara Spa** at the JW Marriott, which recreates the

Hover over to **Dragonfly**. *See p173.*

feeling of a classy old-time Shanghai lane house; or the **Banyan Tree** at the Westin and **CHI** at the Shangri-la, both of which make use of the five elements to bring your body into balance. (Your wallet will lose some weight too.)

For a holistic experience, visit the **VIP Clinic of Shanghai Qigong Institute**, where for as little as RMB 250 doctors will work to bring your *qi* into complete balance through a personalised programme of acupuncture, *tuina*, *qigong* (regulated breath work paired with physical movement) and Chinese medicinal elixirs (scorpion juice, anyone?). Inner harmony may not be priceless, but at least it's cheap.

Traditional Chinese medicine (TCM)

Traditional Chinese medicine (TCM) is rooted in the ideas of balance and harmony. In Chinese cosmology, creation stems from the marriage of two polar principles: yin and yang. Yang

Magpie. *See p175.*

represents active, hot and bright; yin symbolises things passive, cold or dim. The relationship between the two elements is fundamental to the traditional Chinese outlook, and is seen to affect all aspects of life, from personal health to the state of the weather.

In TCM, yang represents the energy and movement of the body, while yin is the flesh, blood and bone. Harmony of this union means good health, while disharmony leads to disease. The strategy of TCM is to redress any imbalances. Diagnosis starts by assessing the patient's pulse, face, tongue and body, and also takes into account their medical history, living habits and emotional well being.

Many Chinese believe that the strength of Western medicine is in its trauma care and therapies for acute problems, while TCM excels in treating chronic problems and applying preventive medicine. Western expats living in Shanghai seem to concur, and many visit TCM doctors for help with asthma, migraines, nicotine addiction and weight loss.

Unfortunately, without a solid understanding of the philosophy or language, trotting off to the nearest Chinese medicine centre can be a thoroughly bewildering experience. For holistic healing in comfortable, English-speaking environs, try the following.

Body & Soul – The TCM Clinic

Suite 5, 14th floor, Anji Plaza, 760 Xizang Nan Lu, by Jianguo Lu, Old City (5101 9262/www.body andsoul.com.cn). Metro Laoximen or Lujiangbang Lu. **Open** 9am-6pm Mon, Wed, Fri, Sat; 9am-8pm Tue; 1-8pm Thur. **Credit** AmEx, DC, MC, V. **Map** p248 L9.

German Doris Rathgeber trained in traditional Chinese medicine, in China, in Chinese. Her clinic offers TCM therapies, complemented with Western medical knowledge, in a comforting environment – not a pickled scorpion in sight. The 15 multilingual physicians specialise in acupuncture, internal medicine, gynaecology, *tuina*, physiotherapy and psychological consulting.

VIP Clinic of Shanghai Qigong Institute

3rd floor, 218 Nanchang Lu, by Sinan Lu, French Concession (5306 4832). Metro Shanxi Nan Lu. **Open** 8am-6.30pm daily. **No credit cards.** **Map** p247 G7.

A classic 1920s home located in one of Shanghai's most evocative neighbourhoods has been converted into a traditional Chinese hospital with a top-floor clinic catering specifically to expats. Acupuncture, Chinese massage therapy, Chinese medicine, scraping and cupping are offered by experienced practitioners. One speciality is a six-week acupuncture weight-loss treatment using dissolvable needles, which are inserted in the body and absorbed over two-week periods. (Don't try this at home). This is also the only official *qigong* institute in China.

Massage & acupressure

Beyond the street-corner blind massage parlours, there is a tier of mid-market body-rub joints. These perfumed sanctuaries of incense candles and Asian-inspired design generally offer a menu of Chinese-style foot and body massages, Japanese shiatsu and aromatherapy oil treatments, as well as additional acupressure treatments such as *guasha* and cupping.

Arts & Entertainment

Dragonfly
206 Xinle Lu, by Donghu Lu, French Concession (5403 9982/www.dragonfly.net.cn). Metro Shanxi Nan Lu. **Open** 10am-2am daily. **Treatments** *Massage* RMB 135-450/hr. **Credit** AmEx, MC, V. **Map** p246 D7.
Having spawned 11 Shanghai branches in five years, this enormously popular therapeutic retreat wins points for its affordability, stylish Zen ambience and simple menu of great massages. If walking into these candlelit, dark-wood and lemongrass-scented oases doesn't instantly relax you, the aromatherapy oil massage or deluxe hour-long foot massage on comfy recliners surely will. Most branches also boast a 'nail spa'. Couples should book the 'Love Nest', a VIP room on the top floor of the Xinle Lu flagship, with two antique beds and its own shower and spa. *Photo p171*. **Other locations** throughout the city.

Green
58 Taicang Lu, by Songshan Lu, Xintiandi (5386 0222/www.greenmassage.com.cn). Metro Huangpi Nan Lu. **Open** 10.30am-2am daily. **Treatments** *Massage* RMB 88-188/45mins. Various acupressure services. **Credit** AmEx, MC, V. **Map** p248 J7.
Green was one of Shanghai's first posh massage parlours. The simple communal rooms with bamboo screens hardly rate as such today, but this affordable neighbourhood joint – boasting some of the most consistent, no-nonsense masseurs in town – continues to be extremely popular with locals and foreigners. Supply has been upped to meet demand:

the original location has recently been renovated to encompass twice as much space as before, and a new branch has been built in Xujiahui. Across the road, the upscale Lotos Spa (2F, West Tower Somerset Grand Hotel, 8 Jinan Lu, by Shunchang, 3308 0088) – which shares its owner with Green – is a little-known gem with ten Balinese-style treatment rooms. **Other locations** 88 Xingeng Lu, by Tianyaoqiao Lu, Xujiahui (6468 7076).

Jade Massage
367 Zizhong Lu, by Madang Lu, Xintiandi (6384 8762). Metro Huangpi Nan Lu. **Open** 11am-2am daily. **Treatments** *Massage* RMB 100-225/hr. *Guasha* RMB 30/20mins. **Credit** MC, V. **Map** p248 H8.
Skip that last drink in Xintiandi and pay the same price across the road for an hour-long treatment at Jade Massage, which scores big for friendly service and fierce yet effective *guasha* (couple it with a *tuina*). Afterwards, relaxed and limp, you might have trouble opening the heavy wooden door of this traditional lane house. Don't worry – the staff are sure to help send you on your way, probably with a large cup of hot jasmine tea for the road. **Other locations** 792 Hongzhong Lu, by Yanan Gao Jia, Hongqiao (6446 2131).

Kangjun Massage Center
436 Dagu Lu, by Nanjing Xi Lu, Jingan (6340 1161). Metro Nanjing Xi Lu. **Open** 10am-2am daily. **Treatments** *Massage* RMB 80-130/hr. **No credit cards. Map** p243 G6.

Bath time

While the Chinese may have been first with inventions such as paper, gunpowder and the compass, the Romans beat them into the tub – public bathhouses didn't appear in China until the Song Dynasty (960-1279). A new egalitarianism came during the Ming Dynasty (1368-1644) after the Emperor Zhu Yuanzhang decreed that labourers could bathe in the same establishments as those of a higher social rank.

While today you'll find mostly BMWs in the parking lots of Shanghai's hot scrub spots, the price is right for those who bus it to their bath: general admission is never more than around RMB 70. Slip in to hot communal pools (single-sex only), sweat it out in the steam room and sauna, or experience an invigorating – if rather intimidating – old-fashioned exfoliation at the hands of a grim-faced attendant who uses a rough cloth to rub off a cloak of dead skin. Make sure to follow up with a milk massage – you'll feel as soft and supple as the day you were born. Afterwards, slip on a pair of pyjamas and

stroll the mammoth halls in search of a foot rub or a game of ping pong, or simply have a drink at the bar or a meal in the restaurant.

Green Water & Clean Sky
Bldg B, 3655 Qixin Lu, by Huqingping Highway, Minhang (5227 7777). **Open** 24hrs daily. **Treatments** *Body/foot massage & skin treatments* RMB 68. **Credit** AmEx, DC, MC, V.

Shanghai Orient Rome
1420 Jiangning Lu, by Aomen Lu, Putuo (6660 0666). Metro Zhenping Lu. **Open** 24hrs daily. **Treatments** *Body/foot massage & skin treatments* RMB 68. **No credit cards. Map** p242 C1.

Xiao Nan Guo
3337 Hongmei Lu, by Yanan Xi Lu, Hongqiao (6465 8888). **Open** 11am-9am daily. **Treatments** *Bath* RMB 58 (RMB 128 VIP). *Foot massage* RMB 78/hr. *Body massage* RMB 128/hr. **Credit** AmEx, DC, MC, V. **Map** p240 A4.

Wanted. Jumpers, coats and people with their knickers in a twist.

From the people who feel moved to bring us their old books and CDs, to the people fed up to the back teeth with our politicians' track record on climate change, Oxfam supporters have one thing in common. They're passionate. If you've got a little fire in your belly, we'd love to hear from you. Visit us at **oxfam.org.uk**

Be Humankind (X) **Oxfam**

This fast-growing chain's excessive use of oil paintings of toucans in the rest areas may attest to the fact that there's no accounting for taste, but at least here you can depend on steady hands that work out your kinks instead of a mere auto-pilot massage. Dagu Lu is home to several other notable chains, but none offer Thai massage with the same contortions or full-body *tuina* with the same personalised targeting at these rates.
Other locations throughout the city.

Magpie
685 Julu Lu, by Shanxi Nan Lu, French Concession (5403 3867). Metro Shanxi Nan Lu. **Open** noon-2am daily; house calls noon-midnight. **Treatments** *Massage* RMB 128-188/hr. **Credit** AmEx, DC, MC, V. **Map** p243 F6.
In contrast to the minimalist calm of other massage parlours, Magpie comes across as positively kitsch, stuffed as it is with antique Chinese furniture amassed by its owner. Rooms are large and can hold several massage beds, so there's not much in the way of privacy. Still, the place offers a divine oil massage: the secret is in the combination of oil and the application of a steam machine. *Photo p172.*

Ming
298 Wulumuqi Nan Lu, by Jianguo Xi Lu, French Concession (5465 2501). Metro Hengshan Lu. **Open** 11am-2am daily. **Treatments** *Massage* RMB 88-248/hr. **Credit** AmEx, MC, V. **Map** p246 C10.
The design is striking: you enter across a small bridge over running water into Japanese-style treatment rooms with whitewashed walls, black beams and vintage wood floors. It's a classy setting – if a little cramped – and the towels are, hands down, the softest in town. Slip into silky pyjamas (provided) to receive treatment from highly professional masseurs. Between 11am and 4pm each day women receive a 20% discount. The full body massage has to be one of the best in town. Afterwards, relax with a cup of complimentary buckwheat tea.

Blind massage

One of the perks of being in Shanghai is that almost every street has a massage centre where you can get a traditional foot and body rub for about the price of a Starbucks coffee. What's most intriguing about the experience is that your masseur will probably be blind.

Massage is one of the few professions open to the blind in China and businesses employing the visually impaired get tax breaks. As a result you pay a lot less than you would at any 'sighted' establishment – and effective pressure point massages are not impeded by lack of sight either. (Note that some 'blind' therapists have an uncanny knack of recognising that you're foreign before you've spoken – the only visual impairment seems to be tinted sunglasses – and levels of cleanliness and service vary.)

The standard blind massage hall has dimmed lights and rows of massage tables with recliners for the footwork. Your feet will be soaked in hot water, dried, wrapped in towels, then massaged. For a standard Chinese body massage, the therapist will put a clean sheet over your (clothed) body – sometimes there will be a curtain for privacy, but usually not. And there's some lingo you should memorise before you go: '*qing/zhong yi dian*' (a little lighter/harder).

Ease Massage Centre
89 Fahuazhen Lu, by Xinfu Lu, Xujiahui (6281 1081). Metro Xujiahui. **Open** 11.30am-midnight daily. **Treatments** *Body massage* RMB 40/40mins, 60/68mins. *Foot massage* RMB 60/50mins.
No credit cards. Map p246 A9.

Feining Blind Massage Centre
597 Fuxing Zhong Lu, by Maoming Nan Lu, French Concession (6437 8378). Metro Shanxi Nan Lu. **Open** noon-1.30am daily. **Treatments** *Body/foot massage* RMB 60/hr. **No credit cards. Map** p247 F9.

JB Massage
New Building, Jingan Hotel, 370 Huashan Lu, by Wulumuqi Bei Lu, French Concession (6248 1888 ext 6660). Metro Changshu Lu. **Open** noon-2am daily. **Treatments** *Body/foot massage* RMB 68/hr. **No credit cards. Map** p242 C6.

Therapeutical Massage by the Blind Doctor
Number 7, Lane 429 Hankou Lu, by Shanxi Lu, Huangpu District (6360 6970). Metro Nanjing Dong Lu. **Open** 9am-8pm daily. **Treatments** *Body/ head massage* RMB 38/45mins; 50/hr; 12 RMB for additional 15mins. **No credit cards. Map** p244 L5.

Spas

Shanghai boasts international luxury spa services with international standards – and prices to match. But it's not all about jet-lag cures for jet-setters; mid-range local options are also entering the scene and offering carefully crafted packages for discerning guests.

Aqua Villa
No.3, Lane 89 Xingguo Lu, by Hunan Lu, Xuhui. (3423 0038). Metro Xujiahui. **Open** 10am-10pm daily. **Treatments** *Facials* from RMB 450/75min. *Massage* from RMB 550/90min. **Credit** AmEx, DC, MC, V. **Map** p246 A8.
This modern three-level reconstruction of a Shanghai lane house offers quiet nooks and crannies for the weary, though some corners may be crammed with decorative kitsch. Groove to yacht rock as you sail the scented waters of a personalised hot tub in a private room – or take along that special someone to a two-tub, two-massage table room. After an invigorating ginger scrub or a Thai massage, clomp down the winding wooden stairs outside to the closed-in flower garden for a spot of Dragon's Well tea.

Underneath the **Banyan Tree**, me honey and me can watch for the moon.

Banyan Tree

3rd floor, Westin Hotel, 88 Henan Zhong Lu, by Guangdong Lu, the Bund (6335 1888/www.banyan treespa.com/shanghai). Metro Nanjing Dong Lu. **Open** 10am-midnight daily. **Treatments** *Facial & body packages* from RMB 1,000. *Massage* from RMB 780. **Credit** AmEx, DC, MC, V. **Map** p244 L5.

Originating in Phuket, the Banyan Tree spas are an Asian success story founded on opulent treatment rooms, and a holistic approach to healing and rejuvenation drawing on ancient Asian remedies and the five elements of Chinese medicine. The rooms are richly decorated in themes of earth, gold, water, wood and fire, which correspond with treatments including facials, scrubs and Balinese, Hawaiian, Swedish and Thai massage (many of Banyan's experienced therapists are Thai). Come to be pampered like royalty – and to pay royally.

CHI, the Spa at Shangri-La

6th floor, Grand Tower, Pudong Shangri-La, 33 Fucheng Lu, by Yincheng Dong Lu, Pudong (6882 8888 ext 460/www.shangri-la.com). Metro Lujiazui. **Open** 10am-midnight daily. **Treatments** *Facials* from RMB 730. *Massages* from RMB 1,330. **Credit** AmEx, DC, MC, V. **Map** p245 O5.

An entire floor of this high-luxury hotel is devoted to this Tibetan temple of tranquillity. The chain's spa concept draws on the mystical aura and ancient healing rituals of the Himalayan region, with 37 body, water, massage and facial therapies designed around the five Chinese elements. Take a brief quiz before your session to determine your element, and therapists will personalise the treatment to bring you back to your most vital self. A reverent atmosphere pervades the soaring space, awash in rich ochre hues, moody candlelight and traditional Tibetan accents. Signature therapies include the mountain *tsampa* rub, and the crystal energising facial. Just as heavenly are the soft chenille robes, cinnamon and mulberry organic teas, and the post-treatment ting of tiny Tibetan cymbals gently coaxing you back to the real world.

David's Camp Men's SPA & Skin Care Centre

2nd floor, 200 Yanan Xi Lu, by Wulumuqi Bei Lu, French Concession (6247 3602/www.davidscamp spa.com). Metro Jingan Temple. **Open** 9am-midnight daily. **Treatments** *Facials* from RMB 400. *Massage* from RMB 150/60mins. **Credit** AmEx, DC, MC, V. **Map** p242 C6.

Expensive treatments for *Vogue Hommes* types in a modern Asian setting. Ascend the sweeping marble staircase for Japanese shiatsu and thorough facials using Swiss products. The Chinese staff have limited English, but deliver treatments with a delicate touch. There are couple treatments in the VIP room.

Diva Life Nail & Beauty Lounge

266 Ruijin Er Lu, by Taikang Lu, Luwan (5465 7291/www.mydivalife.com). **Open** 10am-10pm daily. **Treatments** *Facial* from RMB 200/70 mins. *Massage* from RMB 120/hr. *Manicure/pedicure* from RMB 90/ 35 mins; 130/50 mins. **Credit** MC, V. **Map** p247 F10.

Indulge your inner goddess – or humour your feminine side, guys – at this historic Garden House retreat stuffed with plump purple couches and gossamer drapes. Enjoy some of Shanghai's best nail and waxing services, or let the friendly staff scrub you down with herbal honey before wrapping you up in yoghurt moisturiser – you could almost eat yourself.

Everlasting

380 Shanxi Bei Lu, by Beijing Xi Lu, Jingan (6218 3079). Metro Nanjing Xi Lu. **Open** 10am-10pm daily. **Treatments** *Facial* from RMB 320/90mins. *Massage* RMB 98/hr. **Credit** AmEx, MC, V. **Map** p243 E4.

The grand stone façade and friendly reception lead first-time visitors to expect something more than the basic set-up of the treatment room, but there should be no complaints about the quality of the massage. Specialities include essential oil body massage, hot stone therapy, head yoga massage and slimming treatments (not offered at every branch). **Other locations** throughout the city.

Evian Spa

2nd floor, Three on the Bund, 3 Zhongshan Dong Yi Lu/the Bund, by Guangdong Lu, the Bund (6321 6622/www.threeonthebund.com). Metro Nanjing Dong Lu. **Open** 11.30am-10pm Mon-Fri; 10am-10pm Sat, Sun. **Treatments** *Facials* from RMB 780. *Massages* from RMB 680/hr.* **Credit** AmEx, DC, MC, V. **Map** p245 M5.

Evian's women-only day spa at Three on the Bund has a 35m-high (115-ft) atrium, 14 individually designed treatment rooms, indoor streams filled with Evian mineral water, and a deluxe menu of French beauty treatments (using Clarins products), Eastern holistic therapies and New Age colour- and hydrotherapies. After an exhilarating soak in the colour hydrotherapy bath and an Eve Taylor aromatherapy body treatment, it's time to chill out in the post-treatment lounge and order a bite from chef David Laris's special spa menu.

Mandara Spa

6th floor, JW Marriott, Tomorrow Square, 399 Nanjing Xi Lu, People's Square (5359 4969 ext 6798/www.mandaraspa.com). Metro People's Square. **Open** 10am-10pm daily (last appointment 8pm). **Treatments** *Facial* RMB 520/hr. *Massages* from RMB 680/hr.* **Credit** AmEx, DC, MC, V. **Map** p244 H5.

Located within the Marriot, this is the first Chinese branch of the Asian resort spa giant. Experienced massage therapists offer treatments in 'old Shanghai' themed rooms with traditional grey bricks, antique rosewood furniture and blue and white porcelain sinks. The exotic ambience and scents of sandalwood and lemongrass are a world away from the stark glass and marble hotel lobby outside, and the huge terrazzo bathtubs, soothing music and steam showers make for a thorough pampering. As well as the luscious Eastern therapies like the Pearl of the Orient facial, there's a menu of short and effective treatments for men and women on the go, concentrating on specific areas of the body

La Spa

499 Fuxing Zhong Lu, by Chongqing Nan Lu, French Concession (6387 7708/www.laspa888.com). Metro Huangpi Nan Lu. **Open** 10am-10pm daily. **Treatments** *Facials* from RMB 180/70 minutes. *Massages* from RMB 480/hr.* **No credit cards.** **Map** p247 H9.

This neighbourhood hot spot, a Guangzhou chain, may not boast the luxury of some of Shanghai's finer establishments, but it's an excellent way to experience beauty treatments from a local perspective. Just a short jaunt from Xintiandi, head here for a post-lunch facial before an afternoon walk in Fuxing Park, right across the road. Plop down on a plush sofa with the regulars – a loquacious bunch of Shanghai aunties – and browse the extensive menu of skin, massage and weight loss treatments. The staff here fawn over foreigners, so expect a little extra TLC. Once in the minimal but tidy rooms, attendants deliver fine service and sometimes even throw in free extras, such as eyebrow shaping.

Yuan Spa

Hyatt on the Bund, 199 Huangpu Lu, by Wuchang Lu, the Bund (6393 1234/www.shanghai.bund. hyatt.com). Taxi or bus. **Open** 10am-midnight daily. **Treatments** *Facials* from RMB 680/hour. *Massages* from RMB 780/hour.* **Credit** AmEx, DC, MC, V. **Map** p245 N3.

In Chinese, *yuan* means 'the source', and the new spa at the Grand Hyatt wrings every last drop from its aquatic theme. Follow a waterfall, descending in to a bamboo-ridged river, to the doors of a modern reception room that boasts subtle Chinese accents. Each of the 12 treatment rooms afford a watery view, where talented therapists bring your mind to a glass surface stillness. Afterwards, relax in the sauna.

Yoga

Impressed with locals who lithely squat while waiting for public transport or charge around three to a bicycle? See what they can do on a yoga mat. Try the **Breeze Yoga & Pilates Centre** (7th floor, 120 Xizang Zhong Lu, by Guangdong Lu, People's Square, 6350 1086, www.breezeyoga.com), or check out **Yoga Shala Shanghai** (No.50, Lane 1487, Huaihai Zhong Lu, by Ulumuqi Lu, 6437 5915, www.yogashalashanghai.com). Yoga and Pilates classes are also offered at many gyms (*see p196*).

Water, water everywhere at **Yuan Spa**.

Music

Shanghai rocks. A little.

Despite little support from record labels and the media, and the financial precariousness of being a break-even-at-best musician in a city where the cost of living continues to soar, Shanghai rock keeps on rolling. It has gathered little moss, but has – slowly but surely – been picking up plenty of fans, attention and accolades. Shanghai has some way to go before it can call itself a music city – Filipino cover bands still entertain at the expat pubs and a substance-driven DJ scene dominates the evening offerings – but at least now there is a decent crop of alternatives, with even an outdoor festival mooted; keep an eye on the local press for news.

As you might expect from such a young scene (for decades independent music laboured underground), new venues seem to emerge in spurts and then drop like flies. The same applies to bands, only a minuscule percentage of which get past the thrashing-along-to-White Stripes-in-the-bedroom stage. Still, after many years when the Shanghai rock scene was excited if it produced one album, new releases now dizzy fans in their relative abundance.

Indeed, Shanghai rock, pop, metal and hip hop has been quietly blossoming since around 2000, when the city government lifted the ban on using the word 'rock' and on showing long-haired men in the media. Politics aside, it's hard to define what exactly constitutes rock in 21st-century China. In Shanghai, rockers prefer the term *yuan chang*, as well as indie (*duli*) and alternative (*linglei*), since rock (*yaogun*) has connotations heavily linked to the north-eastern folk-influenced music of Beijing in the late 1980s and early 1990s. The Shanghai sound is all over the map stylistically, but is generally melodic yet hard, with influences from British rock and European electronica.

Continuing to lead the live-music cavalry is **Yuyintang**, a concert venue and organisation founded by Zhang Haisheng, sound engineer and former lead singer of the now disbanded Vicky's Area. It opened its own concert space in 2006, but has been forced to move several times since. Yuyintang regularly showcases local, national and international bands, but they are no longer the only game in town, with **Live**

> ▶ For details of Shanghai's classical music scene, see pp186-190 **Performing Arts**.

Bar, **021**, **Logo** and now **Windows Tembo** giving music fans some pleasant dilemmas.

Shanghai also has a small Chinese folk scene, overlapping on occasion with the rock scene. Cold Fairyland (*see p180* **The fantastic four**) singer Lin Di has a solo career as a folk artist and has cut albums in Taiwan with Liu Xing, who plays the *zhongruan*, a traditional string instrument. Their discs are available care of **Bandu Music**, an aspiring label and bar-café that hosts traditional Chinese music concerts on Saturday nights (call for details).

Hip hop remains a staple of the mainly foreign DJ scene and, among the young Shanghainese, seems more about fashion then music. But a collective of local DJs are – to quote NWA – starting to 'express themselves'. Gary Wang, aka DJ V-Nutz, continues to train and proselytise at the Lab (www.thelab.cn). Last year he paired with several friends to open Shanghai's favourite claustrophobia-inducing night spot, the **Shelter** (*see p185*), which offers hip hop and all varieties of electronica. The same is true of the monthly Antidote parties, at **Cis Bar** (Basement, 685 Dingxi Lu, by Yanan Xi Lu, Jingan, 6294 0547) and other venues, which provides a platform for many of the city's best DJs.

LABELS AND DISCS

Record stores are a dying breed in China, and albums now mostly sell out of bookstores. The selection remains dominated by hits from Hong Kong and Taiwan, including popular favourites like Chinese band Yu Quan and Taiwanese boy band F4. Shanghai has a few start-up indie labels, although they often develop artists then sell the contract to a mainstream label. One indie success of note is Soma's *Easy World* (2007), an English-language electronica-folk album by environmentalist singer Zhong Chi. Most bands sell their albums at concerts, and only a few small stores like 2046 (Rm8, 050 Guoding Lu, by Zhengxiu Lu, Yangpu, 6565 4377) specialise in original Chinese rock. Bandu Music stocks local folk music.

Major venues

Increasingly, big-name Asian and Western performers pack out the city's three large venues. The biggest, **Shanghai Stadium** (1111 Caoxi Bei Lu, by Zhongshan Nan Er Lu, Xuhui, 6438 5200), has featured performers such as Mando-pop stars Faye Wang and Zheng Jun, as well as the Rolling Stones. It consists of the *tiyuchang* or Grand Stage, an 80,000-seat outdoor stadium built in 1997, and the *tiyuguan*, a smaller indoor arena; both are typically called Shanghai Stadium in English. Nora Jones and Deep Purple are among the acts to have played at the **Hongkou Stadium** (715 Dongtiyuhui Lu, by Zhongshan Bei Er Lu, Hongkou, 6540 0009), which was rebuilt in its current 35,000-seat incarnation in 1999. To a lesser extent, concerts are held at the **Changning Stadium** (777 Wuyi Lu, by Zhongshan Xi Lu, Jingan, 6228 9488), also known as the Shanghai International Stadium. Concert tickets for the big stadiums usually go for somewhere between RMB 200-500.

Pop & rock

Bandu Music

1st floor, Building 11, 50 Moganshan Lu, by Changhua Lu, Jingan (6276 8267/www. bandumusic.com). **Open** 10am-8pm Mon-Fri, Sun; 10am-11pm Sat. **Admission** free. **No credit cards**. **Map** p242 D1.
Located in the Moganshan Lu arts district (*see p163*), Bandu Music is an unassuming coffee shop and bar that organises Chinese folk music concerts most weekends (8pm Sat). It also sells the best selection of Chinese folk discs in Shanghai.

Gua'er

685 Ding Xi Lu, by Yanan Xi Lu, Hongqiao (6282 1395). Metro Yanan Xi Lu. **Open** 5pm-2am daily. **Admission** free. **No credit cards**. **Map** p240 B4.

Like 288 Melting Pot (*see p181*), this is a dive run by rockers, for rockers. Gua'er might not have the most consistent of concert schedules but it provides a place for musicians – from novice to veteran – to goof around both on stage and off.

Live Bar

721 Kunming Lu, by Tongbei Lu, Yangpu (2833 6764/www.chinalivebar.com). Metro Dalian Lu. **Open** 8pm-2am daily. **Admission** RMB 30-50. **No credit cards**. **Map** p241 G2.
This oh-so-cool, high-ceilinged dive is out of the way and hard to find, but worth the pilgrimage. There are concerts most weekends showcasing a diverse range of China's alternative bands, plus the occasional foreign import.

Logo

13 Xingfu Lu, by Fahuazhen Lu, Jingan (6281 5646/ www.logoshanghai.com). Metro Yanan Xi Lu. **Open** 8.30pm-late daily. **Admission** free. **No credit cards**.
Formerly known as Tang Hui, this cosy dive has gone from being a live venue to more of a DJ-focused joint, with occasional live gigs (mostly punk bands). It's popular with the student crowd from Jiaotong. On Sunday, all musicians are welcomed for jam night; just bring your instrument to join in.

021 Bar

2925 Yangshupu Lu, by Dinghai Lu, Hongkou (13 91801 5880 mobile/www.shanghairock.org). Metro Hongkou Stadium. **Open** 9pm-midnight daily. **Admission** RMB 30. **No credit cards**. **Map** p241 H2.
A dive bar with heavy metal leanings and a student clientele; situated in Hongkou near the more remote Fudan and Tongji Universities.

Yuyintang. *See p181.*

The fantastic four

Shanghai's bands are nothing if not diverse. Here are four that stand out for endurance, musical variety or exciting potential.

Cold Fairyland

Formed in 2001, Cold Fairyland (Lengku Xianjing; www.coldfairyland.com) defies stylistic pigeon-holing. The music conservatory backgrounds of two of its members help to infuse classical and Chinese folk sensibilities into the band's hard but melodic Gothic rock (it's quite something to see the two women rocking out on a cello and a Chinese *pipa*). The band has performed internationally, and has been unusually prolific, releasing a new album almost every year, mostly self-published. Titles include *Seeds on the Ground* (2007), *Ten Days in Magic Land* (2002/05) and *Kingdom of Benevolent Strangers* (2003).

Crazy Mushroom Brigade

Another stylistic mishmash, Crazy Mushroom Brigade (Fengzi Mogu Jituan) majors in heavy metal and hip hop but adminsters an occasional spoonful of syrupy pop to help the medicine go down. These relative newcomers have yet to release an album, but the past couple of years has seen them change from being a bunch of shy, pimply kids to matching the aggressive confidence of their music, onstage and off. They play regularly at the 288 Melting Pot (*see p181*).

The Honeys

Veteran rockers the Honeys (Tianmi de Haizi; www.the-honeys.net; *pictured*) are something of an urban institution: they have been making their signature Brit pop-inflected rock since 1997. First formed in Hangzhou, where several of its members attended the China Art Academy, the band moved to Shanghai in 2002. That year also saw the release of their first album, *On the Street*, an exercise in youthful exuberance as compared to the mature, slow and defiantly introspective 2008 release, *Shui*, which incorporates a *guzheng* (a traditional Chinese string instrument) on many tracks, some of which have made the domestic charts. Art teachers by day, the Honeys have played in the US, France and Germany.

IGO

Synth-pop duo IGO (www.myspace.com/igoigo) combines the punk swagger of former Terrified Bird frontman JJay Wu and the electronic genius of multi-talented, multi-tasking DJ and designer B6. Singing in English with something of a 1980s Pet Shop Boys feel, the group is still polishing its sound and stage persona, but promises to go far. Formed in 2006, IGO released debut album *Synth Love* in 2007 on Beijing's Modern Sky label, re-releasing it in 2008 with Hong Kong's Universal Music.

288 Melting Pot

288 Taikang Lu, by Sinan Lu, Luwan (6467 9900).
Taxi or bus. **Open** 9pm-late daily. **Admission** free.
Credit AmEx, DC, MC, V. **Map** p247 G10.
Live music runs the gamut of styles nightly, and the sit-down crowd is always mellow and respectful. Featuring local stars like Blue Garden and Crazy Mushroom Brigade on weekends, 288 is also where Shanghai's rockers go to hang out after hours and jam until the sun comes up.

Windows Tembo

66 Shanxi Bei Lu, by Yanan Zhong Lu, Jingan
(5116 8857). Metro Nanjing Xi Lu. **Open** 7pm-
3am daily. **Admission** RMB 30. **No credit cards.**
Map p243 F6.
Formerly just another link in the Windows chain, where impoverished foreign students went to get wasted, in April 2008 Tembo was reincarnated as a live music venue, which has so far attracted some big-name bands from Beijing.

Yuyintang

Tianshan Park, 1731 Yanan Xi Lu, by Kaixuan
Lu, Changning (5237 8662/www.yuyintang.org).
Metro Yanan Xi Lu. **Admission** RMB 30-60.
No credit cards.
The city's premier concert promoter puts on at least one gig a week in its latest venue by Tianshan Park, and also arranges shows elsewhere in town. The mostly-in-Mandarin website details gigs; admission prices vary according to the band. *Photo p179.*

Zhijiang Dream Factory

Tonglefang, 4/F, Building 15, 28 Yuyao Lu, by
Xikang Lu, Jingan (6255 4062). Metro Jingan
Temple then taxi. **Open** noon-10pm Mon-Fri;
noon-midnight Sat, Sun. **Admission** call for details. **No credit cards. Map** p242 C3.
Primarily an independent theatre, Zhijiang also stages concerts by local bands, usually on weekends.

Jazz

Shanghai's jazz scene is almost an exact negative of the rock scene: it is bar-centred, dominated by expats and rarely original. Pretty much every four- or five-star hotel has a resident jazz act, but the bar at the Portman Ritz-Carlton (*see p36*) stands out: streamlined and elegant, with low-slung and comfortable chairs, it hosts excellent American jazzers, changing the roster every few months.

Despite the city's healthy number of independent venues, Shanghainese jazz groups – even individual performers – are thin on the ground. Notable exceptions, like the band Five Guys on a Train and flamboyant gay singer Coco (a semi-celeb), stick strictly to the standards. The imported bands performing in the city's jazz bars are usually tight and professional, injecting verve into their covers and often wrapping up with an energised jam.

The **Glamour Bar** (*see p120*) often hosts weekend gigs of a high quality, while Taiwanese-owned **CJW** (which stands for Cigars, Jazz and Wine: 50th floor, Bund Centre, 222 Yanan Dong Lu, 6339 1777, www.cjwchina.com) appropriates jazz as a lifestyle accessory, but does book competent bands.

Cotton Club

1416 Huaihai Zhong Lu, by Fuxing Xi Lu, French
Concession (6437 7110). Metro Changshu Lu. **Open**
7.30pm-2.30am daily. **Admission** free. **Credit**
AmEx, DC, MC, V. **Map** p246 C8.
No relation to the New York original, Shanghai's oldest outlet of jazz and blues is the closest thing in town to a sure bet for smooth sounds. A good crowd of both Westerners and Chinese packs the small, smoky club for nightly sets. Compared to most clubs, which rotate bands every few months, consistency is key at the Cotton Club; the house band is mainly foreigners, some of whom have been playing there for years. A handful of semi-regulars join in and jam a couple of nights a week.

Five

Basement, M on the Bund, 20 Guangdong Lu,
by Zhongshan Dong Yi Lu, the Bund (6329 4558/
www.numberfive.cn). Metro Nanjing Dong Lu. **Open**
11am-2am Mon-Fri; noon-2am Sat, Sun. **Credit**
AmEx, DC, MC, V. **Admission** free. **Map** p245 M5.
Shanghai's most laid-back jazz house, Five is tucked away improbably at the bottom of the chic M on the Bund building, offering comfy leather chairs and cheap beer. The jazz, five nights a week from 9.30pm, is competent and the atmosphere sultry.

House of Blues & Jazz

60 Fuzhou Lu, by Sichuan Zhong Lu, the Bund
(6437 5280). Metro Nanjing Dong Lu. **Open** 11am-
2am Tue-Sun. **Admission** free. **Credit** AmEx, DC,
MC, V. **Map** p245 M5.
Brainchild of radio and TV personality Lin Dongfu, the House has existed in various incarnations around Shanghai since the mid 1990s. The beloved prior incarnation on Maoming Lu was outfitted in art deco style, and the music was a mixture of blues and jazz fusion. The new two-storey location on Fuzhou Lu had not yet opened at the time of writing, but we are told to expect more of the same.

JZ Club

46 Fuxing Xi Lu, by Yongfu Lu, French Concession
(6431 0269/www.jzclub.cn). Metro Changshu Lu.
Open 9pm-2am daily. **Admission** free. **Credit**
AmEx, DC, MC, V. **Map** p247 C8.
Opened in late 2003 by a local jazz enthusiast who studied music overseas, JZ has established itself as one of Shanghai's leading jazz dives. Its unpretentious but stylish atmosphere and use of young, Chinese musicians makes it more accessible to young Shanghainese jazz aficionados than most of its competitors. Nor is JZ a place for Billie Holiday covers: the three nightly sets focus on contemporary jazz and fusion, often evolving into a rousing jam.

Nightlife

Shanghai nights.

Though still in its salad days (Shanghai's first bona fide dance clubs only got going in 1992, after President Deng Xiaoping opened the city to economic reform), Shanghai's club scene has proved a conscientious and all-too-willing accomplice to late-night hedonism over the past two decades. Long gone are the days when the only option was sleazy expat dives with watery, cheap beer and – dare we say it? – cheaper women. Today, Shanghai's nightspots, with their stylish spaces, well-crafted cocktails and cosmopolitan clientele, give New York, Berlin and London a run for their money.

Though flyers still try to entice with promises of '#76 DJ in the world!' – shamelessly and without a trace of irony – the Shanghai scene has matured and discerning clubbers are now getting the acts they deserve. While lack of variety is no longer a concern, the quality of less mainstream offerings is still inconsistent. Hard house, trance and techno fanatics will have no problems – the Shanghainese love their van Dyks and van Buurens – but those seeking less commercial entertainment may find themselves at the same few venues.

Nevertheless, there are several independent promoters working hard to develop a vibrant, varied scene. The largely expat-driven independent music community is tight-knit and several collectives put on excellent events. Among them are: **Antidote** (electronic; www.antidoteasia.com), **Bananas** (mash-up; www.free-bananas.com), the **Lab** (underground hip hop; www.thelab.cn), **micro** (minimal techno; tootekool.com), **Phreaktion** (drum 'n' bass; phreaktion.com), **STD** (electronic rock; stdpromotions.com), **Uprooted Sunshine** (reggae/dub; uprootedsunshine@gmail.com) and **Void** (underground house and techno; www.void-shanghai.com). If private table bookings and bottles of Grey Goose are more your thing, try promoters **Riviera** (www.rivieraevents.com) – their theme parties and summer poolside fêtes attract a loyal following among those who live and die by styling gel and stilettos.

Though local Shanghainese DJs have been traditionally disadvantaged due to the unavailability of vinyl in China, in the age of digital media, home-grown musical talents are steadily coming to the fore: Ben Huang, V-Nutz and B6 are all at the top of their game, and

global names continue to flock to Shanghai – and not just to tour. In late 2007, three-time world DJ champion Kid Fresh decided to relocate to Shanghai and Hong Kong, citing as motivation his boredom with the German scene and an interest in exploring the newer terrain of East Asian electronica.

As this edition was going to press, *Time Out* caught wind of a new project from nightlife icon Norman Gosney (London's UFO; Munich's P-1; NYC's Palladium and Danceteria). Word is that Gosney, his partner Amelia Kallman, and several heavyweights from NY are reviving the razzle-dazzle of 1930s Shanghai in a new, intimate mock-Victorian venue set to open in October 2008 near Suzhou Creek. Watch the local press for details.

To the club-scene trio of dancing, drinking and drug-taking, Shanghai adds drunken drawling – otherwise known as **karaoke**. Shanghai is lousy with karaoke joints. Many are abysmal, but even the worst should not be confused with KTV bars, many of which are nothing short of brothels. The best are a uniquely Chinese add-on to the clubbing scene in which dancefloors are supplemented by karaoke boxes. Punters use them like chill-out rooms. Stylish karaoke complexes have been set up within stumbling distance of the hippest clubs – **Partyworld** is a popular example, just a short stumble away from the exclusive, Starck-designed **Volar** near Fuxing Park.

Before picking a spot from the list that follows, you may want to consult a listings magazine such as *CityWeekend* (www.city weekend.com.cn) or *SH* (www.shmag.cn), or entertainment website **SmartShanghai.com** for a list of special events. Be sure to call the venues before heading out – Shanghai is notoriously fickle when it comes to nightlife, and it's not uncommon for a club that was turning away people a month ago to close without notice.

In Shanghai, style has long trumped substance and residents are forever chasing each other around the city – it's considered lazy not to pack five stops into one night – in pursuit of the hottest new place to see and be seen. And, though the city seems to shut down in January (unbearably cold) and August (disgustingly hot), the crowds at local favourites don't ever really thin out. So brush up on your bones

Bonbon.

blowing skills – *chui niu* is a popular dice game in clubs – get used to the taste of Chivas and green tea, and get stuck in.

Clubs

Anar

129 Xinfu Lu, by Fahuazhen Lu, Changning (6280 9326) Metro Xujiahui. **Open** 8pm-2am daily. **Admission** free. **No credit cards**.

Over the years, we've seen two places come and go in this space (RIP Shuffle and Pirates), but with Anar it seems like someone's finally getting things right. Up front a cosy café serves tasty Xinjiang-inspired Middle Eastern grub. Pick a flavour of shisha for dessert and plop down with the hookah pipe in the pillowed wonderland out back. The team behind Anar includes some Shanghai indie scene stalwarts who put music ahead of attitude. The line-ups read like a who's-who of local heroes, with regular special appearances by touring guests. While things heat up on the weekends, during the week expect loungey grooves, world music and even the occasional movie night. Here's hoping third time's a charm.

Attica

11F, 15 Zhongshan Dong Er Lu, by Jinling Dong Lu, The Bund (6373 3588/www.attica-shanghai.com). **Open** *Bar* 6pm-2am daily. *Club* 9pm-late Tue-Sat. **Admission** RMB 100 Fri, Sat. Women free before midnight. **Credit** AmEx, DC, MC, V. **Map** p245 M6.

This Bund institution prides itself on its decadence and, true to its aspirations, at weekends both rooms are packed with Shanghai's most primped and primed grooving and grinding, or drenching their fabulousness in champagne suds at private tables. The main space favours hard house, the back room hip pop. Midweek experiments in downtempo;

Friday fiestas are hosted by London's Ministry of Sound; and Saturdays are often theme parties. Formats rotate often, however, so double-check before setting out. In the warmer months, the patio is the perfect place to take in the Bund views.

Babyface

Unit 101, Shanghai Square, 138 Huaihai Zhong Lu, by Pu'an Lu, Xintiandi (6375 6667/www.babyface. com.cn). Metro Huangpi Nan Lu. **Open** 9pm-4.30am daily. **Admission** free. **Credit** AmEx, DC, MC, V. **Map** p248 J7.

With outlets China-wide, Babyface is one of the biggest nightclub brands in the Middle Kingdom and, as such, epitomises the Chinese clubbing experience. Its pull among a mainly local crowd sees business in the 2,000-capacity space booming every night of the week. Babyface, however, is also the mean bitch of the Shanghai scene: sexy, but with a sting. Westerners often complain about rude staff, lack of service and steep prices – problems the locals don't seem to suffer. Resident DJs play a mix of house through to breaks and hip hop, and international names (Tiesto, Judge Jules, Deep Dish) are picked for their dancefloor-filling track selections. Not for the claustrophobic.

Bonbon

2nd floor, 2F-3F Yunhai Tower, 1329-1331 Huaihai Zhong Lu, by Hengshan Lu, French Concession (mobile 133 2193 9299/www.clubbonbon.com). Metro Changshu Lu. **Open** 8.30pm-3am Mon-Thur, Sun; 8.30pm-4am Fri, Sat. **Admission** RMB 50-100 Mon-Thur, Sun; RMB 80-120 Fri, Sat. **Credit** AmEx, DC, MC, V. **Map** p246 C8.

In 2006, Bonbon burst on to the scene care of promoter and global clubbing giant Godskitchen, which hosts a monthly event of its own in addition to supplying the flow of international talent. Both the large

Shelter.

main room and the intimate back room boast impressive sound systems (from Funktion One), and a maze of private booths provide welcome relief for your feet. Bonbon bags more than its fair share of the top touring DJs – Oakenfold, Hawtin, Goldie and Vath have all graced its decks, making weekends here some of the biggest nights in town. While the Wednesday mash-up and Thursday hip hop week-lies are also popular, the real can't-miss is Bonbon's monthly drum 'n' bass knees-up.

Dragon Club

156 Fenyang Lu, by Taojiang Lu, French Concession (6433 2187/www.unionwell.com.cn). Metro Changshu Lu. **Open** 10pm-4am Wed-Thur; 10pm-8am Fri, Sat. **Admission** RMB 50 Fri, Sat. **Credit** AmEx, DC, MC, V. **Map** p246 D9.

It's 3am. You're hugging, um, well, err… names don't matter anyway… your new best friends whom you met three bars and five hours ago. 'You guys are the best!' you find yourself gushing. 'Oh I wish this night didn't have to end!' Well, it doesn't. For the Peter Pan party-goer, Dragon Club is Never Never Land. Things don't generally get going till 3am or so, when Shanghai's children of the night emerge from every smoky nook and clubby cranny for round two at this converted old mansion in the French Concession. The pumping music and flow-ing drinks are geared towards helping you extend the magic for as long as possible.

I Love Shanghai

155 Zhongshan Dong Er Lu, by Jinling Dong Lu, the Bund (6355 8058/www.iloveshanghailounge.com). Metro Nanjing Dong Lu. **Open** 6pm-2am daily. **Admission** free. **No credit cards. Map** p245 N6.

Though it's located smack on the Bund, I Love Shanghai is completely attitude- and pretension-free – it's too busy plotting the wackiest ways to get patrons the drunkest and sloppiest. So far they've come up with theme events such as White Girl Wednesdays, Beer Pong Championships and

Absinthe Annihilation nights, all of which are enthusiastically embraced by a faithful following of frat-boy types. Beers start at RMB 30 and cocktails hover around the RMB 50 mark – reasonable for a Bund spot – and, though tastier versions may be had elsewhere, they're unlikely to be as strong.

Logo

13 Xingfu Lu, by Fahuazhen Lu, Changning (6281 5646/www.logoshanghai.com). Metro Yanan Xi Lu. **Open** 8.30pm-3am daily. **Admission** free. **No credit cards. Map** p240 C4.

A bastion of Shanghai's independent music scene, Logo has solid beats and a cool crowd every night of the week. The reggae night on Friday rarely winds down before sunrise, experimental electronic rock on Saturday usually sees the crowds spill on to the street, and Sunday's jam session (new partici-pants are welcome) is a nice way to unwind at the end of the weekend. There are just two cosy rooms – a dancefloor in the back and an intimate lounge (with table football) up front – at this teeny tiny club; it's a labour of love for local owner Taipei. Drinks are cheap (beers from RMB 20), the music good and the vibe just right.

MAO

46 Yueyang Lu, by Dongping Lu, French Concession (mobile 137 6127 1129/www.maoshanghai.com). Metro Changshu Lu. **Open** 10pm-3am Tue-Sat. **Admission** free. **Credit** AmEx, DC, MC, V. **Map** p246 D9.

MAO (as in 'Music Art Oasis', not China's Moled Almighty One) is a slick spot for the champagne-guzzling socialist. Chrome and concrete dominate the space, relieved by touches of velvet. The sound-track is Eurodance and while the dancefloor is tiny, no one seems to mind – you're not here to dance. The massive floor-to-ceiling bar suggests where your pri-orities should lie. Take one of the fresh puréed fruit cocktails – the kiwi ones are especially good – and enjoy it in the open-air garden.

M2

5F, Plaza 66, 1266 Nanjing Xi Lu, by Shanxi Bei Lu, Jingan (6288 6222). Metro Nanjing Dong Lu. **Open** 9pm-4am daily. **Admission** free. **Credit** AmEx, DC, MC, V. **Map** p243 E5.

Perched at the top of Shanghai's fanciest mall, M2 attracts a well-heeled, local crowd. Though it has played host to some top DJs (Tiesto, Carl Cox), M2 is one of the worst venues in Shanghai for those looking to get down. Good luck finding the dancefloor – a minefield of tables caters to dice, not dance, enthusiasts. This is a place to watch and be watched by those on expense accounts and their hangers-on.

Muse

68 Yuyao Lu, by Xikang Lu, Jingan (5213 5228). Metro Jingan Temple. **Open** 9pm-late daily. **Admission** free. **Credit** AmEx, MC, V. **Map** p242 C3.

Though some way from the heart of the action, Muse is worth the trek up north. It's a good-looking, playful club, with glass rooms, white and silver decor, and disco balls. But the real draw is the crowd: folks wanting nothing more than to let loose. The balance of scenesters, English teachers, locals and suits is just right, with party-goers scattered across the two rooms (one for commercial hip hop, one for house). The music is nothing special, but they are anthems everybody knows and will sing along to. Friendly bartenders, no cover and reasonable drink prices round out the list of reasons to give Muse a try.

Shelter

5 Yongfu Lu, by Fuxing Xi Lu, French Concession (6437 0400). Metro Changshu Lu. **Open** 9pm-late Wed-Sun. **Admission** free. **No credit cards**. **Map** p246 C8.

This cavernous space is home to Shanghai's independent music pushers and lovers. An eclectic line-up sees various collectives take to the stage to show what they're made of and the results usually impress. The space was designed by DJs and it shows; the sound is sultry, the bass sexy. The place goes off till the wee hours of the morning, but a word to the wise: the Shelter's gin bomb, made with fresh basil, is probably the best bar-rail drink in Shanghai – addictive and dangerous, a bit like the atmosphere. Thursdays sees nu jazz/downtempo; Friday is underground hip hop; Saturday welcomes guest DJs – often underground heroes – on to the decks. This is probably the smokiest club in Shanghai.

Volar

99 Yandang Lu, by Nanchang Lu, French Concession (mobile 134 8223 9390/www.volar.com.cn). Metro Huangpi Nan Lu. **Open** 8pm-2am Sun; 8pm-5am Sat. **Admission** free Mon-Thur, Sun; RMB 60-100 (incl 1 drink) Fri, Sat. **Credit** AmEx, DC, MC, V. **Map** p247 G8.

Volar opened in 2007 to fanfare and controversy in equal parts. The interior was conceived by Philippe Starck, the concept by a Hong Kong group who thought 'members only' was the road to cool. The decor won raves but the concept flopped. Though the club is still trying to save face by enforcing the members-only rule (while distributing free tickets around the city), the truth is that as long as you're willing to pay you'll be let in. Special events see some great electro/techno talent, but otherwise the soundtrack is commercial hip hop with some tragically bad MCs. Still, the drinks are some of the best in Shanghai and the upstairs area is great for lounging among Shanghai's bold and beautiful.

Wall

2727 Riverside Avenue, by Oriental Pearl Tower, Pudong (5037 0300/www.thewallshanghai.com). Metro Lujiazui. **Open** 8pm-2am daily. **Admission** free. **Credit** AmEx, DC, MC, V. **Map** p245 N4.

A massive space – it lays claim to the title of 'longest bar in China', a key fact for those who choose venues based on bar length – the Wall is the perfect club to see 'stadium DJs'. Its excellent sound system can do them justice, and, with 2,300sq m (25,000sq ft) of space, there's enough dancing room for all. In its soft opening period, it brought out Sasha for a no-cover, invite-only party. Smart marketing. Smarter still: free drinks for women before midnight, every night (double-check for changes).

Karaoke

Such is the popularity of karaoke that the local pop industry is awash with tunes created specifically to be sung across Asia by millions of kara-cuties – girls with terrible voices who look so good that the men present cheer wildly regardless. However, the traveller looking for something more like Whitney Houston than Faye Wong needn't worry: most karaoke boxes have extensive English song lists. In any case, when lubed up it hardly matters. A new law demands that microphones be switched off at 2am, so lock-ins are becoming widespread.

Gold Glorious

4F & 5F, Golden Bell Plaza, 98 Huaihai Zhong Lu, by Longmen Lu, Xintiandi (5385 8608). Metro Huangpi Nan Lu. **Open** 8pm-2am daily. **Admission** min spend on food & drink RMB 1,700 for 6 people. **Credit** MC, V. **Map** p248 J7.

Langsha KTV

6F, 2018 Huashan Lu, by Guangyuan Xi Lu, Xujiahui (5407 0300/www.langshaktv.com). Metro Xujiahui. **Open** 10am-6am daily. **Credit** AmEx, DC, MC, V. **Admission** RMB 22-280 per room per hr (no min spend).

Other locations 7F, 463 Nanjing Dong Lu, by Fujian Zhong Lu, Bund (6351 2535).

Partyworld (Cashbox)

109 Yandang Lu, within Fuxing Park, French Concession (6311 1111/www.cn.cashboxparty.com). Metro Huangpi Nan Lu. **Open** 8am-2am daily. **Admission** varies; average RMB 27-102/3hr per person. **Credit** MC, V. **Map** p247 G8.

Other locations throughout the city.

Arts & Entertainment

Performing Arts

Precious little funding but plenty of buzz.

On the Shanghai arts scene, size matters. Much of the buzz surrounds big productions staged in big buildings starring big names – which makes for big photo-ops. But when it comes to investing in salaries for actors and musicians, grants for dance companies or money to stage theatre festivals, Shanghai falls short.

Much of the cash for the arts comes via the propaganda bureau, and is earmarked for plays that help advance party campaigns (such as the 'Harmonious Society' drive, introduced in 2005). Fresher events, such as the **Shanghai University Drama Festival**, held every October at the Shanghai Dramatic Arts Centre (SDAC), or the **Ideas Festival**, which grants money to young thespians with bright ideas, are funded by private sources.

Still, Shanghai's performing arts scene is beginning to ferment, even if the wine won't be ready for a few years yet. The **Downstream Garage/Mecooon** (*see p189*) is just as underground as the name suggests and specialises in (way) off-Broadway, experimental productions, often featuring amateurs and/or students. The **Shanghai Theatre Academy** (STA; *see p189*) also stages interesting left-field drama and has raised its profile with a recent renovation of the campus. The move is part of a grand, if slow-moving, plan called 'Theatre Way', which aims to lift the profile of Shanghai theatre by building a pedestrian walkway between the STA and the Shanghai Dramatic Arts Centre to the north, and sprucing up the surrounding streets.

The motherlode of the performing arts scene is the **Shanghai Dramatic Art Centre** (SDAC; *see p190*), the city's largest company. This well-funded institution has been experimenting recently with bilingual productions, such as the *Lu Xun Blossoms*, a physical-theatre performance from Canada's Smith Gilmour Company, which had actors performing scenes from Lu Xun's works. In the same cross-cultural spirit, the company staged *Marguerite Duras*, a Sino-French production based on three of the author's essays.

The SDAC has also been making an effort to link up with Asian neighbours, as with 2008's co-production of *Drif,t*, written by Nick Yu of SDAC and members of Singapore's Drama Box. The storyline flits back and forth between places (Singapore and Shanghai) and eras (the 1940s and 2000s), and examines themes of loyalty and Chinese identity. Many productions, however, don't aim this high and are happy simply to put bums on seats – preferably the bums of Shanghai's large and affluent middle class. 'White collar plays', such as *www.com* and *Singles Apartment*, explore the problems of the rising middle class, putting a glossy spin on issues like infidelity, success and materialism.

Though much of what is staged is oriented towards profit, there are a few producers willing to take risks, commonly by reviving European classics and adding a Chinese twist. A recent adaptation of Ibsen's *Hedda Gabler*, for example, had Hedda performing in red dress with two-metre-long sleeves, and singing Yue opera as she burned up Lovborg's manuscript. Purists may wince at this kind of mucking around for mucking around's sake, but a choice between *King Lear* in drag and *The Phantom of the Opera* is better than no choice at all.

ACROBATICS

Acrobatics in China has a long, rich history, dating back several thousand years to the Warring States Period (475-221 BC). Prior to 1949, it was frowned upon by the well-to-do, but in the 1950s the government recognised it as a national art form. The art has developed to incorporate everyday objects – saucers, chairs, jars, plates – and other traditions such as the Chinese martial art wushu.

The Shanghai Acrobatic Troupe is one of the most famous in China and tours internationally. The best place to see it perform is **Shanghai Circus World** (*see p187*), a futuristic globe in the north of the city with high-tech lighting, stereo sound and rotating stages.

For more traditional acrobatics, call the **Shanghai Centre Theatre** (1376 Nanjing Xi Lu, by Xikang Lu, Jingan, 6279 8663, www.shanghaicentre.com), and ask for details of the next shows by the Shanghai Acrobats (www.shanghaiacrobats.com).

FESTIVALS & EVENTS

Shanghai's government-run festivals tend to suffer from a lack of publicity, planning and diversity. October's **Shanghai International Arts Festival** (*see p153*), for example, typically manages to attract a few big musical acts but very little dance or drama. The city's private festivals tend to be edgier and more interesting. The **Asian Contemporary Theatre Festival** (Nov), October's **Fringe Shanghai** (www.fringeshanghai.com) and May's **Shanghai Dance** (www.shanghai-dance.com), all held at the SDAC, have shown that the city can host successful and challenging festivals.

The Fringe, though troubled by performance permit problems, has great potential and features an exciting mix of local and overseas acts. SDAC's Asian Contemporary Theatre Festival features a range of work from across Asia – everything from Singaporean physical theatre to Filipino musicals. Most performances are subtitled. Shanghai Dance, the city's first modern dance festival, is getting better each year; the highlight in 2008 was Jin Xang's new solo work, *The Closest the Furthest*.

TICKETS AND INFORMATION
The easiest way to get tickets is to buy them at the venue just before the show starts; for popular productions (such as the musicals at the Shanghai Grand Theatre), advance booking is essential. If the box office is sold out, the *huangniu* ('yellow cows', or touts) will be happy sell you tickets at inflated prices. Tickets can also be bought through **China Ticket Online** (800 810 3721, 6374 4968, www.piao.com.cn) or the **Shanghai Cultural Information & Booking Centre** (20 Fenyang Lu, by Huaihai Zhong Lu, French Concession, 6437 0137, www.shcmusic.edu.cn).

For information about what's on, check listings in the local free press, particularly *that's Shanghai* (www.urbanatomy.com).

Major venues

Lyceum Theatre
57 Maoming Nan Lu, by Changle Lu, French Concession (6256 5544/www.culture.sh.cn). Metro Shanxi Nan Lu. **Open** *Box office* 9am-7pm daily. **Tickets** RMB 80-580. **No credit cards**. **Map** p247 F7.

The Lyceum was built in 1931. Several revamps later it still, thankfully, boasts striking art deco architecture. Renowned Beijing opera star Mei Lanfang once trod the boards here and the small intimate space is well suited to all kinds of opera, as well as *pingtan*, a unique Suzhounese form of storytelling involving songs, jokes and various traditional instruments. The crowd is Chinese and middle-aged, and though the technology for English subtitles exists, it is seldom used.

Majestic Theatre
66 Jiangning Lu, by Nanjing Xi Lu, Jingan (6217 4409). Metro Nanjing Xi Lu. **Open** *Box office* 10am-7.30pm daily. **Tickets** RMB 60-4,000. **No credit cards**. **Map** p243 E5.

When it went up in 1941, the dome-shaped Majestic was considered one of the best theatres in Asia and hosted performances with Beijing opera superstars. Nowadays the focus is on local plays, Eileen Zhang dramas, ballet (*Swan Lake*) and musicals (*42nd Street*), folk music, opera and *pingtan*.

Shanghai Circus World
2266 Gonghe Xin Lu, by Guangzhong Lu, Zhabei (tickets 6652 7750/1580 0810 468/venue 6630 0000/www.era-shanghai.com). Metro Shanghai Circus World. **Open** *Box office* 9am-8pm daily. **Tickets** RMB 80-580. **No credit cards**. **Map** p240 D1.

At Shanghai Circus World, which looks like a giant golden golf ball half-embedded in the ground, audiences are treated to fantastic displays of 'new circus' acrobatics. Long-running *ERA: Intersection of Time* (7.30pm daily), choreographed by Canadian Eric Villeneuve, has a distinct foreigner-awed-by-Shanghai flavour, but is no less spectacular for it. It combines graceful moves with slick multimedia touches and enough death-defying moves to keep the adrenalin pumping all around the arena. *ERA* is set to run until late 2010.

Shanghai Concert Hall
523 Yanan Dong Lu, by Xizang Zhong Lu, People's Square (5386 6666/www.shanghaiconcerthall.org). Metro People's Square. **Open** *Box office* 9am-7.30pm daily. **Tickets** RMB 30-1,500. **Credit** AmEx, DC, MC, V. **Map** p244 J6.

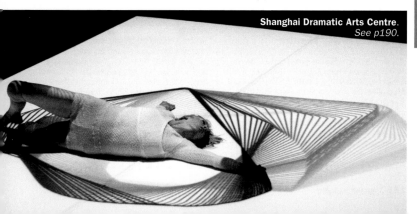

Shanghai Dramatic Arts Centre.
See p190.

Arts & Entertainment

Shanghai Grand Theatre.

Formerly known as the Nanking Theatre, the Shanghai Concert Hall has come a long way – literally. The 74-year-old building was moved 66m (217ft) to the south-east in 2003 – at great cost – to reduce the noise from the Yanan elevated highway. It slid nicely into place above the People's Square metro station. The faint rumble of trains can only occasionally be heard and it has become a top-notch classical music venue, hosting such acts as the Vienna Johann Strauss Capelle, Yo-Yo Ma, Ron Korb and even the occasional rock outfit such as Sonic Youth and local stars Cold Fairyland.

Shanghai Grand Stage
1111 Caoxi Bei Lu, Shanghai Stadium, Xujiahui (6438 5200). Metro Shanghai Stadium. **Open** *Box office 9am-7pm daily.* **Tickets** *RMB 80-3,000.* **No credit cards. Map** p240 C5.
The indoor stage of Shanghai Stadium is neither friendly nor cosy, but this is usually where the shows that are too big for the likes of the Shanghai Centre (*see p186*) end up. Expect stars and a host of wildly popular Canto-pop icons.

Shanghai Grand Theatre
300 Renmin Dadao, by Huangpi Bei Lu, People's Square (6372 8702/www.shgtheatre.com). Metro People's Square. **Open** *Box office 9am-7.30pm daily.* **Tickets** *RMB 80-6,000.* **Credit** *AmEx, DC, MC, V.* **Map** p244 H5.
This impressive modern theatre with a distinctive curved roof is Shanghai's premier venue for staging opera, classical music, ballet and drama performances, as well as being home to the Shanghai Broadcasting Symphony Orchestra. The most popular billings are imported musicals – *Hairspray*, *Mamma Mia*, and so on – which are performed in English, by foreign actors and producers. The theatre also stages occasional classical music concerts featuring the likes of the New York Philharmonic, and even the occasional avant-garde piece such as Tan Dun's *Water Music*. There's also ballet on the bill – mostly the usual suspects such as *The Nutcracker* and *Giselle*, often by the Shanghai Ballet – and Chinese drama (which is sadly often not subtitled), plus a steady stream of Yue and Kun opera.

Shanghai Oriental Art Centre
425 Dingxiang Lu, by Shiji Dadao, Pudong (6854 7757/www.shoac.com.cn). Metro Science & Technology Museum. **Open** *Box office 9am-8pm daily.* **Tickets** *RMB 100-1,800.* **Credit** *AmEx, DC, MC, V.* **Map** p241 G4.
Completed for a whopping US$120 million at the end of 2004, the high-profile Shanghai Oriental Art Centre (SOAC) has been touted as the jewel of Shanghai's financial district, Pudong, or, as its French architect Paul Andreu explains, 'a light in the darkness'. There can be no doubt that it shines, with a glass façade that's simultaneously reflective and transparent, though ceramic tiling on the inside makes it warmer than you might expect. Inside the petals of the orchid-shaped building are three halls (a 2,000-seat orchestra hall, a 1,000-seat lyric theatre and a 330-seat chamber music hall) equipped with state-of-the-art sound and lighting systems and the largest pipe organ in China. SOAC is typical of the Shanghai attitude towards culture – if you build it, they will come – and programming has so far struggled to really find a purpose to match the building, although it is carving out a niche as the venue for both Western and Chinese classical music. The popular Friday Night Jazz Salon makes SHOAC the only venue in town to offer jazz in a concert hall setting.

Yi Fu Theatre

701 Fuzhou Lu, by Yunan Zhong Lu, People's Square (6322 5294/www.tianchan.com). Metro People's Square. **Open** *Box office* 9.30am-8pm daily. **Tickets** RMB 30-500. **No credit cards. Map** p244 J5.

Around since 1921, but massively revamped in the early 1990s, Yi Fu is the main venue for grand Chinese operas, particularly the Beijing variety – as indicated by the huge Beijing opera mask that dominates the entrance. It also stages Yue and Kun opera performances. The regular weekly performances on weekends start at 1.30pm and 7.15pm.

Other venues & companies

Downstream Garage/Mecooon

3rd floor, 100 Longcao Lu, Lane 200, Longcao Lu, by Longwu Lu, Xuhui (6408 9520/www.mecooon. org). Metro Caobao Lu or Longcao Lu. **Open** 6pm-late daily. **Admission** RMB 20. **No credit cards. Map** p240 B5.

This free rehearsal space is a key player on Shanghai's nascent undergound arts scene. Students, amateurs and professionals mingle, performing works (in Chinese) that wouldn't make it to a main stage – call in advance for details. It also hosts the annual Ideas Festival.

Shanghai Art Theatre (Yihai Theatre)

466 Jiangning Lu, by Wuding Lu, Jingan (6256 8282). Metro Nanjing Dong Lu, then taxi or 15min walk. **Open** 9am-7pm daily. **Tickets** RMB 30-280. **No credit cards. Map** p243 E3.

The Art Theatre is used mainly for classical music, plus occasional productions of Yue and Yang opera, dance and sizzling revolutionary shows.

Shanghai Theatre Academy

670 Huashan Lu, by Zhenning Lu, French Concession (6248 8103/www.sta.edu.cn). Metro Jingan Temple. **Open** *Box office* 8.30am-4.30pm daily. **Tickets** RMB 20-80. **No credit cards. Map** p246 B7.

Budding thesps from the Academy periodically stage interesting drama and dance shows at the school's theatre, including some experimental numbers (usually in Chinese). Standouts in 2008 were a production of *Hamlet*, directed by NYU's Richard Schechner, and Cocteau's *La Voix Humaine*.

Classical music

Shanghai's classical music scene suffers from a shortage of nurtured talent, but things are looking up. There are over 20 million young pianists in China, and foreign maestros often offer master-classes when they visit. China now has several superstar ivory-tinklers of its own and pianists such as coiffed prodigy Lang Lang and Li Yundi are making a name for themselves at a national level.

The two major music venues – the Shanghai Concert Hall and the Shanghai Oriental Art Centre – have injected some life into the scene. Although the appetite for classical music among locals and expats remains small, the city hosts a dozen major performances a month by local and international performers. Students of the Conservatory of Music (20 Fenyang Lu, by Huaihai Zhong Lu, French Concession, 6437 0137, www.shcmusic.edu.cn) regularly host 7.30pm weekend concerts, and the Glamour Bar (*see p120*) often hosts international pianists and cellists.

Chinese opera

Chinese opera dates back to the Tang dynasty of the eighth century, and was going strong when Wagner's ancestors were still living in mud-and-straw huts. It still attracts large audiences, but those expecting hum-along Puccini-style arias will be disappointed. The style is wrought from monotone music, simple props and minimalist staging. Dance-like movements are used to express an action such as opening a door or riding a horse. It is fascinating but often difficult to understand, with costumes, make-up and movements freighted with complex symbolism as well as denoting the age, status and personality of a character. The plot fodder is more familiar: heroes slay villains, good kicks the butt of evil, lovers elope to escape domineering parents, and so on. Each

character is from one of four standard types: *sheng* (male role), *dan* (female role), *jing* (painted face) and *chou* (clown).

Add high-pitched voices accompanied by loud gongs, crashing cymbals and droning strings, and you have a performance art that some find compelling, and others torturous.

Though Beijing opera is considered the most refined, China boasts 300 different types of opera distinguished by their use of local dialects and distinct melodies. **Huju**, or **Shenju**, is Shanghainese opera, but **Yueju**, the style from nearby Shaoxing, is better known and more melodic, usually focusing on love stories. The older **Kunju** opera, established in the 16th century, originates from the Kunshan region about an hour from Shanghai.

Jin Xing Modern Dance Company

Jin Xing Modern Dance Company
Office: Room 601, 128 Weihai Lu, by Huangpi Bei Lu, People's Square (6327 0040).
Though her name Jin Xing (Gold Star) is a tad kitsch, no one can dispute the fact that she's earned it. The opinionated choreographer and dancer – formerly a male army colonel – founded her own troupe in 1999, making it China's first privately funded contemporary dance company, and has put endless hours and huge amounts of money into supporting the local dance scene in her role as director of the Shanghai Dance festival. Her latest work, *Made in China – Return of the Soul*, takes a classic scene from the Kun opera *Peony Pavilion* and transforms it into a meditation on the pace of life in modern China.

Shanghai Song & Dance Ensemble
Office: 1650-1674 Hongqiao Nan Lu, by Shuicheng Lu, Hongqiao (6219 5181/www.52921234.com/gewutuan).
This troupe is the result of a recent amalgamation of the Shanghai Oriental Dance Troupe and the Shanghai Song & Dance Ensemble. The dance is contemporary, yet highly influenced by Chinese classical dance. Highlights of the past few years include *Farewell My Concubine* and *Mulan*, both directed by foreign choreographers, and the ever-popular *Wild Zebra*. The biggest name in the troupe is undoubtedly principal dancer Huang Doudou. Using Chinese opera and acrobatics as inspiration, he has created intriguing shows, including *Zen Shaolin* and *Drunken Drum*.

Shanghai Broadcasting Symphony Orchestra
Office: 1498 Wuding Xi Lu, by Jiangsu Lu, Jingan (6252 3277).
Despite its youth (established in 1996), the SBSO has already notched up high-profile collaborations with artists including Placido Domingo, the late and lamented Pavarotti, Isaac Stern and Lang Lang. Under the direction of Chen Zuohang, it is now the resident orchestra at the Shanghai Grand Theatre.

Shanghai Symphony Orchestra
Office: 105 Hunan Lu, by Wukang Lu, French Concession (6437 4685/www.sh-symphony.com).
Asia's oldest orchestra, the SSO began in 1879 as the Shanghai Public Band and was expanded into the Shanghai Municipal Council Symphony Orchestra under the baton of Italian pianist Mario Paci in 1922; its first Chinese director took over – surprise, surprise – in 1949. Current director Chen Xieyi has built himself a reputation and the orchestra has collaborated with the likes of Yo-Yo Ma and Tan Dun.

Dance

Folk dancing performances are numerous but, with dancers commonly kitsched out in sequined costumes, often of dubious authenticity. For something a bit different, look out for the work of choreographer Yang Liping, whose production *Mystery of Tibet* shines a light on the forms of Tibetan dance.

Shanghai sees an endless stream of *Swan Lakes* and *Nutcrackers*, usually performed by touring B-grade Eastern European troupes and a handful of decent contemporary dance troupes such as the Alvin Ailey Dance Company and the Sydney Ballet.

English-language theatre

English-language theatre is on the rise, performed both by local groups and by foreign drama troupes on tour; musicals at the Shanghai Grand Theatre are also performed in English.

Shanghai Dramatic Arts Centre (SDAC)
288 Anfu Lu, by Wukang Lu, French Concession (6473 4567/www.china-drama.com). Metro Changshu Lu. **Open** *Box office* 9am-7pm daily. **Admission** RMB 80-800. **No credit cards. Map** p246 C7.
As the city's largest and liveliest theatre company, SDAC has a staff of over 360 and produces ten first-run plays a year. Though most of the fare is in Chinese (surtitles are often available, though sometimes hard to follow due to poor translation), it occasionally hosts English-language performances of Shakespeare and Ibsen from international theatre companies. One of its founders, Huang Zuolin, was a key figure in the development of Chinese drama theory and, in 2003, it premièred taboo-breaking AIDS melodrama *The Dying Kiss* while in 2004 it was to host Eve Ensler's *Vagina Monologues*, before it was stopped by the authorities. While most of the other venues merely rent out the space, SDAC continually produces interesting new works, such as *And Then There Were None* and *Dog's Face. Photo p187.*

Sport & Fitness

Big-money tournaments buy prestige, but they can't buy fans.

Get up early for **tai chi**. *See p196.*

Attracting major sporting events – and building new arenas to host them – has formed a central part of Shanghai's strategy to become a truly international city. The organisers of headline-grabbing sports events find Shanghai too compelling to pass up: the city is large, loud and, perhaps most importantly, viewed as the master key to the hearts of 1.3 billion sports fans. Shanghai's municipal government and its army of events organisers have splashed out on breathtaking new sporting facilities, like the $200 million Qi Zhong Tennis Stadium, whose retractable roof opens like a giant magnolia flower coming into bloom. Private investors have proved their pockets just as deep, with the construction of the $100 million Tomson Shanghai Pudong Golf Club, which attracted the BMW Asian Open, and the purpose-built Shanghai International Circuit, host of the first Chinese Formula One Grand Prix. As Rubens Barrichello acknowledged the chequered flag, he waved in a lucrative new era of global sporting events in Shanghai, and China.

These events may draw big international names to Shanghai, but they have done little to ingratiate such elite games with locals. Instead, as one Shanghainese sports enthusiast explains: 'Chinese people watch the sports that have Chinese stars.' Indeed, how else to explain the rising popularity of professional snooker? The young and temperamental Jiangsu native, Ding Junhui, has single-handedly created a national audience for this otherwise adrenaline-deficient game.

In Shanghai, as in most of China, sports fans are largely content to watch from the sidelines; the preferred participant game of Shanghainese, both young and old, is the stock market. That said, you can catch glimpses of the local sporting life – at daybreak, in the small local parks that host tai chi groups, and at sunset, as parents take the children into the quiet side streets for an impromptu game of badminton.

Spectator sports

Shanghainese sports fans are largely content to watch the action at home, where beer is cheap and Shanghai's two cable sports channels, CCTV-5 and Shanghai Television Sports Channel, are free. Not surprisingly, then, local sports bars cater to Western sporting preferences. **British Bulldog** (1 Wulumuqi Nan Lu, by Dongping Lu, French Concession, 6466 7878) is the home of rugby and association football in Shanghai. Meanwhile, **Bubba's Texas Bar-B-Que** (2262 Hongqiao Lu, by Jianhe Lu, Changning, 6242 2612) has a monopoly on American football. For games with a more international fan base, your best bets are **Big Bamboo** (132 Nanyang Lu, by Xikang Lu, Jingan, 6256 2265; No.20, Lane 777 Biyun Lu, by Huangyang Lu, Jin Qiao, Pudong, 5030 4228, www.bigbamboo.cn) and **Malone's** (*see p122*).

Athletics

In 2005, Shanghai won the right to host the world's top athletics competition, the **IAAF Grand Prix** (www.iaaf.org), for the following five years. The event has already brought a number of Athens' medalists (and still more Beijing hopefuls) to Shanghai, and will draw even more top names in 2009, when it counts as one of the crucial Golden League meetings. The IAAF Grand Prix takes place in September at the Shanghai Stadium.

All the tees in China

464 yard par

HSBC
Champic

Though the Chinese invented a game similar to golf in the 12th century, the game was outlawed for being a capitalist pursuit in the wake of 1949's Communist takeover. But, like capitalism, golf refused to die, and when clubs were re-established in 1984, Shanghai embraced the game. Three decades of growth created a cashed-up, prestige-hungry business community – and, with plentiful flat land at the urban fringes, all the elements were in place to create a flourishing golfing culture.

In Shanghai, golf and business go hand in hand. The biennial **Asia Golf Show** (www.asiagolfshow.com), held in October 2008 at the Shanghai Exhibition Centre, is co-hosted with the 'Millionaire Fair' and marketed as 'China's leading luxury lifestyle event'. Professional tournaments are also carefully branded: the **BMW Asian Open**

describes itself as 'one of the premier lifestyle events in China'. Small wonder Mao and comrades were anti-golf.

The Asian Open has been held since 2001 at the **Tomson Shanghai Pudong Golf Course** (*see p192*). Among those teeing off in 2008 were three Major champions: Retief Goosen, Michael Campbell and Greg Norman, plus Liang Wen-Chong, the first Chinese winner of Asia Tour's Order of Merit. Since 2005, Shanghai has also played host to the star-studded **HSBC Champions** (www.hsbcgolf. com), held each November at the exclusive **Sheshan International Golf Club** (*see p192*), and featuring title winners from the European, Asian, South African and Australasian tours, plus leading players from the US and emerging Chinese pros. In 2007, American superstar Phil Mickelson clinched the prize money after winning in a dramatic play-off.

For amateur hackers, the corporatisation of golf in Shanghai is a rising barrier: the very best clubs are members-only with long waiting lists, and courses that deign to accept non-members are able to charge inflated prices. The following are more accessible: **Shanghai Grand City Golf Club** (9988 Zhongchun Lu, near Huqingping Gong Lu, Qibao Town, Minhang, 6419 3676, www.grandcity. com.cn), offering a 64-bay driving range, putting green and a par-54 executive course; **Shanghai Golf Hongqiao Golf Club** (555 Hongxu Lu, near Guyang Lu, Changning, 6405 9572), whose nine-hole, par-33 course is floodlit at night; **Binhai Golf Club** (Binhai Resort, Nanhui, Shanghai, 5805 8888, www.binhaigolf.com), designed by five-time British Open champion Peter Thomson, with two 18-hole golf courses; and **Lake Malaren Golf Club** (6655 Hutai Lu, by Yueluo Lu, Baoshan, 5659 0008, www.lmgolfresort. com), also featuring two courses, one of which is floodlit.

Shanghai Stadium

666 Tianyao Qiao Lu, by Lingling Lu, Xuhui (6426 6666). Metro Shanghai Stadium. **Map** p240 C5.

Extreme sports

Skateboarding has a surprisingly long history in Shanghai and, with the new SMP Skate Park, the city has become a destination for several world-class tournaments and, just as important, international name-brand sponsorships.

SMP Skate Park

880 Yinhang Lu, by Xinglongshan Lu, Yangpu (6590 7290/www.smpskatepark.com). Metro Jiangwan Zhhen.

As proof of Shanghai's commitment to extreme sport, the 12,000sq m (129,000sq ft), SMP Skate Park is the world's largest extreme sports facility. The 2,400sq m (26,000sq ft) competition area is strictly for the pros, but the rest of the park is dedicated to all levels. In addition to skateboarding, there are facilities for in-line skating and BMX racing.

Football

Many minds have pondered why football has failed to gain popularity in China. Among the Chinese youth, few play the game seriously – perhaps owing to a lack of game space in the cities, or the lack of Chinese star power to make the sport compelling. Still, at professional games, even if you're not gripped by stunning play, you will be entertained by the pitch etiquette (or lack of it) and the small but animated crowd. Matches take place most Sundays at the Hongkou Stadium; tickets start at around RMB 20 and can be bought on site just before the game. Or, for a listing of match times and ticket prices, visit www.eticketfast.com.

Hongkou Stadium

444 Dongjiangwan Lu, by Sichuan Bei Lu, Hongkou (6540 0009). Metro Hongkou Stadium. **Map** p241 E1.

Golf

See p192 **All the tees in China**.

Sheshan International Golf Club

Lane 288, Linyin Xin Lu, Shanghai Sheshan National Holiday Zone (5779 8088/www. sheshangolf.com). Metro Sheshan. **Rates** *Annual membership* RMB 12,000. *Green fees* RMB 360. Members only (or non-members accompanied by member). **Credit** MC, V.

Designed by Nelson & Haworth and only 35 minutes out of Shanghai, this immaculate – and extremely exclusive – course garnered international attention when it began hosting the HSBC Champions Tournament in 2005.

Tomson Shanghai Pudong Golf Club

1 Longdong Dadao, by Luoshan Lu, Pudong (5833 8888/www.tomson-golf.com). **Rates** *Members* RMB 200-390 Mon-Fri; RMB 300-490 Sat, Sun. *Non members* RMB 700-1,490 Mon-Fri; RMB 1,200-2,290. **Credit** AmEx, MC, V.

This 18-hole course hosts the Asian Open.

Motor sports

The Shanghai International Circuit is the pride of auto fans nationwide. If you miss the annual Formula 1 race (held in October), there are still the Motor GP (motorcycle, May), Formula 3, BMW, Renault, Formula 3000 and new A1 competitions. To get hold of cut-price tickets, try the touts at the Shanghai Stadium shuttle bus stop or at the circuit itself; RMB 2,000 F1 tickets go for as little as RMB 200.

Shanghai International Circuit

2000 Yining Lu, by Jiajin Highway, Anting, Jiading (9682 6999/www.icsh.sh.cn). Shuttle bus from Shanghai Stadium. **No credit cards**.

Table tennis

What better place to soak up some of the local culture than by watching the country's most famous sport? Local and national tournaments take place regularly across the city. Check http://tabletennis.sport.org.cn (in Chinese) or www.ittf.com (in English) for forthcoming events; otherwise, call the venue below. Most table tennis venues also have tables for rent, and curious locals are usually more than happy to educate visitors – and score a few easy victories in the process. Try the Hongkou Stadium (*see above*) or the Yuan Shen Sports Centre; *photo p194*.

Yuan Shen Sports Centre

655 Yuanshen Lu, by Zhangyang Lu, Pudong (5860 1290/5821 4336/www.pd-tyzx.com). Metro Yuanshen Sports Centre. **Open** 8am-10pm daily. **Rates** RMB 30/hr. **No credit cards**. **Map** p241 G3.

Tennis

The striking Qi Zhong Tennis Stadium, in the city suburbs, hosted the Masters Cup until 2008, but as we went to press it was sitting idle awaiting a new role, and hosting the odd pop concert.

Qi Zhong Tennis Stadium

5500 Yuanjiang Lu, by Kunyang Bei Lu, Minhang (6384 6601 ext 88/tickets 962288). Metro Zhuanqiao then 10mins by taxi.

Participation sports

Over the past decade, Shanghai's expat community has become increasingly stable, suburban and community-oriented, resulting in more local leagues and amateur clubs for like-minded enthusiasts. Check out the city's free monthly magazines, especially *that's Shanghai* (www.urbanatomy.com), for details. On the web, *City Weekend*'s user-generated listings (www.cityweekend.com.cn/shanghai) are exhaustive, though some groups listed are inactive. You can also visit the online sports community Active Sports Active Social (www.asas.com.cn) for more on the local sports leagues.

Basketball

Among the younger generation, basketball is Shanghai's most popular participant sport. In-the-know locals play for free at high schools and universities. For foreigner-friendly casual play, try Xujiahui Park (between Zhaojiabang Lu & Hengshan Lu, 7.30am-9pm daily). Games are free and there is no official organiser – you just have to turn up.

Yuan Shen Sports Centre. See p193.

This club, formed in 1999, has been dubbed the 'United Nations Dragon Boat Team' thanks to its mix of nationalities. Practice sessions involve more than one boat, so beginners are welcome. Remember to bring a change of clothes (this is obligatory – everything gets wet).

Football

Shanghai's international league is the most competitive amateur league in China, with 17 teams competing weekly in two divisions. They are sponsored by different bars around the city, which offer pitch rental, team strip, transport and a good chance of a free beer at the end of the match. Top of the league is the Shanghai Shooters. For slightly less formal play, talk to the teams at **O'Malley's** (*see p126*), **Big Bamboo** (*see p122*) or **Eager Beaver** (28 Yueyang Lu, by Dongping Lu, French Concession, 6474 3216).

Shanghai International Football League

Contact Daniel Berger (139 0162 5460 mobile/ www.eteams.com/sifl).
Matches primarily take place at the Tianma Country Club (3958 Zhaokun Lu, Tianma Town, Songjiang, 5766 1666), with 'away' games played downtown.

Cycling

In recent years, the bicycle has lost its status as Shanghai's pre-eminent mode of transport. Now, as the streets teem with electric scooters and mopeds, cycling is reinventing itself as a sporting pursuit. In particular, several expat-oriented groups offer weekly rides through the suburbs and surrounding countryside. Check the websites of these clubs for details of their regular rides: Prodigy Mountain Biking Club (www.mtb.com.cn), Bohdi Biking & Hiking Club (www.bohdi.com.cn) and SISU (www.sisucycling.com).

Dragon boat racing

This Chinese form of rowing dates back to at least 1500 BC and likely originated close to Shanghai, on the shores of the Yangtze River. The long, narrow and colourfully painted boats typically seat 20 rowers, who are kept to their stroke by an onboard drummer. Local teams train year round for the annual Dragon Boat Festival (Duan Wu Jie; *see p150*), which is celebrated in Chinese communities worldwide on the fifth day of the fifth month of the Chinese lunar calendar.

Shanglong Dragon Boat Club

136 6144 7145 mobile/www.shanghaidragon boat.com. **Fee** RMB 50/wk.

Golf

Check the local magazines for golf leagues. Local bar **Sasha's** (*see p127*) runs a corporate league; for up-to-date times and prices, call manager Alan Duffy at 6474 6628. For more on the golf scene in Shanghai, and local courses, *see p192* **All the tees in China**.

Ice skating

Hongkou Swimming Pool Leisure Rink

500 Dongjiangwan Lu, by Dongtiyuhui Lu, next to Hongkou Stadium, Hongkou (5671 5265). Metro Hongkou Stadium. **Open** 7am-9pm daily. **Rates** RMB 30-40/2hrs. **No credit cards. Map** p241 E1.
This outdoor pool is transformed into a partially out-door ice rink in winter. Retired athletes lead group courses and often offer free, informal advice as well. This is also the home turf of Shanghai's only Ice Hockey Club (www.icehockeyshanghai.com).

Super Rink

8/F, Super Brand Mall, 168 Lujiazui Xi Lu, by Fucheng Lu, Pudong (5047 1711). Metro Lujiazui. **Open** 10am-10pm. **Rates** RMB 70/2hrs. **No credit cards. Map** p245 O5.
Shanghai's finest year-round rink is more popular with young couples than it is with serious skaters, but the facilities are adequate for general skating and children's hockey.

Racquet sports

The number of tennis and squash courts increases steadily with the arrival of each new upmarket residence or hotel. Most luxury hotels sell annual memberships to their fitness facilities, but those looking to spend under RMB 10,000 should stick to the public courts. Yuan Shen Sports Centre (*see p193*) or Shanghai Stadium (*see p192*) have excellent, if slightly worn, facilities. For more on squash leagues, contact Esdon Lee (13 7018 49343 mobile, www.shanghaisquash.com).

Jia Bao Tennis Club

Jiading Sports Center, 118 Xinchen Lu, by Puhuitang Lu, Jiading (5999 7151). **Open** *Daytime* RMB 20/hr Mon-Fri; RMB 30/hr Sat, Sun. *Nightime* RMB 40/hr Mon-Fri; RMB 50/hr Sat, Sun. **No credit cards**.
Four floodlit tennis courts are available – reservations are highly recommended. Jia Bao also has badminton and ping pong facilities.

Xian Xia Tennis Center

1885 Hongqiao Lu, by Hongxu Lu, Changning (6262 8327/www.xianxia.com.cn). **Open** 7am-10pm daily. **Rates** RMB 40-100/hr. **No credit cards**.
Call to book one of the four floodlit tennis courts hired out on an hourly basis. The centre also has a small games room with snooker and mahjong tables available for rental.

Running

In a city as hazy as Shanghai, serious runners often debate the health merits of their sport. Many still lace up, though, as evidenced by the local routes listed on www.mapmyrun.com. For solo running, check this site to find user-generated information on scenic paths within city limits. If you prefer to run in a group, the city's weekly hash will not disappoint: Shanghai Hash House Harriers (13 7613 00687 mobile, www.shanghai-hhh.com).

Snooker

Racks (*see p123*) has the swankiest facilities to go with the tables in Shanghai.

Legends Pool Hall

7th floor, 123 Tianyaoqiao Lu, by Xingeng Lu, Xujiahui (6438 25557/www.chuanqi147.com). *Metro Xujiahui.* **Open** 24hrs daily. **Rates** RMB 35-55/hr. *Private rooms* RMB 98/hr. **No credit cards**. **Map** p246 B11.
With 21 locations throughout Shanghai (the Chinese-language website provides full listings), Legends is the undisputed king of the tables. Expect 30 or more tables per hall (mixed pool and snooker), dim lighting and smoke-filled air.
Other locations throughout the city.

Swimming

Shanghai's hotels and upscale apartment complexes usually have pools, and most of them allow visitors for around RMB 100-200 per session. There are more affordable options, but in the sticky summer months, the crowds at Shanghai Stadium (*see p192*) or East China Normal University may leave you feeling like a chlorinated sardine.

Dino Beach

78 Xinzhen Lu, by Gudai Lu, Minhang (6478 3333/www.dinobeach.com.cn). *Metro Xinzhuang, then bus 763 for 4 stops.* **Open** *Late June-early Sept* 9am-9pm daily. **Admission** RMB 100/150/200; RMB 80 children under 1.5m; free children under 0.8m. **No credit cards**.
A water amusement park with an artificial beach, a lazy river, numerous water slides and Asia's largest wave pool. For well-heeled locals and expats of all ages, this is the place to be in the summer.

East China Normal University

3683 Zhongshan Bei Lu, by Jinshajiang Lu, Putuo (6237 3449). *Metro Jinshajiang Lu.* **Open** 8.30-11.30am, 2-9pm daily. **Admission** *Morning* RMB 10. *Afternoon* RMB 12. **No credit cards**. **Map** p240 B3.
One of the city's few public outdoor pools. The pool is clean and well-kept, but, despite its size, has no lane markers – in other words, this isn't a place for serious sport.

Mandarin City

788 Hongxu Lu, by Guyang Lu, Changning (6405 0404 ext 8612). **Open** *Late May-early Oct* 8am-9pm daily. **Admission** RMB 80/day; RMB 50 children. **Credit** MC. **Map** p240 A4.
An open-air pool inside a residential compound (note: some exterior signage erroneously reads 'Mandarine City'). In-the-know visitors come here to enjoy Shanghai's only swim-up bar.

Martial arts

In a city as cosmopolitan as Shanghai, it's fitting that imported forms of martial arts (especially Japanese karate and Korean tae kwon do) are particularly fashionable among the local youth. Visitors, however, might prefer to study the indigenous, and still highly-popular, styles like kung fu and tai chi. Check the local magazines and gyms (*see p196*) for detailed course and class listings.

Kung fu

Most schools teach modern kung fu (Mandarin: *gong fu*), which only covers the basics of the original form. Learning traditional kung fu takes a lifetime's commitment. The instructors below teach the traditional form and expect extreme dedication from pupils.

Hong Wu Chinese Kung Fu Center

Rm 311, Building 3, Lane 210 Taikang Lu, by Sinan Lu, French Concession (137 0168 5893 mobile). **Open** 7-9pm daily. **Rates** RMB 600/mth. **No credit cards. Map** p247 G10.
Traditional kung fu and tai chi classes set in a tranquil, historical lane house.

Long Wu International Kung Fu Centre

1 Maoming Nan Lu, by Julu Lu, French Concession (6287 1528/www.longwukungfu.com). Metro Shaanxi Nan Lu. **Open** 7-9pm daily. **Rates** RMB 1,500/3mths. **No credit cards. Map** p243 F6.
This is Shanghai's most popular location for group classes, with bilingual teachers offering courses in a variety of traditional Chinese martial arts styles: kung fu, wu shu, Shaolin, xing yi and others.

Wang Xiao Peng

135 0173 0640 mobile/Zongteng3@yahoo.com.cn.
Wang (aka Darren) is a sixth-generation member of the Heart and Soul 6 Harmony Boxing Kung Fu family. He teaches tai chi and kung fu motivational training for corporate executives. Private classes cost around RMB 300/1.5 hours.

Tai chi

Tai chi (Mandarin: *tai ji quan*) practice in the early mornings remains one of the most magical aspects of life in Shanghai. Groups start at 4.30am in winter and 5am in summer, continuing until around 9am. You should ask the Master's permission to join in with a particular group and offer payment, although usually it is free. If he sees you are committed, he will guide you, but it may be months before this happens. Fuxing Park, Renmin Park and Liuxun Park (next to Hongkou Stadium, *see p193*) are the most popular locations.

Chongwei Martial Arts Club

64 Wulumuqi Nan Lu, by Hengshan Lu, French Concession (1300 219 0698). Metro Hengshan Lu. **Rates** RMB 80/lesson. **No credit cards. Map** p246 C9.
Classes in tai chi, wu shu and tae kwon do are available in both English and Chinese.

Fitness

Dance

iDancing

2/F, 321 Kangding Lu, by Shaanxi Bei Lu, Jingan (6271 4952/www.idancing.cn). Metro Nanjing Xi Lu then taxi/walk. **Open** 2-9.30pm Mon-Fri; noon-5pm Sat, Sun. **Rates** RMB 100/class. **No credit cards. Map** p243 E3.
The city's hub for ultra-trendy dance styles. In addition to belly dancing, tango and salsa, you can receive instruction in pole dancing and burlesque.

Jazz du Funk

Building C, UDC Innovative Plaza, 125 Jiangsu Bei Lu, by Wanhangdu Lu, Jingan (5239 9922/www. jazzdufunk.com). **Open** 6.30-9pm Mon, Wed; 12.30-1.30pm, 7-9pm Tue; 7-9pm Thur; 11.30am-3pm Sat; 1-5pm Sun. **Rates** RMB 1,600/20 classes; RMB 100/classes. **No credit cards. Map** p240 C3.
Beginner, intermediate and advanced belly dancing, hip hop, tango, jazz, street jazz, jazz ballet, ballet, flamenco, tap and salsa. Children's programmes too.

Souldancing

2/F, 1 Maoming Nan Lu, by Yan'an Zhong Lu, Jingan (6256 4400/139 1876 2681 mobile/www. souldancing.cn). Metro Shanxi Nan Lu. **Open** 7-9pm Mon-Fri; 1-6pm Sat, Sun. **Rates** RMB 680/8hrs; RMB 1,180/16hrs. **No credit cards. Map** p243 F7.
Another option for pole dancing, belly dancing and salsa, with occasional courses in Latin styles.

Gyms

The clubs listed below have a strong local presence. For other clubs, a monthly membership may be the best option; as many local residents can attest, bankrupt gyms do not refund annual membership fees.

Alexander Club

3/F, Building 6-7, Lane 123 Xingye Lu, by Madang Lu, Xintiandi (5358 1188/www.alexander.cn). Metro Huangpi Nan Lu. **Open** 6am-midnight daily. **Membership** RMB 1,000/10 visits; RMB 10,000/yr. **Credit** MC, V. **Map** p248 H7.
Shanghai's finest mass-market fitness centre, with a luxurious swimming pool and plenty of aerobics and yoga classes led by bilingual instructors.

California Fitness

138 Huaihai Zhong Lu, by Puan Lu, Xintiandi (6375 6501). Metro Huangpi Nan Lu. **Open** 6am-12am Mon-Sat; 8am-10pm Sun. **Membership** RMB 180/day; RMB 5,000/yr. **Credit** AmEx, DC, MC, V. **Map** p248 J7.
NBA star Yao Ming has famously invested in (and shamelessly advertised) this mega-gym, known as 24-Hour Fitness in America. No swimming pool.

Kerry Centre Gym

2nd floor, Kerry Centre, 1515 Nanjing Xi Lu, by Tongren Lu, Jingan (6279 4625). Metro Jingan Temple. **Open** 6am-11pm daily. **Membership** RMB 12,000/yr. **Credit** MC, V. **Map** p243 E5.
Small but perfectly formed. Membership is limited, so the place never gets crowded. The facilities include a swimming pool, hot tub, steam room, sauna, solarium and outdoor tennis courts.

Physical

5/F, Metro City, 1111 Zhaojiabang Lu, by Tianyaoqiao Lu, Xujiahui (6426 8282). Metro Xujiahui. **Open** 7am-10pm daily. **Membership** RMB 500/mth; RMB 1,000/season; RMB 3,100/yr. **Credit** MC, V. **Map** p246 A11.
A large, basic gym with swimming pool and sauna.

Trips Out of Town

Tuisi Garden. *See p202.*

Getting Started

Escape Shanghai's frenzied pace for the serenity of local waters and mountains.

Suzhou, city of silk and gardens.

It might be hard to believe amid the bustle of 21st-century Shanghai, but the verdant Yangtze River delta on which the city is built is also home to quiet canal towns and idyllic rural landscapes. These watery towns, which once served as trade hubs and later as film sets, still offer the intrepid traveller glimpses of an older and rapidly disappearing China, if one can navigate past the tourist flotsam.

As the old Chinese saying goes, 'In heaven there is paradise, on earth there are Suzhou and Hangzhou.' **Suzhou** (*see p209*), to the west of Shanghai, is famed for its UNESCO-listed ornamental gardens and gorgeous silk. Most silk for sale in Shanghai is made in Suzhou, so head for nearby markets and bargain hard, or trace its history at the Suzhou Silk Museum, where you can watch the tiny worms work their magic. Once China's cultural capital, it is now renowned as a hub for high-tech manufacturing – the home of operations such as that of famous Chinese entrepreneur Ma Yun, founder of e-commerce group Alibaba, which netted a multi-billion-dollar deal with Yahoo! in 2005.

Currently, the 'it' weekend trip for Shanghai's working weary is **Hangzhou**,

capital of Zhejiang province, to the south of Shanghai, and access point for the most famous lake in China: Xihu (West Lake). Join Shanghai's corporate elite and sip lattes or cocktails along the waterfront at the new Xihutiandi development – brought to you by the architects of Shanghai's own Xintiandi development (*see p75*).

Nearby **Moganshan** (*see p208*), a peaceful village in the hills to the north-west of Hangzhou, is another very popular summer getaway on account of its cooler temperatures and verdant scenery, with several new accommodation options opening in recent years. The lush rolling hills and mountains of Zhejiang also encompass the Zhoushan archipelago, of which the Buddhist holy island **Putuoshan** (*see p212*) is a part.

Hangzhou, Moganshan and Putuoshan are best visited over a couple of days; for the latter two especially, journey times make a day-trip too much of a rush. The other destinations described can all be reached in less than half a day, making them more suitable for day-trippers.

As a general rule, the further you get from Shanghai, the less likely you are to find English speakers, swanky facilities and

Western-style luxuries. But don't let these things put you off – wandering off the well-trodden path and putting up with a lower glitz factor can be the only way to enjoy striking scenery, find some peace and quiet, and meet locals.

TOURIST INFORMATION

Official tourist information and service centres may be hard to find outside Shanghai – some places have a China International Travel Service (CITS), but they aren't always much help. Travel agents within Shanghai are usually able to provide better information, and there are some useful websites: try www.travel chinaguide.com, www.chinatravel.com or www.chinatripadvisor.com. *City Weekend* also has travel listings www.cityweekend. com.cn. For hotel reservations and discounts, try www.ctrip.com or www.elong.com. Some destinations also have dedicated websites with photos and information.

BASICS

Hotel prices given in these chapters are the rack rate. Off-peak discounts of up to 40 per cent can often be negotiated, especially on winter weekdays. Since the week-long public holidays in May and October were shortened in 2008, the formerly prohibitively pricey rates in those months have been discounted to encourage travel. For Spring Festival and the summer season (roughly mid July to mid September), prices may rise much higher.

Getting around

By bus

Local buses run to all the destinations covered in this chapter except Moganshan (which is accessible from Hangzhou). Special sightseeing buses also run from a few venues around town; the buses are used largely by domestic day-trippers and typically leave from 8am onwards and return before dark. For information (in Chinese), call 6426 5555 or go to www.chinassbc.com (also in Chinese). The main terminal is at Shanghai Stadium (666 Tianyaoqiao Lu, by Zhongshan Nan Er Lu, Xuhui, 6426 5555).

Special-interest tour buses also depart from the following locations: Hongkou Stadium (444 Dongjiawan Lu, by Sichuan Bei Lu, Hongkou, 5696 3248), Shanghai Circus World (2266 Gonghe Xin Lu, Zhabei, Zhabei, 5665 9121), Yangpu Stadium (640 Longchang Lu, by Zhoujiazui Lu, Yangpu, 6580 3210) and Huangpu Station (at Nanpu Bridge, 1588 Waima Lu, Huangpu, 6378 5559).

By rail

Rail travel offers a more communal experience and (sometimes) better views. Choose between 'soft seat' or 'hard seat'; the latter is not a choice for the faint-hearted. Trains run to Hangzhou, Suzhou and Wuzhen, as well as cities further away. Tickets can be bought on the day of travel at the train station, where the 'English-speaking' window, rather conveniently, usually has the shortest queue. Tickets are also available through China Youth Travel Service (*see p217*). Find timetables and prices at www.chinahigh lights.com and www.china-train-ticket.com. During Spring Festival, train stations get very crowded and a certain ruthlessness may be required if you want to get tickets.

By car

Except for Putuoshan, the places listed in these chapters are all accessible by car and roads are generally in quite good condition – until you take off down the country lanes. There is usually a car park near the entrance of each of the canal towns, which are all small enough to explore on foot; the sights of Suzhou are all within town, so a car might not be necessary at all. It is, however, especially useful to have a car for exploring Hangzhou and Moganshan, as you can stop at will to explore the surrounding countryside.

By boat

Fast ferries to Putuoshan leave from Luchaogang Dock at 9.30am (5828 2201) in the Nanhui district (to the south of Shanghai); slow ferries leave from Wusong Dock at 8pm (5657 5500), situated where the Huangpu River flows into the sea. Both fast and slow ferry tickets are available from 59 Jinling Dong Lu, 7am to 5pm (6328 3120), which also sells tickets to other domestic destinations. Go in person to buy the tickets, preferably several days in advance. For more details about ferries to Putuoshan, *see p214*.

By bicycle

Weekly cycle trips out of the city offer an interesting way to see the places in this chapter. SISU Cycling Club (138 1663 6060 mobile, 5059 6071, 6471 0877, www.sisucycling.com) offers nice daytrips; Prodigy Mountain Biking Club (6437 7553 ext 8008, www.mtb.com.cn) and Bohdi Bikes Mountain Bike Club (5266 9013, www.bohdi.com.cn) both offer rental and repair services, and organise trips. Cycle China (139 1707 1775 mobile, 6402 5653, www.cyclechina. com) can arrange private bike tours too.

The Canal Towns

Get a taste of the Middle Kingdom of yore in the Venice(s) of China.

Tuisi Garden.
See p202.

The scenic canal towns of Jiang Su Province are a short jaunt from Shanghai – the closest, Zhujiajiao, is less than an hour away – but a world apart in atmosphere and aesthetics. The towns line the banks of the Grand Canal system, the world's longest and oldest man-made waterway, first carved across the mighty Yangtze River delta in 486 BC. When completed in AD 1293, during the Yuan Dynasty, it stretched almost 1,800 kilometres (1,120 miles) from Hangzhou all the way to Beijing, and is considered one of China's greatest feats of engineering. In recent years, the government has realised that it might have something worth preserving here, and deemed the towns 'key state-level cultural relics' in 2006.

Many a Chinese period piece has been filmed in these charming towns and they are popular destinations for domestic tourists. On the weekends, some get unbearably crowded; unless you like to share your vacations with loudspeaker-toting tour guides and their stickered charges, you're advised to stay away.

During the week, however, the towns make for postcard-perfect excursions (and hotels often offer discounts). It's a real shame that many visitors treat the towns as a daytrip – their real magic occurs at night, when strategic lighting throughout the towns (Wuzhen, especially, has perfected this) is enchanting. With the tourists gone, and local residents in their homes, a stroll through the moss-covered lanes and willow-lined river banks can be very romantic. Shadows play among the tiled roofs and intricately carved doors and decorations, while red lanterns swing gently from upturned eaves above lofty gables.

Several of the towns lay claim to the 'Venice of China' title but, really, there aren't huge differences between them except for size. The pedestrian-only town centres feature restored buildings dating back to the Ming Dynasty, labyrinthine lanes bursting with teahouses and local character, and souvenir hawkers peddling various curios and trinkets. In recent years, the tourist boards at the towns have been in fierce competition for tourist dollars, with each claiming to have more authentic cuisine, a richer history and better culture – but, unless you're keen on tracking down the birthplace of a specific poet, you will hardly notice the differences between them. It's best to dedicate your time to one or two rather than trying to do the whole lot – we've shortlisted the most scenic and accessible ones.

Kitschy though it may be, make sure you take a ride on a bamboo gondola through the criss-crossing canals. Homes sit alongside heritage buildings lining the banks – watch the tea-sipping old timers and ponder how much it has actually changed in the last 400 years.

Accommodation, for the most part, remains basic – many a homeowner will be trying to lure you in. If you've got the patience, you can – as with most else in China – bargain. Start your bidding at about half their *kai jia* (starting price). Back in Shanghai, **Jinjiang Tours** (191 Changle Lu, 6289 7830) can help with reservations and even customised itineraries.

QIBAO ANCIENT TOWN
Want to experience Ye Olde water town with minimal effort? Qibao Ancient Town (admission RMB 10) could be your spot. Just 18 kilometres (11 miles) south of downtown Shanghai, in the

Trips Out of Town

Minhang District, it's an easy daytrip (take metro Line 9 to Qibao Station). What you gain in convenience, however, you lose in charm: tourists squeeze into the tiny town, and gondola traffic jams on its sole two canals are not unheard of. A 'model street' has been restored to give visitors a taste of the China of yore, and the adjectives 'old' and 'traditional' seem to feature in the name of every eaterie/shop/residence.

Qibao means 'seven treasures', though most of these ancient treasures (a Buddha statue, a 1,000-year-old tree and a jade axe among them) seem to have mysteriously disappeared. You can still see the world's largest crab claw and a two-headed snake at the local museum of curios – and a temple and a distillery round out the main attractions. Cricket fighting is a popular local pastime, and there are even festivals of cricket culture in early May and early October during national holidays. *Xunlanhamo* (smoked frog's legs) is a local delicacy and, surprisingly, quite a lip smacker.

Tongli

Sightseeing

With seven islets, 15 canals and 49 bridges, Tongli is one of the larger canal towns. Tourist buggies ply between the attractions, but it's

Canal homes in **Zhouzhuang**.

small enough to cover on foot. All signposts are in both English and Chinese. Besides the expected bridges, canals and pretty old buildings, Tongli boasts the **China Sex Museum**. Originally located on Shanghai's bustling Nanjing Road, the museum moved to various city spots – each one more secluded than the last – before being offered a home in Tongli. It's now just behind Tongli's pride and joy: the UNESCO World Heritage site **Tuisi Garden** (*photo p201*). One of the region's finest examples of a late Qing garden – comparable even to the finest in Suzhou – Tuisi was built between 1885 and 1887 by an imperial scholar. Several halls and adjoining corridors were built to create the illusion that they float on water, and the pavilions, rockeries and winding corridors are beautifully conducive to contemplation (*tuisi* means 'retreat and meditate') when hordes of tourists aren't thronging the grounds. A boat service (0512 6063 1987, RMB 180 one-way), departing from the town's entrance, will take you to Zhouzhuang (*see p203*).

China Sex Museum

Tongli, Wujiang city (0512 6332 2973/www. chinasexmuseum.com). **Open** 7.30am-5.15pm daily. **Admission** RMB 20 (over-18s only). **No credit cards**.

Housed in what used to be a girls' school back in the Qing Dynasty are more than 4,000 items of erotica, representing over 5,000 years of Chinese sexual history. You can admire double-headed dildos, brush-paintings of alfresco orgies, sex chairs and tiles that depict a couple enjoying themselves with a variety of animals. Far less amusing but no less interesting are the saddles with wooden erections used to 'ruin' adulterous women and foot-binding equipment. There's also an outpost of the museum at the exit to the Bund Tourist Tunnel.

Where to eat & stay

There are many canalside eateries at Shangyuan Jie, all of which offer similar fare (tea and regional snacks) – and menus in English. **Nanyuan Teahouse** (0512 6332 2677), built in the Qing Dynasty, is a pleasant century-old spot to stop for a cuppa.

Basic accommodation is readily available in Tongli's guesthouses, which are typically above restaurants along the canals – many are less than RMB 100 a night for a standard room. **Wansheng Guesthouse** (0512 6333 1608, RMB 90), a cosy, traditional-style residence, is a good choice. With only nine rooms, the Lu family takes wonderful care of their guests. Ask them for their favourite *xiaochi* ('small eats') place in town; it's well worth the trip. There is a tourist information centre and booking office for accommodation in the town square.

Wuzhen

Sightseeing

Wuzhen is one of the canal towns that escapes being overrun by tourists by virtue of its greater distance from Shanghai. It is about two hours by bus from the city, but just an hour from Hangzhou (buses from the latter leave 12 times a day). Local specialities are rattan baskets and cloth shoes, examples of which are widely available in tourist-tat versions from little alley shops. Admission is a bit pricier (RMB 100) compared to other canal towns (where prices start at RMB 60) but the extra money is well worth it – there is plenty to see and do.

Foremost among the places to see is the **Xiuzhen Taoist Temple**. The temple houses a small but impressive collection of Chinese folk art, with assorted murals, sculptures and woodcarvings featuring scenes from ancient legends. Shadow puppet shows featuring intricately sewn leather puppets and depicting ancient legends are put on at the **Shadow Puppet Play House**, one of the few places where you can still enjoy this dying art. Niche museums exist for all palates; some are dedicated to folk customs, others to Ming and Qing Dynasty beds, and others show footbinding traditions. Centuries-old homes, most with their own docks, line Dongzha Lu. Wuzhen was once the refuge of rich people fleeing the turbulence of the Ming and Qing Dynasties; no doubt part of the attraction was the place's relative inaccessibility and hence greater safety. Many of the residences they built remain well preserved – two examples are the **Zhu Family Hall** and the **Xu Family Hall**. You can also get a taste of local rice wine, *sanbai* ('thrice white'), at the end of a visit to the rice wine distillery.

The **Foliage Dyeing Workshop** is far more fun than it sounds – watch artisans create beautifully coloured and patterned fabrics with tea leaves and mulberry bark. The local water market is a lively affair – from the crack of dawn, town residents gather to gossip, guzzle tea and sell their homegrown produce. Get there at midday and grab a window seat at the aptly named Water Market Restaurant (on Tong'an Dao) for some Cantonese-style dim sum. Afterwards, head upstairs for a soak in the Wujiantang Salt Baths.

Wuzhen is known for its chrysanthemum tea and there are countless teahouses where you can taste it, and even a whole street, Chashi Jie (Tea Street), where you can buy your own to take home. The tea is delicious – delicate, slightly sweet and with a beautiful fragrance.

Where to stay

Basic accommodation can be found all over town, but you can splurge on the **Wuzhen Guesthouse** (Xizha Scenic Zone, 0573 8873 1666, RMB 390-468; RMB 500-1,000 family-size deluxe with balcony & view), with elegant traditional decoration, modern facilities and attentive service. Make sure you get a riverside room. The **Wuzhen Visitors' Centre** (18 Shifo Nanlu, 0573 8873 1088, www.wuzhen. com.cn) is particularly helpful and a good first port of call on arrival. It also has an illustrated tourist map that is indispensable for navigating the small town.

Xitang

Sightseeing

Xitang used to be more low-key than Tongli and Zhouzhuang, being further from Shanghai and, by extension, having relatively fewer tourists. That all changed with the filming here of *Mission: Impossible III*. Still, Xitang remains smaller, quieter and, some would say, prettier than its rivals, and its residents are more laid-back, mostly going about their own business rather then trying to hawk souvenirs.

One of Xitang's designated attractions is the **Pearl Button Museum**, where you can watch buttons being made by hand; further down the cobbled lane is the **Fan Museum**. Unlike other canal towns, many of Xitang's narrow alleys are roofed. At dusk, red lanterns are hung along the length of the 1,300-metre (4,290-foot) main alley – it's a beautiful sight.

Where to stay

There are several Ming Dynasty residences that have been converted into guesthouses, with antique furniture; note that the lack of air-conditioning can make summer nights uncomfortable. Lodgings with air-conditioning are also available, of course, but do cost slightly more. Especially charming Ming-style digs can be found at **Jing Yi Xuan** (8 Shipi Long, 0573 456 5264, RMB 80 Mon-Fri; RMB 100 Sat, Sun).

Zhouzhuang

Sightseeing

This is the largest and most famous of the canal towns – so many tourists come at weekends that it pretty much ruins the experience. The picturesque bridges and well-preserved buildings are featured in a series of watercolours by the late Chen Yifei, one of

Trips Out of Town

China's best-known contemporary artists, and are exhibited in New York. His painting of the Twin Bridges was sold to a petroleum bigwig who then presented it to politician Deng Xiaoping – suddenly, Zhouzhuang's stock went through the roof. Over 60 per cent of the buildings in the town centre date to the Ming and Qing Dynasties or earlier. Tourists flock to experience the town officially identified as 'Number One Water Town' and among the 'Top 50 Destinations for Foreigners' in China. Other attractions include **Shen's Residence**, built in 1742, a rambling residence of 100 rooms surrounding a central courtyard. Down the same lane, **Zhang's Residence** is even older, though smaller.

Where to eat & stay

Finding somewhere to eat in Zhouzhuang is easy: restaurants and teahouses line the banks of the canal near the town square. One speciality is *wansanti* – pig's trotters stewed in brown sauce. On Zhenfeng Jie, a Western-style café serves up freshly brewed coffee and ice-cream. The three-star **Zhouzhuang Hotel** (139 Quanfu Lu, 0512 5721 6666, doubles RMB 380-480) is the biggest hotel in town.

Zhujiajiao

Sightseeing

This is the smallest of the canal towns covered here – and the closest to Shanghai, requiring only a 50-minute bus ride – which is a recipe for claustrophobia, especially at the weekend. Hordes of tourists throng the Setting Fish Free Bridge, where they can toss goldfish into the murky water to chalk up karma points.

There are a total of 36 stone bridges – but it's impossible to keep count as you canter along the labyrinthine cobbled lanes. Zhujiajiao was established in the Song and Yuan dynasties, and became a bustling commercial centre during the Ming Dynasty. These days it is frequented mainly by TV crews from Shanghai.

Getting there & around

By bus

Fortunately, all the canal towns have regular bus connections to Shanghai with Shanghai City Sightseeing Buses (Shanghai Stadium, Gate 5, 666 Tianyaoqiao Lu, 6426 5555, www.china ssbc.com); there are daily departures. The buses for Tongli depart at 8.30am and return at 4pm (RMB 120). Those for Wuzhen depart at 9am and returning at 4.30pm (RMB 150). Xitang tours leave at 9.15am return 4pm (RMB 140); they include a morning at the nearby town of Jiaxing. Zhouzhuang

buses depart at 8.30am and 9.45am (more times are added on the weekend and in the summer) and return at 4pm (RMB 140).

Zhujiajiao tours depart every 40 minutes or so from 7.30am to 1.30pm and return half-hourly until 4pm (RMB 80). All quoted prices are round-trip – overnight stays are possible – and include the entry ticket to the towns. Guides are available for an extra RMB 5 to 20, depending on the tour, but they tend to only speak Chinese – call for details.

By taxi

Most of the four- and five-star hotels in Shanghai can arrange taxis or minivans that will ferry their guests to the canal towns. A taxi from Shanghai to Wuzhen (one of the furthest, at 2 hours away) will cost about RMB 400 (one way).

By train

Visiting the canal towns by train is more complicated than by bus. The best option is to take a train to either Jiaxing or Suzhou and travel onwards to the canal towns from there. Almost every train that heads south, including those to Hangzhou, stops at Jiaxing. Regular services to Jiaxing depart hourly from 7am to noon from the Shanghai Railway Station. From Jiaxing train station there are minibuses to Xitang (RMB 5) and Wuzhen (RMB 12), or you can take a taxi.

Guided tours

Jin Jiang Optional Tours (191 Changle Lu, 6445 9525) offers a convenient one-day group tour with an English-speaking guide. It can also tailor individual tours with drivers and guides. Prices start at RMB 650 per person for its basic Suzhou/Zhouzhuang tour. This lasts 10 hours, departing at 9am daily; it includes lunch and hotel pick-up and drop-off.

Tourist information

The entrance ticket booths in the canal towns double as tourist information centres. The ticket price usually includes an English-language map of each town; ask for one if it is not provided. In Tongli, English-speaking guides are available for hire at RMB 160 per person. Each town has a website (with English translations) that provides an array of background information, enabling you to get an overall feel for the place before you arrive.

Tongli
www.china-tongli.com

Wuzhen
www.wuzhen.com.cn

Xitang
www.xitang.com.cn

Zhouzhuang
www.zhouzhuang.net

Zhujiajiao
www.zhujiajiao.com

Hangzhou & Moganshan

Head to the hills, via China's most famous lake.

Xihu *See p206.*

Hangzhou

The problem with being touted as China's model city is that thousands of people come to see what all the fuss is about. But if you can see past the tour groups led around by guides with little yellow flags you might realise why Hangzhou views have, for thousands of years, been inspiring Chinese poets and writers. The fabled Xihu (West Lake), with the rolling hills behind, now forms the backdrop for hundreds of thousands of wedding photographs.

Marco Polo visited during the Yuan Dynasty and declared Hangzhou one of the most splendid places on earth. These days, the capital of one China's richest provinces has encroaching development to highlight its wealth. Construction dust dirties table tops; Louis Vuitton, Dolce & Gabbana and Giorgio Armani peddle their wares on Wulin Square and the lakefront Eurostreet development; Beemers and Bentleys crowd the narrow streets, making for some of the most expensive traffic jams around. There's also the **China Academy of Art** (218

Nanshan Lu, 0571 8716 4630), one of the nation's best. Specialising in new media, it attracts creatives from around China, many of whom stay on after graduation. Hangzhou's heady student environment nourishes local businesses with talent and forward-thinking ideas. It also makes for a handful of impressive art shows held in the city's lofts and galleries.

HISTORY

The setting of the modern town of Hangzhou was formed in the first century BC, when river currents flowing into the sea threw up enough silt to form a lake. The Grand Canal was then built at the end of the sixth century AD, making Hangzhou the centre of trade between the north and the south. In the Tang era, the city continued to thrive and during the Song Dynasty – when the Tartars invaded the north – the imperial family relocated to Hangzhou (1138-1279), making it the country's imperial city. When the Song Dynasty was overthrown by the Mongols, Hangzhou remained a key commercial centre, revered for the beauty of its gardens. Ming rulers later deepened the Grand Canal, increasing trade

Naked Retreats. See p208.

opportunities by allowing boats laden with goods to sail up to Beijing. Two Qing emperors also favoured Hangzhou as a place of rest, and added to its architecture. However, the Taiping Rebellion in the mid 19th century destroyed much of the city, which was later rebuilt.

Sightseeing

Most visitors arrive by train (*see p208*), usually terminating at the main station to the east of the lake. (The slow, local trains, however, arrive and depart from an older and more remote station in the eastern part of town.) From the main station you can walk to the centre (it's a couple of kilometres or about a mile); head directly west on West Lake Avenue and it runs right to lake.

First stop for most is Xihu, the lake. For less crowded views, there are two causeways – the Baidi, running across the north side, and the Sudi, running from north to south. It is on these paths in the early evening, meandering through the willows with fish leaping out between the lily pads and an orange moon rising above the water, that the enchanting power of the lake begins to make itself felt. Go in the morning for solitude.

Baidi runs on to Gushan (Solitary Hill), the lake's biggest island. Formed by a volcanic explosion, it now has a quieter character, its hillside park dotted with small wooden studios where you can watch members of the Xiling Yinshe (Xiling Seal Engravers' Society) at work. Xiling has historically been a centre of innovation in traditional Chinese art, and in the mid 1800s produced artists like Wu Changshuo, father of the modern Haipai, or Shanghai Style, of brush painting. There is also a small museum of seal carving here, beside Xiling Bridge (0571 8781 5910, admission free). It is possible to rent boats (prices vary, peaking at sunset), which are paddled out into the lake from the south end of the Baidi, or to join the outings aboard a mock

dragon boat for an hour-long tour of the lake's islands (RMB 45, tickets from the pine stands around the lake).

For lake views, head off Beishan Lu, up one of many hidden footpaths, through the moist woodlands to Qixiashan (which means the 'Mountain Where Rosy Clouds Linger'). The stone path meanders past hawkers (woodland dwellers living in tumble-down cottages), Baochu Pagoda (a 1933 reconstruction of a Song Dynasty tower) and, more interestingly, a Baopu Taoist Temple – home to an elegant group of male and female followers of Taoism who can often be heard, or seen, performing traditional ceremonies, especially in the late afternoon.

In the city itself, head to Hefang Lu 'tourist street', a tastefully reconstructed historical road with views of the lake's misty blue mountains. The shops and teahouses sell Chinese medicine, folk art, the area's renowned Longjing tea, woodcarvings and tofu. Nearby there are two sights of interest, both lodged in restored Qing Dynasty houses: the **Guanfu Classic Art Museum** (131 Hefang Jie Lu, 0571 8781 8181, RMB 15) is a fine furniture museum, tracing the social history of furniture in China from straw mats to opium beds, while the **Hu Qing Yu Museum of Traditional Chinese Medicine** (95 Dajingxiang Lu, off Hefang Jie Lu, 0571 8702 7507 ext 8620, RMB 10) does exactly what it says on the plaque.

Excursions

West of the city is perhaps the city's biggest draw, **Lingyin Temple** (1 Fayun Nong, Lingyin Lu, 0571 8796 8665, RMB 30-35), one of the biggest Buddhist temple complexes in China and one of the few that managed to survive the Cultural Revolution intact; it is fully functioning, with daily services. Opposite the temple is **Feilai Feng** (meaning 'Peak Flying from Afar'), with its Buddhist sculptures chiselled into the hillside. Further afield is the village of **Longjing**, set amid lovely emerald-green tea plantations. Just south is the **Hupaomeng Quan park**, where a natural spring produces the only water serious tea-drinkers would consider using to boil their brew. If you want to test that your water is the real thing, bear in mind that Hupao spring water is supposed to have a surface tension so strong that a cup can be filled three millimetres too high and still won't spill.

Those who like to watch others get wet can head up to the **Liuhe Pagoda** (House 8, 147 Nanshan Lu, 0571 8659 1401, RMB 20 park, RMB 10 pagoda), situated on a striking site over the Qiantang River. It was originally built to appease the Dragon King, who was thought to be responsible for the floods that routinely wrecked farmers' crops. Now, ironically, it has become the favoured spot from which to watch the – as yet unsurfed – tidal bore that is at its height every autumn equinox.

Where to eat & drink

To entice more tourists to visit Hangzhou, RMB 1 billion has been invested in the first phase of Xihutiandi ('West Lake Heaven and Earth'), Hangzhou's version of Shanghai's Xintiandi complex (*see p75*). Jamaica Coffee (12 Xihutiandi, 0571 8701 2861) is a good spot for a coffee and a sandwich, and Crystal Jade (Building 10, 147 Nanshan Lu, 0571 8702 7887) is recommended for Cantonese, Shanghainese and South-east Asian cuisine.

For Hangzhou cuisine, don't miss Lou Wai Lou (30 Gushan Lu, 0571 8796 9023), which serves the most famous rendition of local speciality 'beggar's chicken' (a whole chicken cooked inside a ball of mud).

One of the best upmarket restaurants in town is Provence (1 Baishaquan, 0571 8797 6115), which serves French food and fine wines in a quaint, backstreet villa. A duo of interior designers created the quirky but swanky Yee Chino (Yulinglong, 171 Zhongshan Bei Lu, 0571 8707 0777) and Gold Chino (4th floor, 149-2 Qingchun Lu, 0571 8721 0777), which serve Chinese fusion dishes in gorgeous settings.

Wushan Lu is great for local snacks and specialities; it once had a night market – selling an array of goods from *qipaos* and wooden sandals to kitsch Maoist memorabilia and 'antiques' – but it moved to the intersection of Renhe Lu and Huixing Lu.

For nightlife, Hangzhou's professional (not student, in other words) arty types congregate in the laid-back, eclectically designed Common's Place (1 Wanshouting Jie, 0571 8506 2166), near Wulin Square. Casablanca (23 Hubin

Road, 0571 8702 5934) is one of Hangzhou's oldest bars, with décor to match.

For cheap alcohol, thumping tunes and a young crowd, head to one of the lively bars opposite the China Academy of Art on Nanshan Lu (West Town has been around for ages and is packed even on weeknights). Down the street is the best live jazz in town at JZ Club (6 Liuying Lu, 0571 8702 8298), housed in a creatively decked-out villa.

By far the busiest bar street in town is Shuguang Lu, where you'll find Traveller Bar (no.176, 0571 8796 8846), which has live jazz daily; and You To Bar (no.85, 0571 8797 6788), which rocks with live music and rowdy local beer-swillers. Maya Bar (94 Baisha Quan, Shuguang Lu, 0571 8799 7628) serves good *burritos* and some of the strongest long drinks in town. 7 Club (43 Shuguang Lu, 0571 8511 5795) has the best selection of imported beers.

For clubbing, check out SOS (3/F Huanglong Hengli Mansion, 5 Huanglong Lu, 0571 5683 6688), with international DJs and dancers. A more unusual spot is the IN Club (Building 3, 23 Yanggong Di, 0571 8763 4380); it is small but hugely popular at weekends. There's also Club G Plus (6th floor, 169 Qingchun Lu, 0571 8721 5152), which brings in turntable luminaries such as Armin van Buuren, Quivver and Dubfire.

Pick up a *MORE Hangzhou* magazine or visit www.morehangzhou.com to see what's on.

Where to stay

Shangri-La (78 Beishan Lu, 0571 8797 7951, www.shangri-la.com, doubles from RMB 1,600) is a safe bet for those who want to go five-star – but be sure to stay in the west wing for views of Xihu. The Hyatt Regency (28 Hubin Lu, 0571 8779 1234, www.hyatt.com, doubles RMB 1,400) opened in 2005 and is conveniently situated in the middle of the new lakefront development. The New Hotel (58 Beishan Lu, 0571 8766 0000, doubles RMB 780) is a 1920s building with an ugly but unobtrusive add-on. Another mid-range option is the Elan Holiday Hotel (218 Nanshan Lu, 0517 8716 4789, doubles from RMB 280), a cute boutique hotel by the art academy.

For cheap and friendly, plus a site next to the lake and the laid-back Fotoyard Café adjoining, head for the Hangzhou International Youth Hostel (101 Nanshan Lu, 0571 8791 8948/2806 9669, www.yhachina.com, dorm from RMB 45, doubles from RMB 230).

Getting around

The bus network covers most destinations but taxi rides within Hangzhou should not cost much more than RMB 15. Most places round the lake can be

Trips Out of Town

reached on foot, and touring by bike isn't a bad idea; these can be hired from many spots by the lake. Taxi and minibus drivers will approach tourists to offer a variety of excursions, at set day rates; bargain hard.

Getting there

Hangzhou is 170 kilometres (105 miles) south-west of Shanghai. At least nine trains per day leave for Hangzhou from Shanghai Railway Station (12.28am-11.25pm, RMB 25-47, soft-seat). The journey takes two to three hours. Another eleven trains per day leave from the Shanghai South Railway Station (7.45am-9.05pm), most of which are the new bullet lines (with the prefix 'D'), which takes just over an hour. There are buses all day, with most leaving from Shanghai South Bus Station (6.40am-8.20pm). Other stations: Hengfeng Lu Bus Station (7.50am-6.50pm), Shanghai Long Distance Bus Station (6.50am-8.30pm); Shanghai Baishi Hutai Lu Bus Station (7.10am-6.30pm); Shanghai Baishi Pudong Bailanjing Bus Station (8.50am-7.30pm).

Moganshan

The village of Moganshan – up in the cool, green hills of north Zhejiang – originally came to life as a heat retreat for Shanghai's foreign residents and for missionaries from the interior. In 1898, they claimed the peak as their exclusive summer playground, leap-frogging up the slopes past the mountain springs where Song Dynasty emperors once gambolled in the shade of the bamboo. The foreigners rode up on sedan chairs carried by porters, as there were no roads at the time.

Well-to-do Chinese soon followed, and so did the infamous Shanghai gang leader Du Yuesheng. Chiang Kaishek honeymooned here briefly. The original international inhabitants built European-style villas and ran the village like the city concessions they were escaping from, forming an association to decide who was allowed to join their elite community. In 1949, the Communist government turned the village into a retreat for cadres and a state sanatorium. Today the village has resurrected its role as a summer and weekend escape for the international community of Shanghai and Hangzhou, as well as upwardly mobile Chinese. Booking ahead is essential during high season (July-Aug).

Sightseeing

On entering Moganshan visitors pay RMB 80 (plus RMB 10 per car) to access 'the sights', which don't add up to much. There are a couple of waterfalls, the house where Chiang Kaishek stayed – an empty shell with a few pieces of furniture – and the place where Chairman Mao had an afternoon nap – another empty shell with one metal framed bed. You can play at being

decadent with a sedan chair ride, offered by villagers for a fee. The real joy, however, is in wandering off the tourist path and up towards the back of the village. Here you'll find a disused school, a church and chapel built by the original missionaries, and an ageing municipal, spring-fed swimming pool. There is also a market in the middle of the village, selling wild tea and mushrooms picked in the forests.

Other distractions include a walk to an outlying pagoda; follow the road out of the village in a north-westerly direction, past some villas, until the road forks three ways. Take the paved path in the middle to Guai Shi Jiao (Weird Stone Corner).

Maps are available in the village, but they're in Chinese. For directions in English and a sketch map, drop by the Lodge (*see below*). However, a walk off the mountain in any direction will take you through the bamboo forests into the valley below, where you'll encounter plenty of farmers and, eventually, an isolated Buddhist temple.

Where to eat & drink

Eating and drinking can be done at any of the small restaurants on Yin Shan Jie, the main street. Local specialities are bamboo shoots, as well as wild celery and wild partridge. Moganshan Lodge (0572 803 3011, www.moganshanlodge.com, lunch/dinner RMB 60-115) offers good, straightforward Western food. It also serves fresh coffee and has a comfy bar.

Where to stay

The Radisson hotel group manages one villa on the mountain: the luxuriant country pad once belonging to Du Yuesheng (0572 803 3601, rooms from RMB 1,100). Cheaper rooms can be had at any one of the many hotels, some in old villas, all over the mountaintop. Prices range from RMB 150 up to RMB 1,000 or more for a suite. The Songliang Hotel sets a good benchmark (0572 803 3812, rooms with balconies from RMB 280). In the highest hamlet below the old foreign village, Shanghai-based Naked Retreats has converted two farmhouses in impeccable style. (021 5465 9577, www.nakedretreats.cn, rooms from RMB 900-1500; *photo p206*).

Getting there

Moganshan is some 60 kilometres (about 40 miles) north of Hangzhou; from there it's a one-hour taxi journey (RMB 250). Alternatively, you can catch a bus (RMB 19) from Hangzhou North Station (766 Moganshan Lu, 0571 8809 7761) to Wukang, which is at the foot of the mountain. From Wukang a minibus will take you to the top (RMB 60).

Suzhou

Garden city.

Back when Shanghai was still a small fishing settlement, ancient Suzhou was a cultural and fashion leader. Hailed as one of the most beautiful places in the Middle Kingdom, Suzhou attracted the political and cultural elite in droves in the 14th century. In the last decade, it has regained some of that reputation. Like most cities in eastern China, Suzhou has undergone massive new development; however, it still retains much of the flavour that led Marco Polo to declare it the 'Venice of the East'. Pingjiang Lu is a perfect example, with its narrow intersecting streets, ancient buildings, shimmering canal and eclectic shopping. Many of the ornamental gardens and elaborate residences remain remarkably well preserved, and have endured as one of China's favourite tourist attractions.

With a history spanning 2,500 years, Suzhou is also one of the oldest cities in China. Built by Emperor Helu back in 514 BC, it was one of the most prosperous at its peak. Blessed with fertile land, Suzhou is dotted with lakes linked by a criss-crossing network of canals. The completion in AD 600 of the Grand Canal, a trading artery that linked the city to the capital Beijing, turned Suzhou into a major commercial hub. Although less important to the city's economy today, boats still ply the canal and tourists flock to its tree-shaded banks.

The old town reached its present dimensions in the 12th century, and remnants of the city wall that once enclosed it can still be seen. In the past renowned for its silk industry, the canal town is now the world's top producer of notebook computers and digital cameras – a fact that's hard to credit while you amble across another quaint antique bridge. Just take a ten-minute taxi ride from downtown, though, and you'll see Suzhou's other face: the Suzhou Industrial Park. It is this high-tech side of Suzhou that keeps the city one of China's most prosperous. Only 3.5 kilometres (two miles) from the old town, it seems like another world. Only the man-made Jinji lake hints at the famously idyllic ornamental gardens of Suzhou's past.

As a major tourist stop, Suzhou has a well-developed infrastructure. Streets are well laid out and there is easy access to accommodation, transport, entertainment and the tourist sites.

Coiled Gate (Pan Men).

Sightseeing

Suzhou's classical gardens, which date to the Ming Dynasty (1368-1644), and its canals are the city's chief attractions. But you shouldn't be so intent on garden-hopping that you ignore Suzhou's other diversions.

Your first port of call should be the new Suzhou Museum (*see p210* **Pei designs**), designed by IM Pei and housing hundreds of artistic works from the city's rich history, as well as some contemporary art. Getting on the water is an essential Suzhou experience, so grab a **sightseeing boat**. Tours (0512 6752 6931) depart from a landing on the large canal directly across the road from the railway station at the northern end of town. The boats go to four different destinations: Tiger Hill (Huqiu; in the far north-western end of town), Coiled Gate (Pan Men; in the south-western corner), West Garden (Xi Yuan; the western part of town) and Cold Mountain Temple (Hanshan Si; near West Garden). The longest trip – to Hanshan Si –

Pei designs

His striking 1989 design for Paris's Pyramide du Louvre might be IM Pei's most famous work, but it seems to be the new Suzhou Museum, in his homeland, that the architect holds dearest to his heart. Pei refers to his final major project, completed in 2006, as his 'sweetest daughter'. Pei has strong ancestral ties with Suzhou, and he spent his childhood summers in the canal city, giving the project special poignancy.

The architect's only other work in China is a hotel outside Beijing, completed in 1982. So when asked to design the Suzhou landmark that would adjoin a 19th-century residence and the Garden of the Humble Administrator, a project that was to be the last of his long and distinguished career, Pei relished the challenge – and the result is a milestone for modern Chinese design.

For the then 86-year-old master architect, the project was not only physically taxing – after the initial consultation, Pei is said to have left Suzhou in a wheelchair – it was also conceptually demanding. Upon his own insistence, the museum was to be both traditional and modern and, most critically, harmonious with its surroundings. It was these self-imposed conditions that made the project, according to Pei, his most difficult – but the realisation of his vision is impressive.

Architecture and landscape are inseparable as multiple gardens, and courtyards flow in and out of the structures (a central space and two wings). The museum's body itself is a geometric marvel – varying heights, angles and shapes carve out unconventional exhibition areas. A dual-tone colour scheme – white stucco with demure, dark grey detailing – highlights the beauty of contextual design; this is the age-old colour palette of the city.

Fittingly for Suzhou, the garden is the museum's leading lady. Recalling a traditional Chinese painting, it features rock gardens, wisteria and bamboo groves, ponds, pavilions and footbridges, which, when combined, create a serene, Taoist ambience. Latticed windows flood the museum with natural light and connect the interiors with the outdoors. In doing this, Pei honours a key facet of the Chinese design tradition: in China, he said, buildings and gardens are not just related, they are one.

Once a Chinese cultural capital – during the Ming and Qing dynasties, its artistic output was almost that of the rest of the country combined – Suzhou pays tribute to this history in its museum. The permanent collection features works from this period – 250 of its 30,000 ancient relics are considered first-grade national treasures – while a rotating roster of contemporary exhibits keeps things fresh. The structure and its gardens are themselves as much works of art as the pieces they house; – indeed, IM Pei's swan song is alone worth the half-hour ride out to Suzhou.

Suzhou Museum

204 Dongbei Jie, at Qimen Lu (0512 6757 5666/www.szmuseum.com). **Open** 9am-5pm Tue-Sun (last admission 4pm). **Admission** RMB 20. **No credit cards**.

takes about 40 minutes, whereas it takes only ten minutes for visitors to get to the Pan Men Scenic Area.

Pan Men, or Coiled Gate (2 Dongda Jie, 0512 6526 0004, www.szpmjq.com, 7.30am-5.30pm daily, RMB 25), is a good place to disembark for a walk along the old city wall to the top of the original city gate, and to take in **Ruiguang Pagoda**, reputedly the oldest in Jiangsu province. From Pan Men, it is just a short walk north-east to the lovely **Blue Wave Pavilion** (Canglang Ting); this garden's sprawling grounds make some of the others feel decidedly claustrophobic.

Renmin Lu is the main road running north–south across town. At its northern end, near the railway station, is the **Suzhou Silk Museum** (2001 Renmin Lu, 0512 6753 5943, open 9am-5pm daily, RMB 15). The city's 4,000-year-old silk industry comes to life here with displays of antique looms, silk embroidery and, especially, the reproduction of a 13th-century silk farm, complete with real worms. Silk products are sold at the badly lit museum shop; but a better place to buy them is the **Suzhou Embroidery Factory** (262 Jingde Lu, 0512 6522 2403, www.szseri.com, open 8.30am-4.30pm daily).

Further out of town, **Tiger Hill** (Huqiu; 0512 6532 3488, open 7.30am-5.30pm daily, RMB 40) is the final resting place of the Emperor Helu, founder of Suzhou, and is a popular spot for tourists. The man-made hillock got its name, according to local legend, from a white tiger that came to guard the emperor's tomb. Helu had a keen interest in swords, which explains why he was buried with 3,000 of them. On top of the little hill is the 1,500-year-old **Yunyan Pagoda**, propped up by concrete struts. Tiger Hill is four kilometres (2.5 miles) north-west of the city centre and can be reached by tourist buses 1 and 2, or by taxi.

Located in the heart of Suzhou's downtown, on the Guangqian Jie thoroughfare, is the Taoist **Temple of Mystery** (Xuan Miao Guan; *photo p212*). There's nary a hint of mystery about it but the grounds are pleasant and the huge temple hall (Sanqing Dian) is worth a look, as is the busy bazaar that also occupies the square.

The gardens of Suzhou

The famous Suzhou gardens were intended by their creators to contain all the elements of the universe in miniature, manifesting the principles of Taoism, the ancient Chinese philosophy. The gardens once numbered over 200, but only 69 remain well preserved. The attention to detail is staggering, with nothing – neither pebble nor plant – left to chance.

Weekends see crowds thronging Suzhou's top attractions, and it may be necessary to queue and wait your turn to cross a bridge – admittedly, this isn't terribly conducive to experiencing the meditative calm these gardens are meant to instill. If you don't want to spend an entire afternoon moving from garden to garden, the **Garden for Lingering** and the **Humble Administrator's Garden** are generally the best to visit, although the **Garden of the Master of Nets** is perhaps the most beautiful if you can bear the crowds. For more information, visit the Suzhou Municipal Administrative Bureau of Gardens website or call the tourist information line (www.szgarden.sz.js.cn, 0512 6520 3131).

Blue Wave Pavilion

3 Canglangting Jie, by Renmin Lu (0512 6519 4375/www.szwsy.com/clt). **Open** 7.30am-5pm daily. **Admission** RMB 20. **No credit cards.**
Originally built for a prince around AD 950, this is one of the older and bigger gardens. The design is less formal than that of other Suzhou gardens, with wilderness areas and winding, pond-lined corridors replacing the usual fussy pavilions. The carved lattice windows are considered to be among Suzhou's finest and the garden is home to some rare bamboos.

Garden for Lingering

338 Liuyuan Lu, by Tongjing Bei Lu (0512 6557 9466/www.gardenly.com). **Open** 7.30am-5.30pm daily. **Admission** RMB 40. **No credit cards.**
One of the largest of the gardens, with an impressive collection of bonsai and a wilderness area. Fans of traditional horticulture will enjoy the Crown of Clouds Peak, a 6m (18ft) chunk of rock from nearby Taihu Lake. In an attempt to give a sense of the garden being lived in rather than just looked at, women decked out in full Ming Dynasty regalia play instruments and sing in pavilions and walled recesses.

Garden of the Master of Nets

11 Kuojiatao Xiang, down an alley off Shiquan Jie (0512 6529 6567/www.szwsy.com). **Open** 7.30am-5.30pm daily. **Admission** RMB 30. **No credit cards.**
Tiny and charming, this garden is everybody's favourite – which means it tends to be the most crowded. It's home to a group of wood-block painters who sell their work in one of the pavilions. Each night the garden hosts a popular traditional dance and music performance that moves from pavilion to pavilion.

Humble Administrator's Garden

178 Dongbei Jie, by Baijia Xiang (0512 6751 0286/www.szzzy.cn). **Open** 7.30am-5.30pm daily. **Admission** RMB 70. **No credit cards.**
Ming Dynasty courtier Wang Xianchen built this garden in 1513 when he retired. The most talked-about feature is the interconnected, bamboo-covered islands and waterfront pavilions. It is widely considered to be one of the most beautiful gardens in China.

Without a clue? Visit the **Temple of Mystery**. *See p211.*

Lion Grove Garden
23 Yuanlin Lu, by Lindun Lu (0512 6777 3263/
www.szszl.com). **Open** 7.30am-5.30pm daily.
Admission RMB 30. **No credit cards.**
The Buddhist monk Tianru built this garden in
memory of his master Zhong Feng in 1342. It
changed hands a number of times and suffered
many centuries of neglect. The current name comes
from its labyrinthine limestone rockery, for which
stones from Taihu Lake were arranged in the shape
of lions playing, roaring, fighting and sleeping.

Where to eat & drink

The area around the Temple of Mystery
(Xuanmiao Guan) on Guanqian Jie bustles
with a number of eateries, all claiming to
serve authentic Suzhou bites. The city's
native Wu cuisine is known to be soft in
texture and sweet in taste. For the best
examples, try Songhelou Caiguan (72 Taijian
Nong, Guanqian Jie, 0512 6770 0688, RMB
10-138), said to be the oldest restaurant in
town, its history stretching back over 300
years. The house specialities are marinated
duck (*gusu laya*) and 'squirrel Mandarin fish'
(*songsu guiyu*). Caizhizhai (91 Guanqian Jie,
0512 6727 6198, RMB 6-450 per box) has been
in business since the 19th century, and sells
Suzhou-style cakes and sweets.

For Western food, try local expat hangout
Southern Cross (72 Luogua Qiao Xiatang,
Guanqian Jie, 0512 6581 0067, www.southern
crosssuzhou.com, RMB 40-80). Less than a
kilometre from Guanqian Jie, Shiquan Jie is a
bustling bar street. Hotspots like the Shamrock
bar (775 Shiquan Jie, 0512 6520 4270) and
Pulp Fiction (451 Shiquan Jie, 0512 6520 8067,
www.southerncrosssuzhou.com) draw large
crowds of expats.

Where to stay

The Sheraton (259 Xinshi Lu, 0512 6510 3388,
www.sheraton-suzhou.com, doubles RMB 1,880)
is the city's best five-star option downtown. It
is in a replica of a traditional Chinese house and
garden. The Bamboo Grove Hotel (168 Zhuhui
Lu, 0512 6520 5601, www.bg-hotel.com, doubles
RMB 580) was about the smartest lodging in
town before Sheraton arrived. It's still pretty
nice: three interconnected, low-rise buildings
overlook an inner garden courtyard. A former
guesthouse has been renovated to five-star
standards and reopened as the Garden Hotel
Suzhou (99 Daichengqiao Lu, www.garden
hotelsz.com, 0512 6778 6778, doubles RMB 820),
located near the Humble Administrator's
Garden, with lovely secluded grounds.

Getting there

Suzhou is 88 kilometres (55 miles) west of
Shanghai. Trains from the Shanghai Railway
Station take between half an hour and one
hour and cost RMB 13-20; the best option is the
Nanjing express service, which departs hourly
from 5.33am and costs RMB 25 one-way. Going
by coach takes about 90 minutes and costs
RMB 30. Coaches leave hourly between 7.20am
and 5.30pm from the Shanghai Southern bus
station (399 Laohumin Lu) or half-hourly from
7.10am to 8pm from the Hengfeng bus station
(next to the railway station at 70 Hengfeng Lu).
Sightseeing buses depart daily at 8.30am from
Shanghai Stadium (666 Tianyaoqiao Lu) and
cost RMB 168, including bus fare, admission
and a guide. A return trip from Shanghai to
Suzhou by taxi should cost around RMB 500;
ask your hotel to make the arrangements.

Putuoshan

Nirvana on sea.

Putuoshan, one of the 1,000 islands of the
Zhoushan Archipelago in the East China Sea,
attracts pilgrims and tourists in droves. Its
greenery and long golden beaches are as much
of a draw as the temples that dot the island.
This is one of the four holy Buddhist mountains
in China, and devotees travel from far and
wide to worship Guanyin, goddess of mercy.

Unfortunately, it is more Buddhist theme
park than holy ground when the summer
peak season arrives. Between the tour groups
thronging the grounds of the temples, the piped
music in designated 'scenic areas' and the
hawkers of Buddhist paraphernalia, nirvana
couldn't feel further away. However, visiting
off-season should mean you can find yourself
cheaper accommodation – there will certainly
be a calmer atmosphere, much more conducive
to appreciating the island's many charms.

HISTORY

The Boddhisattva Guanyin was enshrined
on the island in AD 916. As the legend has
it, a Japanese monk was travelling with a
statue of Guanyin when a storm stranded
him on the island. The goddess appeared to
him in a vision and promised to return him
home safely if he left the statue behind. He did,
and she hasn't left the island since. Guanyin
literally means 'observing the sounds' and in
Chinese Buddhism the name is taken to mean
'the one who hears the cries of the world'.
Guanyin is revered for her compassion,
as well as for her supposed ability to
grant male children, an extremely useful
ability in a society with draconian one-child
policies and a preference for male heirs.

Pilgrimage site it may be, but Putuoshan
has also been ravaged by fighting and
destruction. The island received imperial
patronage and for centuries enjoyed the
attention and favour of rich devotees. At
its peak, it was home to hundreds of temples
and thousands of monks. But Japanese pirates
and Dutch traders stopped by to plunder
and pillage periodically in the 16th and 17th
centuries. Until 1949, around 2,000 monks
and nuns lived on the island, but the Cultural
Revolution further decimated the temples:
today only three main temples and some 30
nunneries remain. Continuing the theme of
conflict, the island is now home to a naval
base – be careful what you photograph.

Sightseeing

The three biggest temples on the island are Puji
Temple, Fayu Temple and Huiji Temple. The
main area of worship is **Puji Temple**, which
houses a handsome bronze statue of Guanyin.
Old cobblestone streets lead to Haiyin Pool in
front of the temple, where pilgrims set turtles
free as a gesture to gain karmic merit. Before
sunrise, visitors can join the monks and nuns in
early morning chanting to the deities. Around
the main temple are smaller shrines and
pagodas, as well as stalls selling Buddhist
trappings, souvenirs and dried seafood – an
island speciality. The area can get crowded
but it is at least smoke-free: burning incense
has largely been banned in the temples.

Fayu Temple, the second-largest, is two
kilometres (1.2 miles) north of Puji Temple.
It's arranged into six ascending tiers up a hill,
beginning from the stone gateway. About a
kilometre (half a mile) north of Fayu is **Huiji
Temple**, built in the Ming Dynasty. It sits on
top of Foding Hill, which, at 300 metres (1,000
feet) above sea level, is the highest peak on the
island. Visitors who choose to proceed on foot
will be rewarded with the sight of small shrines
and, more rarely, pilgrims prostrating
themselves on each of the 1,000 steps. For those
who don't fancy the climb, take the cable-car.

A giant **statue of Guanyin** looking out to
sea at the southern tip of the island has become
an iconic Putuoshan sight. The 33-metre (108-
foot) statue in bronze and gold was built in 1997
and depicts the goddess holding a ship's wheel,
supposedly watching out for seafarers. Her
four grizzly-faced protectors are the Buddhist
guardians of the world, each leading an army
of supernatural creatures to keep evil at bay.

Around the island are various 'rock stars' –
rocks with special markings that can be easily
identified by the crowds of tourists wanting
to be photographed beside them. One such
rock, which has the Chinese character for 'heart'
engraved on it, is about 500 metres (1,640 feet)
west of Puji Temple. Supposedly, 100 people
can stand on it at the same time.

Near the oversized Guanyin statue is
Chao Yin Dong, or the Cave of Tidal Sounds.
Guanyin is said to have appeared here to visitors
throughout the ages. These visions eventually
led to a cult of suicide after a monk burnt his

fingers in offering to the goddess, who then appeared before him. Following his example, dozens of believers during the Ming Dynasty flocked to the site and threw themselves on to the rocks below in the hope of attaining nirvana. Suicides at this spot are now expressly forbidden – by a sign on the rock. On the easternmost part of the island, a small temple sits wedged in a gully between two cliff-faces at **Fan Yin Dong**, which means 'Sanskrit Sound Cave'.

Sun worshippers can get their fix at **Hundred Step Beach** or the **Thousand Sand Beach**, which lie next to each other. The Hundred is a hive of activity in summer, with water sports equipment available for rental, and sand sculptures (of Buddhist symbols, naturally) adding to the festive atmosphere. The pleasant **Golden Sand Beach** in the south of the island is smaller and quieter.

Where to eat & drink

Seafood is an island speciality. Simple dishes prepared in the Chinese style – complete with bones and shells – can be had at any one of the numerous small restaurants on the island. Clusters of restaurants can be found near the harbour along the road at Xishan new village (near the naval base) or Longwan village (near Golden Sand Beach). The buildings themselves are rather ugly and the food is served on rough-shod outdoor tables, but the fresh seafood and seasonal vegetables are delicious. Near Puji Temple, the Putuoshan Teahouse (6 Xianghua Jie, 0580 609 1208) provides vegetarian Buddhist options and Shanghai cuisine. Note that hotel food has a bad reputation in Putuoshan.

Where to stay

There are two Chinese four-star hotels on the island: the **Putuoshan Hotel** (93 Meicen Lu, 0580 609 2828, www.putuoshanhotel.com, doubles RMB 658-1,188) and **Xilei Xiao Zhuang** (1 Xianghua Jie, 0580 609 1505, doubles RMB 600-1,280). Both are near Puji Temple and the Hundred Step Beach. For something with more character, try **Xilin Hotel** (next to Xilei Xiao Zhuang, 0580 609 1119, doubles RMB 240-688), which is converted from a small monastery. Failing these, hotel touts at the harbour hawk double rooms from around RMB 200 in two-stars; bargaining is expected. Many restaurants also offer accommodation, but the condition of the rooms and the legality of their offers are uncertain. Book ahead during peak season, but at other times hotels are mostly empty. Prices vary greatly according to the season.

Getting around

Putuoshan is only 12 square kilometres (4.5 square miles) long, making exploration easy. Air-conditioned minibuses pick up and drop off passengers at all the attractions; fares range from RMB 2 to RMB 10. The cable car to Foding Hill costs RMB 40 return or RMB 25 one-way.

Getting there

By air

Flights from Shanghai's Hongqiao Airport to Putuoshan Airport (located on nearby Zhujiajian island) are operated by China Eastern (95108, www.ce-air.com); the journey takes 50 minutes and there are two flights daily. From the airport, take a taxi to Wugongzhi Dock before zipping across on a five-minute speedboat to Putuoshan.

By sea

Slow ferries leave from Wusong Dock (251 Songbao Lu, timetables 021 5657 5500), situated where the Huangpu River flows into the sea. (The journey takes 90 minutes to half an hour; the easiest way to get to the dock is by taxi but you can also take buses nos.51, 116, 522 or 728.) The slow ferries leave Shanghai at 8pm daily and arrive in Putuoshan at 7.30am the next morning; they return at 4.40pm daily and arrive in Shanghai at 6.20am the following morning. One-way tickets are RMB 109 to RMB 499, depending on the class of travel.

Fast ferries leave from Luchaogang Dock (timetables 021 5828 2201) in the Nanhui district (to the south of Shanghai). A bus service runs to the dock (8am) from 1588 Waima Lu (near Nanpu Bridge, just out of central Shanghai). The ferry crossing takes four or four and a half hours; tickets are RMB 253. The ferry leaves at 9.30am, and the price includes both the bus and the ferry legs of the journey. There is a return ferry from Putoshan at 12.30pm daily. Both fast and slow ferry tickets are available from the Wusong dock ticket office at 59 Jinling Dong Lu. Go in person to buy the tickets, preferably a few days in advance.

An alternative 15-minute ferry goes from Shenjiamen Dock in Zhoushan. Bus tickets to Shenjiamen Dock are available at Shanghai South bus station; departures are hourly from 7am to 7pm (journey time approximately six hours), and tickets are RMB 125. The ferry, costing RMB 18, leaves for Putuoshan every ten minutes from 6.30am to 5.30pm. For the return leg, bus tickets from Shenjiamen to Shanghai can be bought from ticket offices at Putuoshan harbour.

Tourist information

Entrance to Putuoshan is currently RMB 140, and RMB 160 in high season, payable on arrival. Each site visited within the island costs an additional fee (RMB 5-50).

Directory

Features

Directory

Getting Around

By air

Shanghai has two airports: all international and some domestic flights go through the newer Pudong, while Hongqiao handles domestic flights only. Shuttle buses (6834 6612) run between the two every 20 to 30 minutes (Hongqiao 6am-9pm; Pudong 7am-last flight; RMB 30).

Pudong International Airport

96990/www.shairport.com
Most international flights arrive at Pudong International Airport, 30km (18 miles) from the city proper and 40km (25 miles) from Hongqiao Airport. A new terminal opened in March 2008, and further expansion is planned. A **taxi** to downtown Shanghai will cost around RMB 160 and takes 45-60mins. To downtown Pudong it's around RMB 130 and will take roughly 30mins. Avoid the touts: they charge four times the rate.

The bullet-quick **Maglev train** connects the airport with Longyang Lu metro station on the outskirts of Pudong. The journey only takes seven minutes, but on arrival you are still a half-hour taxi or metro ride from downtown Shanghai – and the metro from Longyang Lu is inconvenient with heavy luggage. Tickets are available at the entrance gates to the Maglev (with same-day plane ticket single RMB 40, otherwise single/return RMB 50/80; VIP single/return RMB 100/160). The service runs every 20mins, 6.45am-9.30pm.

Public **airport shuttle buses** (6834 1000) depart from outside the baggage claim to different locations around the city. Useful lines include bus no.5 (6834 6830), which departs to Shanghai Railway Station every 30 minutes (5am-9pm, RMB 18) and stops at People's Square. Bus no.2 (6834 6612) goes to Shanghai Exhibition Center and leaves every 20-30mins (7.20am-9pm, RMB 19). These shuttle buses are much cheaper than taxis. Many hotels also offer shuttle bus services.

Left-luggage facilities are situated in the domestic arrivals hall (6834 6324), and departures hall (6834 5201); and the international arrivals hall (6834 6078) and departures hall (6834 5035). Rates are low, and depend on the size of the piece of luggage. The service is open from 6am until last flight.

Lost property is located between the 8th and 9th door of the domestic arrivals hall (6834 6324).

There is a reliable HSBC **ATM** near the visa section in the international arrivals hall.

China Telecom has a **cybercafé/ business centre** (6834 5092, open 7am-9pm) in the international terminal; business-class passengers can use machines in the lounges.

Hongqiao Airport

5260 4620/www.shairport.com
Hongqiao is the closest airport to downtown Shanghai, with most central destinations ten to 15km (six to nine miles) away. A taxi should cost no more than RMB 45 and will take around half an hour. Hongqiao also has many public **buses** (5114 6532), which depart from in front of the arrivals hall. Useful lines include the Special Line, a direct service to Jingan Temple (every 15mins, 6am-9.30pm, RMB 4), bus no.938 leaves for Pudong (10-15mins, 6am-9.30pm, RMB 2-4) and bus no.925 for People's Square (10-15 mins, 6am-9pm, RMB 2-4).

The **left-luggage facility** is in the domestic arrivals hall (5114 4520). Rates depend on bag size.

ATMs are located in the arrivals hall, near the customs office, and in the departure hall, near the airport tax booth; the Bank of China ATM is the most reliable.

For domestic travellers, Shanghai Airlines offers a **downtown check-in facility** (1600 Nanjing Xi Lu, 3214 4600), which only operates if your scheduled departure is after 11am. Check your luggage in two and a half hours before departure, get your boarding pass, then hop on the direct airport bus (RMB 19).

AIRLINES

Major airlines currently flying to Shanghai include:

Air Canada *Room 3901, United Plaza, 1468 Nanjing Xi Lu, by Tongren Lu, Jingan (6279 2999/ www.aircanada.ca). Metro Jingan Temple.* **Map** p242 D5.
Air China *Room 307, 2550 Hongqiao Lu, in Hongqiao Airport area, Hongqiao (400 810 0999/ www.airchina.com.cn).* **Map** p240 A4.
American Airlines *Room 702, Central Plaza, 227 Huangpi Bei Lu, People's Square (400 886 1001/ www.aa.com). Metro People's Square.* **Map** p244 H5.
British Airways *Suite 703, Central Plaza, 227 Huangpi Bei Lu, People's Square (400 650 0073/ www.ba.com). Metro People's Square.* **Map** p244 H5.
Northwest Airlines *Room 207, East Tower, Shanghai Centre, 1376 Nanjing Xi Lu, by Xikang Lu, Jingan (400 814 0081/www.nwa. com). Metro Jingan Temple.* **Map** p243 E5.
Shanghai Airlines *212 Jiangning Lu, by Beijing Xi Lu, Jingan (6255 8888/www.shanghai-air.com). Metro Nanjing Xi Lu.* **Map** p243 E4.
United Airlines *Room 3301-3317, 31F, Shanghai Central Plaza, 381 Huaihai Zhong Lu, by Xintiandi (3311 4568/www.united.com). Metro Huangpi Nan Lu.* **Map** p248 H7.
Virgin Atlantic Airways *Suite 221, 12 Zhongshan Dong Yi Lu, by Fuzhou Lu, the Bund (5353 4605/www.virgin.com/atlantic). Metro Nanjing Dong Lu.* **Map** p245 M5.

Rail services are generally used for short-distance travel within China. In Shanghai, trains run from **Shanghai Railway Station**, in the north of the city, and the new **Shanghai South Railway Station** (*see p217*). For more info on travel by train, visit www.rail.sh.cn. Buying tickets at the Shanghai Railway Station requires patience and persistence. Try the English-language counters or better still one of the conveniently located ticket offices around town, such as the ones on Nanjing Lu (108 Nanjing Xi Lu, by Xizang Lu, Jingan, 6327 8430) or Fuzhou Lu (431 Fuzhou Lu, by Fujian Lu, the Bund, 6326 0303 ext 3109).

Shanghai Railway Station

303 Moling Lu, Zhabei (6317 9090/6354 5358). Metro Shanghai Railway Station. **Map** p243 F1.
This is the terminal for services to Beijing, Hong Kong and Suzhou. Beware of pickpockets.

Shanghai South Railway Station

289 Laohumin Lu, Xinlonghua (6317 9090/5124 5040). Metro Shanghai South Railway Station. **Map** p240 B6.
Trains for Hangzhou.

By sea

Located at the mouth of the Huangpu River, Shanghai is in an excellent position if you want to cruise down the coastline of China and beyond. Most domestic ships/ferries dock at the **Wusong Passenger Terminal** (251 Songbao Lu, Baoshan, 5657 5500), 1.5km (one mile) north-east of the Bund. Overseas ships dock at the **International Passenger Terminal** (800 Dongdaming Lu, 6537 2299), also 1.5km (one mile) north-east of the Bund.

Tickets

Tickets can be booked directly at the ferry offices or through one of the following agencies:

China International Travel Service (CITS)

2 Jinling Dong Lu, by Zhongshan Dongyi Lu, the Bund (6323 8771/6321 0737). Metro Nanjing Dong Lu. **Open** 9am-5pm daily. **Credit** AmEx, DC, MC, V. **Map** p245 M6.

China Youth Travel Service/STA Travel

2 Hengshan Lu, by Dongping Lu, French Concession (6433 0000 ext 2036). Metro Changshu Lu. **Open** 9am-6.30pm daily. **Credit** (plane tickets only) AmEx, DC, MC, V. **Map** p246 C9.

Public transport

Shanghai's public transport system is near unfathomable without some fluency in Chinese. Buses are plentiful, but lack of English signage – not to mention overcrowding – makes using them a headache. The metro is an exception – it is efficient and has some English signs (for a metro map, *see p256*). Again, though, it suffers from too many bodies in too little space. It's best for longer journeys, such as to Pudong. For convenience and minimal stress, taxis are usually best.

Fares & tickets

Visitors planning to use public transport fairly frequently over a week or more can buy a **stored-value card** (*jiaotong ka*). Available at metro stations, they are valid for the metro, buses and even taxis, and cost RMB 100 – the stored value is RMB 70, with RMB 30 a deposit refundable when the card is returned. The card deducts a fee when scanned by the reader above the metro turnstile, or by scanners on bus and taxi dashboards. There is no expiry date on the credit. Note that on Shanghai's public transport discount tickets for children, students and the elderly are only valid for Chinese nationals.

Metro

Metro stations are identifiable by their red-on-white 'M' signs. Not always easy to spot, signs in English are present in stations; announcements are also bilingual.
After the completion of extensive renovations in late 2007, there are now eight metro lines in total. **Line 1** runs south from Baoshan, through the Shanghai Railway Station down through People's Square, the French Concession and Xujiahui to Xinzhuang in the southern suburbs. **Line 2** runs west from Zhangjiang (which is out beyond Pudong) via the Bund area, People's Square (where it connects with Line 1) and Jingan to terminate at Songhong Road. The partially elevated **Lines 3** and **4** loop out around the city centre; with the exception of the extension north of the Shanghai Railway Station, which runs via East Baoxing Lu (for Duolun Lu) and Hongkou Stadium, they're little use to tourists. Likewise, **Line 5** is a suburban line running

from the western terminus of Line 1 into Minghang district. **Line 6** explores the outer stretches of Pudong, and **Line 9**, located in the far western reaches of the city, is only reachable via bus. **Line 8** passes through Yangpu, Hongkou, Zhabei, Huangpu, Luwan and Pudong (passing by the fabric market); for a metro map, *see p256*.
The metro runs from 5.30-6am to 10.20-11.30pm and trains are very frequent. Note that Lines 3, 4 and 5 start later (6-7am) and close earlier (9.30-10.30pm). Ticket machines or staff at the metro stations sell single-journey metro tickets costing RMB 3-7, depending on the distance travelled. Keep your ticket until you exit.

Buses

There are over 1,000 bus lines in Shanghai. Prepare to hit a major language barrier when using them – the destinations are listed only in Chinese and there is no English-language phone line. Chinese speakers can contact the **Shanghai Urban Transportation Bureau** (6317 6355).
Don't expect peaceful rides – buses are crowded, unbearably so during rush hour. Air-conditioned buses have a snowflake symbol by the bus number. There is also the added stress of potential pickpocketing. Buy tickets from the on-board conductor (RMB 2-3) or use a stored-value card (*jiaotong ka, see above*).

Taxis

Travelling by taxi is not an extravagance. Fares are cheap and taxis plentiful; the only noticeable shortages are during rush hour or in rain. If you're having trouble finding a taxi, head to a five-star hotel and you should find plenty waiting at the forecourt taxi rank.
Taxis are metered and, in our experience, drivers are scrupulously honest about observing them. Fares are set at RMB 11 for the first two kilometres (1.2 miles) and then RMB 2 for every additional kilometre. Fares rise after 11pm.
Tipping is not expected. Cash or stored-value cards (*jiaotong ka, see above*) are accepted forms of payment.

Directory

Most drivers have only limited English, so you must get your destination written in Chinese – most hotels supply cards with the addresses of major sites in both English and Chinese. Failing that, ask the concierge to write it out for you. Keep hold of business cards for places to which you might return.

The driver will supply you with a receipt (*fapiao*). This shows the taxi number and the company telephone number – useful if you discover you've left something in the cab.

The number for complaints is 962000 (Chinese only).

Those with mobile phones can take advantage of the **Guanxi SMS service** to access bilingual addresses. Simply type in the name of the restaurant, hotel or bar and text it to 1066 9588 2929. Seconds later you receive a message asking you to chose a location; press C for addresses in Chinese.

Taxi companies

Bashi Taxi *96840.*
Dazhong Taxi *96822.*
Jinjiang Taxi *96961.*
Qiangsheng *6258 0000.*

Cycling

Cycling is a popular way to get around the city. Cyclists should, however, be cautious of Shanghai's aggressive drivers and its dangerously ill-kept roads. Bikes should be registered at a police station, but bike shops can offer this service. The Captain Hostel (*see p32*) offers bike rental and tours. For cheap cruiser bikes equipped with a basket, head to the strip on Xiangyang Lu by Fuxing Zhong Lu and be prepared to bargain hard. It's possible to pick up a decent bike for as little as RMB 120.

BOHDI Adventure
Suite 2308, Building 2, 2918 Zhongshan Bei Lu, by Caoyang Lu, Putuo (5266 9013/www.bohdi.com.cn).

Metro Caoyang Lu. **Open** 8am-7pm daily. **Credit** AmEx, DC, MC, V. **Map** p240 C2.
Top-of-the-line mountain bikes and flash racing machines with expert German service.

Driving

Tourists are not forbidden from taking to Shanghai's roads, but there is plenty of red tape to deter them.

Licences

Most expats apply for Chinese licences at the **Shanghai Vehicle Management Bureau** (179 Qinchun Lu, Minhang, 6498 7070, open 9am-4pm Mon-Fri). To do this you will need your passport, residence permit, health certificate and a driving licence held for over three years, plus an official translation of that driving licence. You will also have to undergo a short written driving test and a medical examination. The total cost of the application is RMB 210. Drivers with less than three years' experience are also required to take a road test. The length of licence issued depends on your residence permit.

If you do not have a foreign driving licence, you will be required to attend driving lessons for 70 hours at the **Shanghai Tongrong Traffic Rules Education School** (2175 Pudong Dadao, by Yangpu Bridge, Pudong, 5885 6222).

Car rental

Those visiting Shanghai on tourist L-visas are unable to drive rental cars, but they are allowed to hire a car with accompanying driver. The average daily rental costs are in the region of RMB 600 to RMB 800.

Dazhong Car Rental
100 Guohuo Lu, by Zhongshan Nan Lu, Old City (3376 5666). **Open** 8.30am-5pm daily. **Credit** AmEx, DC, MC, V. **Map** p249 M10.

Hertz Car Rental
Suite 306, Chengfeng Centre, 1088 Yanan Xi Lu, by Panyu Lu, Hongqiao (6252 2200/www.hertz. com). Metro Yan'an Xi Lu. **Open** 9am-5pm daily. **Credit** AmEx, DC, MC, V. **Map** p240 B4.
Other locations Pudong Airport.

Shanghai Anji Car Rental
Hongqiao Airport, 528 Konggang Yi Lu, Hongqiao (6268 0862). **Open** 8am-8pm daily. **Credit** AmEx, DC, MC, V. **Map** p240 A4.
Avis partner in China.

Walking

Distances are such that the city centre is easily navigated on foot. But beware: pavements double as express lanes for bicycles and scooters, but at least they are well maintained. Crossing can be a challenge – look left, then right, then left again and be careful not to step into Shanghai's busy bike lanes. Nor should you risk jaywalking: green-hatted traffic controllers now patrol zebra crossings and will impose RMB 50 fines.

Travel advice

For up-to-date information when travelling to a specific country – including the latest news on safety and security, health issues, local laws and customs – contact the department of foreign affairs of your home country government. Most have websites packed with useful advice for would-be travellers.

Australia
www.smartraveller.gov.au

Canada
www.voyage.gc.ca

New Zealand
www.safetravel.govt.nz

Republic of Ireland
http://foreignaffairs.gov.ie

UK
www.fco.gov.uk/travel

USA
http://travel.state.gov

Directory

Resources A-Z

Addresses

All street signs are written in both Chinese and Pinyin (romanised Chinese) but, in a recent fit of Anglicisation, in some areas of the city the authorities have erased certain useful Pinyin bits and used English (worthless to the average cabby). In a more recent backlash regulation, all establishments in Xintiandi were required to provide Chinese names with Chinese character placards of designated size hung prominently near the door. Aside from such lingual squabbling, keep in mind these simple pieces of Chinese: *lu* means street or road; the prefix *bei* is north, *dong* is east, *nan* means south, *xi* is west. When getting around it is common to give the cross street of the address, for example Nanjing Xi Lu, by Jiangning Bei Lu; 'by' is *kaojin*.

Age restrictions

The legal age for marriage (implying consensual sex) is 22 for men and 20 for women; there's no age of consent for homosexuals as gay sex is not officially recognised. Under-18s are considered minors and are not allowed to smoke (though 'carding' is virtually unheard of here) and there is no clear legal drinking age.

Attitude & etiquette

See p221 **Attitude problems**.

Business

Business travellers should first visit the business site of the Shanghai government: **www.investment.gov.cn**.

Business cards

Business cards are offered or accepted with both hands. Cards can be printed at **Easy Document** (Rm.1301, 18 Xizang Zhong Lu, by Yanan Dong Lu, 5385 2225).

Chambers of Commerce

American Chamber of Commerce *Portman Ritz-Carlton, East Tower, Room 568, 1376 Nanjing Xi Lu, by Tongren Lu, Jingan (6279 7119/ www.amcham-shanghai.org). Metro Jingan Temple.* **Map** p242 D5.
Australian Chamber of Commerce *Room 6709,1440 Yanan Zhong Lu, by Huahsan Lu Jingan (6248 8301/www.austcamshanghai.com). Metro Jingan Temple.* **Map** p242 C6.
British Chamber of Commerce *17th floor, Room 1703 Westgate Tower, 1038 Nanjing Xi Lu, by Jiangning Lu, Jingan (6218 5022/ www.sha.britcham.org). Metro Nanjing Xi Lu.* **Map** p243 F5.
Canada China Business Council *Suite 912, Central Plaza, 227 Huangpi Bei Lu, by Renmin Dadao, Huangpu (6359 8908/www.ccbc. com). Metro People's Square.* **Map** p248 J7.

Convention centres

These are the major conference and convention venues:

Shanghai Everbright Convention & Exhibition Centre *66 Caobao Lu, by Caoxi Lu, Xuhui (6484 2500/ www.secec.com). Metro Caobao Lu.* **Map** p240 C5.
Shanghai International Convention Centre *2727 Riverside Avenue, by Lujiazui Lu, Pudong (5037 0000/www.shicc.net). Metro Lujiazui.* **Map** p245 N5.
Shanghai Mart *2299 Yanan Xi Lu, by Gubei Lu, Hongqiao (6236 6888/ www.shanghaimart.com.cn). Metro Hongqiao Lu.* **Map** p240 A4.
Shanghai New International Expo Centre *2345 Longyang Lu, by Fangdian Lu, Pudong (2890 6666/ www.sniec.net). Metro Longyang Lu.* **Map** p241 G4.

Couriers

DHL Sinotrans *2201 Yanan Xi Lu, by Loushanguan Lu, Hongqiao (6275 3543/www.dhl.com). Metro Hongqiao Lu.* **Open** 9.30am-7.30pm Mon-Fri. **Credit** AmEx, DC, MC, V. **Map** p240 B4.

FedEx *10th floor, Aetna Building, 107 Zunyi Lu, by Xianxia Lu, Hongqiao (6275 0808/www.fedex. com). Taxi or bus.* **Open** 9am-6pm Mon-Fri. **No credit cards**. **Map** p240 B4.
UPS *Suite 23, 166 Lujiazui Dong Lu, by Pucheng Lu, Pudong (3896 5599/www.ups.com). Metro Lujiazui.* **Open** 8.30am-6.30pm Mon-Fri; 9am-2pm Sat. **No credit cards**. **Map** p245 O5.

Office hire & business centres

Most major four- and five-star hotels offer business services, but you'll pay premium rates.

Executive Centre

3501 CITIC Square, 1168 Nanjing Xi Lu, by Shanxi Bei Lu, Jingan (5292 5223/www.executivecentre.com) Metro Nanjing Don Lu. **Map** p243 E5. Full-service office rental with complete secretarial support.

Translators

Shanghai Interpreters Association

Room 702, 66 Nanjing Dong Lu, by Henan Zhong Lu, the Bund (6323 3608). Metro Nanjing Dong Lu. **Open** 9.30am-4pm Mon-Fri. **No credit cards**. **Map** p244 L4.

Speed Shanghai

Room 1409, Fei Diao International Building, 1065 Zhaojiabang Lu, by Tianping Lu (5489 6060/www.speed-asia.com). Metro Xujiahui. **Open** 8.30am-5.30pm Mon-Sat. **No credit cards**. **Map** p246 A10.

Consumer

Buyer beware. Returning faulty products is a trial, even with a receipt or guarantee. Consumers can file an online complaint with the Shanghai Bureau of Quality & Technical Supervison at www.shzj.gov.cn (or call 12365) but it's in Chinese only.

Customs

Visitors can bring in 400 cigarettes and two 0.75-litre bottles of alcohol, plus one each of the following items: camera, portable tape-recorder, portable cine-camera, portable video-camera and portable computer. There are no restrictions on the amount of foreign currency you can bring in to the country. It's forbidden to take any antiques over 200 years old out of China. Check with the shop when you make your purchase, and keep the receipt and the shop's business card to present to customs if necessary.

Disabled

Shanghai poses problems for disabled travellers. Wheelchair access is provided at airports, metro and train stations, and at a handful of the international five-star hotels, but nowhere else. Pavements on major streets have raised strips for the visually impaired to follow. The amount and quality of special-needs facilities have improved somewhat with the introduction of 30 wheelchair-accessible buses on the 926 route, and increased wheelchair ramps around the city's parks and in restaurants, but there is still much to be done. City planners are now promising wheelchair ramps and special taxi accessibility before the city's 2010 World Expo, including more accessible buses and a fleet of cabs.

Shanghai Disabled Persons' Federation

189 Longyang Lu, Pudong (5873 3212/www.shdisabled.gov.cn/english @shdpf.org.cn).

Drugs

Street drugs are becoming more readily available, especially in nightclubs, but the punishments for drug use remain harsh. Consulates can offer only very limited legal assistance to those caught with illegal drugs.

Electricity

China runs on 220 volts.

The most common type of plug is the dual prong, either parallel or at a 45° angle, as in Australia. 110-volt appliances may be redundant – adaptors have been known to overheat.

Embassies & consulates

All foreign embassies are located in Beijing, but many countries also maintain a consulate in Shanghai.

Australian Consulate

22nd floor, CITIC Square, 1168 Nanjing Xi Lu, by Jiangning Lu, Jingan (5292 5500/www.shanghai. china.embassy.gov.au). Metro Nanjing Xi Li. Open 8.30am-12.15pm; 1.15-5pm Mon-Fri. Map p243 E5.

British Consulate

Room 301, Shanghai Centre, 1376 Nanjing Xi Lu, by Tongren Lu, Jingan (6279 8918/www.uk.cn). Metro Jingan Temple. Open 9am-noon; 2-4.30pm Mon-Thur; 9am-noon; 2-3pm Fri. Map p243 E5.

Canadian Consulate

Room 604, West Tower, Shanghai Centre, 1376 Nanjing Xi Lu, by Tongren Lu, Jingan (6279 8400/ www.shanghai.gc.ca). Metro Jingan Temple. Open 8.30am-noon; 1-5pm Mon-Fri. Map p243 E5.

Irish Consulate

Room 700A, Shanghai Centre, 1376 Nanjing Xi Lu, by Tongren Lu, Jingan (6279 8729). Metro Jingan Temple. Open 9.30am-12.30pm; 1.30-5.30pm Mon-Fri. Map p243 E5.

New Zealand Consulate

Room 1605-1607A, The Centre, 989 Changle Lu, by Changshu Lu, French Concession (5407 5858/ www.nzembassy.com). Metro Changshu Lu. Open 8.30am-12.30pm, 1.30-5.30pm Mon-Fri. Map p246 C8.

South African Consulate

Room 2706, 222 Yanan Dong Lu, by Jiangxi Zhong Lu, the Bund (5359 4977/sacgpolitical@yahoo.com). Metro People's Square. Open 8am-4.30pm Mon-Fri. Map p245 M5.

US Consulate

1469 Huaihai Zhong Lu, by Wulumuqi Nan Lu, French Concession (6433 6880/http:// shanghai.usembassy-china.org.cn). Metro Changshu Lu. Open 8am-5pm Mon-Fri. Map p242 C6.

Emergencies

For more useful numbers, see below Health; and p225 Police.

Useful numbers

Ambulance 120.
Directory assistance 114.
Police 110.
Fire service 119.
IDD code enquiry 114 or 10000.
Operator-assisted Yellow Pages 96886.
Time 117.
Weather forecast 121.

Gay & lesbian

See pp166-170 Gay & Lesbian.

Health

China does not have reciprocal healthcare agreements with other countries, so it is advisable to take out private insurance. However, some clinics do accept private international insurance such as BUPA or TIECARE. Check with your insurance provider before departure. Vaccinations against hepatitis A and B, polio, tetanus, flu, chickenpox, typhoid, tetanus-diphtheria, Japanese encephalitis (if travel plans include rural areas) and rabies are the most commonly recommended; there are major problems with tuberculosis and hepatitis A here, so be sure to get those shots before travel. Some travellers may complain of stomach upsets due to the change in diet. Tap water should be avoided, not so much because of bacteria but due to potential heavy metal content. The bottled water sold everywhere is fine, and ice made from purified water is common.

Attitude problems

The intricacies of Chinese etiquette mean that it's all too easy for beginners to feel lost or embarrassed. The pitfalls are many.

Face off

You've enjoyed a feast in a restaurant with your local host and the bill arrives. Your host reaches for his credit card. 'No,' you say, 'I'll pay.' A period of to-and-froing ensues and, to end the discussion, you grab the bill and pay. You've just committed a serious faux pas. Your host has lost 'face' and that's the cardinal sin in Shanghai.

Face is a peculiar Chinese concept and its importance can never be underestimated. Some folk go to great lengths to acquire it by displays of wealth or generosity.

Complimenting someone on their appearance or business acumen – especially in front of their pals or colleagues – is a sure-fire winner. Confrontation and criticism are guaranteed face-destroyers. When in doubt, be lavish with compliments.

Greetings

Chinese people have a family name, followed by a first name – Chen Wu, for example. To address someone, use their family name together with their professional title or 'Mr', 'Madam' or 'Miss', plus the family name – eg Mr Chen. Only family members or close friends use first names. Always acknowledge the most senior person first.

The Chinese will nod as an initial greeting. Handshakes are popular, but wait for your Chinese counterpart to initiate the gesture.

Public behaviour

Avoid expansive gestures, unusual facial expressions and sarcasm, as these can generate confused reactions.

The Chinese, especially those who are older and in positions of authority, dislike being touched by strangers. Conversely, the Chinese generally stand closer to each other than Europeans and North Americans.

Do not put your hands in your mouth – it's considered vulgar. Hence nail-biting, flossing and similar practices are also no-nos. Post-dinner tooth picking is acceptable with one hand covering the mouth.

Conversation

Negative replies are considered impolite. Instead of saying 'No', answer 'Maybe', 'I'll think about it' or 'We'll see.'

Questions about your age, income and marital status are common. If you don't want to reveal this information, remain unspecific.

In Chinese culture, the question 'Have you eaten?' is the equivalent to 'How are you?' in Western culture; it's a superficial inquiry that does not require a literal answer.

Do not be surprised if there are periods of silence during business or dinner. It is a sign of politeness and of thought. Do not try to fill the silence with words.

Gestures

Shanghainese body language has several gestures that appear strange. These include touching one's own face several times quickly in a similar manner to scratching, but with the forefinger straight. This means 'Shame on you!'. It is a semi-joking gesture.

Pointing to the tip of one's nose with raised forefinger means 'It's me' or 'I'm the one'.

Using both hands in offering something to a visitor or another person equals respect. When one's tea cup is being refilled by the host or hostess, tapping index and middle finger on the table twice means 'Thank you'.

Gifts

Official policy in Chinese business culture forbids giving gifts, though enforcement of this policy is rather sporadic; the practice is seen as akin to bribery. Consequently, your gift may be declined. In many organisations, however, attitudes towards gifts are beginning to relax. Discretion is still important, and if you wish to give a gift to an individual, you must do it privately, in the context of friendship, not business. The Chinese will sometimes decline a gift three times before finally accepting, so as not to appear greedy.

Numbers

Eight is considered one of the luckiest numbers in Chinese culture. If you receive eight of any item, consider it a gesture of good will. But avoid four of any item – in Mandarin, the word 'four' sounds similar to 'death'. Likewise, because 'ten' sounds like the word 'is', 14, or 'is dead', should also be avoided. Six sounds similar to 'stay' and nine similar to 'a long time'. Scissors or knives can be interpreted as the severing of a friendship or other bond, as can eating pears, since the word for the fruit sounds like 'separate'.

Directory

Contraception & abortion

Due to its one-child policy China has cheap and available contraception and abortion. Contraceptives are available over the counter at pharmacies throughout the city. Abortions are available at the hospitals listed. For help, contact the American Sino OB-GYN Clinic (6249 3246).

Dentists

The following services are all English-speaking.

Arrail Dental

Unit 204, Lippo Plaza, 222 Huaihai Zhong Lu, by Songshan Lu, Xintiandi (5396 6538/www.arrail-dental.com). Metro Huangpi Nan Lu. **Open** 9am-8pm Mon-Thur; 9.30am-6.30pm Fri-Sun. **Credit** AmEx, DC, MC, V. **Map** p248 H7.
Dental treatment by American-trained staff, with strict CDC/ADA infection control protocols. Popular with US Consulate staff.

DDS Dental Care

B1-05 Evergo Tower, 1325 Huaihai Zhong Lu, by Changshu Lu, French Concession (6466 0928/www.dds dentalcare.com). Metro Changshu Lu. **Open** 10am-6pm Mon-Sat. **Credit** AmEx, DC, MC, V. **Map** p246 C8.
Affordable and complete dental treatment. The Western-trained Chinese staff speak English.

Dr Harriet Jin's Dental Surgery

Room 1904, Hui Yin Plaza, 2088 Huashan Lu, by Hengshan Lu, Xujiahui (6448 0882). Metro Xujiahui. **Open** 9am-6pm Mon-Fri; 9am-1pm Sat. **Credit** AmEx, DC, MC, V. **Map** p246 A11.
A small clinic with a big following among expats – Dr Jin used to work in the UK.

KOWA Dental

3N1-3N3, Jin Mao Tower, 88 Shiji Da Dao, Lujiazui, by Lujiazui Dong Lu, Pudong (5108 2222/www.kowa-dental.com). Metro Lujiazui. **Open** 9am-8.30pm Mon-Sat. **Credit** AmEx, DC, MC, V. **Map** p245 O5.
This ADA-certified German practice boasts comfortable private rooms in a white and chrome space-age setting – but for a price.

Hospitals

Shanghai has some good public hospitals and private international clinics. The main public hospitals

(yiyuan) will treat visitors on an outpatient or emergency basis, often in a special foreigner ward. For international and local clinics you will need to bring your passport and cash for the consultation fees, which vary wildly (RMB 100-500).
Be aware that Chinese hospitals often prescribe antibiotics and drips regardless of whether the cause of illness merits such action. The tendency to overprescribe is exacerbated because hospitals in China also act as general pharmacies, and upwards of 60 per cent of their income is made from drug sales. Make sure you're clear about the necessity of any medication prescribed. The following hospitals provide comprehensive medical care. Levels of hygiene are well maintained and staff are knowledgeable, but comfort and privacy may be lacking. Both Chinese- and Western-style treatment is available at these hospitals. In an emergency, dial 120.

Huashan Hospital Foreigners' Clinic

8th floor, 12 Wulumuqi Zhong Lu, by Huashan Lu, French Concession (6248 3986). Metro Changshu Lu or Jingan Temple. **Open** *Clinic* 7am-5pm Mon-Fri. *Emergencies* 24hrs daily. **Credit** AmEx, DC, MC, V. **Map** p246 C7.
Part of one of Shanghai's largest hospitals, with modern facilities. Staff outside the Foreigners' Clinic may only have limited English.

Ruijin Hospital

197 Ruijin Er Lu, by Yongjia Lu, French Concession (6437 0045). Metro Shaanxi Nan Lu, then 20mins walk/taxi. **Open** 24hrs daily. **Credit** AmEx, DC, MC, V. **Map** p247 F9.
The full range of medical facilities; some English is spoken.

Mental health

Lifeline Shanghai

6279 8990/www.lifelineshanghai.com. **Open** 10am-10pm daily.
English-speakers are almost always available.

12-Step Meetings

www.aashanghai.com
Find information and contact numbers for AA, Al-Anon, and other 12-step programme meetings.

Opticians

Most optical shops will grind lenses (after an on-site eye exam or to a prescription) within a few hours and at a reasonable price. Opticians can be found on Nanjing Xi Lu in

Jingan and Huaihai Nan Lu in the French Concession.
Try Shanghai Sanye Wholesale Eyeglasses Market (515 Shenjiazai Lu, by Shanghai Train Station, North Square, Zhabei, 5632 1259, map p243 F1) for great deals. Prices start as low as RMB 90.

Pharmacies & prescriptions

All medication is available over the counter, although certain antibiotics require a prescription. It is always advisable to purchase medicine at larger pharmacies to avoid the risk of counterfeit drugs.

Huaihai Pharmacist

501 Huaihai Zhong Lu, by Chongqing Nan Lu, French Concession (5383 2101). Metro Huangpi Nan Lu. **Open** 24hrs daily. **Credit** MC, V. **Map** p247 H7.

Huashi Pharmacist

910 Hengshan Lu, by Tianping Lu, French Concession (6407 8985). Metro Xujiahui. **Open** 24hrs daily. **No credit cards. Map** p246 B10.

No.1 Pharmacy

616 Nanjing Dong Lu, by Zhejiang Lu, People's Square (6322 4567). Metro Nanjing Dong Lu. **Open** 9am-10pm daily. **Credit** AmEx, DC, MC, V. **Map** p244 K4.

Private clinics/ doctors

International Medical Care Centre of Shanghai

People's Hospital No.1, 585 Jiulong Lu, by Wusong Lu, Hongkou (6324 3852). **Open** 24hrs daily. **Credit** AmEx, DC, MC, V. **Map** p245 M1.
This private health centre, attached to a teaching hospital, offers all medical services, including dentistry. The standard of care in the Medical Centre is higher than in other departments.

Parkway Health

203-4 West Retail Plaza, Shanghai Centre, 1376 Nanjing Xi Lu, by Tongren Lu, Jingan (6445 5999/www.worldlink-shanghai.com). Metro Jingan Temple. **Open** 9am-7pm Mon-Fri; 9am-5pm Sat, Sun. **Credit** AmEx, DC, MC, V. **Map** p243 E5.
One of several Parkway Health clinics in Shanghai. Doctors are from the US, UK, Canada and Japan, and assistance is available in English, Japanese and Chinese. Clinics offer a

complete range of services from walk-in treatment for minor ailments to internal medicine. Dental treatment is also available.

Shanghai East International Medical Centre

551 Pudong Nan Lu, by Pudong Dadao, Pudong (5879 9999/ www.seimc.com.cn). Metro Dongchang Lu. **Open** *Clinic* 9am-8pm Mon-Fri; 9am-6pm Sat, Sun. *Emergencies* 24hrs daily. **Credit** AmEx, DC, MC, V. **Map** p241 F3.
Joint-venture clinic run by Shanghai East Hospital and a US healthcare group. Expat doctors and English-speaking nurses provide experienced, world-class family healthcare.

STDs, HIV & AIDS

For hospitals, *see p222.*

AIDS Information & Counselling

1380 Zhongshan Xi Lu, by Hongqiao Lu, Hongqiao (6437 0055). Metro Hongqiao Lu. **Open** 8.30am-5pm Mon-Fri. **No credit cards.**

Shanghai Venereal Disease Association

196 Wuyi Lu, by Anxi Lu, Changning (6251 1807). Metro Jiangsu Lu. **Open** 8.30am-4.30pm Mon-Fri. **No credit cards. Map** p246 A7.

Traditional Chinese medicine (TCM)

See pp171-177 **Mind & Body.**

ID

Chinese citizens are expected to carry photo ID at all times. Foreigners should carry their passport or a photocopy of its information page and the page with the China visa.

Insurance

China has no reciprocal agreements with other countries: be sure to take out adequate health and travel insurance before you arrive.

Internet

Most hotels offer internet services for a fee. Top-end joints usually offer free

broadband to anyone with a laptop. Otherwise, there are internet cafés on every corner, most of them (especially 24-hour ones) gaming dens. An hour's surfing in such places can be as cheap as RMB 2; take ID with you. Wireless connections have begun to catch on in the city, so travellers with laptops can access the net at locations such as Xintiandi. If during web searches, you find yourself blocked, you could try going through a proxy server, such as www.proxy4china.com.

Cyber Bar & Café

77 Jiangning Lu, by Nanjing Xi Lu, Jingan (6217 3321). Metro Nanjing Xi Lu. **Open** 24hrs daily. **Rates** RMB 5/hr. **No credit cards. Map** p243 F5.
This cyber café is in an all-night bang-bang arcade. As a consequence, it is very loud – notwithstanding the noise-reducing computer headsets.

O'Richard's Bar & Restaurant

2nd floor, Pujiang Hotel, 15 Huangpu Lu, by Garden Bridge, the Bund (6324 6388 ext 175). Metro Nanjing Dong Lu. **Open** 7am-2am daily. **Rates** RMB 8/hr. **No credit cards. Map** p245 N3.
Get some Qingdao beer and noodles while you surf.

Shanghai Library

1555 Huaihai Zhong Lu, by Gaoan Lu, French Concession (6445 5555). Metro Hengshan Lu. **Open** 9am-8.30pm daily. **Rates** RMB 4/hr. **No credit cards. Map** p246 C8/9.
Here you'll catch the silver surfers getting online. No smoking or drinks, and you must show a passport or library card to use one of the 24 terminals. Some sites (eg hotmail) are periodically blocked.

Language

China, a huge country, has a corresponding range of dialects (Hong Kong people speak Cantonese, people in Shanghai speak Shanghainese), but standard Chinese is called Mandarin or Putongua.
For those who do not read Chinese characters, there is a romanised alphabet called Pinyin. English is not widely

understood outside the top hotels and businesses, so it is wise to get a copy of the address you're heading to written down in Chinese so that you can show it to the driver. Most business cards have Chinese and English addresses listed on them, making them a valuable tool for getting around. Listings magazines such as *that's Shanghai* and *City Weekend* have Chinese addresses for popular venues, and the Guanxi SMS-based directory *(see p218)* is good. *See also p230* **Vocabulary.**

Left luggage

Luggage can be left at Pudong International Airport and Hongqiao Airport (for both, *see p216*). Shanghai Railway Station (6354 3193) and Shanghai South Railway Station (5122 5114) also have left-luggage services. Many of the better hotels can arrange long-term luggage storage for their guests.

Legal help

For help finding a lawyer and basic information on Chinese law, call the Jun He law firm (32nd floor, Shanghai Kerry Centre, 1515 Nanjing Xi Lu, by Tongren Lu, Jingan, 5298 5488/ www.junhe.com/en/index.asp). For more information, *see also p220* **Embassies & consulates.**

Libraries

Shanghai Library

1555 Huaihai Zhong Lu, by Gaoan Lu, French Concession (6445 5555). Metro Hengshan Lu. **Open** 9am-8.30pm daily. **Map** p246 C8/9.
The Shanghai Library is the largest of its kind in China. It has an outstanding collection of Chinese-language books, both antique and modern, but the range of foreign-language books is limited. The library also houses an art gallery and a reasonably priced internet café *(see above).*

Directory

Lost property

To report a crime contact the police hotline (110). For items left in taxis, look at the receipt the driver gave you when paying and use the contact number on the back to trace the vehicle. Hotel concierges can also be helpful when it comes to tracking down lost items. If your passport is lost, contact the relevant consulate immediately (*see p220*).

For Pudong International Airport lost property, call 6834 6324; for Hongqiao Airport, call 6268 8899 ext 42071.

Media

Magazines

Shanghai, the most international of China's cities, has a multitude of free English-language magazines with listings. The most popular are *City Weekend* (www.cityweekend. com.cn) and *that's Shanghai* (www.urbanatomy.com). *City Weekend* is a bi-weekly focusing on how to access the city's hottest events while *that's Shanghai* is a hefty monthly that takes a more in-depth literary view. Other titles include *Shanghai Talk* (www.talkmagazines.cn) and *SH* (www.shmag.cn). Pick them up free at cafés, restaurants and bars.

Newspapers

Newsstands offer two main English-language newspapers, the locally produced *Shanghai Daily* (www.shanghaidaily.com) and the Beijing-printed *China Daily* (www.chinadaily.com.cn). The *Shanghai Star* (www.shanghai-star.com.cn), which is published every Thursday, is also owned by *China Daily*. The Chinese-language *People's Daily* can be read in English at http://english.peopledaily.com.cn. The *Oriental Morning Post* includes an English-language supplement on Friday. Newspaper editorial is scrutinised by the government, necessitating self-censorship.

It is very difficult to get hold of international newspapers in Shanghai, but the Portman Ritz-Carlton should be able to provide a copy of *The Times* or the *Financial Times* – although you'll pay for the privilege. For more on where to buy international newspapers and magazines, *see p133*.

Online

Net-savvy travelers should check out Shanghaiist (www.shanghaiist.com), a hip young website with news, events and commentary, or cruise the sexy yet snarky webzine Smart Shanghai (www.smartshanghai.com) to tap in to the pulse of the expat scene. Those looking to understand local events through the Chinese language can visit ChinesePod (www.chinesepod.com) to brush up on their language skills while learning about current events or cultural practices.

Radio

The BBC World Service can be picked up at 17760, 15335, 11750, 6195 and 9740 kHz. The Voice of America (VOA) is at 7430, 11705, 1575, 1170, 9645, 7125 and 11725 kHz. For tuning information click on 'Radio Schedules' at www.bbc.co.uk/worldservice or on 'Radio: Frequencies' at www.voa.gov. If these sites are blocked, go through www.anonymouse.org to reach them.

Television

Shanghai premiered its first local international channel (ICS) in 2008, which mostly features English-language programming, sprinkled with a few other foreign-language shows. English-language news is also shown on CCTV 9 at noon, 4pm, 7pm and 11pm on weekdays and at noon on weekends. Most top-end hotels have at least BBC, CNN, ESPN, HBO and Star World.

Money

The monetary unit in China is the RMB (*renminbi*), also known as the *yuan* (written) or *kuai* (spoken). Bills come in denominations of RMB 100, 50, 20, 10, 5, 2 and 1; coins include 1 *yuan*, and 5 and 1 *jiao* pieces (10 *jiao* equals RMB 1).

The exchange rate is usually in the region of RMB 7 to the dollar, RMB 14 to the pound. Note that few countries outside Asia recognise RMB, so change any leftover cash at the airport as you leave. Bring receipts to prove that the amount you want to change back is less than the amount first changed into RMB. ATM receipts don't count; you'll need official receipts from exchange counters or bank tellers.

ATMs

ATMs are widely available but they don't necessarily accept foreign cards even if they do display the Interact

logo. HSBC provides some of the more reliable ATMs; try one the following locations:

HSBC the Bund *15A Zhongshan Dongyi Lu, by Jiujiang Lu, the Bund.* Map p245 M4.
HSBC Hong Kong Plaza *Hong Kong Plaza, 282 Huaihai Zhong Lu, by Huangpi Nan Lu, Xintiandi.* Map p248 H7.
HSBC Shanghai Centre *Shanghai Centre, 1376 Nanjing Xi Lu, by Tongren Lu, Jingan.* Map p243 E5.
HSBC Tower *101 Yincheng Dong Lu, by Pudong Dadao, Pudong.* Map p245 P5.

Banks

ABN AMRO *26th floor Huiya Building, 1233 Lujiazui Ring Road, Pudong (3861 5888). Metro Lujiazui.* **Open** 10am-noon, 2-5pm Mon-Fri. **Map** p245 O5.
Bank of China *200 Yincheng Zhong Lu, by Lujiazui Lu, Pudong (3883 4588). Metro Lujiazui.* **Open** 24hrs Mon-Fri. **Map** p245 O5.
China Construction Bank *1632 Yincheng Dong Lu, by Lujiazui Lu, Pudong (5888 0000). Metro Lujiazui.* **Open** 8.30am-5pm Mon-Fri. **Map** p245 O5.
CitiBank *20th floor, Marine Tower, 1 Pudong Dadao, by Shiji Dadao, Pudong (5879 1200). Metro Lujiazui.* **Open** 9am-5pm daily. **Map** p245 O5.
HSBC *101 Yincheng Dong Lu, by Pudong Dadao, Pudong (6841 1888). Metro Lujiazui.* **Open** 9am-5pm daily. **Map** p245 P5.

Bureaux de change

There are two desks just beyond customs at the airports for changing cash or travellers' cheques. In the city itself, only certain banks, including those above, offer this service. Hotel guests can usually change money at their reception desk.

Black-market money changers are often found on the Bund or outside banks. Some established money changers even do business inside bank premises, next to official exchange counters. Black-market traders offer slightly better rates, but there's no receipt and no comeback if you're shortchanged or slipped bogus notes (common in RMB 100 and 50 denominations).

Credit cards

China has limited infrastructure in place for use of credit cards. They are most commonly accepted at four- and five-star hotels and high-end restaurants. Be warned, though: an extra four per cent handling fee is usually charged on all credit card transactions. Visa and MasterCard are the most widely accepted; American Express and Diners Club are also recognised, but less commonly so.

Lost/stolen cards
AmEx 6279 8082
Mastercard 010 800 110 7309
Visa 6323 6656

Tax

A 15 per cent surcharge is added to bills at high-end hotels, but there is no departure tax levied at the airport.

Natural hazards

There are limited natural hazards in Shanghai. The occasional typhoon has swept through the city causing minor floods and wind damage. Warnings will appear in the Chinese media. Although aftershocks were felt in Shanghai from the Sichuan quake in 2008, Shanghai is not located on any major fault lines. At present there is no English-language warning system, but the English-language weather forecast hotline is 12121.

Air pollution varies depending on location. For details of air quality, call 969221 (Chinese only). Mosquitoes are an annoyance during the summer months, but repellent is widely available.

Opening hours

Opening hours are similar to those in the West; museums are usually open seven days a week.

Banks 9am-5pm Mon-Fri. (Some banks open seven days a week.)
Bars 11am/noon-2am daily.
Businesses 9am-6pm Mon-Fri.
Municipal offices 8am-5pm Mon-Fri. (Some offices may close for one hour at lunchtime.)
Post offices 9am-6pm daily.

Police

Police stations can be identified by a red light and a sign that says 'Jingcha'. Police

wear a dark navy uniform. There are numerous private security guards throughout the city who do not enforce the law but wear a similar uniform to local police.

Traffic crossing guards armed with shrill whistles are also prominent at every major road junction in Shanghai; disobey them at your peril – jaywalking can be punished with a RMB 50 fine.

Police stations

Huangpu Police Sub-bureau 174 Jinling Dong Lu, by Henan Nan Lu, Old City (6328 0123). **Map** p244 L6.
People's Square Policemen Admin 499 Nanjing Xi Lu, by Chengdu Bei Lu, People's Square (6327 0729). Metro People's Square. **Map** p244 H5.

Postal services

The Chinese mail service is reliable, though slow. Postcards to any destination around the world cost RMB 4.50. Letters under 20 grams to Europe, Australia and North America cost RMB 6. Letters over 20 grams are charged an additional RMB 1.80 per 10 grams. Packages cost RMB 18 for 100 grams, then RMB 15 for every additional 100 grams. It's best to write the address in both English and Chinese.

There is a post office in every district – either call 11185 or 6325 2070, or go to www.chinapost.gov.cn to find local addresses. The main post office (see below) is in Hongkou and as such is not particularly convenient for most visitors. More useful branch offices include one at the Shanghai Centre (1376 Nanjing Xi Lu, by Tongren Lu, Jingan) and one at Xintiandi shopping plaza (No. 3, Lane 123 Xingye Lu, by Huangpi Nan Lu). Both have English-speaking staff. See also p219 **Couriers**.

Main post office
1 Sichuan Bei Lu, Hongkou (6324 0425). **Open** 7am-10pm daily. **Map** p245 M3.

Property

Finding a home

The number of agencies targeting foreign clients in Shanghai has ballooned in recent years. Most are legit, but there are lots of unlicensed agencies; exercise caution.

The only legislative requirement of the Shanghai Municipal Government is that foreigners must register themselves at the relevant Foreign Affairs Police station (see the list below for the office closest to you) within 72 hours of signing a lease on any property.

Changning 201 Weining Lu, by Maotai Lu (6290 6290).
Hongkou 260 Minhang Lu, by Wusong Lu (6324 2200).
Huangpu 174 Jinling Dong Lu, by Henan Zhong Lu (6328 0123).
Jingan 415 Jiaozhou Lu, by Kangding Lu(6258 8800).
Jinshan 110 Mengyuan Lu, by Mengzi Lu (3799 0110).
Luwan Zhongshan Nan Yi Lu, by Mengzi Lu (5302 5110).
Pudong 655 Dingxiang Lu, by Minsheng Lu (5061 4567).

Real-estate agents

Phoenix Property Agency
Yujia Building, 1336 Huashan Lu, by Pingwu Lu, French Concession (6240 4052/www.shanghai-realty.com). **Open** 9am-6pm Mon-Fri. **Map** p246 A8.
Established in 1999 and noted for its nose for unique properties. The website has extensive listings.

Space
No.16, Lane 76 Wuyuan Road, by Changshu Lu, French Concession (5404 0110/www.space.sh.cn). Metro Changshu Lu. **Open** 9am-6pm Mon-Fri. **Map** p246 D7.
Space specialises in high-end residential property. The firm's up-to-date online property search engine is useful for finding properties for a variety of budgets and locations.

Precautions

A few things to be aware of:
● Any property that has a management company will have a monthly management fee. Check with your agent to see if this is a separate payment or whether it is included in the negotiated rent.
● Test to see that you can run your air-conditioning at the same time as the microwave and other appliances. If in doubt, insist on an opt-out clause in your lease.

- Determine which parts of the house being shown to you are for private and which parts are for common use.

Types of housing

New flats

High-rise developments with Western standards and amenities. Dependent on layout, size and location, prices range from $500 to $4,500 per month, with the top end running to penthouses, roof gardens, multiple bedrooms and the like.

Old flats

Generally apartment buildings with individually owned flats (or flats granted to a family by the government). They are largely tenanted by local Chinese families due to convenient central locations and reasonable prices. If you can manage to rent one, expect prices in the order of $400 to $2,000 per month.

Old houses

The city's old (Concession era) terraced and fully detached houses are, of course, over-subscribed. It you can find one, it'll cost $3,000 to $7,000 per month, depending on location, state of renovation and whether it has a garden.

Serviced apartments

These often offer concierge services and/or hotel-quality facilities and are generally the only places available for short-term lease. Apartments range from studios to six-bedroom affairs, with city-centre prices per month ranging from $2,500 to $15,000.

Villas

These are sterile, gated communities located on the outskirts of town in such districts as Hongqiao, Xuhui and Pudong. Expect gardens, service-oriented management, security and a high standard of facilities – and prices in the order of $7,000 to $20,000 per month.

Religion

Religion is still a sensitive topic. While long-established religions such as Christianity, Islam, Buddhism and Taoism are recognised (Judaism seems a borderline case), the primacy of the Communist Party must always be acknowledged. Steer clear of sensitive topics such as Falun Gong or religious freedom in Tibet.

Buddhist

Jingan Temple
1686 Nanjing Xi Lu, by Wanhangdu Lu, Jingan (6256 6366/www.shjas.com). Metro Jingan Temple.
Map p242 C5.
Longhua Temple
2853 Longhua Lu, Longhua (6457 6327). Metro Longcao Lu.
Map p240 C5.
Temple of the City God
249 Fangbang Zhong Lu, by Anren Jie, Old City (6386 5700).
Map p249 M7.

Catholic

All Saints' Church
425 Fuxing Zhong Lu, by Danshui Lu, Xintiandi (6385 0906). Metro Huangpi Lu. **Mass** 7pm Tue, Fri; 1-3pm Wed, Thur; 7.30pm Sat; 7.30am, 9.30am, 7pm Sun.
Map p247 H8.
Dongjiadu Lu Catholic Church
185 Dongjiadu Lu, by Wanyu Jie, Old City (6378 7214). **Mass** 6am Mon-Sat; 7.30am Sun. **Map** p249 O9.
St Ignatius Cathedral
158 Puxi Lu, by Caoxi Bei Lu, Xujiahui (6438 2595). Metro Xujiahui. **Mass** 5am Mon-Fri; 1-4pm Sat, Sun. **Map** p246 A11.
St Joseph's Church
36 Sichuan Nan Lu, by Jinling Dong Lu, Old City (6328 0293). **Mass** 7am Mon-Sat; 6am, 7.30am Sun. Map p245 M6.
St Peter's Church
270 Chongqing Nan Lu, by Fuxing Zhong Lu, French Concession (6467 8080). Metro Huangpi Nan Lu. **Mass** 5pm Sat; 10.30am Sun. **Map** p247 H8.

Jewish

Jewish Community of Shanghai
62 Changyang Lu, by Zhoushan Lu, Hongkou (6537 1238). Metro Dalian Lu. **Map** p242 F2.

Muslim

Jingxing Mosque
No.117, Lane 302, Jingxing Lu, by Pingliang Lu, Yangpu (6541 3199). Metro Yangshupu Lu. **Map** p241 G2.

Protestant

Hengshan Community Church
53 Hengshan Lu, by Wulumuqi Lu, French Concession (6437 6576). Metro Hengshan Lu. **Services** 2pm, 4pm Sun. Map p246 C9.
Moore Memorial Church
316 Xizang Zhong Lu, by Jiujiang Lu, People's Square (6322 5029). Metro People's Square. **Services** 7am, 9am, 2pm, 7pm daily. Map p244 J5.
Shanghai Grace Church
375 Shanxi Bei Lu, by Beijing Xi Lu, Jingan (6253 9394). Metro Nanjing Xi Lu. **Services** 7.30pm Mon-Fri; 9am Sat; 9am, 7pm Sun. **Map** p243 F6.

Safety

Shanghai is remarkably safe. Crime against foreigners is negligible and what little occurs tends to be limited to pickpocketing. Women usually get about independently without harassment.

Smoking & spitting

Shanghai is a smoker's paradise. Cigarettes are inexpensive and smoked by many, though some restaurants are finally starting to offer smoke-free environs.

Spitting is the most beloved non-spectator sport in town. From a mild spittle to a full-on, lung-rattling, expectorant cough, it is a prevalent and revolting habit. The belief that it is healthy to expel noxious fluids from the body may have something to do with spitting's popularity. Although ubiquitous Chinese signs encouraging civility forbid it, it's hardly on the wane.

Study

Chinese-language schools

Creative Methodology

8C Xinan Building, 200 Zhenning Lu, by Yuyuan Lu, Jingan (6289 4299/www.talkingchina.com). Metro Jiangsu Lu. **Rates** RMB 50-70/hr for small classes (up to 10 students); RMB 135/hr for individual classes. **No credit cards**. **Map** p242 B6.
The centre offers eight different levels of classes in addition to business Chinese, Shanghai dialect and Mandarin for Cantonese speakers. Tutoring is by bilingual teachers from a variety of respected Shanghai universities.

Ease Mandarin

Room 101, No.2, Lane 25, Wuxing Lu, by Kangping Lu, French Concession (5465 6999/www.easemandarin.com). Metro Hengshan Lu. **Rates** RMB 6,000/2mnths (at 4hrs per wk). **No credit cards**. **Map** p246 B9.

One of the most popular schools for expats wanting to study Mandarin. Friendly, helpful and dedicated teachers make the programme effective and engaging. Classes incorporate work on speaking, writing and reading.

Learning Mandarin Centre

Room 6012, 887 Huaihai Zhong Lu, by Ruijin Er Lu, French Concession (6431 6104/www.l-e-c.net). Metro Shaanxi Nan Lu. **Rates** RMB 110/hr. **Credit** MC, V. **Map** p247 F7.

In a convenient central downtown location, this school focuses on teaching English to Mandarin speakers but also offers classes for students of Mandarin.

Mandarin Center

16 Songyuan Lu, by Hongqiao Lu, Hongqiao (6270 7668/www. mandarin-center.com). Metro Hongqiao Lu. **Rates** 65/hr for small classes (3 students); 125/hr-150/hr for individual lessons; RMB 2,500-11,000/2- to 5-month term. **Credit** AmEx, MC, V. **Map** p240 B4.

Offers morning, afternoon and evening classes; popular with expats. Classes range from two- and five-month programmes. Instructors follow a traditional approach to teaching Chinese, as the centre is affiliated to Fudan University.

Telephones

Dialling & codes

The country code for China is 86 and the city code for Shanghai is 021. Drop the prefix zero when dialling from overseas. Domestic calls require the city code but it is not necessary within Shanghai.

For outgoing international calls, dial the international access code, 00, followed by the country code, the area code and the local telephone number. The US and Canada country code is 1; the UK 44; Australia 61; and for New Zealand 64.

Useful city codes

Hangzhou *0571.*
Moganshan *0572.*
Nanjing *025.*
Putuoshan *0580.*
Suzhou *0512.*

Faxes

Most hotels are willing to accept incoming faxes for guests. Faxes can be sent from hotel business centres or the front desk and are charged at around RMB 10 per page.

Mobile phones

The two mobile phone providers in Shanghai are China Mobile and China Unicom. Both use the GSM system. China Mobile uses GPRS phones and China Unicom uses CDMA phones. China Mobile is the larger of the two, but Unicom has lower rates. Mobile users from Japan and North America should check that their roaming service will operate in China. Both providers offer prepay and billed services. With the prepay system users can purchase a SIM card, put it into any GSM phone and add value to the account with a prepaid card. The billed system requires Chinese ID or a Chinese guarantor.

Local prepaid phone cards and SIM cards can cut the cost of mobile use in Shanghai. They are priced at RMB 100 and are sold at newsstands, subway station kiosks and convenience stores. Incoming and outgoing calls are charged by the minute.

Operator services

Local directory assistance 114. For international enquiries and reverse-charge/collect calls, try phoning one of these numbers:
AT&T 108-11.
Global One 10817/6279 8538.

Phonecards

Internet calling cards (or 'IP' cards), which are widely available in Shanghai, make for an economical option for overseas calls. The access codes for US phone card users are: Sprint (10813); MCI (10812); and AT&T (10811).

Public phones

Chinese public phones take prepaid phone cards (IC Cards) with values of RMB 20, RMB 30, RMB 50 and RMB 100 – you should try to bargain the price for these cards if you buy them at small kiosks or in subway stations. A card with a value of RMB 100 can be bought for as little as RMB 30 with a little haggling. Users of public phones can make domestic and international calls. The latter can be pricey – over RMB 10 a minute. Rates for domestic long-distance calls are RMB 0.20 for three minutes, with calls longer than three minutes charged at RMB 0.10 for every further six seconds.

Telephone directories

To order a copy of the *Yellow Pages*, call 5385 4017 (Chinese only).

Operator Assisted Yellow Pages 96886 (the service is in Chinese only).

Time

China is eight hours ahead of GMT. The country does not operate daylight-saving time.

Tipping

Hotel restaurants and other high-end, foreigner-aimed places usually add a 15 per cent surcharge to the bill. Everything else is at your discretion. Tour guides usually expect to be tipped.

Toilets

Public toilets are available throughout the city but standards vary tremendously, and it is definitely worth taking an emergency tissue supply with you. They charge a marginal fee and also sell tissues, feminine hygiene products and cosmetic items. The squat toilet is most common, but some facilities have Western-style commodes. Hotels, bars and restaurants have Western-style toilets.

Tourist information

There are various tourist information lines you can try, among them the 24-hour helpline (with English service) of the Tourist Bureau on 962020, the Shanghai Spring International Travel Service (6252 0000, open 10am-9pm daily) and a new 24-hour Shanghai Call Center hot line (962288), staffed by English-speaking university graduates who can handle most tourist queries. The tourist offices themselves offer a limited selection of free information in English – the services tend to be geared toward local Chinese rather than international travellers. Concierges at top hotels offer a much higher standard of customer service.

Directory

There is a tourist bureau in every district. We list below the the best but this really isn't saying very much:

Jingan District Tourist Information & Service Centre
1699 Nanjing Xi Lu, by Huashan Lu, Jingan (3214 0042). Metro Jingan Temple. **Open** 9am-5pm daily. **Map** p242 C6.

Luwan District Tourist Information & Service Centre
127 Chengdu Nan Lu, by Huaihai Zhong Lu, French Concession (5382 7330). Metro Huangpi Nan Lu. **Open** 9am-9pm daily. **Map** p247 G7.

Pudong New Area Tourist Information & Service Centre
168 Lujiazui Lu, by Yincheng Lu, Pudong (6875 0593). Metro Lujiazui. **Open** 9am-6pm daily. **Map** p245 O5.

Yuyuan Tourist Information & Service Centre
Yu Bazaar, 149 Jiujiaochang Lu, by Fangbang Zhong Lu, Old City (6355 5032). **Open** 9am-7pm daily. **Map** p249 M7.

Visas & immigration

All visitors to China require a visa. These are obtained through a Chinese embassy or consulate. Most tourists are issued with a single-entry visa, valid for entry within three months of issue and good for a 30-day stay. Processing times and fees vary. In the UK the cost for a citizen is £30, while it's £65 for Americans. You need to allow three working days for processing. Two passport photos are required for the application. A next-day express service is available for twice the standard fee.

Business visas are usually multiple entry and valid for three to six months from the date of issue. They allow the visitor to stay for the full specified period. These require a letter of invitation from the host business or corporation and in some cases a copy of the business licence.

For more information on current visa regulations and application procedures, check the following websites:

UK citizens
www.chinese-embassy.org.uk.
US citizens
www.china-embassy.org.
Canadian citizens
www.chinaembassycanada.org.

Visa extensions of 30 days are easy to get. They take three days to process, and cost RMB 160 for Britons and RMB 125 for Americans.

PSB
1500 Minsheng Lu, by Yinchun Lu, Pudong (2895 1900). Metro Science & Technology Museum. **Open** 9am-5pm Mon-Sat. **Map** p241 G4.

Long-term residency

Long-term residency requires a 'green card' or residence permit (*xukezheng*). The formidable amount of paperwork that is needed for a green card requires at least ten passport photos to go with it – one to go with each of the ten completed forms necessary for the application. It's a five-step process beginning with the acquisition of your initial tourist visa (*see above*). Beyond this you need a certificate of health, an employment visa, your company's business licence and a work permit: only then can you apply for the green card. Employers will need to help you with the process.

For the health certificate, the required examinations and tests can be done in your home country, but it's much easier to do it in Shanghai. There is a new, efficient and clean testing facility (1701 Hami Lu, Hongqiao, 6268 6171, open 8.30am-11am, 1.30-3pm Mon-Sat). Get there early (by 8am) and you should be out within the hour. To take a 'health exam' you'll need a copy of your passport plus a copy of the photo and China visa pages, two passport photos and RMB 700. The exam includes tests for STDs, chest X-rays, a sonogram, a vision test and general health queries.

For the employment visa, you need an invitation letter from your company, your company employment licence and your newly obtained health certificate.

For the work permit (or 'red book') you'll need your employment application letter and CV, the contract you've signed with your company, your health certificate, your passport (plus photocopies of the photo page) and three passport photos.

Finally, for the residence permit ('green card') you will need the completed application form, the original and a photocopy of your

entire (!) passport, two passport photos, your health certificate, your work permit (the original and a photocopy) and a copy of your company's business licence. The green card is valid for 12 months.

Water

Don't drink tap water – bottled water is widely available.

Weights & measures

China uses the metric system for measurements.

What to take

Everything you are likely to need can be found in Shanghai, although it may take some finding. Prices may be slightly more expensive for foreign or imported goods. Although most medications, from aspirin to Zoloft, are available in China, it's wise to bring all essentials with you – important medication may not be available here, and foreign prescriptions will not be accepted at pharmacies unless endorsed by a certified local practitioner.

When to go

Climate

The weather is a major factor in planning a visit to Shanghai. There are times of the year when the city's high humidity can be seriously debilitating, making a visit to the city distinctly uncomfortable. A summary of what to expect during the year follows, but bear in mind that Shanghai's weather can be very unpredictable; *see p229* **Average climate**.

Spring (March to mid May) is often pleasant and is one of the best times to visit weather-wise, although some of the heaviest rainfall is recorded during this time. Bring a medium-weight jacket or sweaters for the evenings, which can be cool. Spring is also the time of fresh blooms, so it's great for visits to the Yu Gardens (*see p67*) and the gardens of Suzhou (*see p209*).

Summer (late May to mid September) is hot, hot, hot and

stiflingly humid. Ironically, you'll probably still need to bring an extra layer for when you're indoors, as shops, restaurants, bars and hotels tend to crank up the air-conditioning to icy levels. Also be aware that in the month from mid June – Mei-Yu Season – the city receives perhaps a quarter of its annual rainfall. Summer is also prime festival time.

Autumn (late September to early December), along with spring, is generally the best time to visit Shanghai; temperatures are comfortably warm, and humidity drops to a bearable level. Sunny days and clear skies are quite common.

Winter (mid December to February) gets chilly, windy and cloudy, so you need to bring extra layers of clothing. Although the temperature rarely drops below zero, it seems much colder due to the humidity – this is really not a good time to be around Shanghai, although the New Year festivities bring a little colour and warmth.

Public holidays

In 2008, China lost many of its formerly beloved but always chaotic week-long public holidays in order to adopt day to two-day breaks (in addition to traditional Chinese holidays). They are dependent on the lunar calendar, so each year the dates change.

New Year's Day 1 Jan
Chinese Lunar New Year 3-7 days in Jan/Feb
Tomb Sweeping Festival 1 day Apr
Labour Holiday 1-3 May
Dragon Boat Festival 1-3 days in June
Mid Autumn Festival 1 day Aug/Sept
National Day Holiday 1-3 Oct

Women

Shanghai is a very safe city for women. There is minimal harassment and crime rates are low. Women can travel independently at night, but it's still sensible to be cautious. Some useful women's groups in Shanghai include:

American Women's Club
www.awcshanghai.org
Australian Women's Social Group
www.awsg.org
Brits Abroad
www.britsabroad.org
Expatriates Professional Women's Society
www.epws-shanghai.org

Working in Shanghai

Expect to spend about two months searching for a job; www.chinahr.com and www.51job.com are good starting points, as are *City Weekend* and *that's Shanghai*'s websites. Many temporary jobs in China for English-speakers pay quite well. For English teaching and contract jobs, check out the China job board on Dave's ESL café www.eslcafe.com/jobs/china. Typically, part-time jobs for English-speaking foreigners include voice recording, writing, teaching English or even modelling. Wages

generally start at RMB 100/hr and are paid in cash. Contracts for this type of work are uncommon. Although it is illegal, some foreigners work on this basis until getting a full-time job. The police rarely monitor this type of activity but significant fines can be levied on anyone who is caught out.

Internships are a good way into the system if you have limited China-based work experience. Many consulates, US and European companies offer internships. These positions can and do often turn into paid employment on completion.

Work visas

For a work visa you need:
● A passport with at least six months' validity and at least one blank page.
● One completed visa application form with one additional passport photo.
● A visa notification issued by the authorised Chinese unit.
● Your company's business licence.
● Either a work permit issued by the Chinese Labour Ministry or a Foreign Expert's Licence issued by the Chinese Foreign Expert Bureau.
● A visa notification issued by the authorised Chinese unit or proof of kinship is required for spouse or accompanying family members. Allow three to four days for processing the documents. For more information, go to www.molss.gov.cn.

Average climate

	Temp (°C)	Temp (°F)	Humidity (%)	Rainfall (mm)	Sunshine (hrs)
January	7-9	45-48	18	45-50	131
February	8-10	46-50	22	60-65	158
March	12-14	54-58	27	80-85	58
April	18-20	65-68	48	90-95	159
May	23-25	74-78	54	110-115	180
June	27-29	80-84	73	160-165	103
July	31-33	88-92	76	140-145	96
August	31-33	88-92	75.5	140-145	99
September	27-29	81-84	73	136-141	145
October	22-24	72-76	52	55-60	104
November	16-18	61-65	45	50-55	112
December	10-12	50-54	25.5	40-45	186

Directory

Vocabulary

In Shanghai people speak Shanghainese (*see p223* **Language**). It is substantially different in pronunciation from Mandarin and Cantonese, with several sounds that are not found in any other Chinese dialect. The bulk of the vocabulary is the same, but there are lots of variations, and unique words and phrases. It is considered a coarse and uncultured dialect, unsuited to formal occasions. In such cases, people typically switch to Mandarin, which is the city's second language.

Grammatically, Chinese is actually easier than many other languages. There are no tenses – Chinese words have only one form. Suffixes are used instead to denote tenses. There are no comparative adjectives. The most challenging part of learning Chinese is often the tones, as each sound has four different inflections, each of which can change the meaning of a word. Even for the Chinese, the various tones only avoid confusion up to a certain point: complete understanding is gained from the context.

In the written language, characters take the place of an alphabet. A character can be a word or part of a word, but normally a word consists of two or more characters. There are about 20,000 characters in a normal Chinese word processor. For those who do not read characters there is a romanised alphabet called Pinyin. However Chinese rarely understand it when spoken by non-natives. Note that not all consonants in Pinyin are pronounced as in English:

c   like the 'ts' in 'hits'
q   like the 'ch' in 'chase'
r   like the 's' in 'measure'
x   like the 'sh' in 'shop'
z   like the 'dz' in 'duds'

Phrases

yes (to answer a question)	*shi*
(to indicate correct)	*dui*
no (to answer a question)	*bu shi*
(to indicate incorrect)	*bu dui*
my name is...	*wo jiao...*
my last name is...	*wo xing...*
I am	*wo shi*
American	*meiguo ren*
British	*yingguo ren*
Australian	*aodaliya ren*
European	*ouzhou ren*
hello	*nihao*
goodbye	*zaijian*
thanks	*xiexie*
how are you?	*ni zenmeyang*
you're welcome	*bu keqi*
sorry	*duibuqi*
correct/right	*dui*
incorrect/wrong	*bu dui*
don't want	*bu yao*
don't have	*meiyou*
I don't know	*wo bu zhi dao*
I don't understand	*wo bu mingbai*
please speak more slowly	
	qing shuo de man yidian

Getting around

Is this taxi free?	*Zhe gei che you ren ma?*
turn left	*zuo guai*
turn right	*you guai*
go straight	*yizhi zou*
stop the vehicle	*ting che*
I want to go to	*wo yao qu*
hotel	*da jiu dian*
airport	*feijichang*
train station	*huochezhan*
metro	*ditiezhan*
this place (point)	*zhe ge difang*
I want to return home	*wo yao hui jia*

Shopping

how much is it?	*duoshao qian?*
too expensive	*tai gui le*
cheaper?	*pianyi dian?*
too big	*tai da*
too small	*tai xiao*
please give me a receipt	*qing gei wo fapiao*

Eating & drinking

beer	*pijiu*
water	*shui*
English tea	*yingguo cha*

the bill please	*mai dan*
telephone	*dianhua*
bar	*jiuba*
pub	*jiuguan*
café	*kafeiguan*
restaurant	*fandian/canguan*

Dates & times

Monday	*xingqiyi*
Tuesday	*xingqier*
Wednesday	*xingqisan*
Thursday	*xingqisi*
Friday	*xingqiwu*
Saturday	*xingqiliu*
Sunday	*xingqitian*
morning	*zaoshang/shangwu*
afternoon	*xiawu*
evening	*wanshang*
today	*jintian*
tomorrow	*mingtian*
yesterday	*zuotian*
day after tomorrow	*houtian*
day before yesterday	*qiantian*

Numbers

zero	*ling*
one	*yi*
two	*er*
three	*san*
four	*si*
five	*wu*
six	*liu*
seven	*qi*
eight	*ba*
nine	*jiu*
ten	*shi*

Emergency phrases

There's an emergency!
Zheshi ge jinjide qingkuang
Please can you help me?
ni neng bu neng bang wo ge mang ma

I lost my passport	*wo de huzhao diu le*
I need to see a doctor	*wo yao kan bing*

Call an ambulance!
qing jiao jingcha jiuhuche!

Fire!	*zhao huo le!*
Police!	*jingcha!*

Mobile phones

I'd like to buy a mobile charge card *wo xiang mai chongzhie ka*
I'd like to buy a SIM card
phone charger   *dianhua chongdianqi*

Further Reference

Books

Memoirs

Jung Chang *Wild Swans* (1992) A moving memoir that spans three generations of women in China.
Nien Cheng *Life and Death in Shanghai* (1987) Cheng, accused of being a British spy, was put under house arrest in 1966 and jailed. On release she was told her daughter had committed suicide; in reality she was beaten to death by Red Guards.

Non-fiction

Jung Chang & Jon Halliday *Mao: The Unknown Story* (2005) Controversial biography of Mao Zedong, banned in China.
Christian Datz & Christof Kullmann *Shanghai: Architecture & Design* (2005) A CD-sized primer to Shanghai's fabulous modern buildings, lavishly illustrated.
Edward Denison & Guang Yu Ren *Building Shanghai: The Story of China's Gateway* (2006) Terrific book about Shanghai's rapid growth and troubling lack of coherent planning.
Stella Dong *Shanghai: The Rise and Fall of a Decadent City* (2000) The tabloid version of high-jinks and low life as played out in the Shanghai of the 1920s and '30s.
John Fairbanks *The Great Chinese Revolution 1800-1985* (1987) An approachable, thorough guide to Chinese history for the layman.
Greg Girard *Phantom Shanghai* (2007) Beautiful photographic look at rapidly disappearing remnants of Old Shanghai.
Lynn Pan *In Search of Old Shanghai* (1982) Waxes historical on Shanghai's glory days. Her more recent offering is *Shanghai Style: Art and Design Between the Wars* (2008).
Harriet Sergeant *Shanghai* (1991) Vivid portrait of life in the 'whore of the orient' in the 1920s and '30s, compiled from first-hand interviews.
Sang Ye *China Candid: The People on the People's Republic of China* (2006) Chinese journalist's interviews about life in modern China.

Fiction

JG Ballard *Empire of the Sun* (1984) Part fiction, part autobiography, the chilling story of a young boy separated from his parents in wartime Shanghai and interned by the Japanese.
Tom Bradby *The Master of Rain* (2002) A young Englishman battles Chinese gangsters, distracted by a Russian whore, in this 1920s thriller.
Bo Caldwell *The Distant Land of My Father* (2001) Young girl leaves millionaire dad behind in Shanghai. Dad interned by Japanese, loses all, travels to America, reunion. Aww.
Wei Hui *Shanghai Baby* (2002) Semi-autobiographical tale of a Shanghai 'bad' girl.
Kazuo Ishiguro *When We Were Orphans* (2000) An Englishman raised in Shanghai returns to find the dark truth about the deaths of his parents. No happy endings.
André Malraux *Man's Fate* (1933) Malraux's characters pierce the quandaries of ideology and loyalty posed by the early days of the Cultural Revolution.
Mian Mian *Candy* (2003) Semi-autobiographical tale of the other Shanghai 'bad' girl.
Anchee Min *Becoming Madame Mao* (2000) Patchy but brave attempt to get inside the mind of China's very own Lady Macbeth.
Qiu Xiaolong *Red Mandarin Dress* (2007) The most recent of the captivating Detective Chen series, which follows the sleuth through reconstructed 1990s Shanghai.

Film

Code 46 (Michael Winterbottom, 2003) Moody sci-fi thriller in which Shanghai stars as a Brave New World, a job it performs matchlessly.
The Empire of the Sun (Steven Spielberg, 1987) Terrific adaptation of JG Ballard's extraordinary story, demonstrating that old Shanghai wasn't all glamour.
The Goddess (Wu Yonggang, 1934) Ruan Lingyu ('the Greta Garbo of China') as a single mother trying to pay for her son's education – but there's only one way to earn the money and it's not typing.
Jasmine Women (Hou Yong, 2004) Visually stunning tale about three generations of Shanghai women.
Home Song Stories (Tony Ayres, 2007) Chronicles the life of a Shanghainese nightclub singer who marries an Australian sailor and migrates to Melbourne.
Lust, Caution (Ang Lee, 2007) Set in Shanghai in World War II; a young woman finds herself entangled in a political game of emotional intrigue and steamy sensuality with a political figure.
Mission: Impossible III (JJ Abrams, 2006) Tom Cruise swings from the city's skyscrapers and drops in on canal town Xitang in the franchise's palatable third portion.

Shanghai Baby (Berengar Pfahl, 2007) A flat-footed attempt to capture the novel featuring the scandalous Chinese actress Bai Ling.
Shanghai Express (Josef von Sternberg, 1932) Kidnapped foreigners on the Beijing–Shanghai line. None of it was shot in China but it's Dietrich at her best and still outshone by Anna May Wong.
Shanghai Story (Peng Xiaolian, 2004) Subtle film about a group of feuding siblings brought back together by their ailing grandmother.
Shanghai Triad (Zhang Yimou, 1995) Classic gangster pic set in 1930s Shanghai, considered China's answer to *The Godfather*.
Suzhou River (Lou Ye, 2000) Surreal tale of lost love and betrayal set on the industrial banks of Shanghai's murky creek. Modern film noir, Chinese style.

Music

Cold Fairyland *Seeds on the Ground* (2007) The latest offering from the prolific, much-beloved experimental Shanghai band. The best live show in town.
Coco Zhao *Dream Situation* (2007) Masterful modern arrangements of 1920s and 1930s tunes.
Crystal Butterfly *Mystical Journey* (2005) Debut by one of Shanghai's oldest and most famous bands. Filed somewhere between U2 and the Cure, with a Shanghainese twist.
The Honeys *On the Street* (2002) Debut album of long-time local pop-rock favourites runs the gamut from fast, catchy tunes to soaring ballads.
Night Bus *Night Bus* (2004) Perky pop-rock with jazzy influences.
Various *Shanghai Jazz: Musical Seductions from China's Age of Decadence* (2004) Jazz musos contribute to a lively collection of jazz faves from Old Shanghai.
Various *Fanyin Music Box* (2003) Twelve tracks by nine Shanghai bands showcase everything from pop to rock to metal to grunge.
Ian Widgery *The Original Shanghai Divas Collection* (2003) Top Chinese pop stars from the '20s and '30s, remixed with uptempo grooves and laid-back break beats for one of the hippest CDs in town.
Li Xianglan *Fragrance of Night* (2003) One of Shanghai's most enduring anthems from its 1930s heyday. Combines the original version with 16 other tracks.
Xiao Yao *Lost Topic* (2004) Singer-songwriter Xiao mixes hard beats and electronica into surprisingly pleasant melodies.

Index

Index

Advertisers' Index

Please refer to the relevant pages for contact details

Airline flights are one of the biggest producers of the global warming gas CO_2. But with **The CarbonNeutral Company** you can make your travel a little greener.

Go to **www.carbonneutral.com** to calculate your flight emissions then 'neutralise' them through international projects which save exactly the same amount of carbon dioxide.

Contact us at **shop@carbonneutral.com** or call into the office on **0870 199 99 88** for more details.

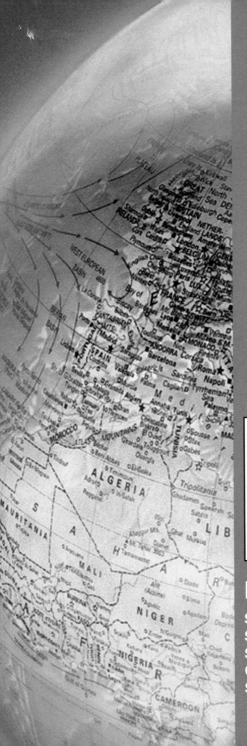

Major sight or landmark	. . . .
Railway station	. . . .
Park	. . . .
Hospitals/universities	. . . .
Hotels	. . . .
Area name	. . . . JINGAN
Metro station	. . . . ⊖
Motorway	. . . .
Raised highway	. . . .

Maps

Shanghai Overview

1

Circus World

Zhabei Park

To Anting New Twon

QILIANSHAN LU

ZHENBEI LU

WENSHUI LU

HUTAI LU

GUANGZHONG LU

ZHENBEI LU

LINGSHI LU

XINCUN LU

RONGHE XINLU

2

Shanghai West Railway Station

JIAOTANG LU

LANGAO LU

XINCUN LU

HUTAI LU

PUTUO

TAOPU LU

ZHENBEI LU

WUNING LU

Caoyang Park

ZHONGSHAN BEI LU

Zhangtai LU

Zhenping Lu

HENGFENG LU

GONGHE XINLU

Shanghai Railway Station

Shanghai Railway Station

See pp242-243

Caoyang Lu

WUNING LU

CAOYANG LU

CHANGSHOU LU

JIANGNING LU

TIANMU XI LU

Hanzhong Lu

SHIMENER LU

Jade Buddha Temple

Jinshajiang Lu

JINSHAJIANG LU

Jinshajiang Lu

WANHANGDU LU

JINGAN

Beijing XI LU

Nan Jing Xi Lu

3

East China Normal University

Changfeng Park

ZHONGSHAN BEI LU

CAOYANG LU

JIANGSU LU

Jingan Temple

NANJING XI LU

Changfeng Ocean World

CHANGNING LU

Zhongshan Park

Zhongshan Park

Jiangsu Lu

YANAN ZHONG LU

Shanxi Nan LU

Changning Stadium

CHANGNING LU

Zhongshan Park

Changshu Lu

HUAIHAI ZHONG LU

RUIJIN ER LU

Fuxing Park

Tianshan Park

Yanan Xi Lu

67

FUXING LU

CHONGQING NAN LU

Hongqiao Airport

GUBEI

Hongqiao Central Garden

YANAN XI LU

HUAIHAI ZHONG LU

Hengshan Lu

HENGSHAN LU

FRENCH CONCESSION

Shanghai Zoo

Marriott Hongqiao

HONGQIAO LU

HONGQIAO LU

63

35

ZHAOJIABANG LU

4

Soong Qingling Mausoleum

HONGXU LU

HONGQIAO LU

Hongqiao Lu

XUJIAHUI

XIETU LU

68

HONGKU LU

HONGQIAO

WUZHONG LU

Xujiahui

66

65

ZHONGSHAN NANER LU

Yishan Lu

YISHAN LU

Shanghai Stadium

Shanghai Stadium

Unique Hill Studio

WUZHONG LU

5

Guilin Lu

Caoxi Lu

CAOXI BEI LU

Longhua Temple

HONGMEI LU

YISHAN LU

Caobao Lu

CAOBAO LU

Guilin Park

LONGWU LU

LONGHUA

Huangpu River

6

HUMIN LU

Shanghai South Railway Station

Shanghai Botanical Gardens

JINJANG LU

Jinjiang Park

BAISE LU

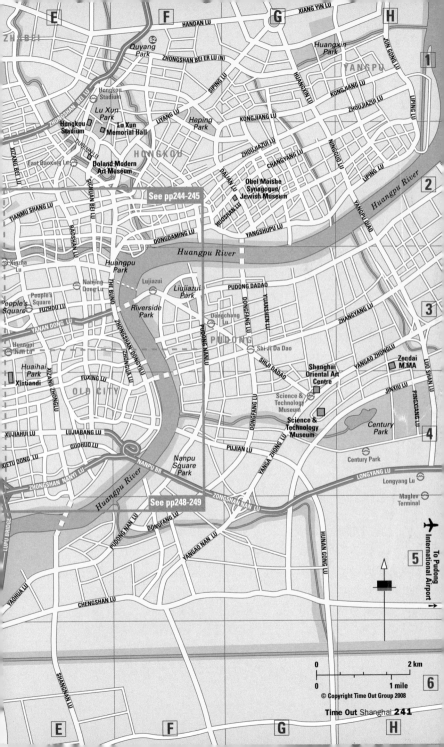

1

0   500 m
0   500 yds

© Copyright Time Out Group 2008

DONGXIN LU

GUANGFU XI LU

YICHANG LU

SHANXI BEI LU

AOMEN LU

JIANGNING LU

CHANGHUA LU

PUTUO LU

Art Warehous
District

AOMEN LU

XIKANG LU

CHANGDE LU

PUTUO LU

CHANGSHOU LU

CHANGHUA LU

2

WUNING LU

CHANGSHOU LU

XINHUI LU

SHANXI BEI LU

Jade Buddha
Temple

ANYUAN LU

JIAOZHOU LU

ANYUAN LU

CHANGDE LU

XIKANG LU

HAIFANG LU

SHANXI BEI LU

JIANGNING LU

YUYAO LU

CHANGNING LU

3

19

CHANGPING LU

SHANXI BEI LU

CAO JIA DU

YUYAO LU

WUNINGNAN LU

KANGDING LU

WANGCHUN JIE

YANPING LU

KANGDING LU

CHANGDE LU

JINGAN

XIKANG LU

WULING LU

20

4

WANHANGDU LU

WUDING LU

JIAOZHOU LU

XINZHA LU

NANCAOJIAZHAI

WUDING XI LU

11

XINZHA LU

18
19

Yunfeng
Theatre

BEIJING XILU

CHANGDE LU

TONGREN LU

12

5

15

ZHENNING LU

WANHANGDU LU

YUYUAN LU

NANJING XI LU

TONGREN LU

Jiangsu
Lu

WULUMUQI BEI LU

Paramount
Ballroom

Jingan
Temple

Jingan
Temple

City Plaza

CHANG DE LU

YUYUAN LU

YUYUAN LU

Municipal
Children's Palace

Jingan
Park

ANYI LU

6

JIANGSU LU

XUANHUA LU

ZHENNING LU

XUANHUA LU

NANJING XI LU

12

CHANGNING

ANHUA LU

Hilton
Hotel

FUMIN LU

36

YANAN XI LU

See
p246

WULUMUQI ZHONG LU

CHANGSHU LU

JULU LU

28

25 54
57

7

36

A   B   C   D

CHANGSHU LU

32

31

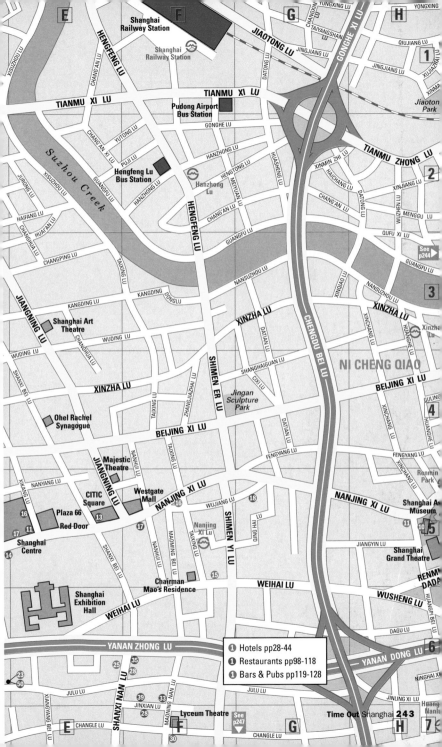

H · YONGXING LU · **J** · **K** · BAOSHAN LU · **L** · ZHI LU · XINGJIANG LU

1

QIUJIANG LU · QIUJIANG LU · ZHONGZHOU LU

YUYINGTANG LU · MINDE · HUIWEN LU · JIAOTONG LU · QIUJIANG LU

QIUJIANG LU · WANGJIAZHAI LU · DONGXINMIN LU · WUJING LU

JINGJIANG LU · XINMA LU · XUJIAZHAI LU · North Railway Station · HENAN BEI LU

Jiaotong Park · HAINING LU

TIANMU DONG LU · HAINING LU · TANGGOU LU

HUAXING LU · KANGLE LU · ANQING LU · SHANXI BEI LU

2 · XINJIANG LU · HAINING LU · QIPU LU · Qipu Lu Market · JIANGXI BEI LU

WUZHOU LU · XINJIANG LU · XINYANG LU · QIPU LU · ZHEJIANG BEI LU · FUJIAN BEI LU · QIPU LU

MENGGU LU · KAIFENG LU · WEN AN LU · HENAN BEI LU

QUFU XI LU · QUFU XI LU · QUFU LU · TIANTONG LU · SHANXI BEI LU

See p243 · GUANGFU LU · BEISUZHOU LU

3 · NANSUZHOU LU · *Suzhou Creek* · NANSUZHOU LU · BEISUZHOU LU · NANSUZHOU LU

XINZHA LU · XIAMEN LU

XINCHANG LU · HUANGHE LU · Xinzha Lu

BEIJING DONG LU · BEIJING DONG LU

NI CHENG QIAO · ZHIFU LU · HENAN ZHONG LU · NINGBO LU · JIANGX

BEIJING XILU · GULING LU · GUIZHOU LU · GUANGXI · ZHEJIANG ZHONG LU · FUJIAN · NINGBO · SHANXI NAN LU

XINCHANG LU · HUANGHE LU · BAHE LU · XIZANG ZHONG LU · NINGBO BEI LU · LUHE LU · TIANJIN LU · TIANJIN LU

4 · FENGYANG LU · LUHE LU · Shanghai No.1 Department Store · Shanghai No.1 Foodstore

XINCHANG LU · NANJING DONG LU · **PEOPLE'S SQUARE** · JIUJIANG LU · Nanjing Dong Lu

Moore Memorial Church · JIUJIANG LU · HANKOU LU · HENAN ZHONG LU

NANJING XI LU · Shanghai Art Museum · *Renmin Park* · HANKOU LU · HUBEI LU · ZHEJIANG · SHANDONG LU · FUZHOU

5 · MoCA · Urban Planning Centre · Raffles City · FUZHOU LU · Train Ticket Office · Bund Centre

City Hall · Yifu Theatre · ZHONG · FUJIAN NAN LU · SHANDONG NAN LU · HENAN ZHONG LU

Shanghai Grand Theatre · RENMIN DADAO · *People's Square* · GUANGDONG LU · **HUANGPU**

Shanghai Museum · BEIHAI · WUHU LU · Natural History Museum

Bus Station · ZININ LU

WUSHENG LU · YANAN DONG LU · Great World · SHANDONG NAN LU

6 · DAGU LU · Shanghai Concert Hall · NINGHAI DONG LU · ZHEJIANG · JINLING DONG LU · FUJIAN NAN LU · SHENGZE LU

NINGHAI · SONGSHAN LU · JINLING ZHONG LU · PUAN LU · LONGMEN LU · XIZANG NAN LU · YUNNAN NAN LU · RENMIN LU · Fuyou Lu Mosque

JINLING XI LU · HUANGPI · **ZHONG LU** · *See p248* · CHENXIANGGE

7 · **244** Time Out Shanghai · Huangpi Nan Lu · **HUAIHAI** · **J** · **K** · Dajing Lu Market · HENAN NAN LU

Huaihai Park · TAOYUAN · LIUJIN LU · DONGQINGLIAN JIE

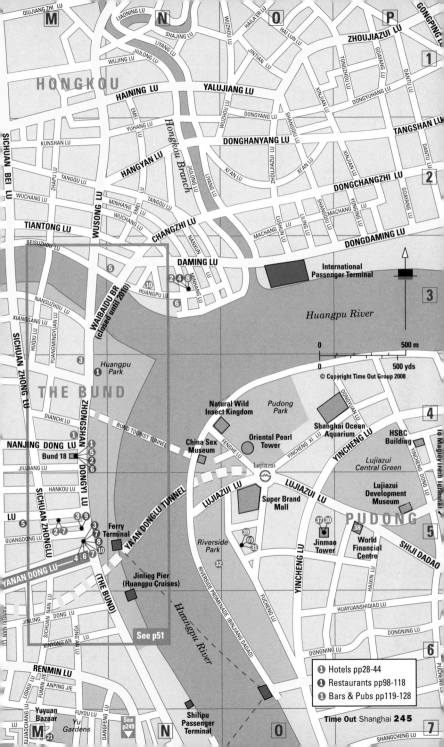

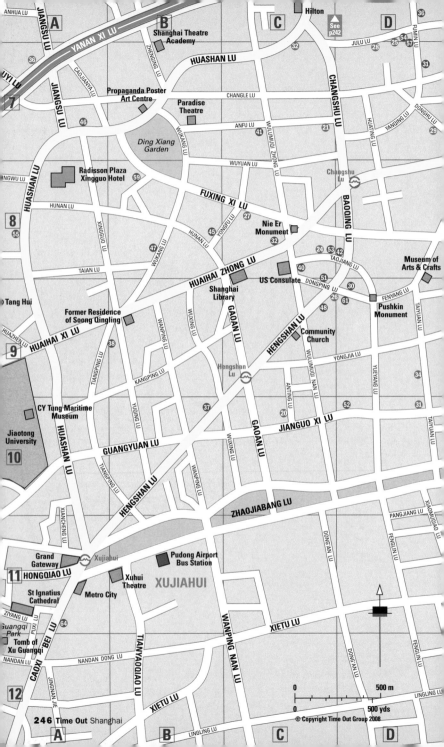

© Copyright Time Out Group 2008

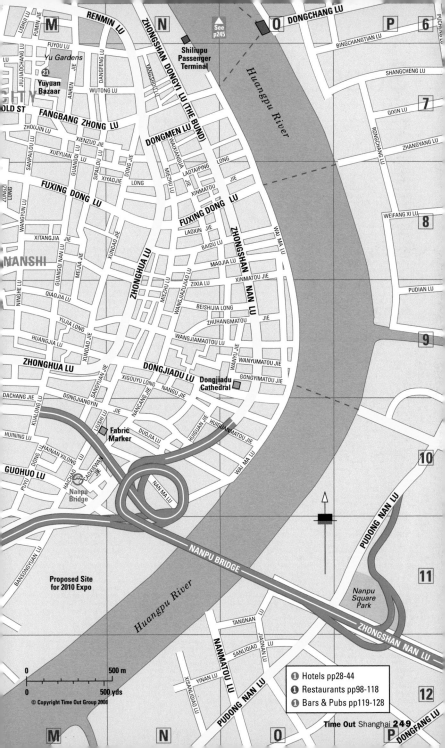

LISHUI LU
FUMIN LU
JIUJIAOCHANG LU
LU
ZHONGSHAN DONGYI LU (THE BUND)

See p245

PUCHENG LU

BINGCHANGTIAN LU

FUYOU LU

Yu Gardens

DANGFENG LU
YANGSHUO LU

Shiliupu
Passenger
Terminal

SHANGCHENG LU

Yuyuan
Bazaar

WUTONG LU

ANREN

OLD ST
FANGBANG ZHONG LU

ZHOUJIN LU
XIENZUO JIE

DONGMEN LU

WAKIANGJIA

LAOTAIPING

LONG

QIXIN LU

RONGCHANG LU

ZHANGYANG LU

SANPAILOU LU
XUEYUAN
GUANGQI
SIPAILOU LU
DONG JIE

MIEZHU LU

LONG

JIE

XINMATOU

ZUNGZI
LONG
FUXING DONG LU
XIYAOJIE

LONG

WEIFANG XI LU

8

WANGYUN LU
XITANGJIA
JIE
KUNDAO JIE
FUXING DONG LU

LAOXIN JIE

ZHONGSHAN

WAI MA LU

NANSHI
GUANGBI NAN LU
MEIJIA JIE
ZHONGHUA LU

MIEZHU LU

BAIDU LU

MAOJIA LU
ZIXIA LU

NAN

XINMATOU JIE

PUDIAN LU

NINGHE LU
QIAOJIA LU
YUJIA LONG
KUNDAO JIE

WANGJIAZUOGU LU
BEISHIJIA LONG

LU

JIE

9

HUANGJIA LU
ZHUHANGMATOU

JIE

ZHONGHUA LU
DONGJIADU LU
SANGYUAN JIE
NANCANG JIE
WANGJIAMAOTOU LU
WANYU JIE
WANYUMATOU JIE

GONGYIMATOU JIE

Dongjiadu
Cathedral

DACHANG JIE
XIGOUYU LONG
NANGU JIE

DONGJIANGYIN
KUALONG JIE

HUINING LU
LIUSHI LU
JIE
DUDJIA LU
HUIJUAN LU
HUIGUANMATOU JIE

WAI MA LU

Fabric
Marker

HAINAN XILONG

GUOHUO LU
PUYU
HAICHAO
LAODEWAN

10

Nanpu
Bridge

NAN MA LU

PUDONG NAN LU

BANSONGYUAN LU

NANPU BRIDGE

11

Proposed Site
for 2010 Expo

Nanpu
Square
Park

Huangpu River

ZHONGSHAN NAN LU

TANGNAN

LU
JIAONAN LU
SANLIQIAO

0   500 m

NANMATOU LU

YINAN LU

XISANLIQIAO LU

PUDONG NAN LU

0   500 yds

© Copyright Time Out Group 2008

1 Hotels pp28-44
1 Restaurants pp98-118
1 Bars & Pubs pp119-128

12

Street Index

Chinese Translations

THE BUND 外滩
Bund Centre 外滩商贸
Bund Historical Museum 外滩历史博物馆
Bund Museum 外滩博物馆
Bund Tourist Tunnel 外滩人行观光隧道
Chinese Post Office 邮政局大楼
Garden Bridge (Waibaidu Qiao) 公园桥(外白渡)
Huangpu Park 黄浦公园
M on the Bund 米氏餐厅
Metropole Hotel 新城饭店
Natural History Museum 自然博物馆
Shanghai Friendship Store 上海友谊商店
Shanghai Mansions 上海大厦
Suzhou Creek 苏州河
Three on the Bund 外滩三号
Streets 街道
Beijing Dong Lu 北京东路
Jiulong Lu 九龙路
Nanjing Dong Lu 南京东路
Yanan Dong Lu 延安东路
Zhapu Lu 乍浦路

PEOPLE'S SQUARE &
NANJING DONG LU 人民广场和南京东路
City Hall 大会堂
Great World 大世界
Hong Kong Shopping Centre (D Mall) 香港购物中心
Moore Memorial Church 沐恩堂
Shanghai Art Museum 上海美术馆
Shanghai Concert Hall 上海音乐院
Shanghai Grand Theatre 上海大舞台
Shanghai Museum 上海博物馆
Shanghai No.1 Department Store 上海第一百货公司
Tomorrow Square 明天广场
Urban Planning Centre 城市规划中心
Yi Fu Theatre 逸夫舞台
Streets 街道
Huanghe Lu 黄河路
Fuzhou Lu 福州路
Guangdong Lu 广东路
Renmin Dadao 人民大道
Xizang Zhong Lu 西藏中路

Yanan Dong Lu	延安东路
Yunnan Nan Lu	云南南路

JINGAN 静安
Antiques, Bird and Plant Market	古玩、花鸟市场
Chairman Mao's Residence	毛泽东故居
Children's Palace	上海市少年宫
CITIC Square	中伬泰富广场
Jade Buddha Temple	玉佛寺
Jingan Park	静安公园
Jingan Temple	静安寺
Ohel Rachel Synagogue	摩西会堂
Plaza 66	恒隆广场
Shanghai Centre	上海商城
Shanghai Centre Theatre	上海商城剧院
Shanghai Exhibition Centre	上海展览中心
Westgate Mall	梅龙镇广场

Streets 街道
Maoming Bei Lu	茂名北路
Moganshan Lu	莫干山路
Nanjing Xi Lu	南京西路
Weihai Lu	威海路
Wujiang Lu	吴江路

OLD CITY 老城
Chenxiangge Nunnery	沉香阁
Cixiu Nunnery	慈修庵
Confucius Temple	孔庙
Dajing Pavilion	大镜亭
Dongjiadu Cathedral	董家渡天主堂
Fabric Market	布料批发市场
Fuyou Lu Market	福佑路市场
Fuyou Lu Mosque	福佑路清真寺
Hua Bao Building	华宝楼
Kuixing Pavilion	魁星楼
Nanpu Bridge	南浦桥
Peach Garden Mosque	小桃园清真寺
Shanghai Museum of Folk Collectibles	上海民间收藏陈列馆
Temple of the City God	城皇庙
White Cloud Taoist Temple	白云寺
Yu Gardens	豫园
Yuyuan Bazaar	豫园小商品市场

Streets 街道
Anren Lu	安仁路
Dongjiadu Lu	董家渡路
Fangbang Zhong Lu	方浜中路
Fuyou Lu	福佑路
Henan Nan Lu	河南南路
Jiujiaochang Lu	旧校场路

Lishui Lu	里水路
Renmin Lu	人民路
Wenmiao Lu	文庙路
Zhenling Jie	真灵街
Zhonghua Lu	中华路

XINTIANDI — 新天地

Dongtai Lu Antiques Market	东台路古玩市场
Fangzangjiang Buddhist Temple	法藏将佛寺
Museum of the First National Congress of the Chinese Communist Party	中国共产党一大会址纪念馆
Shikumen Open House Museum	石库门博物馆
Wanshang Bird and Flower Market	万商花鸟市场
Streets	**街道**
Huaihai Zhong Lu	淮海中路
Huangpi Nan Lu	黄陂南路

FRENCH CONCESSION — 法国花园

Cathay Theatre	国泰电影院
Church of St Nicholas	金巴仑教堂
CY Tung Maritime Museum	董浩云航运博物馆
Former Residence of Soong Qingling	宋庆龄故居
Former Residence of Sun Yatsen	孙中山故居
Former Residence of Zhou Enlai	周恩来故居
Fuxing Park	复兴公园
Lyceum Theatre	兰心戏院
Museum of Arts & Crafts	手工艺博物馆
Museum of Public Security	公安博物馆
Old China Hand Reading Room	汉源书店
Propaganda Poster Art Centre	宣传画艺术中心
Shanghai Library	上海图书馆
Xiangyang Market	向阳市场
Streets	**街道**
Changle Lu	长乐路
Changshu Lu	常熟路
Fenyang Lu	汾阳路
Gaolan Lu	高拦路
Huaihai Zhong Lu	淮海中路
Maoming Nan Lu	茂名南路
Ruijin Er Lu	瑞金二路
Shanxi Nan Lu	陕西南路
Shaoxing Lu	绍兴路
Sinan Lu	思南路
Taikang Lu	泰康路
Taiyuan Lu	太原路
Xinhua Lu	新华路

XUJIAHUI, HONGQIAO & GUBEI — 徐家汇·虹桥和古北

Hongqiao Airport	虹桥机场

Longhua Martyrs Cemetery	龙华烈士陵园
Longhua Temple	龙华寺
Shanghai Botanical Garden	上海植物园
Shanghai Zoo	上海动物园
Soong Qingling Mausoleum	宋庆龄陵墓
St Ignatius cathedral	圣依纳爵主教座堂
Streets	**街道**
Hongqiao Lu	虹桥路
Zhongshan Xi Lu	中山西路

PUDONG 浦东

Bund Tourist Tunnel	外滩人行观光隧道
Century Park	世纪公园
Jinmao Tower	金茂大厦
Lujiazui Development Museum	陆家嘴发展陈列馆
Lujiazui Financial and Trade Zone	陆家嘴金融贸易区
Natural Wild Insect Kingdom	上海自然野生昆虫馆
Oriental Pearl Tower	东方明珠电视塔
Pudong International Airport	浦东国际机场
Science & Technology Museum	上海科学馆
Shanghai History Museum	上海历史博物馆
Shanghai Ocean Aquarium	海洋馆
Streets	**街道**
Lujiazui Lu	陆家嘴
Shiji Dadao (Century Boulevard)	世纪大道

HONGKOU 虹口

Doland: Shanghai Duolun Modern Art Museum	多伦现代美术馆
Former Residence of Lu Xun	鲁迅故居
Huoshan Park	霍山公园
Jewish Refugee Museum	犹太难民博物馆
Lu Xun Memorial Hall	鲁迅纪念馆
Lu Xun Park	鲁迅公园
Ohel Moshe Synagogue	摩西会堂
Streets	**街道**
Dongdaming Lu	东大名路
Duolun Lu	舵轮路
Huoshan Lu	霍山路

TRIPS OUT OF TOWN 周边地区

Hangzhou	杭州
Moganshan	莫干山
Putuoshan	普陀山
Suzhou	苏州
Tongli	同里
Wuzhen	乌镇
Xitang	西塘
Zhouzhuang	周庄
Zhujiajiao	朱家角

Shanghai Metro

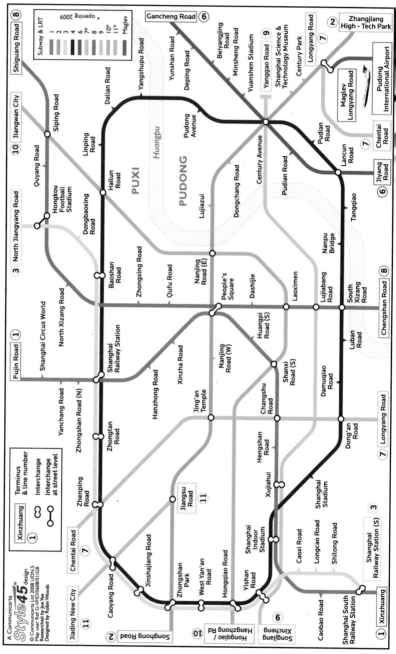